"I have been lucky enough
tor for a few decades now, an(
same birthday. His knowledge of astrology is both deep and broad
and, like most gifted people, his intuitions and interpretations are
exceptional. He will reveal both your highest potential and lowest
nadir for any given time, and I enjoy being his student almost as
much as I enjoy making movies."
 —Trudie Styler, Founder of Maven Pictures and Co-Founder
of the Rainforest Fund

PRAISE FOR STEVEN FORREST

"Steven, you carry the noble art of Astrology so faithfully. I have
had several charts done in my lifetime, and none of them but yours
have escaped the astrologer mistaking so much of the chart as a
sounding board for his own ego. You have restored the divine art to
its noble status."
 —Robert Johnson, author of *We*

"Looking back at Steve's readings, they just increase my faith in
life as a 'team sport,' which is to say that skilled support can make
all the difference on game day! He insists that nothing is so grave
as to be beyond repair, and correspondingly that there is no rainbow
that won't be evaporated by poor judgment in the now. So I guess
'benevolent realist' would best describe his approach . . . I can't recommend him highly enough."
 —Robert Downey, Jr.

"No matter what you think of astrology, if you appreciate humor,
insight, poetry and astute, articulate observations of human nature,
you will appreciate Steven Forrest's fascinating book *The Inner Sky.*"
 —Calli Khoury, screenwriter, *Thelma and Louise*

On *The Book of the Moon*: "Steven Forrest's warmth and accessibility will immediately draw you to this gem of a book. With a twinkle in his eye, he shakes up our habitual thinking about the Moon and challenges us to see Her again with new eyes. Not only does he remind us that the Moon is much more than we imagined, he brings a distillation of deep practice and creative thinking to his writing on the lunar phase. He makes complexity fun and adds his inventive, evolutionary twist."

—Lynn Bell, Centre for Psychological Astrology

The Book of Air

Also by Steven Forrest

The Inner Sky

The Changing Sky

The Night Speaks

The Book of Pluto

Measuring the Night (with Jeffrey Wolf Green)

Measuring the Night Vol. 2 (with Jeffrey Wolf Green)

Stalking Anubis

Skymates (with Jodie Forrest)

Skymates II (with Jodie Forrest)

Yesterday's Sky

The Book of the Moon

The Book of Neptune

The Book of Fire

The Book of Earth

The Book of Air

The Art of Paying Attention

by Steven Forrest

Seven Paws Press, Inc.
Borrego Springs, CA

Published in 2020 by Seven Paws Press, Inc.
PO Box 82
Borrego Springs, CA 92004
www.sevenpaws.com

ISBN 978-1-939510-06-8

Cover art by Diren Yardimli

Printed in the United States of America
LCCN 2020936769

ACKNOWLEDGMENTS

Once again, my gratitude to my manager, web-wizard, and friend, Tony Howard. He remains the brains behind my world, even as he helps to create astrology's future with Astrology University.

The Book of Air was truly *written* rather than simply transcribed from talks. Still, it was an enormous help to be able to refer to a transcript of my original "Air" program – "The Shock of the Senses" – offered back in November 2015 at my bi-annual Apprenticeship Program meeting in Alpine, California. For the painstaking, tedious work of producing that transcript, I thank my student, JoAnn Anderson.

My gratitude also to my editor Shelley Madsen for skillfully removing my typos, *non-sequiturs*, and other evidence of literary malfeasance.

A profound *gracias* to the people who have run my various Apprenticeship Programs around the world over the years. The workload is enormous and I wouldn't have had enough patience to do it myself. Even though all but two of those programs are currently on hiatus in order to make time for me to write these Elements books, I can honestly say that I have learned at least as much by teaching as I hope my students have learned from listening to me. Here are the names of those leaders, in no particular order. In southern California: Ingrid Coffin and her team at the Blue Sky Ranch Fellowship, with special thanks there to Cristina Smith, Jonathan Sacks, Paula Wansley, and Carey Nash. In China: Felicia Jiang and David Railey, along with the amazing NoDoor team. In North Carolina: Kathy Hallen and her able assistants, Carol McLauren and Tricia Mickleberry. In Nelson Bay, Australia, and various places around Europe: the indomitable Mercurial Connections team, Lisa Jones and Christine Murfitt. Finally, in northern California, I thank Joyce Van Horn, Kathy Jacobson, and Deni Mateer. My Apprenticeship Programs have come and gone, as have the people who have made them possible. Thanks, *emeritus*, to Karen Davis, Vinessa Nevala, Barbara King, and the late David Friedman.

I would like to offer special gratitude to two dear friends and colleagues, Dr. Catie Cadge and Jeff Parrett, with whom I am currently working hard to create the Forrest Center for Evolutionary Astrology – stay tuned, you will soon hear more about that project.

Finally my gratitude to the following people who were actively engaged with me in various ways during the writing process: Scott Ainslie and Barbara Ackerman, Virginia Bell, Cheryl Benedict, Lonnie and Josh Busic, Matt Cohen, Chip Conley, Cui "Chloe"Ying – my intrepid Chinese translator, Carol and Mike Czeczot, Rona Elliot and Roger Brossy, Michael Faith, Hadley Fitzgerald, Rishi Giovanni Gatti, Robert and Diana Griffin, the Grossenbacher clan: John, Tracy, and Ryan, Pamela Hoback, Susie and Mark Hodge, Sylvia Hsiao, Bariş İlhan, Bill Janis, Sherry Jayne, Kelly Jean, Mark Jones, Kathy King, Peter and Ingrid Kondos, Lisa Kostova, Kate and Alex Laird, Jackie Larsen, Rick Levine, Laurie Lindgren, Elizabeth Long, Ralph MacIntyre, Barbara Matson, Mary Ann McGuire, Kym and Scott McNabb, Cristin McVey, Randy Meeks, Linnea Mirron and Ricky Williams, Dominic Miller, Elizabeth Motyka, Jim Mullaney, Rafael Nasser, Brian O'Flynn, Annette O'Neill, Marie O'Neill, Nina Ortega and Miguel Bracho, Carol Peebles, Joey Paynter, Steven Poster and Susan Williams, Aminah Raheem and Fritz Smith, Claire Rauwel, Dusty Recor and "Indian Joe" Stewart, Ray Ristorcelli, Evelyn Roberts, Paige Ruane and Jack McDonald, Fran Slavich, Katie Sloan, Debbie and Scott Steingraber, Sting and Trudie Sumner-Styler, Tem Tarriktar, Kay Taylor, Elaine and Mark Thomas, Julia Trawick, Jaan Uhelszki, Dick and Artemisa Walker, Cindy Wyatt, and Helen Zou.

TABLE OF CONTENTS

PART TWO: MASTERING THE ALCHEMICAL MARRIAGE OF SIGN, HOUSE, AND PLANET

PART THREE: MERCURY, VENUS, SATURN, AND URANUS THROUGH THE TWELVE SIGNS AND HOUSES

PART FOUR: SEEING FUTURES

*For Michelle Kondos, with gratitude for reminding me of Spring
back in a season of cold and fading light.*

FOREWORD BY DAVID RAILEY

When Steven Forrest asked me to write a foreword to his *Book of Air,* I felt genuinely honored, but then . . . my second thought was, "Sure, *The Book of Air* . . . but Air! I didn't get to write about action-oriented, exciting, adventurous Fire, or deeply feeling intuitive Water, or even practical down to earth – Earth! No. I get to write a foreword about Air . . . Air! You know, devoid of feelings, chattering on and on about ideas without regard to practical application, a noisy bothersome and often intellectually conceited group of annoying do-nothing, gossiping, lightweights!"

Sure, I laughed alongside my streaming thoughts about Air signs, thoughts that reflected stereotypical prejudices about the element of Air. I'd heard such statements about Air signs since first beginning to seriously study astrology fifty years ago. As you probably guessed, I was born with five planets in Air. Yep, my Sun, Mercury, Venus, and Neptune are in Libra and my chart ruler, Jupiter, is in Aquarius. So for me, and perhaps for many of you born with a majority of Air signs, these complaints about the Air signs are familiar.

Nonetheless, whatever you think about Air signs and the Air element, just take a deep breath (that's air), relax and open your mind. For in this *Book of Air,* Steven sets the record straight about this misunderstood element, with insightful, entertaining conversational examples and graphic prose. He makes a clear case that we all have access to Air, thank goodness! Even without any personal planets in Air signs or Air houses, everyone has a Mercury, a Venus, a Saturn or Uranus and experiences this element one way or another. Most of all Steven underscores the essential importance and meaningfulness of Air. He writes:

"Bottom line, air is what connects our hearts and our minds to the world around us. Astrologically – but also in plain speech – "Air" is the linking element, telegraphing an endless stream of information to us – and letting us send a few telegrams in return. Air makes a mockery of the delusion that we are separate

from each other – or, for that matter, from anything else. Air connects. It is what allows us to pay attention, and perhaps to create some good reasons for other people to pay attention to us."

I love this. It's beautiful and eloquent.

But here's something else to consider. We can survive without food (earth) for about twelve weeks, without water for four to seven days. Without sufficient body heat (fire) – i.e. hypothermia – death occurs within forty-five minutes to six hours, depending upon the temperature. But how long can we survive without air? Answer: somewhere between three minutes, maybe up to twenty minutes, absolute maximum. So, how important is air? Pretty darn important. Death occurs faster without it than any other element. Even with drowning the problem is lack of air.

Bottom line: we need air.

Air is the atmosphere. We take air for granted until it's so polluted that it burns our eyes and hurts to breathe. Air to us is like water to a fish, it's the last thing we think of until we lack it and become terribly and briefly desperate.

Air moves things too! Think of a windy day with dust and papers swirling all about, or the air that turns a windmill. Consider the heavy winds of a hurricane battering a coastline, or the cold winds blowing across a lake, or a tornado sucking up trailers and neighbor's cows into a hellish blender of spinning air. Wind erosion wears down mountains over time and carries the seeds of spring and summer for hundreds even thousands of miles. Hawks and vultures soar on currents of air, while hot air lifts balloons, which float on the breeze.

Astrologically, Air is about *ideas* – and ideas bring change too, sometimes swirling about like a windy day, or creating a better windmill. Ideas spoken or written down can become like a hurricane battering the consciousness of a people, eroding cliffs and mountains of calcified thoughtless routine, or bringing chaos like a tornado. Just like those hawks, vultures, and hot-air balloons, our thoughts can soar too. Ideas motivate us, sending us gliding over our mental landscapes, perhaps high enough to gain new perspective.

I know that Steven understands all of these things about air deeply, because I know Steven. I first spent time with Steven when I interviewed him for my TV show *Astrology Today*, in the early 1990's. He was visiting the Metropolitan Atlanta Astrological Society, and I did an on-location interview that was broadcast later on my show. I wish I still had a copy of that interview, I'm sure we'd both get a chuckle out of it.

However, since 2011 Steven and I have become close friends as a result of his visits to China every year, sponsored by the Nodoor School of Astrology in Beijing. His workshops in China have been inspired, and students there love him. When you're reading this book you should know you are getting a lifetime of thinking about and practicing astrology, from a truly gifted teacher. This is especially important for those of you who are "new" to astrology. The rest of us already know this, and we eagerly pour through his books, hearing in our minds the familiar voice we've grown to love at his workshops and lectures.

Steven speaks from his heart, a heart connected to a brilliant mind. His *Book of Air* is quite a ride. He gives you the full view. It is a panoramic journey. With Steven you know how much "words matter." Not only in writing but likewise in astrological consultations. As he writes near the end of his book:

"It is the Air element that we are talking about, and Air is always about paying attention. That includes paying attention to glazed-over eyes and other signs of befuddlement in our clients if our choice of words is not working."

This is good advice to counseling astrologers, especially those of you just starting out. However, when reading this book you can tell that this man Steven Forrest has been *paying attention* for quite a while, and we are all joyfully indebted to him for that. No matter how long we've practiced astrology, we are always students of astrology, and every birth chart we look at represents the opportunity of a lifetime. And what is that birth chart calculated for? For the moment of first breath. Our first independent intake of air.

– David Railey
Beijing, China

1

PAYING ATTENTION

A moonless desert night, coolness in the air. A coyote yaps in the distance – *or could that have been a faint human cry?* The sounds are similar, but the distinction could be critical: I listen closely, trying to focus, trying to sort it out. If I am lucky, maybe the sound will come again. Waves of fresh information may crash and break against my eardrums – literal waves, airborne on the sea of oxygen and nitrogen that I am breathing.

I listen carefully.

Nothing. There is no further yap . . . or cry, or whatever it was.

I now find myself paying very close attention to the sound of a coyote *not* yapping – my consciousness experiencing a total, enraptured, immersed focus *on nothing at all*.

Didn't I read something about that *state of Absolute Attention to the Eternal Now* once in a book about meditation? Suddenly, I am *paying attention* in a very different way. That unnamed sound has triggered a thought, and thought spins kaleidoscopically down its own chaos-theory pathways.

Air carries me from coyotes to metaphysics in a tenth of a second.

We smell the perfume of honeysuckle on the evening zephyrs – or, if we find ourselves downwind of a burning building, the telltale stench of oily smoke. Maybe the perceptions trigger memories, happy or sad. Senses stimulated, we tumble down the mind's gravity-well, surfing those unpredictable and serendipitous waves of free-association.

Honeysuckle in the thick humid air of summer when we were children walking the park with mom and dad.

A campfire.

A car in flames.

Just before we touch it, we feel the warning heat of the burner on the stove. In the nick of time, we pull back. Once again, Air – ever the great messenger – has saved us from a nasty burn. Gratefully, we pay attention to the scar we do not have – and perhaps quickly recall the stories behind scars of body and soul that we do have.

We step into a room where a week ago someone died in a state of bitterness. No one told us about that death, but we feel a chill in the ambiance of that room anyway. Would a thermometer register it? I don't know – but I've felt that chilly death-vibe, and I bet you have too.

That's Air again, at least in some etheric sense, commanding our attention as it always does.

Data, data, data . . .

Bottom line, *Air is what connects our hearts and our minds to the world around us.* Astrologically – but also in plain speech – Air is the *linking* element, telegraphing an endless stream of information to us, and letting us send a few telegrams in return. Air makes a mockery of the delusion that we are separate from each other – or, for that matter, separate from anything else. Air *connects.* It is what allows us to *pay attention,* and perhaps to create some good reasons for other people to pay attention to us.

Saying that the Air element is about "information" and "data" is true, but those words are dry and narrow. They leave out too much of the magic. It would be very much like saying that life was about making money or that sex was about bodies.

In the conventions of astrology, the Air element – embodied in the signs Gemini, Libra, and Aquarius – is typically described as *mental* and *cognitive.* That perspective is accurate, although as we will soon see, such words do not cast the net widely enough to capture all the nuances of this third astrological element. Reading between the lines of what astrologers have written about the Air Family, we might get the impression that it stands aloof from life – the cool, detached observer. It is as if while you might *learn* something from Air, you wouldn't want to *sleep* with it.

I promise we will go far deeper than that in the pages that follow. We will confirm those mental and cognitive dimensions of the Air element – but we will also encounter realms of pure magic and mystical transcendence, not to mention some genuine *woo-woo* strangeness.

Remember that chill in the air of the room where a man had just died?

THE TRADITION

In *The Only Way To Learn Astrology* by Marion D. March and Joan McEvers, we read of the Air element, "These signs can communicate well; they tend to be intellectual, and are able to handle abstract reasoning. They are logical, broad-minded, objective, idealistic and unprejudiced. Misused, they can be cold and impractical."

True dat, as they say in New Orleans.

As a young astrologer, I cut my teeth on one of modern astrology's founding fathers, Great Britain's Charles E. O. Carter. In his *Principles of Astrology*, he writes, "Air is intellectual, refined, thoughtful, and devoted to the arts and sciences, especially from a more abstract and theoretical point of view . . . By itself, it tends to become divorced from the real and the practical, and to spend its time day-dreaming; it works with ideas rather than concrete objects . . ."

Again, all that is reasonably accurate – and I applaud these astrologers for recognizing both the higher and the lower ground with this third element. None of them were "evolutionary astrologers" *per se*, but their affirmation of the fact that humans can respond well or poorly to any symbolism is really the heart of the matter.

In *Relating*, Liz Greene writes, "All three airy signs, although different in their modes of expression, share the need to relate life experiences to a preconceived framework of ideas. This framework may come from outside, culled from the books, teachings and conversations of others, or it may come from within, painstakingly created by one's own laborious mental processes; but the existence of the framework is all-important and there is a tendency to take all experiences and seek in them the underlying pattern of logic which will make them conform to this preconceived structure."

Once more, in Greene's words, we see that classic Airy emphasis on ideas and the stream of data that fuels them. It is that latter clause – *the stream of data that fuels them* – which will be the foundation of much that we explore in this book. That "data" is how we map what we think of as reality.

But what is reality – and what about the gap between reality as it actually is "out there" and the version of it you carry between your ears? This is not an abstract, philosophical issue. This is an everyday matter. Maybe, for example, you *just know* that you left your car keys exactly where you always leave them, on the kitchen counter.

Ten minutes later you find them beside your toothbrush.

There is a reality in your head and there is another reality out there. The source of most human folly is the belief that the two are the same thing.

WHAT IS ACTUALLY OUT THERE?

There's the question!

Air, symbolically, but often quite literally too, provides *the bridge that links the internal realities of consciousness to the external realities of the objective world.* There are deep philosophical dharma-waters here, but for starters let's just dangle our toes in the shallow end of the pool.

The second sentence of this book was, "a coyote yaps in the distance – or was that a faint human cry?"

You heard . . . *something.*

Maybe you were out here in the desert sitting beside me. Exactly the same sound waves struck your ear as struck mine. But we heard different things – me, a coyote announcing his position to the other members of the pack, and you: someone crying out for help. Or maybe just someone who was startled by something.

What was actually out there in that cool, moonless night air? I have connected the perceptual dots one way. You have connected them in a different way. Maybe we are both wrong. Maybe it was a bird. Maybe it was somebody's radio.

Who knows? Who ever knows what is really out there? None of us live in reality; we all live inside an *interpretation* of reality. We navigate by that map in our heads. It can be dangerous or comically incorrect, but it is all we have.

Sometimes the authorities have re-directed a cloverleaf exchange on the highway, but your GPS has not been updated.

Trusting such a map can kill you.

Sometimes you think that you have found your true love.

Trusting that map can kill you too.

The Air element, when it is healthy, is *constantly updating your inner maps*, pressing endlessly toward the impossible, unreachable goal of aligning what is in your head with what is actually happening. That line, by the way, is a pretty effective working definition of sanity: having your beliefs and reality in reasonable alignment.

When you finally locate your car keys beside your toothbrush, you might casually announce, "I must be going crazy." Well, probably not truly *crazy* . . . but as Confucious said, "the journey of a thousand miles starts with a single step."

Blind faith that what we *think* is real is *actually* real is a good way of thinking about that first single step in the direction of madness. That particular madness quickly leads us into a deep dark forest of illusion, delusion, and error. The good news is the fact that this catastrophe is avoidable. It only happens *if we fail to pay attention*, only if we fail to heed the corrective messages that constantly come to us, borne on wings of Air.

COBRAS

Buddhists tell a story that takes us straight down to the bones of the Air element. A master is meditating alone in his monastic cell. An idea strikes him for how he might startle his disciples into grasping some wisdom. He spreads a striped necktie out crookedly on his bed, then he runs in apparent panic from the room, yelling, "A cobra! A cobra!"

The disciples take a peek. *They see a cobra in the cell*, and general pandemonium ensues. Of course all they have actually seen is the master's necktie. Because of his words, they *imputed* "cobraness" to the necktie, and so that is exactly what they experienced. It was as real as a venomous snake to them. Their hearts beat faster and adrenaline flooded their bloodstreams.

And what horrified them was nothing but their imaginations.

That is our Air lesson in a nutshell: we believe that we are looking at reality, but the joke is almost always on us. Our interpretations may be completely wrong – and we may be the last ones to know it.

A false belief that there was a venomous snake in the room would lead me to behave in apparently crazy ways – I would be terrified of a necktie. *But I am not really crazy.* I am just navigating on the basis of bad information. If I were to look very carefully at that "cobra" – if I were to truly and skillfully *pay attention* to it – I would quickly realize that it was actually nothing but a necktie. My craziness would vanish.

There in this little anecdote, as we will see, is the Airy pathway to the higher evolutionary ground: *it is not simply that we are learning to "trust our senses;" it is that we are learning to make our senses trustworthy.*

A ROGUE'S GALLERY OF FAILED RESPONSES TO THE AIR ELEMENT

- Humans, for a long time, believed that the Earth was flat. Have a peek – it certainly *looks* flat . . .
- Pick your prejudice: sexism, racism, homophobia. In each one, we see a vivid illustration of the triumph of erroneous belief over actual observation.
- An insecure partner fears infidelity on the part of a lover who is actually faithful. How does that relationship go?
- The stock market is in free-fall. Many people, in a froth of panic, stampede to sell. A few cooler heads choose that moment to start buying. Who gets rich?
- Someone brashly announces, "I've been smoking cigarettes for thirty years and they've not done me any harm yet."
- "There is nothing new to be discovered in physics" – words spoken by a celebrated 19th century physicist, just dogs' years before Einstein published his Special Theory of Relativity.
- My personal favorite: people, completely ignorant of astrology, who "don't believe in astrology."

OPINION AND INTERPRETATION

No one can escape the *zeitgeist*. The times in which we live, especially in youth, always leave a mark on us. That mark typically takes the form of certain assumptions that we make about life and our place in it – assumptions which people might find laughable or worse in ten years' time. The casual racism we see, for example, in the films and novels of a few generations ago was mostly unnoticed at the time, at least by people of the privileged Caucasian persuasion.

Were these bad people? That interpretation seems harsh; my interpretation is that they were simply products of their time.

But that is only my interpretation. That is just my opinion, in other words – one which I, like you, may be inclined to mistake for reality.

Is my belief actually a mistake? I don't know. Were those people actually bad human beings? What is your *opinion?*

And be careful: what you think is only an interpretation as well.

Welcome to the kinds of sensitivities we need to develop if we are truly to understand the Air Family. These sensitivities are about the ways that *all interpretations of reality are potentially blinding.*

And yet, they are all we have.

BACK TO CHARLES E.O. CARTER

Charles E.O. Carter, whom I mentioned a little earlier, was a man of his times. He wrote a century ago, when the Sun was just beginning to set on the British Empire. See if you can detect the signature of his place in history in these words of his from *An Encyclopedia of Psychological Astrology*: "Air, however, is distinctly related to the Intellect and is only fully manifest in human beings . . . This may be seen in gregarious animals, but it is most obvious when it is set in motion consciously by mankind. Indeed, man owes his supremacy upon the globe to his conscious and unconscious recognition of its value."

Carter, from the modern point of view, is being awfully hard on the chimpanzees, dolphins, elephants, and ravens. We now understand that these creatures are capable of feats of logic and reason that overlap with human capabilities. And of course where our vaunted brains have actually

brought us in terms of our continued "supremacy upon the globe" is looking increasingly shaky.

Simply said, all creatures great and small – not to mention every event,
institution, or thought that has *a moment of birth* – reflects some aspect of
the Air function. All entities swim in a sea of data – and all live or die based
on their ability to align their perception of reality with reality itself.

Otherwise they slip on unseen banana peels while running in panic
from "cobras" that are actually neckties.

AIR IS THE HUMAN ELEMENT

With all that said, right in the core of the ancient astrological symbolism
there remains a clue we cannot ignore. Aries is a ram, Taurus is a bull,
Capricorn is a goat – they are all animals, in other words. But what about
the three Air signs? Gemini is represented by *human* twins, Aquarius by a
human Water-Bearer, and Libra, while not human, is symbolized by a human invention: the balance scales.

Not a beastie among them.

Virgo – an Earth sign – is a human virgin, but the other two Earth
signs are animals. Water is all "creatures" too: a crab, a scorpion, and a fish.
Leo is a lion, and Sagittarius is a Centaur – a weird melding of a human
and horse.

Only the Air element lacks a single animal symbol – that is, unless
we view *homo sapiens* as an animal. And of course that is exactly what we
are. Still, we cannot ignore this clue without doing some serious denial and
compartmentalization.

So, to what *interpretation* shall we fall prey here? Are humans "higher"
than the animals? And, if so, is Air "higher" than the other three elements?

Before you answer, here is a better question: *do you feel that unmistakable tug of "opinion" trying to take hold of you?*

DZOGCHEN PONLOP RINPOCHE

Once, many years ago in North Carolina, I had the privilege of attending a
talk offered by the great *vajrayana* teacher, Dzogchen Ponlop. By a miracle
for which I will ever be grateful, I even had lunch with him, chatting about
astrology, enjoying the ease his fluent English afforded me.

Ponlop was born in 1965 in Sikkim, India. Early in his life, he was recognized as the reincarnation of a great teacher. In the Tibetan Buddhist traditions of which he is a part, there are many treasures. Perhaps the most precious of them are instructions around the process of dying and death, and about the experiences that lie just beyond that mortal door. If you are interested in learning more about any of that, I would heartily recommend Dzogchen Ponlop's book, *Mind Beyond Death*. In the eternal fashion of the Air Family, that book changed my life by changing my mind. Maybe it will perform that same magic for you too.

As astrologers, we are obviously quite focussed on birth rather than death – the process of *in*carnation. But what about what we might call *ex*-carnation – the process of exiting the flesh? To the Tibetans, that process is also quite astrological in nature. I bring up Dzogchen Ponlop here because of a traditional teaching about death that he recounts in *Mind Beyond Death*. According to this understanding, on our death-beds, attachment to our worldly bodies and our worldly minds unravels in an astrological order. Here is how it is described: *Earth dissolves into Water, Water dissolves into Fire, and Fire dissolves into Air.*

Air, in turn, dissolves into *Space*. But that is the actual "moment of death," at least as it would be defined medically. In that final moment, we are carried beyond the universe as it is described by astrology.

In simple terms, to the best of my own understanding, the Earth element represents the *physical body* and our attachment to it. That attachment and identification is the first thing to dissipate when we come to the end of the trail.

Water is the *emotional body* – when it is done dissolving, some of the emotional drama connected to dying fades away. Acceptance arises.

Fire? The fighting spirit of the survival instinct – the *will to continue living* in the physical form – surrenders to the larger framework of Grace.

Finally, with the Air dissolution, *our identification with our own thoughts* is released. We no longer let an *interpretation* of what is happening to us blind us to the mysterious processes of waking up from the dream of physical life.

These are profound subjects, and if you would like to learn more, I again refer you to Dzogchen Ponlop's work. But I am bringing up this elemental dissolution-sequence of Earth to Water to Fire to Air for a very specific reason: according to the Tibetans, *Air is the last element to go.*

Another way to say it is that, in a sense, Air is the highest and most subtle of the four elements.

What is closer to your essence than your own thoughts? *Are* you your thoughts?

Charles E.O. Carter may have been a little too cocky about being human and a bit disrespectful to the other creatures with whom we share our planetary home. But he was in harmony with one fundamental truth: that Air – *awareness itself* – is the element closest in nature to the human soul. Perfecting our response to it – which is to say, perfecting our ability to truly *pay attention* – is perhaps our clearest path to a state of enlightenment.

And what does Air look like when it is perfected?

A flawless mirror placed before reality as it actually is.

No opinions, no interpretations, no arguments.

Only what is.

How do we get there? Follow the treasure map:

- First you *learn how to Gemini*, then you *learn how to Libra*, then you *learn how to Aquarius*.

Eighteen words, but they also serve pretty well as an outline of this book. "*To*" Gemini – I like to make the signs verbs rather than nouns, by the way; I like to make them active. That is because the signs of the zodiac are *evolutionary pathways*, not pre-recorded, immutable "personality traits" inserted between your ears at birth.

Master those three active steps and the mirror of consciousness and the mirror of reality dissolve into each other.

Read on and we will explore this ancient mystical pathway together.

2

THE GRAND SCHEME

The three Air signs – Gemini, Libra, and Aquarius – should all marry each other and live happily ever after. That, at least, is the conventional astrological dogma. The truth is far more complex. While it is true that the three Air signs share a lot of common ground, rumors of their "harmony" have been greatly exaggerated.

Still, as we have already begun to explore in our opening chapter, all three of them are about one unified theme: various ways of "paying attention." That gives them significant common ground. Despite my hesitation to pronounce them happy bedmates, I do believe that it is true to say that these three zodiacal signs form a natural marriage. The trick is to remember that "marriage" is a loaded word. As soon as we begin to think about it realistically, we instantly dive a lot more deeply into the actual mysteries of the symbolism.

Marriage, as we all know, is not always an easy road. Again, as almost all of us have learned from experience, partners often find themselves "paying attention" to exactly the same subject, while reading it in wildly divergent ways.

Going deeper, as we generally figure out by the time we are twenty years old, "living happily ever after" is a fairytale. Life is rarely that simple, for starters. Delving deeper yet, we might also recognize that such a "supernaturally harmonious" couple would actually learn very little from each other. A healthy marriage needs some grit in the system – and, as we will soon see, the three Air signs provide each other with plenty of that creative tension.

Claiming that Gemini, Libra, and Aquarius "get along harmoniously" entirely misses the underlying point of their relationship. Equally simply – and with a lot more accuracy – we can instead say that they are *good for each other.* Each one brings something fresh to the table – something that is completely alien, not easily digested, and yet totally nutritious to the other two.

As with the elements Fire, Earth and Water, the Air Family forms an *interdependent whole.* It is this very *interdependency* which puts life in the system. These three need each other and feed each other.

And, as in any truly living human marriage, they drive each other crazy sometimes.

Just to put some lead in our shoes, let's start with a simple, almost "Sun Sign," view of Gemini, Libra, and Aquarius. Let's also ask some questions that Sun Sign astrologers tend not to ask. Our aim here is not to demolish the idea that these three signs can exist in some degree of harmony, but rather to grant their interdependent relationship the complexity, tension – and ambivalence – it deserves, and on which it thrives.

- Libra – the Balance Scales – is looking for peace, unity, and equilibrium. How does it react when scattered, hyperkinetic Gemini crashes into the room? Or when rebel Aquarius takes a contrary position for the sheer joy of argument?
- Aquarius wants to change the world. It understands that you cannot make that particular omelet without breaking a few eggs. How does Aquarius react when Libra suggests that we should all just live and let live in a spirit of mutual tolerance and courtesy? Or when Gemini prefers a discussion group over a revolution?
- Gemini is endlessly curious. How does it feel when Libra indirectly implies that certain lines of inquiry are off-limits, being too indelicate or graceless? Or, when fixed-sign Aquarius already has its mind made up and "doesn't need any more stinking talk?"

It will take us many pages to do justice to these three Air signs; Lord knows we have not done it with these three almost cartoonish sketches. Each of these signs is a very deep well of human evolutionary meaning. A hundred words about the creative tensions that link them together can only begin to scratch the surface – but hopefully we are already bidding adieu to the dead-end notion that they simply "like each other."

Their dance has vastly more vitality than that.

TEN SYMBOLS (NOT NINE)

As with the two previous volumes in this series, *The Book of Fire* and *The Book of Earth,* in these pages we are not only exploring Gemini, Libra, and Aquarius. We are also considering the three "Air houses" which correspond to them – houses three, seven, and eleven. Rounding out our view of the Air element, we will also consider the planets that rule the three Air signs.

And that is where things begin to get complicated.

With Gemini and Libra, determining rulership is straightforward enough – Mercury rules Gemini and Venus rules Libra. But a great way to start a food fight at any gathering of astrologers is to feign a beginner's ignorance and say, *"I forget . . . which planet rules Aquarius?"* You will get staunch traditionalists who point to Saturn and modernists who prefer Uranus. Often the resultant discussion gets acrimonious.

Later in the book, we'll have a lot more to say about that question, but for our purposes here, let me simply state that we will be using both ruler-ships. Bottom line, both Saturn and Uranus share many common agendas with Aquarius, and, to me at least, that is the essence of the idea of rulership.

So, with Fire and Earth, we had to master a vocabulary of nine words. With Air, given the dual rulership of Aquarius, we are up to ten.

Another complication, at least for me as an author, is that since Venus, Mercury, and Saturn rule Taurus, Virgo and Capricorn, respectively, I've already written extensively about them in *The Book of Earth.* Even so, I can't leave them out of this book – that would put a huge hole in the picture. At the same time, I'm loath to simply copy/paste what I've already written about those three planets in the previous two books and just insert it here – to make you buy it all twice, in other words.

What I have decided to do in these pages is to take a more "Airy" spin on all three of these planets, emphasizing some fresh dimensions of their natures. Inevitably there will be some repetition from the earlier book, but I will try to minimize it.

In *The Book of Earth*, we also covered Venus, Mercury, and Saturn in "cookbook" fashion – that is to say, individually, sign by sign, house by house, and in terms of aspects. That kind of material remains the same no matter which element we are discussing, and so for the sake of making this volume self-contained and complete, all of those paragraphs appear once again here in identical form. We also looked in similar cookbook fashion at the transits, progressions, and solar arcs of those three planets. Again, for the sake of completeness, most of that material is repeated *verbatim* in this book – but with one major exception: in *The Book of Earth*, we considered the meaning of all ten planets as they moved through Taurus, Virgo, and Capricorn. In these pages, we will replace those Earth signs with Air signs. We will reflect on the meaning of each of the planets as they enter Gemini, Libra, or Aquarius via transit, progression, or solar arc.

All of that "entering an Air sign" material is fresh writing.

Since Uranus is new territory, in these pages we will delve into it more deeply than we do Saturn. Later on, we will also devote an entire chapter to the *Uranus cycle*, which illuminates the critical developmental steps we are all invited to take around the ages twenty-one, forty-two, sixty-three, and finally at age eighty-four when Uranus returns to its starting point. Together with the Saturn cycle which we covered in *The Book of Earth* and the cycle of the progressed Moon which lies ahead in *The Book of Water*, an understanding of the Uranian cycle unlocks the astrological dimensions of the mysteries of aging and maturation.

In *The Book of Earth*, we delved into Mercury's retrograde cycles, both by transit and, more importantly, by progression. None of that material will be repeated here, even though for a complete understanding of Mercury, understanding it is essential. I encourage you to read the previous volume if you have not done so already.

Balancing the void where Mercury retrograde should go, in Chapter Twenty-One, we'll fathom a mystery of Venus which we ignored in *The Book of Earth*: its elegant eight-year pentagonal cycle, as Venus's successive alignments with the Sun spin out a nearly perfect five-pointed star.

So, in summary, we need to master a vocabulary of ten words, and lucky us – if you've been following this elements series, some of the words are already familiar.

Underlying everything is one critical, pivotal idea: each of these ten symbols is about a different dimension of the art of *paying attention*. And each one captures the attention of the other nine simply by asking them some very unexpected questions.

A QUICK WORD ABOUT SIGNS, PLANETS, AND HOUSES

Since the beginning of human time, people have been feeling their intuitions pulling them in one direction while logic and reason pulled them in another. Our heads and our hearts operate *interdependently*, in complementary fashion – either that, or they simply argue. Either way, together, head and heart form a very simple *model of the mind*.

In similar fashion, Freud suggested dividing the mind into *ego*, *id*, and *superego*.

Then there's the *enneagram*, with its nine orientations of mind, each with their own strengths and interests.

In astrology, the planets, taken together, do the same thing as the rest of these mind-maps. Together, they also form a model of the human mind. For example, everyone has an ego, even though those egos can take many forms. Ego is equivalent in many ways to the Sun.

Everyone has some degree of self-discipline. That is Saturn.

Everyone *thinks*. That is Mercury – but Mercury gives us an example of how astrology quickly gets more complicated: *not everyone thinks in the same way*. Not everyone has the same interests or curiosities. Still, in every case, all *styles of thinking* boil down to the same planet: Mercury.

What gives astrology its uncanny ability to reflect human differences is that Mercury can occupy any one of the twelve signs *and each one orients a person's thinking according to a different set of values, attitudes, interests, and motivations*. We might find Mercury in Sagittarius, for example. In that sign, the planet takes on philosophical curiosity and an interest in other cultures. In Cancer, Mercury's orientation becomes more psychological, familial, and domestic.

Signs condition planets, in other words. They give the planets style and individuality.

We take it all a step further when we recognize that each planet-sign combination falls in a different house. In essence, houses are the more concrete, outward arenas of life – *theaters of action* which we enter and in which we make the decisions that shape our biographical lives. There is a house of money, and a house of relationships, and a house of work, and so on. Houses are particularly tied to *synchronicity* – they reflect the *circumstances* which life is guaranteed to thrust upon us . . . "by chance," as people say. For example, somebody might have a lot of planets in the eleventh house, which refers to *group affiliations*. Even if that person is an introvert, he or she will constantly be faced with situations involving movements, organizations, teams, or clans. Meanwhile, his or her *attitude* towards those group circumstances is much more connected to the signs.

In one pithy line, it is fair to say that we *are* our signs and we *do* our houses.

The planets themselves, taken together as an integrated system, represent something akin to the "blank slate" of human identity. They then need to be colored by signs and houses before they become recognizably human.

Pulling together these *triads* of planet, sign, and house is perhaps the most primary astrological skill. We saw many examples of it in the previous two books in this series. We will see many more in the pages that follow.

THE INTERDEPENDENCY OF THE AIR FAMILY

Gemini, Libra, and Aquarius, taken together, can be understood to represent about one quarter of the universe and one quarter of all the possibilities in it. They are, in other words, vast subjects. Keep turning these pages and you will learn a lot about all three of them. Here, in this initial overview, I want to introduce them in simple terms and underscore their essential interdependency.

One thing you will certainly learn as we go forward is that Gemini, Libra, and Aquarius are very different from each other. As we saw in the previous chapter, pop-astrology rumors of them all "getting along harmoniously" have been grossly exaggerated. It is truer to say that they *need* each other than it is to say that they *like* each other. They can potentially compliment and balance each other. That sounds good and ultimately it *is* good – but think of a socially-skillful friend of yours "balancing" you one afternoon by pointing out that you ran your mouth a little too long at the party last night.

You may *need* to hear it, but that does not mean that you *want* to hear it. That is how it is with Gemini, Libra, and Aquarius.

Let's begin our study of the "Unified Field Theory" of the Air Family with a quick look at the three Air signs individually, then we will move on to reflect on the dance of *mutual rescue* that they do together.

GEMINI

Perception – if I were limited to one single word for Gemini, that would be it. For clarity's sake, I want to remain focused on signs here, but perception would also be my first choice for Mercury and for the third house – for the whole Gemini Clan, in other words.

In more conventional astrology books, for Gemini we might hear the word "communication" rather than perception. Communication is a useful word too – but before we have anything to communicate, we need to have *seen something* in the first place, and in the second place, to have *thought about* what we have seen. Thus we have, in Gemini, a three-layered cake: *speech resting upon the foundation of thought and thought resting upon the foundation of perception.*

Remove perception, and thought and speech disappear. They would have no ground on which to stand.

And true perception always leads us directly to that Geminian evolutionary superhighway: *questions.*

Women and men with a lot of Gemini planets of course have opinions about things. They have tastes and interests, and also areas of life which hold no fascination for them at all. They are as human as anyone else, in other words. But if we could somehow pull the elixir of Gemini out of them, distill it down to its essence, crystalize it and strip it of any admixture of the other signs, we would see only the *raw interface of consciousness and the five senses* – or six senses, for that matter, counting our psychic faculties. No interpretation, no judgement – just the *act of seeing* itself, and a relentless, gnawing hunger for experiencing it, which is also known as *curiosity.*

Gemini is ultimately about *paying attention* with absolute clarity, no agenda and no attachments. It is the *witness*. It is the perfect mirror held before reality. It is about asking the kinds of questions that knock the stilts out from under our assumptions and our certainties, opening the doorway to fast-track evolution.

LIBRA

Relationship – were I limited to one word, that is the one I would choose to represent Libra. I would quickly add that as I am using the word here, *relationship* does not refer in a narrow sense to romantic sexuality. We will definitely include that kind of love in our Libran mix; it's just that "relationship" has a far wider meaning. We include the relationships among friends – or between enemies, for that matter. More broadly, under the Libran banner, we must also include a sensitivity to the *aesthetic relationships* that exist between colors, words, and musical notes. Also the relationships between ideas, especially ideas which exist in *fruitful tension* with each other.

Libra is symbolized as the Balance Scales. Imagine a measured ounce of lead on one platform, and gold dust carefully poured out onto the other. Eventually these two very different substances find a point of equilibrium. Thus, in that Balance Scale you might detect a metaphor for every partnership that has ever survived happily in human history: *lead and gold, finding a way to balance each other,* just like two human beings working things out between themselves. It is also how democracy works, when it works. And how humans get along with each other, once they get over themselves. And why drums sound good with guitars, and a dash of orange paint lights up a field of green, and sweet balances sour, and the good guys are no fun at all without a few bad guys in the mix.

Libra is about *duality reconciled.* It is about the Hermetic Law that we live in a universe in which *opposites define each other* – where up has no meaning without down, nor wet without dry, nor hot without cold. Nor me without you.

Another way to express it is the notion that everything has two sides: every coin, and every story.

The *close attention we pay to each other* is very near the heart of Libra.

AQUARIUS

One word for Aquarius? *Individuality* – or if you grant me three words, I will say the *process of individuation*. Those are really just fancy ways of saying that most of us benefit from spending some time trying to sort out who we actually are from what we have been trained to be.

One corollary is that people who are not actively drawn to engage in that kind of critical Aquarian self-examination all look a lot more alike than they prefer to admit.

One of the reasons that this individuational process requires a lot of effort is because since infancy we have all been pressured into adopting a false, socially-conditioned identity. One of my favorite ways to go directly to the heart of the matter with my Aquarian-inflected clients is to pose an unanswerable question: *who would you be today if you had had a different mother?* Everyone immediately understands that the answer is huge – but no one can answer the question. The mind just boggles. In your head, where does your mother stop and the real you start?

That simple insight brings us to the essence of Aquarius: *trying to sort out our soul's true path from the ocean of influences that have shaped us.* Mom is on the list, but the line-up of suspects is far longer. None of us, for example, are personally responsible for the existence of sexism, but male or female, it has had an impact on your life. Ditto for the digital revolution, capitalism, global climate disruption, the movie industry, racism, William Shakespeare, birth control, advertising, body-image fascism, politics – the list would be longer than this book. You are swimming in a sea of distorting social influences. Furthermore, they got to you when you were young and defenceless and they began to inflict "normalcy" upon you. Culture is inseparable from brain-washing.

Can you "be true to yourself?" That is not just a question of courage. It is closer to a question about the kind of wisdom that comes with fearless self-inquiry, along with a willingness to tolerate judgment and disapproval – or at least to avoid becoming a dancing monkey in an effort to please or impress everyone else.

Aquarius is about *paying attention* to the guidance – and sometimes it is very subtle guidance – of our own souls in the face of all the training, indoctrination, bribes, and threats that constitute modern society.

1+1+1= 3 = HOW TO PAY ATTENTION

So what about our Unified Field Theory of the Air signs? What about the *interdependency* of Gemini, Libra, and Aquarius? Here at the outset, let me spell it out very simply. In later chapters, we will honor all the nuances, counter-currents, and complexities.

Let me begin by affirming that even if you are "a Gemini," you have Libran and Aquarian elements in your psyche. That remains true even if you have seven planets in Earth signs.

Remember too that Gemini, Libra, and Aquarius are approximate stand-ins for houses three, seven, and eleven. Even if you have no planets in Air signs, there is a good chance that you have a planet or two in at least one of those houses. These houses are not interchangeable with the Air signs, but, as we will soon see, they do raise parallel issues and concerns.

And of course we can absolutely guarantee that you have Mercury, Venus, Saturn, and Uranus somewhere in your chart. They too carry some of the energetic signatures we are exploring.

Going further, almost certainly at least a couple of those Air signs fall on the cusps of houses. That is true unless those signs are *intercepted* – that is, completely swallowed up by a house. They are still part of you even in that case, but they'll be less visible in your outward life.

Nobody escapes the Air Family, in other words. They are part of everyone.

Here is how they dance together.

To pay attention effectively . . .

- We light the fuse with Geminian curiosity, questions, and open-mindedness. We take a wide-open, fresh look at everything that arises on our path. We must cultivate the "beginner's mind," free of the traps created by our own self-perceived expertise. Everything is a surprise. We watch, we read, we commit to endless learning. *We try to see everything as if we are seeing it for the first time.* It all starts with our eyes and our ears, and the fine art of keeping them wide open. We resolve to live in a state of perpetual wonder and amazement. We assume that whatever we see, the truth is more than that. We expect miracles.

- Then, in a spirit of cooperation, openness, and humility, we *compare notes,* Libra-fashion, with a few, consciously-chosen soul-friends who are our worthy companions – and, sometimes, our adversaries. Who among them will challenge us with exactly the right questions? Who among them *sees what we are missing?* Going further, we must also learn to live with *paradox* and *ambiguity* since they are inherent to the actual nature of reality. We learn about them by finding respectful points of balance with people whom we *perceive as our equals* and yet who see the world differently from the way we see it. Above all, we learn that taking a breath and letting it out before we jump to any conclusions – cultivating mindful *serenity of spirit,* in other words – supports us in finding balanced, fair understanding.

- Finally, having observed life for ourselves and then having availed ourselves of the *alien wisdom* of trusted others, we come, Aquarian-fashion – that is to say, independently, honestly, and bravely – to our own *personal conclusions,* even if they run counter to what everyone else is thinking. Gemini and Libra taught us that contradictory truths can exist simultaneously – so which truths actually work best for us personally? We do not require anyone else's agreement in order to have faith in our own views. We must learn to navigate our lives according to the realities that have been revealed to us, even if the social price is high. We value love, but we prize truth even more highly. And we recognize that of all the negative forces that might block this understanding from arising in us, our *social conditioning* tops the list.

That is how the three Air signs can potentially cooperate. That is how they help us learn the fine art of paying close attention. That is how we distill our raw sensory experience into the elixir of true wisdom and meaningful understanding. That is how we endlessly correct the alignment of our beliefs with what is actually happening.

That is how we accurately *impute meaning* to what our six senses are registering as we experience this wrap-around dream we are taught to call reality.

PART ONE

THE THREE AIR CLANS

3

THE GEMINI CLAN: MERCURY, THE THIRD HOUSE, AND THE SIGN OF THE TWINS

Growing up, I was not much drawn to the Greek myths. As an astrologer, some knowledge of them comes packaged with the drinking water, but I've still not dived very deeply into them with any kind of scholarly ambitions. Gemini-fashion, I'm not particularly proud of that lapse in my knowledge – being proud of any kind of ignorance never struck me as a virtuous condition, even for someone who isn't a Gemini.

Wait a minute . . . I forget what I was talking about . . . oh yes, it was Greek myths – but I wanted to say something about stars too. Did I tell you that? I can't remember . . .

And there was something else as well . . . what was it?

Simply with the title of this chapter, I have already invoked the great god Gemini, as you can perhaps detect in my intentionally rambling opening here. Invoking that particular god entails certain risks: in classic Gemini style, my mind is already merrily *free-associating*. My thoughts are scattering down four or five pathways simultaneously, all of them fascinating, all of them interconnected somehow . . . I think.

Ignorance is never a virtue: that's definitely a Gemini-point.

But wait a minute: stars!

I remember now: I wanted to talk about two bright stars, Castor and Pollux. They're both in the *constellation* Gemini . . . which isn't exactly the same as the *sign* Gemini – but that's another story. Ever heard of the Precession of the Equinoxes? That's why there's astrological and astronomical Gemini. Anyway, what was I saying? Castor and Pollux are stars – but they're not actually in *astrological* Gemini. They are also brothers in a Greek myth.

See?

I also wanted to talk about the Roman Empire and how we are all still awaiting its eventual fall.

And stars remind me of telescopes – and telescopes remind me of eyes, which are actually yet another Gemini-thing: the five senses.

Or six senses, if you count our psychic perceptions.

Now, where was I?

Are you following?

Am I making any sense?

Welcome to the realm of Gemini, where everything quickly leads to everything else.

EVERYTHING IS CONNECTED

If I assert that "everything is connected to everything else," I doubt that anyone with the inclination to read this book would quibble. But when we start actually trying to embody that big idea, you might detect a certain loss of focus. I've tried to embody that careening experience in these opening lines.

"Everything" turns out to be a very big subject.

You might also observe precisely this same *free-associative* quality in your Gemini-inflected friends. Trying to follow their threads of reason can be a roller-coaster ride. As we will see, there is a definite quality of genius in it, provided we can surf the colliding waves of universal interconnectedness without losing our balance.

I have often thought of two of those colliding Geminian waves as *Order* and *Chaos*. That's not exactly the point of the Greek myth about the brothers, Castor and Pollux, but ... *oh yeah, I remember now:* as I was saying, growing up I was not much drawn to Greek mythology.

So let's start with the stars instead.

CASTOR AND POLLUX

Those are the two brightest stars in the constellation Gemini. Once you know what to look for, they are easy to recognize in the sky since it is unique to have two "first magnitude" (really bright) stars so close together. As a kid, I suspect Gemini was the first constellation I learned to spot after Orion and the Big Dipper. Not only was it easy to think of the stars Castor and Pollux as twins, but the heavens made it even easier: two lines of dimmer stars parade under the bright pair, representing their bodies.

In Greek mythology, we learn that Castor and Pollux were twins *sired by different fathers*, just like a litter of kittens might reflect mama-cat's expansive approach to dating. *Superfecundation* is the word, by the way, and it does actually happen with humans sometimes.

Castor's dad was Zeus, the king of the gods. That made Castor immortal.

Pollux, on the other hand, had a mere mortal for a father: Tyndareus, the king of Sparta. Having a mortal father made him subject to death, and thereby hangs the tale.

When Pollux was killed, heartbroken Castor intervened with his dad, who was the king of the universe. A deal was struck: the two brothers would be immortalized together in the heavens.

And that is where the constellation Gemini originated, at least if you take your Mediterreanean mythology literally.

THE FALL OF THE ROMAN EMPIRE

Mahatma Gandhi was asked what he thought of western civilization. He famously responded, "I think it would be a good idea." (His Mercury was in acerbic Scorpio, but I am getting ahead of myself.) I bring up Gandhi's words because I feel the same way about the fall of the Roman Empire. It too would be an excellent idea.

(Remember: I am talking about Gemini – and, truth said, I am actually trying to live it right here before your eyes, which is no mean feat for an orderly Capricorn.)

The Romans basically inherited the Greek gods and goddesses. And when the Roman Empire fell as a political entity, who then inherited that same ancient hand-me-down pantheon? The answer is looking back at you from your mirror: a millennium later, the main heirs of those same gods and goddesses are we astrologers. Who else today has such a personal relationship with Mercury and Jupiter and Neptune and the rest of them? Who else cares? We inherited the treasure.

Everybody else thinks Pluto is a cartoon dog.

Each and every culture on the face of the earth has something helpful to teach us. And that coin has two sides: each and every culture also has its own biases and limitations. Romans, Greeks, or Eskimos – they export those poisons too.

The Graeco-Roman mythology is precious and powerful. Modern astrology would not be nearly as rich a treasure as it is without those stories. And it is truly weird and wonderful that when Neptune and Pluto were discovered and *astronomers* named them, those mythological names worked out quite accurately in terms of the observed meanings of the two planets.

That is pure synchronicity, by the way.

Still, I often wonder about the Meso-American god-figure, Quetzacoatl, and what we astrologers might learn from those half-forgotten stories – at least once we mapped them into the familiar signs and planets.

In *The Book of Earth*, we looked specifically at the old northern European god, Woden or Odin, and related him directly to Mercury – and thereby learned a thing or two about Mercury that the Romans did not teach us.

What about *Yemaya*, the West African goddess of childbirth and water? Or *Kwan Yin*? Or *Green Tara*? Might the cultures that spawned those stories have also seen a few things the Greeks and Romans missed?

I am part of the problem; I'm an old astrologer now, immersed in the old Greek and Roman perspectives, even if I'm not a scholar of mythology. But I do expect that a day will come when an astrologer – maybe one not yet born – turns to a client and says, *"Your progressed Quetzacoatl is trine your natal Yemaya . . ."*

Quickly note four observations:
- That last sentence may be among the weirdest that you have ever read.
- But that is *exactly what astrologers do today*. The only difference is that we mostly use the names of *Roman* gods and goddesses rather than Mexican or African ones.
- I hope that I have just triggered some cognitive dissonance in you, followed closely by the light bulb lighting over your head.
- If so, welcome to Gemini, where shock and surprise lead directly to insight.

MORTALITY VERSUS IMMORTALITY

Castor was immortal, but brother Pollux could die. Reincarnation aside for a moment, which condition would you prefer for yourself? There is, of course, a reflexive response in all of us: *give me immortality*. Who wants to die?

But with a bit of deeper scrutiny, the question becomes profoundly tricky.

Science fiction writers have often wrestled with this theme, positing the existence of an alien culture that has conquered death, or at least learned to extend life by centuries. In almost every such story, these people are absolutely miserable. How would you like to wake up 8278 years from now and see that same old face in the mirror? That's a little over three million mornings from now, day by day by day by weary day.

Upon reflection, we might begin to have a suspicion that the only thing more frightening than death might actually be immortality. Could physical death be one of life's fierce mercies?

The question is becoming less abstract by the minute too. There's much speculation lately about medical advances that might lengthen human life exponentially.

Let's say that happens. Do you take the pill?

Or not.

Let's just agree that all of this qualifies as a Discussion Group question, or perhaps a vigorous debate. *"In this corner, weighing in intellectually at 275 pounds, representing Immortality, we have Castor . . ."*

And in the other corner, we have Pollux. Remember: one brother was immortal, while the other one was not.

That discussion could go on for millennia and be no closer to resolution. *But what an interesting conversation!* That is Gemini paradise.

What year did Napoleon die? I say 1825. You say 1821. One of us whips out a cell phone, Googles the answer, and the debate is over: you win. He died in 1821.

Life abounds with simple yes/no questions such as that one. *But immortality versus mortality?* Google that question, and all that you will learn is that a whole bunch of really smart people have been wrestling with it since time began, and still no one is any closer to an answer.

It is these *unanswerable questions* that endure. *And it is these unanswerable questions that are the heart of Gemini.* The conversation between "Castor" and "Pollux" never ends; it is the engine that animates the Geminian soul.

Remember: *signs supply underlying agendas, values, and motivations for the planets that occupy them.* For any planet in Gemini to be happy and on its evolutionary track, it must be in a state of *endless learning*. It must be defeated by ever-vaster questions.

Defeated? Yes, that is what keeps the fun alive.

And to kill such a Geminian planet?

Easy: all you have to do is to *bore it to death.*

Next time you are at a dull party, try putting any one of the following conundrums on the table. Watch the Geminis (and the folks with big Mercury influences or planets in the third house) instantly perk up:

- At the end of your life, would you rather regret what you did or what you were not brave enough to do?
- Is time an illusion?
- Are human beings naturally monogamous or is that just a cultural thing?
- If you won a billion dollars, would you really be any happier in the long run?
- Are there really angels and miracles?
- Is there any such thing as a mistake?
- Who killed John F. Kennedy?

- Can humanity survive its own folly?
- Is there life after death?
- What was popular music's best decade?
- Which is more important – kindness or truthfulness?
- Do you believe in UFOs and aliens?

Guaranteed, any one of these questions will liven up that boring party – or anyone who is a son or daughter of the Gemini Clan. Again, it is *questions rather than answers* which underlie and animate this sign. It is on an eternal quest for information. In pursuing that path, it pays particular attention to the loose ends and the pieces that don't fit, sensing that it is there in those cracks that it will find the most illuminating clues.

THE VALUE OF A DATUM . . .

. . . is in inverse proportion to its predictability. That, as I understand it, is a basic principle of formal Information Theory. Translated, it boils down to a simple, intuitive idea: *the less we expect something, the more interesting it is.*

Johnny hits Billy and Billy hits Johnny back. We break up the fight and give the boys a quick lecture about world peace. Then we forget about it. Little boys fighting is hardly one for the history books.

Johnny hits Billy and Billy puts his palms together in the familiar *namaste*, and says, "Johnny, I hope that someday you can work through your anger issues."

That is a story people will still be telling about our Billy when he is forty-five years old. We never would have expected that reaction from a little boy. Therefore it is more valuable information.It tells us something useful about Billy.

What propels the evolution of Geminian planets is that unpredictable information, that exact *willingness to learn*, that *openness to the unexpected*, that sense that *whatever I see, the truth is more than that.*

Reduced to a single word, the Geminian north star is *curiosity.* Equally, we might say that it is all about *questions.*

Your best friend is Geminian. She lies dying in a hospital. You pay a visit. Gently, you ask her how she is doing. She says, "Dying is actually very interesting . . . I think my left leg died about an hour ago." . . .

Dying is *interesting* . . . your friend is somebody still making an A+ on the Gemini road, even though she is nearing the end of it, at least as far as this body goes.

TEACHER AND STORYTELLER

In silly pop astrology, there is a standard giggle: you can always recognize the Gemini. He is the one with his mouth open.

Slander! – well, at least sometimes.

The idea that Gemini people tend to chatter is an astrological commonplace. To simply call that observation wrong would be misleading. Gemini can indeed get off track and go down that chatterbox road, especially when feeling nervous.

Still, the twin archetypes of *Teacher* and *Storyteller* are both fundamental to this sign. And those two archetypes must *talk* in order to be themselves. There are not many other ways to teach or to tell a tale.

We cannot understand Gemini without thinking about language. I suspect that when the first hominid uttered the first meaningful human syllable, that hominid was a Gemini. "Communication" is a keyword here, for sure. But true communication is a two-way street. If we forget that, we miss half the point.

Verbal communication between people is just a small part of how the larger universe communicates with us. And those dispatches from everywhere – especially the unexpected ones – are what keep Gemini cooking. Everywhere in astrological literature and tradition, Gemini is tied to speech. Still, I've intentionally saved talking about language until near the end of this section. Perception itself – and most especially *radically open-minded perception*, unblemished by distorting opinions, theories, and axes-to-grind – must come first in our understanding of Gemini.

With those qualities, Gemini can indeed rise to its highest mission in the world, which is to be the Teacher or the Storyteller. With them on its side, *Gemini can find its voice.*

Without them, Gemini is just one more talking head – one more pedant with his or her mouth moving.

TEACHERS

Gemini, when truly manifesting as the Teacher, *plants the seeds of questions* in the minds of anyone who listens. The trouble is that when we hear the word "teacher," we naturally think of *expertise*: the teacher is the person who *knows the answers*. Gemini can play that role, no problem – but rote answers are tangential to its real purpose. Questions that take root in us, and ramify into more questions, more doubts about what we *thought we knew* – that is the soul of Gemini.

An old college professor of mine, Ruel Tyson, is on my short list for the wisest human being I have ever met. One day, he walked into my Religion class and said, "I am only interested in the obvious." Ruel passed away a few weeks ago, but I've been thinking about that line of his ever since I first heard him say it. A long meditation on "the obvious" – the *surfaces* of things – had led him to depths of understanding far beyond my own orbit. It seems that the harder we stare into the realm of "the obvious," the more mysterious it becomes.

Ruel Tyson was a solar Sagittarian, but I thank him for that very Geminian lesson early in my life.

When I first met my root spiritual teacher, Marian Starnes, I was a young testosterone-addled lion and I had a bit of attitude toward her "guru" status. After a lecture she gave, some friends marched me up to her to be introduced. Marian had heard of my astrological work, which was just beginning to take off in those days. Looking right into my eyes, her first words to me were, "Hello. I am a myth. *Are you a myth too?*"

An explosive, unexpected *question:* my mind spun; a seed germinated; I surrendered.

Those were Marian's exact words, spoken nearly half a century ago. I remember them as if she said them yesterday. That's the shape of true Geminian verbal magic. It is not "just talk." It has far more *mojo* than that. With Gemini at its best and most magical, something far more than "words" is going on. Suddenly everything looks different. Certainty evaporates.

In his haunting song, *That Voice Again*, the great British composer and performer, Peter Gabriel, sings, "It's only in uncertainty that we are naked and alive." Just ten words, but they stand as a good summary of almost everything in this chapter so far. Marian asked me if I were a myth; in one instant, all my cognitive defences were in a shambles. Ruel Tyson's reference to "the obvious" impacted me like a psychedelic; *what was right before my eyes that I was missing?*

Ruel Tyson and Marian Starnes were two of my greatest teachers. Neither one was a Gemini, and neither am I – but they each triggered a classic Geminian breakthrough in me.

How?

By saying words that stopped my mind in its accustomed tracks. By saying words that stopped the endless flow of business-as-usual, reality-affirming words in my own head.

THE STORYTELLER

What about Gemini the Storyteller? It is really nearly the same thing as the Teacher. When the story is pure Geminian elixir, *it stops the mind.* We are full of wonder and surprise. A space opens up in our awareness for something we never before knew, considered, or understood.

When I was a kid, I read a science fiction story about astronauts finding the ruins of a dead civilization on another planet. On that faraway world, they encountered wise aliens who were also exploring the same ruins. The astronauts asked the aliens if the ruins were theirs.

The aliens said, *"No, they are yours."*

That line knocked me out. Human ruins on another planet we thought we had "just discovered?" Humans had been there thousands of years earlier. How could that be? And yet it was true – at least, in the story. Gemini goosebumps. Sixty years on, and I still remember it exactly.

That's the Storyteller archetype in its full glory: the mind flips. You remember lines like that; they change you. Words such as those have magic. They do more than convey information. They do more than entertain us. They open our minds to unimagined possibilities.

On the other hand, every plodding, didactic story written by some preachy person with an axe to grind is soon forgotten. There is nothing unexpected in such tales; nothing to fascinate or beguile our attention. Just think of all the dumb movies you've seen. What do you actually remember? *There were some explosions, then the good guys won.*

The stories that endure are the ones that make us think and wonder. That is Gemini at its best.

Was Don Quijote really crazy?

Could Darth Vader have turned out to be a better man?

What if the Montagues and Capulets had cut Romeo and Juliet a little slack?

If you are carrying a lot of Gemini-energy, the evolutionary formula is simple to say: *start with questions.* The laws of synchronicity guarantee that you will be presented with many of them. Follow the loose threads. The most productive clues lie in the realm of the unexpected. Look for what undercuts your theories and your expectations. Pay attention to the obvious – and beware of letting a curtain composed of your own opinions, preconceptions, and "position papers" stand between you and being naked and alive.

Pull that thread, and your higher destiny as a Teacher or a Storyteller will crystallize before you.

And it is a destiny which is inseparably bound to language.

MERCURY: THE MESSENGER OF THE GODS

The planet Mercury whips around the Sun in just eighty-eight days. That is its "year" – and it is also actually its "day." With Mercury, the two are the same length. That is because one side of Mercury always faces the Sun and the other face is in perpetual darkness.

Feel some "Castor and Pollux" in that astronomical fact?

Here's another synchronicity: Mercury is the second-hottest planet in the solar system (after Venus, with its runaway global warming) – and weirdly it is also one of the coldest planets. That's because the dark side that faces away from the Sun is warmed only by the light of distant stars.

I've always marveled at how the universe seems to bend over backwards to spell out its astrological messages to us.

Going further down that road, Mercury – the fastest planet – corresponds to the fastest dimension of your psyche: it moves at the *speed of thought* itself. Many of us have some facility with a second language. Until we become fluent, we all have the same problem: understanding native speakers is often difficult because *they talk too fast.* Yet language, despite its high-velocity transmission, is slow compared to thought. *Saying something always takes longer than thinking it.*

Feel that zooming signature of Mercury and how closely it is connected to Gemini? Castor and Pollux are twins who are opposite each other in fundamental ways – and here is Mercury, half blinding light, half perpetual darkness, half-hot, half-cold. And it is as fast as greased lightning.

Geminian paradox is woven into the physical, material reality of Mercury. The solar system is an open book.

But only a poet can read it.

To the Romans, Mercury was *the messenger of the gods,* among other roles. Naturally, as soon as we think about messages, we are in familiar Geminian territory: language, whether it is spoken or written. To be painfully modern about it, Mercury translates to *data in and data out.*

That two-way street is critical here. Mercury leaves its fingerprints on how you speak. But it also leaves them on how you listen.

And how do we actually listen? How do we *pay attention* to the world?

Selectively must always be part of the answer.

When I think of Mercury, Gemini, or the third house, I always think of my favorite Hindu proverb: *When the pickpocket meets the saint, he sees pockets.* We all see the world according to our own natures and interests, in other words. I walk into a crowded social event. Spying a stranger, I might think, *"Ah! – a textbook example of a lunar type, but with perhaps just a dash of Uranus . . ."* Meanwhile, a life insurance salesman is looking at exactly the same person, thinking, *"Asian . . . prosperous . . . probable age: mid-fifties . . . probable life-expectancy: maybe forty more years. A good prospect . . ."*

Pickpockets see pockets.

One of the grandfathers of the Impressionists, Claude Monet, once said, "To see we must forget the name of the thing we are looking at." For us humans, that is a very tall order.

Who can see this world as it actually is? Again, we all look at it through the lens of our natures, our interests, and our appetites – not to mention our wounds, our educations, our cultures, and so on.

Unless we start talking about enlightened beings, probably no one can see the world as it actually is.

Here is an absolutely pivotal point in our understanding of Mercury. In reading these last few words, you may sense something akin to regret about how our own natures limit and distort our perceptions.

Don't worry about it! You have exactly the Mercury that you need. Read on, and you will see why that is true.

MERCURY AS THE FILTER

As abstract ideals, both Mercury and Gemini represent an open mind, unprejudiced, free of judgments, as neutral as a perfect mirror, and eager to *know everything.* In practical terms, we can balance all that with another principle: even one single moment of that degree of openness would probably put us all in mental hospitals. For the sake of sanity, we all need *filters* between ourselves and the overwhelming reality of the mystery "out there." Otherwise, it would bowl us over.

That is why, in a moment of consummate mercy, the Universe decided that, for humans, Mercury must always be in a particular sign and a particular house, while making a particular set of aspects. It must, in other words, experience the world in a filtered way.

But each person's filter array is distinct. *It is perfectly attuned to paying attention to exactly the kind of material that he or she most needs to perceive.*

To keep a roof over his head, our life insurance agent must make calculated length-of-life estimates. He does not want to sell a million-dollar policy to someone who will fall over dead before the end of the year. *Maybe his Mercury lies in clear-eyed, detail-oriented Virgo. Maybe it is functioning behaviorally in the context of the eighth house – the classic house of death.*

His perceptions serve him well.

And, at a deeper level, maybe some days he looks at himself in the mirror with that same objectivity about his own mortality. His death is always with him, counseling him, maybe haunting him. In the end, these more personal statements are closer to the true evolutionary purpose of his Mercury. He just happens to be able to make a living with those perceptual filters as well.

As with the rest of us, there is much in life that this life insurance salesman misses – but what he does see feeds his journey.

YOUR MERCURY IS JUST PERFECT

- Someone with Mercury in Scorpio might be told to "lighten up" from time to time. Here's the right response: *"If God wanted me to lighten up, She would have given me Mercury in Libra."*

- In parallel fashion, someone with Mercury in Gemini might be advised to try to concentrate on just one thing at a time. Meanwhile, he is noticing a song on the radio in the next room that reminds him of someone he once kissed in high school. Funny how that person gave him *exactly* the same advice about concentration . . . but her hair was red while yours is really more auburn. Might that path of free-association lead him to an important insight? Let's not rule out that possibility.

Your Mercury – and really, your entire chart – is ultimately a reflection of your natural evolutionary path. There are no errors in it at all. *You* may make mistakes, but your chart itself is perfect. Astrologers who speak of good charts and bad charts are missing the point. The idea that *you always have exactly the right chart* is bedrock. If we ever lose sight of it, astrology comes adrift from its metaphysical roots.

Of course, you are also in a karmic predicament. That's why you are here. Your chart reflects that less-flattering reality too. Each symbol can thus also be a trap for your evolving consciousness.

Still, each symbol also shows the *remedy* – how to escape the trap.

Mercury in Scorpio can sink into darkness, suspicion, bitterness, and misery. It can also penetrate down to the wounds and hurts that trigger those conditions, and thereby help us find liberation.

Mercury in Gemini can indeed dissipate its energy by never following through with any one thing. On the other hand, maybe that red-haired girlfriend made a wise comment that can only now be understood years later. A lightbulb lights up over our hero's head, all because of noticing that song on the radio in the other room while you were offering him a stern lecture about . . . something.

If you are starting to feel a little bit confused, you are probably right on target. That is the way it always is with true questions.

Let's spell out the underlying Castor-and-Pollux paradox:

- Your Mercury is perfect, and . . .
- You are trying to perfect it.

Those are both true statements, each one in its own way. The *sign* your Mercury occupies orients your intelligence and your curiosity to certain areas of interest. It also gives a particular style to your thinking. Master them and you will learn what you need to learn.

The *house* in which your Mercury is located takes it further: here is an area of life which will keep popping up and demanding your attention. Notice it; it has something to teach you.

Aspects spice the stew even further. And every piece of the Mercury puzzle represents new information – input that bears real fruit if you attend to it. There is always something there that you need to learn.

If you learn it, it triggers breakthroughs in terms of your understanding of your path.

If you don't learn it, you will find yourself stymied by bad information and distorted thinking. It will be as if you've got to travel from Madrid to London in this lifetime, but you are sure that traveling due west is how to get there.

How do you correct your map? You pay attention. And you particularly pay attention to the clues hidden in the loose ends, the unexpected, and that which is cognitively dissonant *in the categories of experience, learning, and perception represented by the position of your Mercury.*

That's where the magic lies.

SPEAK YOUR MIND

People who press you to "speak your mind" want to hear your straightforward opinion about some subject, even if they suspect they may not agree with it. That's what the phrase implies. But the reality is that all of us are *always* speaking our minds – whatever comes out of your mouth had its origin in your mind, and reveals its nature.

Someone telling lies had constructed those lies in her mind before her lips moved. Someone expressing appreciation had just felt a mental impulse of gratitude.

We sometimes say, "I spoke without thinking." But no one ever actually does that. Without the mind moving, there would be no basis for our saying anything at all.

These points are pretty obvious, but let's take them a step further.

There are some people to whom you naturally want to listen, even if you disagree with them. They are not necessarily eloquent; their verbal magnetism derives from a different source. They are speaking from their hearts.

We sense that kind of sincerity when it is present, and it invariably lends gravity to anyone's speech.

That is especially clear when we contrast such a soul-centered style of self-expression with the speech of someone who is just talking in order to be heard. Even if the words are eloquent, they are still reminiscent of a dog barking in the night – "I'm here! I'm here! I exist! Make note of me!"

You hear it, but it is meaningless and soon forgotten.

FINDING YOUR NATURAL VOICE

The point of all this is that the position of your natal Mercury represents your *natural voice*. When you speak from that part of your mind, there is a compelling authenticity to what you are saying. People listen; they can't help it. They sense that, unlike those "barking dogs," what you are saying is *worth* saying. And therefore it is worth hearing.

The person with Mercury in Capricorn might speak "conservatively" of *moral values* he or she thinks are worth preserving. And people listen, even wild people, even criminals.

Meanwhile, the person with Mercury in Aquarius might speak compellingly of justice and a better future, in contrast to the *status quo* – and the most conservative person *hears*. Those words sink in. Even if that conservative person is hesitant to agree, a seed is planted.

A person with Mercury in the eighth house makes a comment about the "Right To Die" movement. That is a charged subject; there are many strong opinions. But no one interrupts him or her; the words have authority. Five minutes later, a person with Mercury in any other house starts making the same point – and barely gets to her first comma before someone pipes up with a contrary view.

We all like to be taken seriously. Follow your Mercury path and people will listen to you. Just remember: *your Mercury path does not start with speech. It starts with learning.*

Humans have been comparing notes for a very long time now. Maybe it is my own Mercury in Capricorn, but I tend to fantasize about a past in which wise, simple ancestors sat around a campfire in mostly-silent support of each other. After half an hour, one of them might speak. Then there would be five or ten minutes of quiet reflection, until someone else was moved to respond.

Words were measured, treasured, given enough time to be powerful. That's Capricorn.

Now, of course, we have the twenty-four hour news cycle, with a talking head yammering away on all ninety-seven channels. We have the advertising industry and all of its lying faces: we know this toothpaste is not really going to improve our sex lives, but that face assuring us that it will looks so sincere.

We've had to become *defended against words*. Our defences are strong too – but there are still people who can break through them. These are the ones who have attuned themselves to their own distinct Mercurial energy. These are the ones who have found their *natural voices*. And their words are compellingly potent.

Some are scoundrels.

But most of these *true teachers* are people who are simply speaking to us directly out of their hearts and souls. And that statement is a plain English way of describing people speaking from the strong foundation of their natal Mercury.

- Each one of us was born with something important to say – something worth hearing, something that needs to be heard. Offering it is a gift to our community. On top of that spiritual benefit, it simply feels really good to be taken seriously and to have our words remembered.

Here is an excerpt from one of the most famous speeches of history. These words, from Winston Churchill, stirred the fainting hearts of Britain as the Nazi *wehrmacht* was storming across Europe, seemingly unstoppable.

The whole fury and might of the enemy must very soon be turned on us. Hitler knows that he will have to break us in this Island or lose the war. If we can stand up to him, all Europe may be free and the life of the world may move forward into broad, sunlit uplands. But if we fail, then the whole world, including the United States, including all that we have known and cared for, will sink into the abyss of a new Dark Age made more sinister, and perhaps more protracted, by the lights of perverted science. Let us therefore brace ourselves to our duties, and so bear ourselves that, if the British Empire and its Commonwealth last for a thousand years, men will still say, "This was their finest hour."

Might you guess that Churchill had his Mercury in Scorpio opposing an eighth-house Pluto? The point is not simply about his eloquence – the point is that he was speaking directly from the heart of his dramatic, "do-or-die" Mercury. As ever, that attunement to the unique nature of this natal configuration lent a higher *psychic harmonic of power and authority* to his voice. Churchill's words will be remembered forever.

Rev. Martin Luther King made many an eloquent oration, but none are recalled so readily as his famous *"I have a dream"* speech, delivered during the March on Washington in 1963. Speaking of his vision for a livable human future, King's words still stir the heart:

"And when this happens, and when we allow freedom to ring, when we let it ring from every village and every hamlet, from every state and every city, we will be able to speed up that day when all of God's children, black men and white men, Jews and Gentiles, Protestants and Catholics, will be able to join hands and sing in the words of the old Negro spiritual: 'Free at last! Free at last! Thank God Almighty, we are free at last!'"

These words are probably familiar to you, but let me just point out that M.L.King's Mercury was in Aquarius. Here he is, *speaking of a revolutionary future* which he can already feel in his bones. *He is speaking with the kind of authority and power that only comes out of the mouth of someone who has followed his or her Mercurial heart straight to the perceptions and understandings it promised – and which he or she has signed up to share with the human community.* There is history-shaping power in doing that. The people whose words are remembered have successfully created that exact alchemical transformation in their consciousness.

Would you like to be taken that seriously? Would you like to have your words remembered and treasured that way – and, more importantly, to know that what you said made a difference in the world? Or at least in someone else's life? You may not be as eloquent or as historic a figure as Winston Churchill or Martin Luther King, but if you honor the path Mercury has laid before you, your words will reflect the gravity and authority of truth you have actually experienced.

When you speak, people will listen – and they will remember.

MERCURY RULES TWO SIGNS

In teaching, I have often noticed that students quickly grasp Mercury's rulership of Gemini, but often have questions about its rulership of Virgo. In this volume, we are concentrating on the easier Mercury-Gemini connection, but to keep perspective, let's include a few words about Virgo too. In *The Book of Earth*, we learned that Virgo is associated with the master-student relationship: *apprenticeship*, in a single word. That notion derives from the common association of Virgo with the archetype of the Servant. All we need to do is to remember that *servants serve masters,* and the door of understanding opens wide. Any *unequal relationship* is in the Virgo (or sixth house) category. Those relationships run the gamut from true darkness (*master and slave*) to sweetness (*spiritual master and disciple; grandma teaching little Debbie how to knit*).

We humans learn in two ways: by listening and by questioning. There are two distinct insights there. Listening is the Virgo face of Mercury, while questioning is its Gemini face.

- Virgo: Anyone too arrogant to be a disciple will never become a guru. Humbly listening to those more advanced than ourselves is a fast-track to evolution in any category from meditation to brick-laying.
- Gemini: Anyone afraid to ask questions becomes a sheep, blindly following the footsteps of a teacher – and never adding anything new or correcting existing understandings.

When I teach my apprenticeship programs, I insist that everyone use my methods: Placidus houses, the Mean nodes rather than the True Nodes, electro-convulsive shock for saying "good" or "bad" aspects, an evolutionary perspective. I "batch process" questions in long Q&A sessions that are interspersed through the teaching days – and I discourage questions and comments while I am presenting the material in my Goaty linear fashion.

That admittedly totalitarian teaching path is effective; people quickly learn a solid, reliable method of practicing astrology.

Most likely, my students with Mercury in Virgo enjoy this approach more than my students with Mercury in Gemini.

Is the "Steven Forrest" method of doing astrology flawed? Probably. Does it reflect the limited values, interests, and language of one human being? Absolutely.

Still, *direct transmission* is an effective way of keeping a particular flame burning beyond one human lifespan. And it is efficient – no one spends years re-inventing the wheel.

All of that is Mercury-rules-Virgo wisdom.

The trouble is that such memorized, inherited systems often become static. Some essential element of creative life-force can go out of them. That is where the fact that Mercury rules Gemini enters the equations, ready to throw a monkey wrench into the smoothly-turning gears that Virgo created. People carrying such Geminian energy make fresh trouble. They ask the questions, find the loose ends, and they help to keep things alive.

We can learn from teachers or we can learn from life. Both methods work and both are necessary. Learning from teachers might limit our creativity. But another word for "learning from life" is "learning from our mistakes." And while that is a time-honored method, those mistakes can be costly in terms of the time they waste and the scars they leave.

It would be folly to try to decide which sign expression of Mercury's is the right one. We need them both. And Virgo and Gemini are of course in square aspect to each other – these two methods clash.

Like cougars and deer, they keep each other in balance.

THE THIRD HOUSE

Ask any astrologer the meaning of the third house and there is an excellent chance you will hear something about speech. If the astrologer is an astute one, you might also hear a word or two about *listening* as well. The third house is a two-way street; it has as much to do with *reception* as it does with *transmission.*

Without much of a stretch, we can extend our understanding of the third house to include reading and writing, teaching and learning. The word *media* is relevant here too, and indeed among people with packed third houses we often find videographers and documentarians, along with journalists, broadcasters, screenwriters, and authors.

When I sit with such a person, I often say that his or her destiny is "inextricably bound to language." In response, I generally see a head nodding in agreement – if not a paragraph or two of confirmation.

Having advanced this far into the Elements series, you have probably internalized the idea that *we are our signs and we do our houses*. Gemini thus provides energy and attitude, while the third house represents the *behavioral expression* of those same motivations.

If Gemini represents the *motivation* that we call "curiosity," then the third house represents the *action* of reading an informative book – or of asking a question.

If Gemini represents the *urge to experience surprise*, then the third house represents the *behavior of going to an unfamiliar restaurant or visiting a foreign country.*

If Gemini represents a *fascination with the phenomenon of language*, then the third house represents *adding a new word to our vocabulary* – or simply the act of speaking up.

Divide the entire universe into twelve boxes: those are the houses of the horoscope. Obviously, each one is huge. But if I had to reduce the third house to one single word, the one I would choose would be *perception*. The quintessential third house action lies in taking in fresh information.

It is the very essence of the behavioral act of paying attention. Get it right, and the third house is what paying attention should look like.

WHEN THE PICKPOCKET MEETS THE SAINT . . .

. . . he sees pockets. I've used that line before. I got it in *Miracle of Love*, Ram Dass's paean to his guru, Neem Karoli Baba. And don't those nine words say it all? We all see the world according to our natures and our interests – that is an idea that we have already encountered frequently in exploring the planet Mercury. You may remember our life insurance salesman and his astute ability to estimate how many years you have left in this world. Or my own tendency to immediately package everyone I meet in astrological categories.

In a similar vein, we might speak of someone who "sees the world through rose-colored glasses." And we all know what that phrase means: such a person, while he or she might look kindly upon all beings, is also likely to learn some hard lessons about the dark side of life due to his or her naiveté.

The broad point here is that we all see the world through some kind of glasses. No one can see as it really is.

Any planet in your third house reveals much about the color of the glasses you are wearing.

The sign which that planet occupies adds its own tint to the lenses, as does the sign on the cusp of the house.

Do remember to be gentle with your interpretation here: the glasses with which you were born might benefit from a little "tuning," but they are the right ones for you!

If, for example, you have Neptune in the third house, you will probably have a natural interest in metaphysical or spiritual topics. You will likely have some inexplicable, otherworldly experiences as well – psychic phenomena, extrasensory perception, sensing the presence of spirits, and so on.

With Jupiter in the third house, you live in a world of exciting possibilities.

With Saturn there, you have catalogued the day's obstacles before other people have finished their morning coffee – and by the time they get to their donuts, you've come up with a fallback plan just in case . . .

Adding a sign to the mix deepens our understanding, as always: with a third house Mars in skeptical, analytic Virgo, you are constantly assailed by people with erroneous ideas that require your correction. We can laugh at that line for all the obvious reasons – but their ideas might indeed benefit from your input.

THE PRIVATE EYE

Pluto – the Lord of the Underworld – is naturally oriented to the unconscious mind. When someone is born with Pluto in the third house, there is a tendency to look deeply into things. Such a person's "glasses" possess a psychological tint, even a suspicious one. The mind can be astute about secrets, wounds, and so on. Such people *hear a lot of confessions* in the course of their lives – people often open up to them, in other words.

When a client with Pluto in the third house walks through my door, I will often say that he or she "would make a good psychoanalyst." That metaphor usually starts the bridge-building process quite effectively.

One day it didn't.

I was doing private astrological readings up in Manhattan. A very "New York" guy with Pluto in the third house walked through the door. One look, and I was pretty sure why he was there: it was because his girl-friend had insisted. He was a muscular man, bulging out of his tight T-shirt, wearing reflective aviator sunglasses, which he did not remove. He was not my typical client.

He sat down, crossed his arms, and basically said "show me what you've got." He wasn't hostile, but he obviously did not expect very much of our session. My impression was that he was only there in order to prove a point about his status as an open-minded person.

I looked at that Pluto in the third house and thought about rolling out my usual approach – but in the light of this gentleman's elevated testosterone levels, I immediately knew that suggesting "a career as a psychoanalyst" would fall catastrophically far from the mark. Any patients he might have had would be too terrified to speak. They would be certain that they had wandered into the wrong office.

I knew I had to improvise. Mixing the intense perceptual powers of Pluto in the third house with his extremes of "traditional masculinity" led me instantaneously to the perfect metaphor: *I told him that he would make an excellent private detective.*

His jaw dropped. He took off his reflective aviator glasses and, wide-eyed, pulled his wallet out of his pocket. He showed me his private detective's license. That was actually what he did for a living.

The rest of the reading went splendidly. But I am sure that he over-estimated my powers, not to mention the powers of astrology. I merely improvised a metaphor and I got lucky.

Through what kind of glasses was this man contemplating the world? They were of a color which revealed the shadow dimensions of anyone and everyone.

Like any good detective, he knew that, even though she baked excellent apple pies and remembered all the kids' birthdays, grandma might very well be the murderer.

That's Pluto in the third house.

THE HERESY OF PERCEPTION

Robert Hand practices a very different kind of astrology than I do, but he has been a good friend and colleague of mine for thirty years. With his Mercury in Sagittarius, Rob has always been a far-ranging scholar – and with that Mercury in opposition to his Saturn, he has an intellectual affinity for the wisdom of our ancestors. Accordingly, he has devoted himself to re-animating the astrology of the European Renaissance.

He offered a lecture once, which I attended and which fundamentally impacted my understanding of the third house.

Robert started off by describing the ninth house – always opposite the third – as the "house of religion," among other things. That understanding is still an astrological commonplace and quite valid – something we investigated back in *The Book of Fire*. Then Robert invited us to put on our medieval thinking caps. In the Europe of half a millennium ago, "religion" basically meant the Roman Catholic Church – which was of course, by definition, *right about everything.*

So what *opposed* the "one true faith" back then? In other words, what did the third house mean?

The answer was *heresy.*

Nowadays, we might have to hunt for someone who could even spell the word "heresy" the same way twice. But a few centuries ago, it was a word of fearful portent. Heresy could get you burned at the stake – or burned in Hell for eternity. Questioning the one true faith was dangerous business.

If the ninth house is about answers, then the third house is about questions.

And among dogmatic people, there is nothing more heretical than a penetrating question.

This connection between the third house and heresy is no abstraction. The evidence for it is abundant. The arch-heretic of Western history is undoubtedly Martin Luther, who triggered the Protestant Reformation. We actually have a fairly accurate birth time for him. He was born with Pluto, Jupiter, and Mars all in his third house.

By the way, Luther's Mercury was in Sagittarius conjunct Neptune and Uranus. I suspect that he was a man with no shortage of answers – but what makes him interesting was his questions.

They changed the world.

In parallel fashion, Albert Einstein had rebel-Uranus in his third house. He was thus looking at the world through "genius-colored" glasses. And of course Einstein was a heretic relative to the "religion" of nineteenth century physics, which he essentially overthrew.

How much of what we see boils down to what we have been *taught* to see? Earlier I mentioned the "innocent" racism, sexism, and homophobia of the fading world order. I felt the need to put the word "innocent" in quotation marks since those three poisons did so much damage for so long. Yet not everyone who bought into the underlying assumptions in these prejudices did so with evil intent. I suspect most of them did it because they were taught to think that way from an early age. *Of course* it's a man's world − anyone can see that. Women have babies and make homes. *Of course* Caucasians are the master race − look at what they have accomplished. Look at their sheer dominion. *Of course* it is unnatural for people of the same gender to be couples − that is not what God intended, just look at the obvious anatomical and reproductive facts.

That world and those attitudes are fading now. For some of that estimable blessing, I thank people born with planets in the third house. They are the ones with a knack for recognizing underlying assumptions and challenging them. They are the ones who doubt the "received wisdom." They are attuned to their own senses rather than to the collective agreements. They are the questioners.

They are the ones who practice the heresy of true perception.

IN SUMMARY

A planet in the third house? Throughout this series of books, we consider each planet individually as it plays its role in the third house, both natally and in-motion. For now, here are a few general interpretive guidelines:
- Trust that planet. Whatever interests and curiosities arise naturally with it are exactly attuned to what you need to learn. Uranus: *think outside the box.* Mars: *you do not need to please everyone.* Venus: *you catch flies with honey*
- Flavor the third house planet with a sign; let those particular sign-values further focus the planet's natural interests and curiosities.

Cancer: *family experience; psychology.* Taurus: *the wisdom of Mother Nature.* Leo: *self-expression.*

- Spice the third house planet with aspects. Squared by Neptune? *Believe your senses, even when they seem to be presenting you with impossibilities.* Trine Venus? *Listen carefully to your friends, especially when they say something you do not understand and are thus inclined to dismiss as unimportant.*

- Educate that planet; never be afraid to seek teachers, read books, listen to lectures.

- Finally, speak up; when that planet prompts you to express your thoughts, do so. You have something to say which other people need to hear. The Moon in the third house? *Speak words of comfort and kindness.* Saturn? *Facts, limits, and realism – people need them more than they want them!*

4

THE LIBRA CLAN: VENUS, THE SEVENTH HOUSE, AND THE SIGN OF THE BALANCE SCALES

Three thousand years ago in a market in old Damascus, a merchant carefully parses out gold dust on a platform balance, letting it find a point of equilibrium with a measured lead weight. Lead and gold: that is Libra. As soon as we invoke the seventh sign of the zodiac, we have entered the realm of *paradox* – a realm where opposites converge, where balances are struck. Or where two truths might perceive each other as lies. We come to a place where Yin and Yang must find a way to live in peace with each other.

Being symbolized by the Balance Scales, Libra is the only sign represented by an inanimate object rather than by a living creature, human or otherwise. Yet Libra is ruled by Venus, the famous "goddess of love," and it is associated with the classical "house of marriage."

How can the only symbol in astrology represented by a physical object made of cold metal find any correlation with the warmest and most intimate of human interactions?

More paradox.

It will be a little while before we fathom that mystery. Let's start at the beginning, with the symbol itself.

THE SCALES

Here we are talking about an old-fashioned platform balance, the kind that has been around for thousands of years helping people make accurate measurements of weight. Forget those modern digital units – we are talking about the real deal: 100% steam-punk, no batteries needed or included, no menus to figure out, and not a microchip anywhere in sight.

Again, return with me on the wings of your imagination to the markets of old Damascus in the second millennium B.C. An ounce of lead equals an ounce of gold. Merchant and customer are satisfied that the transaction was fair; coins are exchanged, the deal is sealed.

But an ounce of lead equals an ounce of gold *only in weight*. Which would you prefer to have? Gold dust is obviously a very different substance, and far more valuable.

Here is our elemental Libran principle in three words, all based on balancing lead and gold: *equality between opposites.*

You may already sense which way the wind is blowing here: Libra is the sign of human love, where that same *equality between opposites* must always be a critical ingredient if any marriage or partnership is going to prosper.

I am getting ahead of myself though. We will have a lot more to say about Libran intimacy down the road. At this point, we still need to work with the symbolism of the sign at a more fundamental level.

ON ONE HAND, BUT ON THE OTHER HAND . . .

People have been using that expression for a long, long time. They correspond to a fundamental *template of perception* in our heads: the ability to recognize a paradoxical situation. That appreciation of paradox is one of the ways in which we can pay a particularly acute form of attention. Here is why: *life is complicated and full of hard choices.* Should you accept the wonderful job – meaningful work, a handsome paycheck – in Rapid City, South Dakota, *where you do not know a soul?* The job is yours if you want it, but they need to know one way or the other by Monday. Will moving there make you happy in the long run?

Well, *maybe* . . . who knows, your true love might be waiting for you there in Rapid City.

Or not.

Is getting married a good idea? What about buying that elegant old farm-house built in 1887? What about having a kid? What about getting a cat or a dog?

I would not want to have dinner with anyone who had quick, simple answers to any of those kinds of questions. And in discussing such difficult, uncertain, life-shaping choices with an intelligent, helpful friend, I can almost guarantee that you will find yourself repeating those eight classic Libran words: *on one hand, but on the other hand . . .*

THAT'S A REAL TAIL-TWITCHER

Love cats? If so, you have doubtlessly seen one sitting there twitching its tail back and forth. It's classic cat behavior. What is going on? Is it simply feline nervousness?

God only knows with cats, but here's the most cogent explanation I've ever encountered: a *cat twitching its tail is confronted with a choice and is uncertain about what to do.* She stands in front of the open door, not sure if she wants to go out or stay in . . . twitching her tail in a profound, and perhaps lengthy, feline meditation upon paradox – while you await her pleasure.

A cat twitching its tail is having a Libran moment. Translating, she is basically saying "on one paw, but then on the other paw . . ."

Should you move to Rapid City, South Dakota, to take that job?

If you had a tail, you'd be twitching it too.

NIELS BOHR

Niels Bohr is on most people's short list for the smartest science-side person who ever lived. He was one of the originators of Quantum Theory. He was also very Libran, although I am not sure that he knew that. No matter – no one has to believe in astrology for it to work. Bohr was born with his Sun, Moon, Mercury, and Uranus, all in the seventh sign. Thus, Libra represented the most fundamental *template of perception* in his consciousness. Deep down inside, Bohr knew that everything in the cosmos was built around paradox. For him, the universe itself was a tail-twitcher, right down to the subatomic atomic level.

Bohr's son, Hans, wrote a book about his father, which included this exact quote from Bohr senior: *"(There are) two sorts of truth: profound truths recognized by the fact that the opposite is also a profound truth, in contrast to trivialities where opposites are obviously absurd."*

I'm a writer, not a scientist, so in presenting Niels Bohr's words to a Libran client, I streamline them down to simpler wording: *"The opposite of a Great Truth is always another Great Truth, while the opposite of a small truth is always a falsehood."*

I doubt that Bohr would quibble with that translation – in fact, he went me one better. When he was granted membership in the prestigious Order of the Elephant in Denmark in 1947, he needed to come up with a motto for his newly-minted coat of arms. He chose, *"Contraria Sunt Complementa."*

Translated, that simply means "Opposites are complementary."

. . . which brings us right back to lead and gold in that Damascus marketplace three thousand years ago.

Welcome to the heart of Libra, where opposites complement each other . . . although sometimes they only do that after considering the possibility of slitting each other's throats.

WE SHOULD ALWAYS STRIVE TO BE KIND . . .

. . . but we should also always strive to be truthful.

Who would argue seriously against either virtue? Unless we socialize with absolute scoundrels, kindness and truthfulness are universally recognized as good moral goals for everyone. Even scoundrels Tweet angrily when they feel they have been treated unkindly or dishonestly.

And yet truth and kindness have to duke it out in your head sometimes. Libra is the part of your consciousness which then functions as the referee.

It can be a thankless job.

A friend of yours recently married a gentleman toward whom you took an instant feeling of mistrust. But you attended the wedding and wished them well, all the while trying your best to be positive and supportive.

Kindness won. No fault, no penalty.

A year later, you chance upon her husband speaking in apparent intimacy with another woman in a crosstown restaurant. It could be innocent, but every intuitive bone in your body feels suspicious that he is cheating on your friend.

Do you mention that "data" to her?

Doing that would be truthful . . . but would it be kind? Is this situation any of your business? Might you set wheels turning that should not be turned, at least not yet?

Sometimes telling the truth *is* in fact the kindest thing we can do, even if the truth hurts. But on the other hand, there are times when kindness might take natural precedence.

See how tricky this gets? The part of you that is surfing over this dilemma with me *without feeling the need to take sides* is called Libra. No matter our charts, we all have some of it in us.

Libra is about balancing lead and gold. *It is about making peace with paradox.* And as Niels Bohr expressed it, such oppositions are fundamental to the nature of the universe.

When you gaze at the universe through Libran eyes, those paradoxical oppositions are what you see. It is to them that you are invited to *pay attention.*

THE NORTHERN STAR

Up periscope for a moment. Let's temporarily leave the realm of the Balance Scales and think some big thoughts about astrology in general.

Each sign of the zodiac is a rich, complicated field of symbolism, and yet at a kind of "quantum" philosophical level, each sign is actually very simple. Paraphrasing Niels Bohr, each one of them represents a "profound truth," while also simultaneously representing "trivialities" galore.

Libra actually does represent scales, quite literally – your bathroom scale is a Libra. The avionic instrument that tells the pilot whether he or she is flying level is a Libra too.

Those are true, but trivial, statements, far from the heart of what astrology is about.

What is the *profound truth* about Libra?

In common with the rest of the signs, Libra represents an ideal – an *idea in the mind of God*, so to speak. It is impossible for me to write about the signs at that lofty level without using capital letters: *Perfect Courage* (Aries). *Perfect Open-Mindedness* (Gemini). *Perfect Self-Discipline* (Capricorn)

What about Libra?

Perfect Equilibrium.

In a nutshell, the evolutionary goal of any Libran planet *lies first* in simply *calming down*. That peace is the heart of the matter; that is what has primacy. The opening line of the famous Serenity Prayer comes immediately to mind: *"God grant me the serenity to accept the things I cannot change."*

Easier said than done, of course! In the face of the jangly stress of daily life – the news, money worries, family, the endless, headbanging battle of staying alive and afloat – maintaining "perfect equilibrium" is a tall order.

Each sign is an idea in the mind of God – but it also shows a practical path toward it, a set of steps that, if you follow them persistently, will eventually lead you closer and closer to that ideal.

We have already covered one of the major steps in that calming Libran direction: the development of a *tolerance for paradox*. Let's understand why.

A REALLY MELLOW FANATIC

Try wrapping your head around that one! There is no way anyone can simultaneously be mellow and a fanatic. The two are opposites. Looking at it rigorously, every fanatic who has ever lived has one quality in common with the rest of them: *he or she wants the universe to be more one-dimensional than it actually is.*

 • Fanaticism invariably involves oversimplification – which is the precise opposite of "tolerance for paradox."

In fanaticism, one extreme is underscored, while the existence of the other extreme is typically denied or at least denigrated.

Consider for a moment a fanatical Christian's perspective on Islam – and as quickly as you can, please turn that around and consider a fanatical Muslim's perspective on Christianity.

Consider an angry feminist's perspective on the innate selfishness, violence, and infidelity of men – or a phallocrat's perspective on women's intelligence and capacity for reason.

Those poor fanatics! They have to sleep with one eye open, constantly ready to bat down the ugly head of life's true complexity. A fanatic can never relax. Such a person is under constant attack from the actual realities of human existence.

If the evolutionary goal of Libra lies in attaining – or at least approximating – Perfect Equilibrium, it follows logically that a tolerance for paradox is a good tool for getting there.

Up periscope once again. In the foregoing words, Libra presents us with a concrete expression of the fundamental paradox which lies at the evolutionary core of this zodiacal sign.

- On one hand, a Libran planet is naturally inclined to see that there are two sides to every story. An expectation of paradox is simply built into its perceptual style.
- On the other hand, any Libran planet is actively exploring and expanding its innate tolerance for paradox. That is how it evolves. That is how it moves toward the higher ground.

In other words, Libran planets simultaneously *have* that inborn quality of sensitivity to paradox – *and they are also developing it.*

It is as if the universe has offered them the starter kit. Their job is to take it from there.

This principle, by the way, can be applied across the spectrum of all the astrological symbols. The universe plants the seed, for free. We need to then start watering it, weeding it, and fertilizing it with experience.

WHY?

Why exactly would the development of serenity of spirit be such a central spiritual goal for anyone? It sounds desirable enough of course – but life is short and we could easily catalog other goals whose development would sound equally noble: kindness, truthfulness, courage . . . the list is long. Why is reaching toward inner equilibrium so centrally relevant to anyone with Libran influences?

Once we start thinking about astrology in evolutionary terms, the answer to our question is not difficult to find. After a war, everyone needs peace. After trauma we need healing. After shock we must remember to breathe.

Born with planets in Libra? That implies, in this meaningful, non-random universe, that before taking birth this time around, you experienced something like war, or at least some kind of trauma or shock. *In this lifetime, you are in recovery from those wounding past-life experiences.* This is why "perfect equilibrium" is such a meaningful goal for you – and cultivating a tolerance for paradox is simply an effective *yoga* to get you down that path.

That is because there is no such thing in this universe as a mellow fanatic.

SYNCHRONICITY

A non-random universe? Certainly, in the modern age, the notion of life being a fundamentally random affair has taken over the *zeitgeist*. If I were to casually announce that "some people just get lucky," who would argue with me today?

But long ago, Carl Gustav Jung realized two things: first, that there were too many coincidences for the word coincidence to be meaningful. Secondly, that there were patterns in those so-called coincidences: *patterns of meaning.* Hence his term *synchronicity*, without which astrology – and life – would not make very much sense at all.

Nothing is ever really quite as random as "common sense" might suggest.

For Libra, encounters with paradoxical situations are meaningful. Libra-inflected people attract those kinds of tricky circumstances into their lives, almost as if they are radiating a magnetic property. Maybe they are.

Remember our straying husband in the crosstown restaurant? Let's imagine that it was a Libran woman who observed the apparent infidelity. By a Libran woman, I might easily mean someone with the Moon or Ascendant in that sign, or even a strong Venus signature. We are not simply talking about Sun signs.

She may not have wanted that information. She did not ask for that "truth versus kindness" situation to arise; she did not *have* to ask for it. All she had to do was to be born with Libran planets, and the synchronistic magnet does the rest.

So what should she do? It's a tail-twitcher . . .

While this pattern of complexity that Libran people attract is easily recognized if we simply keep our eyes open for it, let us not forget the heart of the matter: for Libran people, it is *meaningful* – and spiritually helpful – for them to develop and expand their fluency in the language of paradox. That is where the rubber meets the road. Should she tell her friend what she saw – or not? Was the husband actually involved with that other woman – or was he just helping a friend? How much time in her head should she allot to sorting all this out? How great a price in terms of her own serenity should she pay for it?

The universe, in its relentless way, is helping her along that path via the mechanism of synchronicity, just as it is helping the rest of us. She attracts what she needs to experience – and one of the things she needs are complicated situations where right and wrong are not so clearly labeled.

As she digests them and learns to live with them, she evolves.

LIBRA AND ART

The idea that "all Libras are artists" is a gross exaggeration. Substitute the word "many" for "all," and the statement becomes a lot more solid. But a better way of saying it is that Libra correlates with *aesthetic sensitivity*.

This brings us right back to the metaphor of the Balance Scales, with lead and gold finding a point of equilibrium. In parallel fashion, we might feel the *harmony between a particular shade of green and a particular shade of yellow*. Or the pleasing harmony between musical notes or the words in a poem or a song.

Or the pretty way the furniture is arranged or how the garden grows.

None of these forms of uniquely *Libran perceptual intelligence* are even slightly connected to the kind of intelligence that allows you to balance your checkbook, learn the laws of physics, or figure out your taxes. *Aesthetic intelligence* – commonly known as *taste* – can have intellectual components, but intellect alone can only take us so far.

Most of us know that we should not wear our chartreuse hat with our favorite hot pink shirt – that kind of formalized "color coordinated" taste is something we can learn. There is even some science behind it. A computer could make those choices for you.

It takes a true artist to know that one dab of hot pink in that field of chartreuse is going to set the painting on fire.

That's Libra.

BUT WHY ART?

You have tickets for the symphony. The performance is downtown, and hard to get to with the traffic. Parking is difficult too. By the time you arrive in the lobby, you are a nervous wreck. The traffic was indeed terrible. All the way there, you were afraid you were going to be late, if not a victim of Road Rage. You finally make it to your seat on time – barely. On your way to it, you step on several people's toes.

If looks were microwaves, your coffee would be boiled.

You settle into your seat. Almost immediately the orchestra begins to perform Ralph Vaughan Williams' *The Lark Ascending*. Instantly, the vibe changes. Those haunting opening passages for solo violin lift you instantly into a higher world – one in which your stress-load instantly evaporates.

How do you respond to this very Libran moment *physically*?

Simple: *you sigh*. We always sigh when we are confronted with beauty, whether it is humanly-created or part of the natural world.

But what is a sigh *from a physiological point of view*?

A release of tension.

And what is the evolutionary purpose of Libra?

Again: the release of tension.

Why does Libra correlate with aesthetic sensitivities and motivations? It is not simply a random personality trait. Rather, Libra's orientation to beauty is an *evolutionary method*.

In a nutshell, *immersing one's senses in aesthetic experience triggers the release of accumulated tension.*

And for Libra, that release is the evolutionary goal. The release of tension is just another term for *serenity* – just another way of saying *calming down*. Exposing oneself to beauty is a method for getting there. That beauty can be created by humans, as in our example of the concert. Or it can be our taking a mindful moment to sigh at the beauty of a sunset or the falling light of a perfect autumn afternoon.

WHAT ABOUT LOVE?

Mention Libra and most astrologers, myself included, immediately *segue* to the word *partnership*. And it is true – human love in all of its myriad forms is in the Libran domain. In affirming this piece of the puzzle, it is pivotal that we do not limit our understanding of partnership to sexual relationships. They are certainly on the list, and perhaps even on top of the list – but coupling is not the only form of love in this world. Libra represents all of it.

- *Where would we be without our friends?* Could we survive without them?
- What about *family love* – the love we might feel for our children or our parents?
- What about our *animal companions*? Do we not often love them in almost the same way that we might love our children?

All of these kinds of relationships are Libran territory. Such connections typically dominate astrological investigations of this sign. They certainly dominate our motivations – who would not crawl over forty miles of broken glass to be with the one he or she loved?

As much as I love *The Lark Ascending*, I doubt that I would crawl over forty miles of broken glass just to hear it. But if that crawling were the only way I would ever see my partner again, I would be on my hands and knees in one second.

Still, I have saved looking at this critical "intimate" dimension of Libra for last. It is not simply so that love can be "our dessert;" I have saved love for last because if I put it first, it might eclipse everything else we have said.

Such is the nature of the human psyche. When love calls, we drop everything else. We start crawling.

To understand how intimacy connects with everything else we have explored, let's go right back to the beginning – right back to the lead and the gold dust on the platforms of that scale in ancient Damascus. Two entirely different substances find a point of equilibrium: *could there be a better metaphor for the process of forming a healthy human partnership?* I am lead and you are gold – and only in a spirit of mutual respect and "meeting in the middle" can we avoid a crushing burden of conflict.

Love is always a balancing act, and love – when it goes well – *calms us down*. Think of our language: two people fall in love and *settle down* together. They *put down roots*. Van Morrison sang, "She makes me righteous. She makes me whole. She makes me mellow down to my soul." Those are simple words that pretty much say it all.

Love soothes us. And any Libran planets in your birthchart hint at a mystery, probably a dire one: you need some soothing.

You really need a hug.

TWO PEOPLE ARE FALLING IN LOVE . . .

. . . and there is a conversation they are bound to have. Here is how it goes: *"You and I are so alike."* They catalog their symmetries. "We both love Thai food and jazz. We each like to sleep for seven hours. We agree that a house should be kept at 72 degrees Fahrenheit. We vote for the same rascals. We are both neatniks. Amazingly, we both have always felt that we had many past lives in Egypt. *It is so obvious that we are soul mates. It is so clear, with us being so alike, that we were born to be together."*

Cynicism might come easily here, but let's not succumb to it. Let's say that these two lovebirds are not fundamentally wrong about their relationship. They were in fact "born to be together." They make that commitment to each other. They jump over the broom backwards, the way the slaves used to do in the old South. They set out to live happily ever after.

Call them "married." Even call them "well-married."

Three years pass. They still love each other – but now they have entered the real world of human intimacy. Now there is another conversation they are guaranteed to have. It begins with *"you and I are so different . . ."*

Again, I do not intend this little anecdote in a cynical way. I do, however, encourage you to run a quick reality check on it: doesn't it ring true?

No two people are ever so much in agreement as new lovers imagine themselves to be.

We can take the point further. If through some miracle – one that incidentally violated all the laws of the known universe – we were to meet someone with whom we actually had that degree of personal symmetry, there would be no evolutionary dynamic in the bond.

In a nutshell, we would have nothing to teach each other. Pointing as surely as a compass needle right back to the core of our general theoretical model of the Air element, there would be nothing in the other person to which it benefited us to *pay attention.*

Thus we see the eternal "Balance Scales" of human intimacy. Each partner needs to learn to see the world through the other one's *very differ-*

ent eyes. No one ever perfects that art – but every human bond that truly works approximates it.

"Informed mutual respect" might not be a sexy term, but it has a lot more utility in marriage counseling than it does in romance novels.

One morning each of the partners in this story wakes up realizing that "I am in bed with an alien – *but actually kind of a cute one* . . ."

Our lovers need to begin to learn the *fine art of compromise* – and the equally-fine art of not compromising too much, to the point that they have given themselves away. Love is always a Libran balancing act that way. It is always about lead and gold dust learning to dance the dance of paradox: how to be true to oneself and simultaneously true to the needs of a committed relationship.

No one has ever called that path an easy one. And yet something deep inside of almost everyone longs to be on it.

I knew a couple who got married. They rewrote the traditional wedding ceremony in order to reflect their own values and beliefs. They vowed to "love, honor – and *negotiate*."

Everyone laughed when they delivered that line in their ceremony, but I think we all heard its undercurrent of modern wisdom.

A ROTTEN DAY

You have "one of those days." Everything goes wrong. Everyone is uncooperative. Your tax bill arrives, and it's higher than what you expected. Something under your sink is leaking ooze. You have a six-hour headache. And it is raining.

You know that before the end of the week, all of these little miseries will be forgotten. But right now you are feeling as if you have been "ridden hard and put away wet," as horse-people say.

You are walking down the street, finally heading home at day's end. "By chance," you encounter a dear friend. She takes one look at you and immediately asks what's wrong. She can see that you look exhausted and bedraggled. There is no way to hide it, and no need to – she is a pal. You and she are close enough that honesty has simply become a natural reflex between you.

You briefly recount the horrors, injustices, and indignities of the day. Without a word, she spreads her arms wide, inviting you into an embrace. *As your friend holds you in her arms, what exactly happens?* Just before you met her on the street, you were braced for the next blow. You were tense, ready to defend yourself. *Just let one more person try to give me the slightest grief.* But now, locked in the embrace of a dear friend, you *sigh.*

Remember that very Libran word?

You relax into your friend's embrace. Perhaps you notice a bit of moisture forming in the corners of your eyes.

That hug is helping, that's clear enough – and it is such a common human reality that we hardly need to think about it.

But let's think deeply about it anyway: *hugs relax us.* Touch relaxes us.

Going further, hugs and touch come in a lot of flavors. Some of them work more effectively than others. Maybe you are attending one of those spiritual gatherings where the hug is the new handshake. You may find yourself *socially required to hug someone* for whom you do not feel much affection, or even much trust. We all learn to endure that kind of interaction, but obviously we do not derive much Libran benefit from it.

At the risk of belaboring the obvious, the hugs and the touches that carry the true healing magic are the ones we get from the people whom we love.

Knowing that the evolutionary aim of Libra lies ultimately in the release of tension, we begin to fathom this dimension of the mystery of the Balance Scales. *As we build trust and affection with other human beings – always in a spirit of equality and respectful mutual dialog – we move effectively toward healing our ancient wound of trauma and disequilibrium.*

And that is why we have those Libran planets in the first place.

VENUS, GODDESS OF LOVE – AND OF PEACE AND OF THE ARTS

I am going to defy astrological custom and make Venus an "it" rather than a "her." I know the Roman goddess was female, but I don't want to perpetuate the old gender stereotypes – and with Venus correlated primarily with *relationships, a willingness to compromise,* and *concern with beauty,* the obvious gender stereotypes loom like black holes.

Some astrologers today still feminize Venus, but I am betting that such language will seem (at best) "quaint" in another twenty years, and probably worse. I am hoping that these four Elements books are still being read in a generation or two. I have no crystal ball for discerning their fate in that regard, but in order to do my part, I am going to assert the radical position that men have Venus in their charts too.

As the ruler of Libra, Venus shares many of the same aims and methods we have just been exploring. Again like Libra, the ultimate evolutionary aim of Venus lies in the *establishment of equilibrium.*

It is "the goddess of peace," after all.

Signs are motivational, while planets are the basic "circuit boards" in your head. Even when life gut-punches you with some terrible shock, you eventually return to a state of balance. That is Venus doing its job in your psyche. *It is what reminds you to breathe.* Once you have gotten some control of your heart rate and your blood pressure, Venus might suggest a hot bath, maybe with some soothing music.

Loud rock'n'roll or hip-hop? They have their place, but here I doubt it – how's about Ralph Vaughn Williams' *The Lark Ascending* again. That is more likely to do the trick. You need calming, not stimulus.

Dreadful, stressful things happen to us all from time to time. That is clear enough. It is a Venusian miracle that we *get over them.* That recovery is one fundamental mechanism of this planet.

Imagine what life would be like if every stressful moment was simply added to the pile. How long could you survive? Why would you even want to?

Later, in chapters eleven and twelve, we investigate Venus sign by sign and house by house. Here, let's begin to consider these varying Venusian mechanisms for the restoration of equilibrium at a broad level, using Gemini and the fifth house as demonstrations.

As with our previous consideration of Libra, I want to start with the pursuit of serenity.

We'll save the comforts of intimacy for a little later.

VENUS IN GEMINI

Let's say that you were born with Venus in Gemini. Let's say that you have just experienced a very challenging year in your career. You took a new position, one for which you were barely qualified. You've succeeded at it, but only by working twelve hour days under killing pressure. You are being well paid, but you've not even had a moment to spend your money. It has been a steady diet of work and stress.

Finally, you have a week's vacation. Understandably, you are eager to relax. Perhaps you decide to go to a *chi-chi* beach resort – one of those all-up places where you never have to lift a finger. Just lie in the sun, get massages, and drink *Mai-Tai's* at the Tiki bar.

It might sound like just the ticket after all that career stress – but your vacation falls flat. You are no better off at the end of it than you were at the beginning. That laid-back week at a beach resort might work fine if you have Venus in Taurus – but in Gemini? Forget about it. Paradoxically, what you need in order to relax is *stimulus*. You need to *learn something*, to see something you have never seen before. That is the Gemini path, as we learned in the last chapter.

If Gemini animates your Venus, then that stimulus is the optimal path toward the release of tension.

Let that last sentence sink in for a moment: *what you need in order to relax is stimulus*. On the face of it, the words sound counter-intuitive. Flopping under a *palapa* on some tropical beach seems like a better idea. *But what are the values that animate Gemini?* We learned the answer in the previous chapter: amazement, variety, wonder, and surprise. With Venus in that sign, those are the things that will actually help you to relax.

My suggestion? You might go to a cultured city – say, New York or Vienna. Take in some museums. See some historical sights. Go to a play or a concert.

If Vienna is your destination, try learning some of that Austro-Bavarian variant on standard German that the Viennese speak. What if you never use a word of it again in your life? Wasted effort? No matter – it was fun to learn it, plus you will never forget that delightful, fragmented conversation you tried to have with that sweet bartender who didn't speak a word of English.

Obviously other Venus-in-Gemini illustrations would work just as well. It is the underlying principle that counts: relaxation through stimulus. When it comes to recovering from the "slings and arrows of outrageous fortune," Venus is your ally. But you have to feed your Venus the correct nutrients.

Do that, and peace will pervade your body-mind-spirit system.

VENUS IN THE FIFTH HOUSE

One core behavioral expression of the fifth house is the *act of creativity*. We explored that idea thoroughly in *The Book of Fire*. Born with Venus there, devoting yourself to some form of art is a powerful path toward peace and the release of accumulated tension.

You do not need to be impressively skillful at your art either – although there is a good chance that with this configuration, you were indeed born with some innate talent. Still, let's hear it for singing loudly and badly in the shower. The reverberation in there is excellent, and the audience is always on its feet – provided that no one else is home, at least.

Seriously: *sing.* Off-key is just fine. It is the *act of self-expression*, not the "critical reviews," that carries the healing energy.

If you do not want to sing, no worry. Then just bang a drum or put paint on a canvas or join a local theater group – and if you don't want to be on stage, then help out backstage designing the sets or making the lighting look magical.

Again, with Venus in the fifth house, you probably actually *do* have some talent, at least lying latently in your psyche awaiting discovery. But talent is not the point. The point is that the actual behavior of creative self-expression is a highly efficient road toward freeing yourself from the grip of accumulated anxiety.

Another classic fifth house behavioral arena lies in the area of *sports* and *games*. These too can be effective arenas for the release of tension. With social Venus in that house, we might think of *team* sports and the *camaraderie* that naturally arises there. For similar reasons, in terms of games, we might recommend Poker over Solitaire – with Poker, you are constantly reading another person's signals.

And reading other people's signals is pure Venus.

Speaking of reading another person's signals, the fifth house is much connected with sexual expression and love-making. And yes, when it comes to releasing accumulated tensions . . . well, if you need a note from your astrologer, shoot me an email.

With that remark, we shift our focus unashamedly to . . .

THE REALM OF APHRODITE

I guess it is because of the word "aphrodisiac" that "Aphrodite" sounds sexier than Venus. Actually, as I understand it, they are more or less the same goddess. Greek or Roman, either way, we are now on that most compelling of wavelengths: *human sexuality*.

Venus, like Libra, actually embraces all forms of love, including the non-erotic kinds. In the Libran section of this chapter, we celebrated *friendship*. That applies equally to Venus as well. But let's begin our spelunking with a long look at Venus the Lovemaker: the planet of romance.

We will start with a meditation upon a slippery word, one that is easily trivialized, but which actually contains some of the deeper mysteries of Venus. The word is *cuteness*.

We all know the feeling that such a perception of another person inspires, even if "cute" is not the exact word that we would use. Some people just carry themselves in a way that beguiles us. It is not exactly the same concept as "beauty" – a beautiful person might feel remote to us; intimacy with such a person would feel awkward and unnatural. But cuteness: we are drawn to it with equal measures of desire, surrender, and joy. We meet someone and, in the words of Sting, *"every little thing she does is magic, magic, magic."*

Falling in love, one lover might say to the other, "I love the way you breathe when you are listening to music."

Are there any other human circumstances in which one might be tempted to utter a line like that one?

But in the grips of falling in love, in the grips of cuteness – Vensuian *bonding*, that is – a mixture of fascination and delight accompanies every observation of the beloved. That perceived "cuteness" we see in certain other people has many effects on us, and many of them are potentially dangerous.

We are instantly blind to their flaws – temporarily at least.

At the same time, we exaggerate their virtues.

Complicating it further, we flatter them with our unbroken attention – who can resist being seen as a flawless, magical being? Additionally, our flattery is 100% sincere; there are no tell-tale signs of manipulation or any kind of sexual con-game. So not only are we seeing them in a distortedly attractive light, we are also enchanting them with our absolute fascination with their every quirk, trait, or distinguishing physical mark.

Without getting too Darwinian about it, one can easily see how "cuteness" plays a role in pair-bonding, and thus in fertility and the survival of the species.

What triggers this strange and powerful phenomenon in us? What makes someone look cute? That's a complicated, multi-dimensional question. Ultimately, answering it astrologically gets into full-blown *synastry* – the interactions of two complete birthcharts.

But our point here is that the planet Venus plays a huge role in that perception – or projection – of cuteness.

Anyone with the qualities implicit in our own Venus is already on first base when it comes to generating feelings of attraction in us.

One look and we are thinking, "What a cutie . . ."

We may fall for someone, beguiled by their cuteness – only to discover down the road that we actually *didn't like him or her* very much. Simply "liking" someone has Venusian components too, and we will get to that – but the perception of "cuteness" is in another category. We can be ninety years old, and still not immune to its effects.

Still, we all know that the word "cuteness" reminds us all of high school.

And marrying your high school sweetheart is not always a formula for lasting happiness.

Long-term, grown-up, mutual appreciation between two people stems more from shared values than from an initial response to anyone's "cuteness."

And those shared values are more a solar question than a Venusian one.

Still, if you trigger a Venusian response in me, I will always tend to look at you through the eyes of generosity, forgiveness, and radical acceptance of who you are. I will celebrate your existence. "Cuteness" offers that gift.

That will remain true until or unless you actually hurt me badly through gross insensitivity or some kind of fundamental betrayal.

Generosity. Forgiveness. Radical acceptance of the other's nature, quirks and all – regardless of age or maturity, how could love survive for long without those three allies?

So, cutting to the chase, here is the Venusian paradox:

- Venus can beguile, seduce, and trick people, sometimes without them even knowing that is what it is doing. *We can trick ourselves into tricking others into tricking us.*
- Without a Venusian response of *generosity, forgiveness* and *acceptance* toward another human being, intimacy simply does not endure. The other person soon becomes repellant. Only with generosity, forgiveness and acceptance can human love thrive in the long term.

Remember how much we spoke of paradox in connection with Libra? Here we see it raising its slippery head again.

How can we stay on the right side of the paradox? Hearts are delicate: how can we know *whom we can safely trust?* Then how do we trust in a way that builds on that shared generosity, forgiveness, and acceptance – without going so far in those directions that we have lost track of our own centers?

Read on.

VENUS: THE RIGOROUS DEFINITION

Sweet, sappy rhapsodies about true love, soul-mates, and sexual magic are *absolutely welcome* in our thinking about Venus – no shame, and no need here to apologize or to feel self-conscious about getting in touch with your inner romantic. Openness to such perceptions and preoccupations plays a critical role in any astrologer actually *feeling* Venus inside herself or himself. Without such a feeling, there is little chance any astrologer could speak in a meaningful, connecting way to anyone else.

Icing the cake is the fact that it is the rare astrological client who steps into the office without at least a few pressing questions about intimacy.

"Love and work . . . work and love, that's all there is," said Sigmund Freud.

Personally, I would add spirituality and physical health, and make it a foursome. And those four together have accounted for nearly all of my hours in the counseling room over the years.

We cannot talk about Venus without entering the Venusian framework of language and values. They are soft and sweet, and that is fundamental. But in honor of the Air Family and its ability to think in abstract conceptuality, let's propound a rigorous definition of the action of Venus in the human psyche.

- Venus represents the drive to establish a bridge of rapport with another human being, and to maintain that bridge, come what may.

In support of that drive, Venus brings the bridge-building skills of *courtesy,* the conveyance of *respect,* the ability to *identify* with another person, *diplomacy,* a capacity for *compromise, listening skills, social strategies, grace,* and the right use of *humor* as an intimate lubricant.

With those skills in place, there simultaneously arises in Venus a set of interpersonal *risks,* starting with *too much compromise,* then adding: Superficiality. "Niceness" to the point of dishonesty. A potential for *co-dependent* behavior. A loss of self-awareness. Allowing oneself to be defined by a relationship. Seductiveness, even if it is unintentional. A vulnerability to seduction.

As ever, the sign and house in which Venus is located further specifies the way these highs and lows might operate. Certain signs and houses may minimize some of these risks, while underscoring others.

We can say the same for the potential virtues.

A little while ago, we looked at Venus in Gemini from the perspective of the *release of tension.* Let's consider it now from the perspective of love.

VENUS IN GEMINI, PART TWO

Gemini seeks experience. Mix that hunger with the erotic side of Venus and you might quickly suspect that we are not talking about Sunday School. Fair enough. But let's be careful: when we consider this configuration from an evolutionary point of view, we are not looking at any kind of exploitative or purely appetite-driven expression of human sexuality. We are simply exploring the classic Geminian territory of eagerness for wide experience – open-mindedness leading to the right questions, and eventually to answers that work.

Kiss anyone when you were in high school? Most of us did. And for all the emotional ups and downs of being a teenager, people don't *grow up right* if they try to by-pass all that proto-intimate experience. It is all part of life's learning curve.

If we have a seventeen year old child, the last thing we ever want to hear from her is that a baby is on the way and she is getting married. That teenager is almost certainly too young for those kinds of commitments.

But "too young" is too simple a way of saying it. "Too inexperienced" is more accurate – and the proof of that pudding lies in this little tale:

A fifty-year-old Roman Catholic nun or priest – still a virgin – leaves the Order. Such a person is in mortal danger of marrying the first person she or he kisses. It is, in other words, *experience,* not simply age, that makes the difference in terms of the kinds of judgement and self-knowledge good relationship decisions require.

In this regard, it is fair to say that age is just a number.

What if someone has been a celibate nun or a priest for their last seventeen lifetimes? They might need some courtship experience. They might need to kiss a few frogs, so to speak.

For those reasons, they might manifest a birthchart with Venus in Gemini.

And that is a completely honorable, completely natural, and completely logical evolutionary development.

Does Venus in Gemini imply that we are doomed to "date forever?"

Not at all – but we do have to embrace the fact that we need to do *some* "dating." Call it what you will: courtship, adventures, experimentation.

With Gemini, we are always learning through experience. That is bedrock. We need to gather data – and in this case the data is Venusian: it is, in part at least, *sexual data,* both about ourselves and about others and how we interact with them.

Let's just remember to be adults here and recognize that by "sexual data," we mean a lot more than what physical bodies do; we must include minds and hearts as well.

With that solid foundation of experience established, then, even with Venus in mutable Gemini, we have created the possibility of moving into more stable forms of intimacy.

Such relationships must also have a Geminian basis if they are to continue to thrive. That is to say, the two people must actually *enjoy* communicating with each other. The conversation never ends. They both also need to be capable of being articulate and clear about difficult subjects – and, equally, they need to *listen well* to each other, even when they do not like what they are hearing. For Venus in Gemini to thrive, they must share life as an adventure, always eagerly open to new experiences.

And they must avoid boredom the way cats avoid the beach.

When it comes to "living happily ever after," that is the Venus in Gemini formula.

VENUS IN THE FIFTH HOUSE, PART TWO

The fifth house is famously the "house of love affairs." Naturally that intimate face of the house is underscored when romantic Venus lies there.

Note that the term "love affairs" includes the simple reality of *honorable courtship,* as well as more salacious possibilities. At the deepest level, it is helpful to extend the meaning of love affairs even further, to include certain kinds of affectionate non-sexual interactions, although with Venus in the mix, romance tends to be in the spotlight.

Metaphysically, I believe that the clearest way to read the interpersonal dimensions of the fifth house is to see it through the lens of the phrase, *I feel like I've known you before.*

Let's assume that we can take that line straightforwardly: *you actually have known each other in prior lifetimes.*

Fifth house "love affairs" are relationships in which we are aiming to *tie up karmic loose ends:* unfinished business with other people from past lives. And so we actually *have* "known each other before."

That is why, when someone triggers a fifth house planet in us, so often there is that baffling sense of instantaneous familiarity.

Typically the aim of these fifth house relationships is simply to *finish them* – the goal being a clean goodbye. Even if the soul-intention is for the two people to go forward in a long-term way, there is still remaining "old business" that must be cleared up, lest it sink the ship of love before it gets far from port.

Broadly, from this reincarnational perspective, the fifth house might reference unresolved family dynamics, rivalries, murder most foul – you name it. But with Venus in the fifth, the nature of this unfinished business does tend to be romantic and sexual.

Let me quote two lines from just a few paragraphs back: *"Venus can beguile, seduce, and trick people, sometimes without even knowing that is what it is doing. We trick ourselves into tricking others into tricking us."*

All that is obviously about the darker dimension of Venus – and if Venus lies in your fifth house, we can guarantee that you will meet some "strangely familiar" people in this lifetime – people regarding whom those words we just quoted provide a warning that can potentially save you a lot of heartache.

Please note that, while exploitative sexual seduction is hardly a rarity in human history, in some ways the most insidious version of this unresolved karma has a more innocent origin: two people, desperate for love, who "invent each other." That means each one projects onto the other some kind of ideal out of his or her own unconscious mind – and falls in love with the projection. Eventually the illusion unravels, and is replaced by emptiness and feelings of betrayal.

Maybe you did exactly that together in a prior life. The question is, will you again fall into that same heartbreaking trap?

BACK TO THE PRESENT TENSE

Prior-life perspectives often open the deepest doorways in evolutionary astrology. But what about Venus in the fifth house here and now, today?

With Venus in that position, you might be "in love with falling in love." That is far from boiling down to nothing but bad news – but there is a need to do some serious reality-checking before you are blinded by your own hormonal fog. Even if that fog was generated five hundred years ago, you still need to deal with it in the here and now. No one has to believe in reincarnation in order to resolve past-life karmic entanglements.

We might say that Venus in the fifth indicates that you are "better at falling in love than you are at staying in love." While that phrase might have an ominous ring, it actually bridges us into happier territory. Here is the key question: *what is the "statute of limitations" on how long a couple might spend falling in love?*

The truth is, there is no such limit. The kind of love that can last in a happy way for you needs to be romantic, and there is an art to sustaining those kinds of feelings. That's an art you must share with anyone who is a good choice for you. He or she knows that art too.

Taking it further, what are the *behaviors* (remember: we are talking about an astrological *house*) we expect when two people are falling in love with each other? We'll provide a quick, specific list in a moment – but let's start with two bottom line statements:

- What follows are examples of exactly the "courtship" behaviors whose expression you must learn to cultivate in yourself and thus offer to a partner.
- Simultaneously these are behaviors that arise naturally in anyone who is a suitable partner for you.

Here is our list:

People falling in love *pay a lot of attention to each other.* They *notice changes* in each other; they *make inquiries* about the other one's mood or the nature of his or her day. They *celebrate minor anniversaries.* They tend to eat in restaurants and go to concerts. They buy each other flowers. Perhaps they write love poetry or love songs for each other. They relish time alone together. *They look into each other's eyes.*

If you have Venus in the fifth house, you have some interpersonal business to finish. Synchronicity guarantees that you will meet them. You need to claim something back from them before you can move forward in your personal intimate life – which very likely does not include those people once you have released each other and thus "finished your business".

Once that karma is cleared, go back to that checklist – and find someone who has the same list. With projections withdrawn, you will now be seeing each other clearly. No one will be tricking anyone into anything.

WELCOME TO THE FAR HORIZON: THE SEVENTH HOUSE

In trying to understand the astrological Descendant, it is helpful to start with the Ascendant, which is the eastern horizon – that is to say, where the Sun rises.

I picture a little man rising there too, in the east, his nose resting on the edge of the world, with him peering over its rim, looking to the mystical west.

Before him the road of his life winds off into the distance. Far away, many uncharted miles to the west, lies his goal, lost in the mists. I picture it as an idealized mountain range, made purple, soft, and mysterious by sheer distance.

For our little man, the journey of a thousand miles starts with a single step – and continues for a billion more steps. He does not know what he will find in those western mountains – but his heart is filled with the certainty that the journey will be worth the effort. Whatever is out there in that violet distance, he is viscerally hungry for it, knowing that it will fulfill him, giving purpose and meaning to his life, even though he cannot begin to define its exact nature so early in his westward passage.

These words represent the symbolic tonality of the Descendant. It marks *the missing half of what we are.* It represents that which *promises to complete us.* We do not understand it – but our attraction to it is compelling and instinctual. *We sense that if we can only somehow manage to arrive there, the purpose of our lives will be fulfilled.*

Note that so far in these introductory comments about the seventh house I have not said a word about relationships, even though that subject is usually taken to be absolutely central to our understanding of it. Don't worry – we'll get there. This is indeed the famous "house of marriage," so we can expect that it will represent a concrete, behavioral expression of Libra and Venus and their connections to intimacy in all its forms.

Yet in choosing to begin this section in the way that I have, I hope that I have sown the seeds of a far more fundamental understanding of the seventh house – one that embraces a wider horizon than the question of *"when will I meet someone . . . ?"*

In looking at the Descendant more broadly this way, we position ourselves to unravel one of the most fundamental of all the human mysteries: *why coupling relationships are simultaneously so utterly compelling and yet often so difficult.*

With the imagery of our little man with his nose on the horizon and the road of his life lying ahead of him, we sense the *mystical longing for something transcendent* that underlies all romance and every vibrant, healing partnership – not to mention every mad one.

STARTING IN THE EAST . . .

Let's soften a word that is often used in a hard way: *ego.* We all need one or we just stare out the window, unmotivated by anything at all.

I often reference the astrological Sun as a kind of shorthand for the ego. That idea is effective and helpful – but actually to understand the true nature of anyone's ego, we would need the whole chart. Every planet in it is part of what makes us tick as individuals, and thus plays a role in forming the ego-structure.

That wider astrological definition of ego includes the Ascendant, which is where I want to begin our excavations.

At a simple level, the Ascendant represents your *style*. As the sign that was dawning – literally – at the moment of your birth, it represents how you *dawn on people*. The Ascendant is thus inextricably connected to the way people you are meeting for the first time size you up. Whether you like it or not, whether or not you are even *aware* of it, it mirrors how you carry yourself in the world.

I think of the Ascendant as *stained-glass,* such as you might see in the window of a church. As the light of your soul passes through it, it is given a "tint" – hence, back to your style. To know what a given Ascendant will actually look like, you need to know the color of the light that is shining through its stained glass. Put a fierce Aries Ascendant on a nurturing solar Cancerian, and people will see a Protector – *Mama Bear,* so to speak. Put the same Ascendant on a Gemini, and it looks like a *daredevil* – or at least a trial lawyer.

To know the color of the light coming through stained glass, you need to know two things: what is the color of the stained glass and what is the color of the light shining through it.

Similarly, to know what anyone's Ascendant is going to look like, you need to know the rest of that person's chart.

That stained-glass is a two-way street: as you gaze upon the world around you, the glass is tinting your own view of things as well. This is all fine and exactly as it should be. You have the Ascendant that you need to have. The universe makes no mistakes, ever, at that level.

Still, every Ascendant is attuned to a certain perceptual wavelength. It flavors how we *pay attention* to everything – and flavors it in a way that *narrows and focuses the spectrum of our attention.* Therefore, inevitably, in being true to ourselves, there is much that we miss.

Some of what we miss is too important to ignore. *And yet we cannot see it:* our very natures forbid the perception.

Think of a pilot, with his eyes trained on the far horizon – while a black widow spider is slowly crawling up his leg . . .

Wouldn't it be helpful if someone mentioned the spider to him?

That's where our friends come to the rescue. That is where we enter the intimate realm of the seventh house. *We all need people in our lives who can see what we must see, but could never see, without a little help from our friends.*

LOOKING AT THE WORLD THROUGH THE LENS OF SCORPIO RISING

That last "black widow" image perhaps gives you an insight into my own Ascendant, which is Scorpio. Who else would come up with such an unsettling metaphor? Who else would come up with the idea of a poisonous spider crawling up someone's leg?

With seventy years of practice, I have become very accustomed to peering out at a world that is tinted with Scorpionic tones. That is my Ascendant at work. I think psychologically. I've got a dramatic streak, maybe even a morbid one. Death is always close to me. I tend to look people directly in the eye – and under "people," I am including the devil.

One might say that as *I am looking deeply into myself, similarly I am looking deeply into everyone else.* My Scorpio side *shows*, in other words – that is the nature of the Ascendant. People have often described me as "intense." Let me be the first to say that "I resemble that remark."

Scorpio-fashion, I sometimes tend to blurt out the truth as I see it. This has not always garnered me the blue ribbon in life's endless popularity contest. I know I've hurt people that way. I'm not proud of that. Like everybody else, I am here on the planet in order to learn – and that means I am going to make mistakes sometimes.

On the other hand, for the past fifty years many thousands of people have trusted me with their deepest, most vulnerable secrets. Listening to people that way is basically how I have always made my living. My Scorpio Ascendant has served me well, in other words – but like all Ascendants, it has come with a price tag.

If people think I am "too heavy" or "too psychological" for their taste, they tend to go away after a while. No problem – quite the opposite, in fact.

We both benefit. The way my Scoprio Ascendant helps to sort out my true friends from "future strangers" is not the price tag to which I am referring.

The price tag is that my seeing the world in Scorpionic terms leaves out so much of what is really out there. We might say that it leaves out "almost everything" that is true and real – even though Scorpio is true and real itself.

The point is that there are eleven other signs – eleven other *equally legitimate wavelengths of perception.*

To get past my perceptual blockages, I need some help.

There is no way that any one of us can do it alone.

Now, the sovereign remedy for any kind of Scorpionic blindness is the opposite sign: Taurus. That is a core principle here: *opposite signs balance each other's blind spots.* People carrying a strong dose of the energy of Taurus are looking at the world in a very different way than how I see it.

Thus they can be enormously helpful to me, provided that I am willing to listen to them, trust them, and love them.

- Sometimes I might think that what I need is a brilliant psychological insight; my Taurean friends suggest that ice cream or a shot of tequila might work better. Sometimes they are right.
- I might be exhausted; I blame psychological stress. They point out that a simple nap might actually be the cure – something it might take me hours to figure out for myself.
- I'm worried about some possible future-dread; they remind me that it probably will not happen – and that even if it does, it is not the apocalypse.

In this balancing, correcting process, we observe one of the most elegantly benign principles of the universe. By definition, everyone with Scorpio rising has a Taurus Descendant – therefore everyone with Scorpio rising finds themselves connected with Taurean people, either through "random" circumstance or through direct attraction in love or friendship.

We are drawn to them, just as they are drawn to us. It is an ancient symbiosis.

You have heard it before: *opposites attract.* The mysterious interdependency of the Ascendant and the Descendant is what lies behind the truth of that piece of folklore.

Balance all this with one simple proviso: in speaking of "Taurean people," don't limit yourself to thinking only of Sun Signs: there are many other ways that Taurean energy can manifest in a person. Is it the Moon? Might it be a stellium in that sign? Might it even be a strongly-placed Venus – that is not quite the same as Taurus, but it can carry a similar energy, especially if Venus is in an Earth sign.

A QUICK TECHNICAL NOTE

In what I have written so far, I have been using the word "Descendant" and the term "the seventh house" interchangeably. That way of thinking does not get us into any serious trouble, but let's split a few hairs.

The Descendant is literally the *cusp* of the seventh house. If you have 17° of Gemini rising, then you have a 17° Sagittarian Descendant. Your seventh house *starts* with that degree, but extends for many degrees beyond it – almost certainly including some of Capricorn. (Houses average 30° in breadth, but that varies enormously.)

In that case, it is quite possible that you might have a planet in Capricorn that also falls in your seventh house.

That Capricorn planet then too would be inseparable from any complete astrological understanding of your intimate karma and dharma. You would need to include its message, along with the basic way that your Sagittarian Descendent can help to balance your Geminian Ascendant.

Two practical points arise:
- The importance of the sign actually on the Descendant is greater than the importance of the "other" sign that falls within the framework of your seventh house. Don't ignore that second sign – but keep it in perspective.
- Any seventh house *planet* that falls in either sign plays at least as powerful a role in the intimate interpretation as does the sign on the seventh house cusp.

While we are at it, let's affirm that a complete analysis of anyone's intimate life must also include Venus, Mars, houses four, five, and eight – and really an integrated view of the entire birthchart. Synastry is a big subject, in other words. Check out *Skymates*, Volumes One and Two, if you want to dive into that territory. It quickly ranges beyond what we are covering in this chapter of *The Book of Air*.

HOW LIBRA FITS IN

Remember how one dimension of Libra was the reconciliation of opposites? Lead and gold dust finding a point of equilibrium? Tolerating – and in fact expecting – paradox in all of our experiences is one fundamental expression of the perceptual orientation of the Balance Scales. They know that every story has two sides. Those psychological principles are brought into concrete *behavioral expression* in the seventh house.

That is easy to see: nowhere do we humans encounter such a rich matrix of paradox as in our very own bedrooms. Every relationship is ultimately a Libran "balancing act" between two very different human beings.

My Scorpio Ascendant attracts people more "Earthy" than myself – people who are more "in their bodies" than I am, more engaged with the immediate world, Taurus-fashion.

I need that correction more than I want it.

Your own Ascendant does the same thing, drawing healing, illuminating paradox into your life, mostly in the form of the people whom you love, and who are also custom-designed to "press your buttons."

And remember too that Libra and the seventh house have a lot more to do with actually *being in love* than they do with "falling in love." Nothing is wrong with the latter, and obviously when it comes to being in love, falling in love is a necessary first step. Still, it is when we *begin to be aware of our differences* that the true seventh house evolutionary magic begins. It starts when we realize, often with considerable shock, that we have managed to wind up sharing a bed with someone who sees everything in a way that is fundamentally different from how we see things.

Here, in the form of a little soliloquy, is the quintessential underlying structure of any true, healthy seventh house dialog:

I respect you. I take you seriously. This is not about my being nice or fair. This is about who I see when I look into your eyes. Whatever the word evolution means, you are as evolved as I am. We are different, but when it comes to our level of spiritual advancement, we are at similar levels. In a word, you are my equal. I recognize that. I will never deny it.

I resolve never to dismiss you even if I disagree with you.

And yet, if everything you think is true is in fact true, then half of what I think is true must be wrong.

So let's talk about it.

And on that basis we might talk for fifty years. In baffling each other, we learn from each other. In the end, our time spent marinating together in the alchemical cauldron of intimacy leaves us wiser than we could ever have become alone.

A few pages ago, I promised that we would soon "position ourselves to unravel one of the most fundamental human mysteries: *why coupling relationships are simultaneously so utterly compelling and yet often so difficult."*

That is exactly what we have just explored in detail.

Here it is in a nut shell: lead and gold have a lot to learn from each other – provided that they don't murder each other first.

YOU ARE HERE

Remember, in our Grand Scheme for understanding the Air Element globally, we begin with Gemini and that means learning to keep our eyes – and, more importantly, our minds – open to the reality of our own perceptions.

With Libra, we take it further by realizing that *other people's perceptions*, while they might seem wrong to us, often contain information and perspectives that we need more than we want.

Questions we face in Libra-land: can love conquer pride? Can trust overcome fear? And that is not just because love and trust are virtuous qualities, but rather because they *correct* how we go about the endless Air task of learning to pay attention.

In the following chapter, we come to the third point in our Air triangle – Aquarius, and the fine art of *thinking for ourselves*. As we will see, that is something we can only do well if we are first standing on the strong foundation provided by Gemini and Libra.

THE THREE ESSENTIAL SEVENTH HOUSE QUALITIES

We are all capable of getting the seventh house wrong – that is to say, making bad choices in love. Many of us do, and it is nothing to be ashamed of. Love is famously difficult and fraught with psychiatric minefields. We can all misuse the beautiful potentials of the seventh house, miss its evolutionary point, and wind up either in bad relationships – or in no relationships at all.

In a little while, we will catalog some of those particular soul-cages. For now, let's accentuate the positive. Let's focus on the higher ground and how to get there.

When it falls in the seventh house, each planet represents its own set of lessons – and possible pitfalls. Throughout the pages of this Elements series, we will encounter each configuration and the unique face it presents in the seventh house.

No matter which planet we are considering, there are certain immutable realities that apply to it simply because it is in the seventh house, and which define the parameters of any healthy response to the symbolism.

These parameters boil down to three essential qualities, each one of which must be fully present for the higher purpose of this house to be activated. The three essential qualities are:
- Equality
- An Open-Ended Future
- Magic

No relationship is ever perfect. We have to accept that. Still, these three qualities are not very flexible. There is room for some temporary lapses, but the bottom line is that for any human bond to fulfill its seventh house dharma, we need to be averaging at least a B+ in all three of these areas most of the time.

Let's unpack each one individually.

Equality is one concept that we have already explored in some depth. Remember the balance of lead and gold dust? The word "equality" here does not refer to some ethic of fairness between two people – that's a good idea, but it is not the point. The point is that, at some deep-down, gut-level sense, you have only truly entered the seventh house when you know that *your partner is as wise as you are.* We are different, but ultimately we are on the same plane of consciousness. That's why we can teach and learn from each other *about equally* – total up counsel given and counsel received at the end of the year, and it's an even balance of trade. We are *partners in evolution*, without a hint of parent-child or guru-disciple dynamics. That is what *equality* means.

An Open-Ended Future. Our initial launching pad here is the old wedding-bells line, "Until death do us part." Those words may or may not work out literally – we might not actually be together "forever"– but the point is that in the naked truth of our hearts, we know that it *might* work out that way. We are open to that level of mutual vulnerability. We are committed to that level of trust and interdependency. We are willing to take that risk; we have decided in our hearts that this relationship is potentially worth that kind of risk. The affirmations: there is no "statute of limitations" on this bond; I realistically sense that this person might be with me for the rest of my life. I am open to embracing that estimable emotional hazard; I humbly accept it and I surrender to it.

If we cannot sincerely affirm that *open-ended* possibility, we are not yet operating in the framework of the seventh house.

Magic. That is of course the most difficult of the three essential qualities to define. Potter Stewart, the U.S. Supreme Court Justice, when asked to define pornography, said that he couldn't define it, "but I know it when I see it." Magic between two people is exactly like that. Calling it "love" gets us into the right ballpark – yet why do we bond with one person, but not another one who is equally worthy in all the obvious ways? This is a slippery subject, and we will delve into it with a lot more precision in *The Book of Water.* Our bottom line here is that seventh house intimacy can challenge and stretch us to extreme degrees. You really have to love another person very deeply if you are going to hang in there through the rough spots. Magic is what gets us through. That transcendent magic is what motivates us to do the work.

How do you know when magic is present?

You know it when you see it.

THE DARK SIDE OF THE FORCE

So far, we've been mapping the road to the higher ground of the seventh house. It does not take too much imagination to reverse the positive points I have made, and come up with a formula for sinking the ship of love. In that sense, we have already begun writing our catalog of seventh house catastrophes and disorders.

Not really *equals* spiritually? One of you will feel empty, while the other either feels like a failure – or is furious about your "impossible demands that no one could ever understand."

The relationship is not truly *open-ended*? In other words, for whatever reason, at least one of you holds a deep-down belief that the other person "is not the one." How long does it take before that situation falls apart or becomes toxic?

No *magic* – well, without magic on your side, sooner or later you break up over your varying choice of doorknobs, irreconcilable differences over the best restaurant in town, or clashing party affiliations. The truth is that you just don't *want* the relationship badly enough to do the work.

And maybe your guardian angels agree – this one is really not worth the effort it would take to make it work. People aren't *Kleenex*, but leaving a bad relationship can be a gift to all concerned.

Let's take a deeper look at another two classic seventh house dysfunctions before we move onward to Aquarius.

PROJECTION

To understand the psychological phenomenon of *projection*, let's use Mars in the seventh house as a starting point. The fortune-tellers would terrify you with tales of "the god of war" in the "house of marriage," pointing out how at best you were inexplicably attracted to people whom you did not actually like very much – and at worst, to abusers and rage-aholics.

Dark astrological predictions such as that one are always worth knowing! They generally give a fairly succinct definition of what it looks like if we get a configuration wrong by failing to learn its real lessons.

So what is the actual evolutionary purpose of Mars in the seventh house? That's a big topic, but in a nutshell, you have come to a point in the soul's journey in which you must learn *the art of intimate conflict*.

Admittedly, at first blush, that doesn't sound any better than what the fortune-teller predicted. But there are deep waters here. Couples disagree; that is eternal. Sometimes tempers are frayed; it is unrealistic to imagine the situation always being otherwise. But that is where we come to the critical fork in the road.

Two people can be angry and frustrated with each other, *but still listen to each other respectfully.* There can be a shared, underlying, unspoken *faith* that we will work through this issue, whatever it is. Our love is bigger than this problem, and our *mature negotiating skills* are up to this challenge. We both understand that love and anger are not opposites.

That is the *art* of intimate conflict.

Down the other fork in the road, we see hurled crockery, shouted obscenities, and mutually-assured destruction. We have fights that go nowhere. Meanwhile, there is one sure way to make that latter path even more venomous: that is to quietly *harbor unspoken resentments,* letting them gather the kind of inner momentum that eventually leads to a monumental explosion down the road.

With Mars in your seventh house, you are aiming for the "art."

If you reach it, you will never need to worry about hurled crockery. Part of the higher path with Mars in the seventh house therefore lies in 'keeping short accounts" – that is to say, when something is bothering you, you put it on the table with your partner before it becomes truly radioactive.

We are not quite at projection yet . . .

Here is the next link in the chain, and this single, very simple, point actually embraces literally everything we need to know about *any* planet in the seventh house.

You cannot do seventh house evolutionary work all by yourself.

This house is about love and trust, and where the rubber meets the road in those two areas is with another flesh-and-blood human being sitting across the table from you.

The nature of any planet in your seventh house says a lot about exactly who that other person is – or should be.

Venus? He or she had better be courteous. Neptune? There needs to be some evidence of a spiritual life. Jupiter? Generosity of spirit . Saturn? Reliability, responsibility, and trustworthiness.

What about Mars in the seventh house?

Remember what intimate, interpersonal lessons your soul is trying to master in this lifetime – and remember that you cannot learn them all by yourself. To learn "the art of intimate conflict," you *need some help.*

And your natural partners in that enterprise are healthy "Mars types."

(Beware of the sick Mars types, by the way – failing in that discernment is how you make the fortune-tellers' prophecy come true.)

You need someone who can *do battle with you* when necessary – but only in this clean, constructive way we have been describing.

This final insight is what brings us face-to-face with *projection,* which is a classic seventh house dysfunction. Synchronicity guarantees that you will encounter lots of "Mars people" in your life. If you slip into the grips of projection, instead of learning from them, you ask them to *carry all of that Mars energy for you by themselves.*

Meanwhile, you take your job to be "feeling their muscles," admiring their courage, their honor, and their entrepreneurial *chutzpah.* You depend on them to *protect you* and to do most of the "intimate enemy" work of maintaining the relationship.

If we are in a sexual relationship, you need them to always be the one who initiates sex.

What you have forgotten in this dysfunctional scenario is that this seventh house Mars is *your* Mars, not anyone else's. It represents something that *you* need to claim.

The underlying soul-contract here is that your partner is going to "teach you how to fish." It is not a contract that he or she will supply you with fish for the rest of your days.

CODEPENDENCY

Let's stick with Mars in the seventh house, and take it down another dark road: *codependency.*

Every bully needs a victim.

Everyone given to long, angry harangues needs a passive audience soaking up all of that bad *ju ju.*

Every shamer needs someone open to being shamed.

These thoughts get us into some delicate territory. While we must be careful of "shaming the victim," we must also maintain a certain vigilance about unconscious, mutually-destructive arrangements that might be the responsibility of both parties, even if only one of the people appears on the surface to be "the bad guy."

On the other hand, there are the bad guys out there..

There are two sides to this issue, in other words. It is perfectly Libran.

I am personally uncomfortable with the simplistic, reductionalistic notion that there is *always* some kind of soul-collusion behind every act of abuse – that victim and victimizer had some kind of pre-existent metaphysical arrangement. That feels like a terrible over-simplification. I believe that awful things sometimes happen to good people who have no personal responsibility at all in the matter.

But sometimes there is actually such an agreement between souls – and the arrangement is typically most obvious when we tone down the drama and simply look at standard-issue human messes, where we do not need to invoke any abstruse metaphysical explanations.

For example, here's the mother whose thirty-eight year old son still lives at home, mooching off mama. Is that completely and totally his fault? Or is she part of the deal too? Where did he learn those tricks? Does only one person in the story benefit from his agreement never to grow up? What's in it for mama, in other words?

Here is the woman who stays in a marriage even though her husband beats her.

Here's the man who "has no power over" his wife's chronic infidelities.

According to Wikipedia, *"Codependency is a behavioral condition in a relationship where one person enables another person's addiction, poor mental health, immaturity, irresponsibility, or under-achievement."*

Codependency is a seventh house disorder. In a weird, backwards kind of way, it is fair to say that in order to be "a good codependent," you need a lot of love, a lot of "sensitivity toward another person's needs," and "a willingness to compromise."

All of which are seventh house virtues, turned into the service of the Dark Lord.

I loved my dad a lot, but he was a Capricorn and he gave everyone a lot of free advice. He also had a Sagittarian Moon, which gave him a tendency to be "right about everything." And he had an Aquarian Mars on his Midheaven, which added an argumentative streak to the mix.

One day when I was in my thirties, my father was giving me breathing lessons and I just lost it. I slammed my hands down on a boat he was building and said something brilliant and insightful along the lines of "goddamnit, dad."

He loved me and I loved him. Our relationship was not in any serious jeopardy from my explosion. In fact, our relationship improved a lot after that.

Here is my point: my relationship with my father was indeed in deep jeopardy – *not from my outburst, but from the slow rot of my own codependency with him.*

He had a psychological need to give me those unwittingly-belittling, ego-corrosive lectures, *and I let him get away with it for thirty years.*

If we want to use the word "blame," I was as much to blame as my father was, even though anyone looking at the situation from the outside would probably have been thinking "poor Steve, what a saint he is for not retaliating . . ."

I would have displayed every appearance of being "the victim," in other words.

The seventh house is ultimately the house of "the other person." The Air Family is about paying attention, and the Libra Clan within it pays particularly acute attention to whoever is sitting on the other side of the table. The seventh house is about putting ourselves in the other person's shoes, feeling what the other person is feeling or experiencing.

All that is good news.

Where the bad news gets into the mix is that, with seventh house planets, we can *go into orbit* around another person. We can become so attuned to their needs and natures, not to mention their dysfunctions, that we forget all about our own. We can become so *cooperative* that we actually, unwittingly, assist another person in staying crazy.

That hurts both of us.

And it is also pretty much the definition of codependency, along with nicely defining the dark side of the seventh house.

5

THE AQUARIUS CLAN: URANUS, SATURN, THE ELEVENTH HOUSE, AND THE SIGN OF THE WATER-BEARER

Let's aim our mental telescopes at Aquarius, the third and final sign in the Air Family.

Lucky us – as we begin these observations, we are standing on solid Libran ground, having just finished that chapter. To understand Aquarius, we will need every one of those Libran perspectives. That is because if we cannot accept paradox, the best we could ever hope to achieve with Aquarius would be a flawed, one-dimensional understanding.

So: it's about paradox again: There are two sides to Aquarius. They exist – at least at first glance – in sharp tension with each other.

On one hand, this sign is associated with a fierce commitment to *independence, individuality,* and *free-thinking*.

On the other hand, it is irrevocably linked to *group activities* and *collective enterprises* – all of which rather obviously require some submergence of individuality and personal autonomy in service of joint aims.

If the orchestra is playing J.S. Bach's *The Well-Tempered Clavier*, but if, in the holy name of maintaining his Aquarian individuality, the third violinist has independently decided to launch into Antonín Dvořák's *New World Symphony* . . . well, "Houston, we have a problem."

All collective activity demands cooperation and agreement – and "thinking radically for oneself" exists in tension with those diplomatic qualities.

Let's add another paradoxical Libran perspective: both *cooperation* and *individuality* are laudable conditions. Who would oppose either one of them on principle? The world would be a sorrier place if either one of those virtues poofed out of existence.

But they are indeed sometimes hard to reconcile.

And both qualities are utterly Aquarian.

CHARLES E.O. CARTER

I quoted Charles E.O. Carter back in the first chapter. He is perhaps not read so widely today as he was when I was a young astrologer, but he still represents much that was typical of the roots of modern astrological practice. In his 1925 book, *The Principles of Astrology*, he writes of Aquarius, "The native tends to be attracted to societies, clubs, associations, groups of people, and 'movements' of all sorts, easily merging his personality in 'causes.'

Then just fifteen words later, he adds, "Aquarius has a great love of personal freedom and resents enforced obedience . . ."

Go figure, in other words. Cooperation or individuality?

Identifying with groups and causes on one hand, and simply playing out your own independent *identity* on the other hand – they are not precise polar opposites like good and evil or up and down, but they do not sit together easily.

Yet, as Carter points out, both are true of Aquarius.

INDIVIDUATION

The process of figuring out *who we really are as distinct from what we have been trained to believe we are* – to me, that particular evolutionary pathway is the heart of the matter with Aquarius. This sign, above all else, represents the *process of individuation*. Anyone carrying a lot of Aquarian energy has come to a point in his or her evolutionary journey where the kinds of experiences that will prove meaningful to him or her in the long run lie on the other side of some serious cultural and social conditioning.

Further, because of the inescapable laws of synchronicity, such people will constantly find themselves in situations in which they will be punished or "corrected" simply for being true to themselves. Such situations, while obviously regrettable in a simple sense, are also perfect incubators for Aquarian evolution.

- We might be looking at an artist born into a family of accountants – or, just as easily, a natural accountant born into a family of bohemian artists.
- We might see a natural mystic raised in a materialistic, acquisitive, competitive society – I see many Aquarian types who fit that description sitting in my classes.
- We might see a person born to be a farmer raised in an urban ghetto or a sensitive person born into a family of cretins or a particularly sexual person trying to function in prudish society.

You get the picture: for Aquarius, everything spins around tension between one's nature and one's social conditioning and circumstances. That is the basic karma symbolized by this sign. That is the school that Aquarians are attending.

It is only in the face of those particular kinds of social resistance that the Aquarian dharma of *individuation* can be fulfilled.

As is so often the case when we look at life through the lens of evolutionary astrology, what appears to be a curse is actually a blessing.

THE PARADOX RESOLVED

We might plausibly call a person with a lot of Aquarian *ju-ju* a "free spirit." But free *compared to whom or what?* Compared to a lone eagle soaring over the mountain peaks? Or compared to one more ant in a long line of ants?

To recognize that the term "free" is always *relative* is a good start – but far closer to the essential point is that freedom requires the *context of some kind of restraint* in order for it to have any meaning at all. You cannot have a rebel without something against which to rebel. You cannot have a criminal without laws. You cannot have groundbreaking genius without some preexisting ground to break.

- Aquarian individuation can only occur in the context of social expectations, constraints, rules, and threats of coercion.

That simple insight is what actually resolves our paradox. Individuality and group dynamics are interdependent. *The social group with all its pressures and expectations is the incubator of Aquarian freedom.* That is where it must be won.

Thus we have C.E.O. Carter writing about how Aquarians are " . . .attracted to societies, clubs, associations, groups of people," while also resenting "enforced obedience."

Here's a pivotal point: *Just try to find a coherent identity-group that does not somehow "enforce obedience."*

Illustration: try advocating the many benefits of socialism while trying to make friends at the conservative country club – or try wearing your baseball cap with the brim forward among hip-hop artists or skateboarders. Try singing James Brown's tune, *"It's A Man's, Man's, Man's World"* to a group of feminists – or explaining why you think it is women's turn to rule the world to a bunch of phallocratic C.E.O'.s in the trucking industry.

All cultures are conservative – the statement might sound dogmatic, but I think it can be easily defended. Every culture, by definition, represents a set of values, norms and tastes. In every one of them, those who embody those idealized qualities are rewarded, while those who do not are marginalized, or worse.

That is how a culture seeks to "conserve" itself and thus to exist eternally and unchanged as the centuries and millennia roll slowly by . . .

BUT THAT NEVER WORKS . . .

Cultures do change. We can see that. We have all experienced it, provided we have passed our twentieth birthdays. And, at the risk of over-simplification, let me say that *cultures change because of Aquarians.* People often speak today of "paradigm shifts." But no paradigm will ever simply shift of its own accord. They shift because of people – *paradigm shifters,* also known as Aquarians.

To clarify my last few words, I would only add that I am not just talking about "Sun Sign" Aquarians. I am talking about people with those same doubting, questioning attitudes that are symbolized by having *any* planet in the sign Aquarius. As we will see, this "Aquarian" principle extends to embrace people with significant Uranian signatures as well.

All of this also raises some telling and paradoxical points about the simultaneous rulership of conservative Saturn over Aquarius, along with its more intuitively obvious Uranian rulership. We will get there soon. The short version is that maintaining awareness of Saturn's rulership of Aquarius is absolutely essential to any full understanding of this sign.

- Rules and rule-breakers are interdependent; you cannot have one without the other. Saturn makes the rules, while Uranus breaks them.

As this chapter unfolds, those same paradoxical points will similarly complicate our understanding of the eleventh house.

Still, the simple insight here is that, if it were not for Aquarians, we would still be hauling rocks for the Pharaoh, building yet another pyramid. We would still think the earth was flat. And we would still believe that boys don't cry and girls do.

There would, in other words, be no change at all in the human world.

DANE RUDHYAR

Aquarius may see the constructive development of State and civilization through inventions, social improvements and the glorification of special social virtues. It may also mean revolution and a complete upheaval of State and civilization by the power of a new type of human being and of new ideals which the existing State blindly refuses to tolerate, or against which it must fight because it cannot possibly assimilate it.

– Dane Rudyhar, *The Pulse of Life*

I have always found reading Rudhyar to be heavy going, but consistently worth the effort. I think that if I had not labored through his masterpiece, *The Astrology of Personality*, when I was around twenty years old, I would have just gone to graduate school in some conventional field.

In his words which I quote above, Rudhyar goes directly to the heart of the Aquarian paradox, which is the essential *symbiosis* between a culture and those who would overthrow it.

He writes, as usual, at a very "macro" level, placing the individual in a majestic, transpersonal context of epochal social evolution.

With my fourth house Moon, I tend toward a more "up close and personal" approach to astrology. Rudhyar had an Aquarian Moon squaring his eleventh house Uranus, so naturally our orientations are distinct. He talks history while I try to talk heart.

Libra-fashion, Dane Rudhyar therefore has had a lot to teach me.

Still, Rudhyar sees Aquarius helping "the constructive development of civilization" and also simultaneously fomenting "upheaval" by becoming "a new type of human being." Tellingly, Rudhyar adds his ominous line – "which the State refuses to tolerate."

When "the State" refuses to tolerate you, get out your hard hat! Being an Aquarian can be tough.

A SAD STORY ABOUT AN OLD FRIEND

In what follows, I need to be a little bit circumspect in order to protect the innocent – and perhaps to avoid the legal wrath of the guilty as well. This is a true story about an older woman whom I loved very much some years ago when I lived in North Carolina. She is gone now. She died fairly recently, spry and intelligent, well into her nineties. She was magnificently Uranian in every way, with that very "Aquarian" planet prominently placed in her first house.

One night, while I was on a teaching trip, I sat alone with her in her rather sumptuous home drinking *Famous Grouse* Scotch whiskey. We talked long into the wee hours. With us both slightly toasted, she told me this hard tale.

She – I will call her "Lily" because using her real name might ring some bells that should not be rung – was born a century ago into a wealthy, conservative Southern family here in the United States. She was carefully trained from the cradle to be anything other than a Uranian type.

When she was about twenty years old, she was placed against her will in a psychiatric hospital. That travesty happened at her family's insistence and it required that two psychiatrists sign off on her internment.

Here was the evidence they found for her madness: *she believed in astrology*.

This really happened.

Eventually she was released – and she went on to exact the kind of revenge that could only be cooked up by a saint who was also blessed with diabolical genius. I am sorry that I cannot include those details here. You would love them.

Now, at a moral level, poor Lily's story is easy to parse: ignorance and evil take horrible advantage of a defenseless young maiden. Power and stupidity triumph over justice and wisdom, at least for a while.

It is not the world's most original storyline.

But let's go a little deeper. Let's add one dollop of wisdom-granting compassion for Lily's oppressors . . .

Did her parents and those two psychiatrists wake up one morning and just decide to do something evil for the sheer joy of it?

That seems unlikely. "The road to hell is paved with good intentions." That's a proverb with a long history – and, sad to say, very likely a bright future as well.

I suspect that Lily's parents' intentions were of the highest order.

Put yourself in the place of those adults, so many years ago. They were living in a world very different than our present one. Imagine that you are Lily's parents and that you love her and that you are deeply concerned for her mental wellbeing.

She "believes in astrology."

You believe that you understand what that means.

You believe that she thinks that planets are telling her what to do.

What if "planets" tell her to jump off a bridge? What if "planets" tell her to shoot the president? What if some unscrupulous astrologer – and everyone knows that *all* astrologers are charlatans and therefore unscrupulous – tells her that "Neptune" wants her to empty her parents' bank account?

In the face of such tragic, psychotic madness, what can any parent do? Addressing this situation by themselves is beyond their scope. For Lily's own sake, it is time to call in the professionals. That is the kindest thing any caring parents could possibly do under these dire and frightening circumstances.

So they called the mental hospital. And two, presumably equally well-meaning, and, not to mention "well-educated," psychiatrists signed off on it.

Lily was "locked up for her own good."

As we explored Aquarius, we recognized the necessary symbiotic tension between culture and the individual. Lily suffered for it. Without that tension, the process of individuation would have no meaning. Not to glibly dismiss her suffering, but Lily probably grew spiritually through it.

Aquarius is about sorting out our authentic self from all of the lies, distortions, and baleful influences to which we are subjected as a result of being social creatures. As we reflect on this dynamic evolutionary process, it is pivotal that we keep perspective: while there are truly cruel and tyrannical forces in this world, *never underestimate the power of blind, well-intended ignorance.*

That is my Uranian friend Lily's story. She was a victim, not of evil, but of something more closely akin to sheer stupidity.

Here is the hardest part to digest: did she attract that kind of empowered ignorance into her life as part of her soul's evolutionary plan? *Could she have individuated had there been nothing to individuate against?*

That question is above my pay grade. But do remember that in the end *Lily thrived.* That which did not destroy her only made her stronger. Her "vengeance" was pyrotechnical in its glory, but her soul burned even brighter than that revenge.

A NEW TYPE OF HUMAN BEING

That is Dane Rudhyar's phrase, which I quoted above. Being one of those "new types" is dangerous business! Again, all cultures are conservative, and they enforce their rules. They do not like change. When they sense the presence of a "mutant cell in the bloodstream," they have a wide array of weapons at the ready, just as your body does. You saw what Lily was up against.

But if it were not for mutation at the cellular level, we would still all be amoebas floating around in the primal stew.

If your chart carries the energies of this Aquarian Family, then *life is experimenting in you with new possibilities for the human future.* Some of the things that might make you look a little strange today will be perfectly normal in fifty or a hundred years.

And a fat lot of good *that* will do you.

But it just might do some good for the world – that is, unless the world locks you up permanently in a mental asylum. Or nails you to a cross or puts you in a prison with a life sentence. When it comes to the way a culture seeks to conserve itself, those are just the big guns. Usually they are not necessary. Usually more subtle methods of enforcement do the trick.

- Keep on acting this way, and we will afflict you with *financial insecurity*.
- Keep on acting this way, and we will simply *marginalize* you. No one will listen to you. We will all laugh at you.
- Keep on acting this way, and we will *smother your voice with our prejudices:* "you have a mental disorder, you come from a culture of violence, you people are all the same."
- Keep on acting this way, and no matter what you say we will *pat you dismissively on the head*.

And here is my personal favorite, and probably Lily's too:
- Keep on acting this way, and we will persist in assuming that your faith in astrology means that you believe that "planets tell you what to do."

What I mean by that last line is that we astrologers are an Aquarian force in the world, regardless of our personal charts. We all embody the heretical notions that life is meaningful, that the sky is the mirror of the mind, and that "something out there" loves us and is guiding the evolution of our consciousness.

Try explaining that to your high school science teacher. Almost guaranteed, you will have an Aquarian experience: he or she will look at you as if you were mad, or just weak in the head.

In the Foreword to my 1993 book, *The Night Speaks*, I was *kvetching* about how hard it was to explain to people what I actually do as a professional astrologer. Someone might meet me and politely ask me "what I do." I wrote, *"When I hear that question, I know I am trapped. I can lie. Or I can tell the truth, and know that what will be heard is a lie."*

Things have improved; astrology's star is rising. But we still have a long – and very Aquarian – road ahead of us. Good news though: nowadays not everyone believes that we think planets are telling us what to do.

HAVE A PLANET IN AQUARIUS?

As we have seen many times, planets represent the basic drives which animate your psyche. Signs flavor those drives with particular values, agendas, and ultimately certain evolutionary intentions.

When a planet is in Aquarius, one point is certain:

- The experiences which will actually nourish that planet in a way that gives you genuine joy, energy, and fulfillment are experiences which will also get you into some kind of trouble.

You are invited to be yourself in that area of life no matter what other people think. That is easy to say, but hard to do. At a simple human level, almost everyone wants to be liked and appreciated. And who does not want to be taken seriously? What if, in order to "be yourself," you must sacrifice some of that moral support? If you get this Aquarian evolutionary process right – that is to say, if you persist in following your own true inner guidance – the pressures of conformity tend to mount.

Here is one insidious way that coercive process can happen:

You may have people *who genuinely love you* sitting before you crying, piteously exhorting you, *"if you cannot think of yourself, perhaps you can at least think of me."* They are *"so worried about you."* As if they embodied the soul of reason and decency, they add: *Why can't you compromise, even a little bit?"*

Their tears and their love are real. The trouble is, their worried attitude is based on a complete misunderstanding of who you actually are. *They themselves never compromised* – not because they are such paragons of courage, but rather because, unlike you, *they were born normal.*

Most people are!

And "normal" here doesn't mean healthy; it only means "average" or "typical" or "mainstream."

Such coercive intimate pressure is difficult to resist. Who wants to harden their hearts enough to be indifferent to the suffering of people who love them? Parents are amazingly skillful at this particular form of soul-sabotage – and typically excel at it without even knowing that is what they are doing.

If that kind of mounting intimate pressure does not bring your Aquarian self back into alignment with the norms of your culture, then out come the big guns we listed earlier: threats of financial insecurity, mental health labels, social marginalization, even possible imprisonment.

FIGHTING THE SURVIVAL INSTINCT

The *herd instinct* is powerful in our species. Back in the days when our evolution was driven by Darwinian principles, our survival and our reproductive success were very much enhanced by membership in a tribal group. To put it simply, most of the truly independent human beings were eaten by sabertooth tigers long before they could have babies.

People who think about instincts often put the *survival instinct* at the top of the list in terms of its power over our behavior. My point here is that the survival instinct and the herd instinct are inseparable. With any planet in Aquarius, in order to be true to yourself, that is the instinct with which you must wrestle. Even if you are not literally faced with a life-and-death situation, these archetypes are still activated in the psyche.

Let's bring these ideas to life with a specific example.

VENUS IN AQUARIUS

Here we have a very interesting combination of planet and sign. The most basic drive of Venus, as we saw in the previous chapter, is the urge to *establish and maintain a bridge of rapport* with another human being. Try reconciling that need with *radical independence* and a commitment to being true to yourself no matter what the price!

Still, synthesis can happen. In fact, if your Venus lies in Aquarius, it *must* happen if you are to evolve spiritually – not to mention, if you are ever to find the kind of intimacy that actually helps you feel happy.

Nowadays, a conventional social agreement is that your sexuality is your own business so long as you don't hurt anyone else. Fair enough in principle – but how true is that really? White people, Black people, Native people, Asian people – all are free to mate across racial lines. Today they sometimes do exactly that – *but actually not that often*. Interracial sexual partnership is still far more the exception than the rule.

Why?

What about crossing lines of religion and ethnicity? Jews marrying Christians, for one example? Again, that does happen and it is fine and welcome – but looking at it statistically, it is clear that the old strictures around religion and ethnicity have not entirely lost their power to influence people's intimate choices. We still often see Jewish people marrying Jewish people, northern Europeans marrying other northern Europeans, and so on.

Think of the pressure on the cutest boy in the sixth grade class to have a crush on the cutest girl, and *vice versa*. It's not so different.

Think of the way upper class parents herd their children into meeting other kids from the same economic plane – or of the parallel improbability of a child from the ghetto having a chance to get close to the son or daughter of the C.E.O.

We do not even have to imagine any dark conspiracies here. We do not have to think about virulent racism, even though it is not in short supply. This is just the way the world works.

The point is that our sexuality, despite our affirmations that "who we sleep with is our own business," is very much the business of the community.

What if your natural partner in life lies on the other side of some such social barrier?

Will you ever even meet?

In those questions, we perhaps enter Aquarian high school – and here is the question that puts you in Aquarian college: even if you did meet, *could you sufficiently penetrate your own internalized social conditioning to even recognize that person? Would attraction arise* – or would social training eclipse it? Here is another way to raise exactly the same questions, except now we place them in astrological language: *can you attune your natal Venus to the Aquarian vibration?*

Your happiness in love depends on it. So does your happiness in that other sacred Venusian category: *friendship*. With this configuration, in order to find meaningful intimacy of any sort, you have to cross some well-defended borders – borders that exist both in the social world and inside of yourself.

So far, I have been writing about only one barrier to joy for an Aquarian Venus: *grossly divisive sociological categories*. There is so much more going on here.

When I was young, the almost universal norm in heterosexual marriage was that the man would almost always be a little bit older than the woman. The roots of that custom clearly arose for practical reasons in patriarchal farming communities centuries ago. In the present world, such a gender-based age difference offers no advantages whatsoever. And today that old custom is often broken – but once again, *not really that often.*

Back to Venus in Aquarius, but now in a milder, less sociological, form: what if your natural partner is "the wrong age" for you? Can you get over your own social conditioning enough even to recognize that person? *Can you think for yourself?* That is always the basic Aquarian question. One of the things that makes the question so hard to answer honestly, is that people everywhere automatically believe that they are *already* thinking for themselves.

But if that were really true, we might expect a higher humans-to-sheep ratio in the general population.

There are obvious LGBTQ issues with Venus in Aquarius too – although I would be quick to say that I've not actually observed any particularly reliable astrological patterns in determining anyone's sexual orientation. Still, LGBTQ folks offer a fairly obvious illustration of Venus in Aquarius – talk about "social strictures" blinding you to the very identity of your true love. People in any of the sexual or gender minority groups still face significant cultural prejudice – but more insidiously, they also face their own social conditioning from an early age. One possible way that a soul might be learning Venus in Aquarius lessons could be "being born that way."

Years ago I had an Aquarian friend who was a lesbian. Much to her surprise, she fell in love with a man. As that relationship became public, she was shocked and hurt by the judgmental, shunning reaction of her community. LGBTQ culture, in other words, is no more inherently immune to "Aquariosis" than is the straight heterosexual one. People are people, and in all cases, it takes a lot of evolutionary effort to free one's self from the tyranny of the conservative instincts of the herd.

I have always loved to quote a line from Sting's tune, *All This Time:* "Men go crazy in congregations, but they only get better one by one."

One of the most numbingly predictable presumptions of every herd is the belief that "we are not like other herds." But all herds ultimately sing from the same liturgical hymnal: repeat after me, in unison: *Yes, we are all thinking for ourselves.*

That's why God made Aquarius. It's the sovereign medicine for that madness.

Aquarius, as we have seen, is fundamentally about the process of individuation. With Venus in Aquarius, here is a good rule of thumb: if you want to have any realistic basis for the anticipation of happiness in your intimate life, *first find yourself.* First figure out who you are. Take your time. Break some rules. Don't be afraid to walk on the wild side for a while. Without that individuation, you will still naturally experience sexual desire and romantic impulses. Trouble is, they are likely to be aimed at the wrong targets – people whom *your culture has conditioned you to see as desirable* rather than the ones whom your soul actually recognizes.

Another line from Sting: *"Be yourself no matter what they say."*

THE SHADOW

True individuality rises from the depths of the soul and immediately encounters a powerful countervailing force: social conditioning. At first that force is often relatively subtle. It literally takes the form of our parents training us to operate within their definitions of normalcy. Most of that training is beneficial, but there are nearly always some complications. Let's start with a line you have heard many times before: *good parents "only want what is best for their children."*

But how do they *know* what is actually best – at least beyond basic nourishment and touch?

Usually what that noble affirmation actually means in practice is that parents want for their children *what would have been best for themselves.* This is not necessarily a selfish motivation, but of course it can go terribly awry. If you have planets in Aquarius, *without our saying one negative word about your parents*, we can assume that your upbringing had a distorting effect upon the expression of your true being.

For practical as well as emotional reasons, children need their parents' love. They often win it by "being good." Mostly that is beneficial for all concerned – but distorting influences can easily sneak in under the banner of good behavior. What if a child who is all hot-wired Aries and trenchant Scorpio is born into a very polite Libra-and-Capricorn kind of family?

Or the other way around?

What if a violinist is born into a family of professional wrestling fans – who might be wonderful, loving, salt-of-the-earth people – but more inclined to *Lynyrd Skynyrd* than to Dvorak?

These are classic Aquarian situations.

Our parents of course get us when we are young, which gives them enormous shaping power. But that is only the beginning.

Then comes the pressure cooker of high school and beyond. We face *fashion*. We face *hierarchies of status*. Throughout, with planets in Aquarius, we are punished when we are being true to ourselves, while being systematically rewarded and reinforced for any conventional behavior. If "we are good," we are offered money, respect, security, and sexual gratification – the whole benefits package.

It is no wonder that such conditioning takes a toll. Gradually, we develop a *false self*, often purely as a survival skill. Generally we have no idea that we are doing it.

This is how the Aquarian shadow arises: slowly, compromise by compromise, until the outer life has come adrift from its roots in the soul.

WHAT SUCCUMBING TO THE AQUARIAN SHADOW LOOKS LIKE FROM THE OUTSIDE

If you fall into the clutches of the dark side of Aquarius, *there is no apparent problem at all*. Everything about you looks terrific – or at least inoffensive. That's because you have successfully learned how to maintain a plausible social facade, one that earns you various advantages and benefits. You have learned how to *fake normal*. You may even have no idea that you are doing it, and others almost certainly have no such suspicions about you. You say what people expect you to say, you espouse the common beliefs of your social class, and you seem to take consensual reality as the real deal. There's not a shocking bone in your body.

In a word, people are going to *like* you.

Because they like you, some of them are drawn to you, looking to get some of that juicy, enlivening energy that arises from deeper exchanges of intimacy. Everyone wants love in its various forms. The "normal people" of the world are as eager for it as anyone else, and every bit as capable of sharing affection. But as they approach you, they experience a shock. It is as if they have unexpectedly walked into a wall of plate glass.

What they have actually walked into is your perfectly plausible hologram of a normal well adjusted modern person. Bottom line, they can get close to your personality, but they cannot get close to your soul.

Open a conventional astrology book, read the chapter about Aquarius, and you will probably learn that "all Aquarian people are emotionally cool and detached." You will read that they are the kinds of people who might have "a thousand friends," but not one single deep friendship."

No astrologer comes out and actually says it, but the implication is that it would be a misfortune to share a bed with any Aquarian type. An unfortunate soul who finds himself or herself in such a position will dine on very thin emotional soup for the rest of her or his days – or so they imply.

All of this is a baseless slander against Aquarians, at least if we take it as a general description of the sign. *But it is an excellent and accurate characterization of the Aquarian shadow as it appears from the outside.* If we succumb to it, that is what we look like: aloof, detached, and emotionally unavailable. It is not that you lack heart; it is that your heart is hidden inside a hologram. You seem doomed perpetually to "run for office," even though it is not an office you particularly want to hold.

What is the alternative?

We already know the answer: *individuation.* The courage to be true to yourself. The courage to let your "weird" soul guide your life, even if that commitment sometimes costs you victories in local popularity contests.

WHAT SUCCUMBING TO THE AQUARIAN SHADOW FEELS LIKE FROM THE INSIDE

It is late at night. You cannot sleep. You are trying to remedy your insomnia by watching a movie. You have chosen one that does not look very promising. That is actually part of your strategy: you are hoping that a boring movie will lull you back to dreamland.

As the story unfolds on the screen, you feel a persistent temptation to just turn off the television. You cannot identify with the motivations or attitudes of the protagonist. He seems like an empty suit. The rest of the characters are wooden as well. And the plot plods onward in predictable fashion, fraught with clichés, and never a surprise or any scenes which hold the slightest fascination for you.

Why don't you turn the movie off? "For two cents," you would do that – except that you have been numbed into a state of torpor. You have no control over the runaway television set.

This is exactly what life feels like from the inside if we go down the Aquarian shadow road: your life has started to feel like a dull movie.

Again, that is because life and soul have come adrift from each other. Your biography has lost its connection with your heart. You might be living *a wonderful life for someone else.* For you, it feels like a movie you might walk out of right in the middle.

In plain English, this dimension of the Aquarian shadow can be called *alienation.* In the language of psychology, we might call it *dissociation.*

Whatever we call it, let us affirm one overriding principle: this miserable state is 100% optional. It is absolutely not hardwired into Aquarius in any inescapable way. If you feel trapped in such a condition yourself, go back and read the earlier part of this chapter again. There is your map. There is your escape route. Your life does not have to be that way. You just have to be brave enough to be yourself.

TRAUMA

Think of the look on people's faces thirty seconds after a devastating earthquake. Think of how they look thirty seconds after a terrorist bomb explodes in a café. Think of the look on a parents' face when he or she has just learned that their child has an incurable, fatal disease.

These are terrible images, but none of us would have any trouble understanding their emotional impact, even if we have never had such an awful experience ourselves. An understanding of how the human psyche responds to *traumatic shock* is in the basic toolbox issued to everyone who takes human birth.

Let us go further. What are these disaster survivors usually saying? You already know the answer: *I cannot believe my eyes. This cannot possibly be happening.*

Those phrases may be clichés, but they are eloquent ones. The senses have had an experience which the mind rejects as impossible or unacceptable. Something in the human heart *reflexively withdraws* from such horror, burrows deep inside the psyche, and refuses to engage with the dreadful reality. Ask anyone who has been raped. Ask any spaced-out soldier, just back from the war. In World War One, they called that condition *shell shock*. The poetry reached its zenith in World War Two, when the condition was often called *the thousand yard stare* – and one can easily imagine that poor soldier staring blankly into the far distance. Nowadays we've mostly all been to college and our talk is fancier. Now this condition is called *Post Traumatic Stress Disorder*.

PTSD may be a relatively new term, but it is an old human condition, easily recognized. Humans have been experiencing these kinds of waking nightmares for a long, long time. Mother Nature has dished up a few of them in the form of earthquakes and *tsunamis*, but many have been "gifts" that our collective madness leads us to offer each other.

- That state of *traumatically-induced emotional distance* is symbolized astrologically by the sign Aquarius and the planet Uranus. The dissociated condition we call PTSD is simply the most extreme expression of all of the issues we have been exploring.

It also leads us straight into the metaphysical heart of the third Air sign.

WHY DO I HAVE AQUARIAN PLANETS IN MY CHART?

As soon as we begin to wrestle with the question of *why* we have the chart that we have, we must contend with one inescapable fact: *you have had that chart ever since the day you were born.* Therefore, whatever *caused* you to have that chart must have happened at an earlier date. This leads us directly into the realm of metaphysical speculation, centered on the question of who we were before we were born.

Anyone who has read this far in my work knows that I frame my response to this issue in the language of reincarnation. I believe that your present birthchart reflects unresolved issues and evolutionary aspirations rooted in prior lifetimes. In other words, I believe that while your chart embodies all of your karmic delusions and attachments, it also offers remedies for them.

Going a little further, *for every astrological configuration, there is a low response and a high response,* as well as many shades of gray in between.

- To state it very simply, the low response simply reflects the persistent, habitual *continuity* of those karmic delusions and attachments into the present life, while the higher possible responses represent the remedy.

Applying these broad ideas specifically to Aquarian planets, there is always one obvious and reliable interpretive principle at the metaphysical level. *In a prior life, that planetary function was socially constrained,* not allowed the breathing room that it needed in order to fully open. Therefore, in this lifetime, we aim to take *remedial action.* There is now a plucky "Aquarian" quality that underlies that planetary function, as if it is hardwired to say, "do not ever tell me what to do (again)."

In acting upon that attitude, we are correcting the prior-life pattern of excessive compromise, surrender, and obedience.

There is another, darker possibility with Aquarian planets – one that brings us face-to-face with that "thousand yard stare." *In a prior lifetime, you were severely traumatized.* You experienced some awful shock, and in response to it, you entered a state of *dissociation.* Something inside of you "went away." You withdrew into the fortress of your heart and refused to come out.

Goodbye, cruel world.

In this lifetime, you are in recovery from that blow, whatever it was. And in order to feel the Aquarian guidance of your own soul, you must first simply learn how to recover your ability *to feel anything at all.*

How do we sort all this out? Does your Aquarian planet reflect this kind of unresolved trauma – or was it simply "bossed around" too much? There are so many past-life possibilities here, and they range all the way from being too constrained by "polite society" to dying in the Black Plague or a death camp. With Aquarian planets, are we looking at something truly hard and overwhelming in the karmic past – or just a little too much social constraint?

That is a big subject.

To say it simply, if these Aquarian or Uranian features are associated with the south node of the Moon, we may very well be in the territory of this kind of traumatically-induced dissociation. That becomes even more reliable if hard planets, such as Mars or Pluto, are tied to the nodal structure through squares or oppositions.

To understand these analytic techniques fully would require me to insert a 357 page footnote. So that is exactly what I am going to do: if you want to learn about karmic analysis, I invite you to read my book, *Yesterday's Sky: The Astrology of Reincarnation*. It contains pretty much everything I know about the subject.

LET'S START WITH URANUS . . .

. . . even though Aquarius has two rulers. And don't worry – we will not forget about Saturn.

When I was learning astrology, I often saw Uranus described as the Lord of Earthquakes and Lightning Bolts. That is just one metaphor, but however we express it, that is a title that the planet has earned over and over again. When you need a monkey wrench thrown into your smoothly running gearbox, Uranus is the god to invoke.

One fine illustration of that "monkey wrench" principle occured in Spring, 1781, when William Herschel discovered Uranus – or more accurately, when he began to realize that it was a planet, not a star.

Well, the tale is actually a little bit more complicated than that.

Herschel thought what he was seeing was a *comet*, not a planet. His real contribution was only to realize that, whatever it was, it was *moving* and so it could not be a star. It took the work of many other astronomers, plus a couple years of tail-twitching before Herschel himself acknowledged Uranus to be a planet. Herschel's hold on the title of "discoverer" is actually pretty shaky everywhere except in high school science books.

There is good evidence that the Greek astronomer, Hipparchos, saw Uranus in 128 B.C., along with a series of other astronomers starting in about 1690. The trouble is, most of them cataloged it as a star – which is an even worse guess than "comet," so let's at least give William Herschel the bronze medal, if not the silver or the gold.

In any case, the discovery of Uranus rattled astrology right down to its roots. Remember our Lord of Earthquakes and Lightning Bolts? Its discovery is a classic example of synchronicity in action. The system of "seven planets" was hallowed ground – Sun, Moon, Mercury, Venus, Mars, Jupiter and Saturn. There were the seven days of the week. The seven notes of the octave. The seven colors of the rainbow. The seven wonders of the world. The seventh seal. The seven cities of gold. The seven chakras. Even the "seven sisters" in the sky – the Pleiades – where most people can actually only see six stars, but no matter – everyone agreed there *should* be seven, so that is what they claimed to see.

Seven was a magic number. The very existence of "seven planets" was *prima facie* evidence of the cosmic validity of astrology.

And then suddenly there were eight . . . and sixty-seven years later, nine.

For astrologers, it was a big blow to public relations.

Mostly undaunted, the astrologers left standing began to work with the new planet. Countless centuries of experience had taught us a few tricks. We knew, for example, that anyone born with Venus conjunct the Sun or the Ascendant would be the embodiment of Venus, for better or worse. Ditto with the rest of the planets. Why would it not work the same way with this new planet?

This leads me to one of my favorite astrological insights. It will seem like a digression, but it isn't.

What is north for Earth is north, more or less, for Venus, Mars, Jupiter, and so on. That means that as planets orbit the Sun, they *rotate* on their axes. Thus we – and they – experience night and day. This is true of all the planets, except for Uranus, whose rotational axis is tilted about 98° relative to the ecliptic.

Translated, that fact means that where other planets spin, Uranus rolls.

As those 18th-century astrologers plugged Uranus into peoples' charts, looking for putative "Uranian types" who would then give them clues about the nature of this planet, they discovered that these people too had a tendency to "roll where others might spin."

I have never actually encountered that exact phrase in any historical document. But what we do find are persistent references to these people's *peculiarity* and *eccentricity*. Saying that they rolled where others might have spun hardly seems like a metaphorical stretch. It worked then, and it still works today.

Peculiarity and eccentricity can be understood as judgemental words. In more contemporary parlance, we might similarly use the word "weird" – and, again, if someone aims that word at you and they aren't smiling play-fully when they do it, you probably bristle a bit.

Think deeply – *and in Aquarian fashion* – about this last point: im-plicit in the judgemental tone of such language, we observe *social pressure to conform.*

You wouldn't want everyone to think you were weird, would you?

Sound familiar? This single point obviously echoes so much of what we have just explored about the sign Aquarius. There we learned that "all cultures are conservative" – which, translated, means that all cultures op-pose individuation. As they say in Japan, "The nail that sticks out gets hammered down." And not only in Japan. Being "weird" might mean be-ing ejected from the tribe – something that is not conducive to health and longevity for anyone. So it frightens us.

The rulership of Uranus over Aquarius hit our astrological ancestors over the head, in other words. It was completely obvious.

And I believe they were correct.

Giving Uranus the rulership of Aquarius has become practically the litmus test that distinguishes a "modern astrologer" from a "traditional as-trologer." When I was young and modern astrology ruled the world, there actually seemed to be some danger that Saturn's connection to Aquarius would be completely forgotten.

And that would have been an epistemological disaster.

SATURN THE LAW-GIVER

There is a famously inappropriate word that begins with the letter "F." Say-ing it is widely described as "dropping the F-bomb." I suspect you know the word I mean. I am going to keep my P.G. Rating here by leaving it to your worldly experience to figure out the word I am referencing.

When I was a kid, I was afraid to say that word. One syllable uttered, and I was afraid that I would be dragged down into the bowels of hell. By the time I was twelve or fourteen, some of my rougher friends would taunt me, trying to get me to say it. But not me, no – not Mister Capricorn with Saturn in Virgo on the Midheaven. I wanted to go to heaven, and I knew that pronouncing that magical, Satanic word was a ticket in the opposite direction. Back then, the F-bomb had that kind of occult power.

Naturally, just a few years later, I had become fluent in the use of that same word. But even back then, it still had some power to shock.

Last week, I was teaching at the Omega Institute in upstate New York, which is sort of a gentle post-hippie spiritual paradise, especially if you are fond of vegetables. I saw a car parked there with a happy-face bumper sticker inviting me to *Have a F**king Mystical Day.*

I think the driver meant something nice by that.

In Chengdu, China, a couple of years ago, in the famous panda park, I saw a Chinese woman with a tee-shirt that announced, in English, that *I Am A Walking F**king Paradox.*

I could launch into that one as a profound insight into modern China, but that's not why I invoke it here. I invoke the F-bomb simply to point out how today it has become a shadow of its former self. Much of the power has gone out of it. It may still shock a little bit, but it no longer has enough amperage to electrocute anyone, even grandma.

In fact, I know a lot of grandmothers who use the term with fluid grace and never a second thought.

The F-bomb is just no fun anymore.

Without the laws against using it, that poor word has practically no *mojo* left at all. If you reflect deeply on that simple point, I believe that you will soon grasp how essential Saturn is to our understanding of the Aquarian Clan in the Air Family.

Among students of modern astrology, I have often heard a question: how can Saturn, this strict, structured, highly moral planet, ever have had anything to do with wild and woolly Aquarius? What were our ancestors thinking?

You probably already see where this is going. Without laws to break, there can be no lawbreakers. Without tyranny, there can be no rebellion. Without tradition, there can be no groundbreaking innovation.

When anyone can use the F-word, why bother using it at all? You have probably noticed how comedians from the 1980s who peppered their routines with that word seem faintly ridiculous and pitiful today.

This is the eternal symbiosis of Saturn and Uranus.

Modern astrologers who ignore Saturn's connection with Aquarius are attempting to define "good" while denying the existence of anything we might call evil or darkness. They are trying to define "up" with no reference to "down" – or "hot" with no reference to "cold."

No one can ever actually succeed at that, except in a glib or superficial way.

This error strikes me as one of the most cogent critiques of twentieth century astrological practice. Later, in *The Book of Water*, we will make similar cases for the dual-rulerships of Scorpio and Pisces. We modern astrologers should never forget about the role of Mars and Jupiter in connection with those two signs, and yet we often do. We can thank traditional astrologers for reminding us all of this critical piece of astrological understanding.

With all that said, I would like to give traditional astrologers – at least the current crop of them – equal time on the rotisserie. *To deny the obviously Uranian dimensions of the observed behavior of large swaths of the Aquarian population is the triumph of biased theoretical perspective over what our eyes can plainly see.*

The original Hellenistic and medieval astrologers can of course be forgiven for this lapse – they did not even know about the existence of the planet Uranus. Astronomically, they were playing with half a deck. But today, it is up there in the sky, speaking with a loud and clear voice for anyone willing to listen. And if our eyes are open, we can see its natural alignment with exactly *half* of what we need to understand about the sign Aquarius.

How to grasp the dual rulership of Aquarius? It is not difficult; in fact, the more you think about it, the more you realize it is actually easier to understand this sign if you use both Uranus and Saturn – and absolutely impossible if you limit yourself to either one of them.

NOT TO GIVE SATURN SHORT SHRIFT, BUT . . .

. . . we already took a long, deep look at Saturn in the previous volume of this series, *The Book of Earth*. Have a look at chapter five of that book for a refresher, if you like. Rather than repeating or paraphrasing all of that material here, let's dive a little deeper into less familiar territory: the action of the planet Uranus.

SELF VS. SOCIETY

Our true nature is pitted against training and socialization – as with Aquarius, that is the basic dynamic of the planet Uranus. Where it lies in your chart, your sanity is inseparable from your ability to sort those two forces out, and commit to simply being true to your own inborn path.

That is easier said than done. In fact, as we will see, it is a bit like asking the rat to guard the cheese. One problem is that we all believe that we *already are* our "true selves." Unless we are spies, few of us get out of bed in the morning with an urge to pose under some fake identity. But in truth, every one of us is an amalgam of two very distinct substances: *a real self and a trained monkey*. And they have a difficult time telling each other apart.

The first step in making a strong response to Uranus is to admit the existence of the question. Many people never even get that far. With a few self-inquiries, we can set the stage for our excavation of this new planet. Here are some examples:

• Who would you be if you had had a different mother or a different father?
A fundamental insight of modern psychology is the extent to which we are shaped by the experience of our early years. What if your mother was distant? What if she felt unprepared and incompetent, afraid of you when you were a baby? What if your father was actually in love with someone else and that secret pervaded the air of the home before you were three years old? Or what if your family was idyllic, not a care in the world – and so you never saw conflict resolution or how to deal with the blows of life?

• Who would you be if you had been born in Botswana instead of where you were actually born?
Presumably, Botswanan humor is different, as are Botswanan sexual customs, attitudes toward child-rearing, aging, gender, disease, money, the dead, nudity, and so on. Had you been raised there instead of where you were actually raised, how would those conditions have impacted your personality? How would you be different? And, more pointedly, how did the culture in which you were actually raised similarly distort your own nature today in ways that you do not understand?

- Who would you be if you had been born in 1652 instead of when you were actually born?

Imagine it: you still have the same soul, with the same wisdom, the same karma, and the same issues to resolve. But you take birth in the human society of centuries ago, when everything was so different that we can barely imagine it. You are raised in that mythic matrix instead of the one into which you were actually born. Step out of the Time Machine and meet your spiritual doppelgän- ger – would you even recognize yourself?

Perhaps the planet Uranus plays a big role in your chart – it is aligned with the Sun, for example, or in strong aspect to the Moon or the Ascen- dant. Then much as we saw with the sign Aquarius, most of the experi- ences that will be meaningful to you in this lifetime come with a price-tag: if you go down those roads, you will begin to look increasingly unusual. You will look as if you were "rolling where other people might spin."

When the Uranian signature is very strong, the biographical pattern of *individuation as an evolutionary necessity* is central and unmistakable.

There is, of course, zero guarantee that you will get this right. The only guarantee – and it is ironclad – is that you *can* get it right. You have that capability. How to exercise it? Answering that question brings us back to familiar Aquarian territory: bottom line, you must accept that your path through life is "the road less traveled." *You must overcome the need to have everyone's approval and good will.*

What if you make a weak response to a strongly-configured natal Uranus? Again, the answer is familiar. It is essentially the same mess we encountered under the banner of the Aquarian shadow: you will feel *dis- sociated* and *alienated.*

A NOT SO PROMINENT URANUS

These last comments have been about having a major Uranian fingerprint in your natal chart. What about a more subtle one? Everyone has Uranus *some- where* in his or her chart. What does it mean if it is hiding out in a corner?

Start with the obvious insight: in such a case, making a vigorous re- sponse to this call to individuation is not quite so pivotal to the success of your soul's journey. Assuming that there is nothing in Aquarius (and no significant Out of Bounds influences – see *The Book of the Moon* if you need definitions there), it is fair to say that "being normal" might be a perfectly natural and appropriate path for you. The world is full of middle class "soccer moms" and "soccer dads" living steady, if predictable, suburban lives *who are highly evolved souls.* They of course have Uranus somewhere in their charts – and where it lies, all of our basic principles apply. In that particular area of life, even the mildest person must make some kind of stand against being steam-rollered into a false identity. The nature of that area of life is naturally spotlighted by the house in which Uranus lies, the sign which conditions it, and the aspects which tie it into the rest of the chart.

Let's bring this to life with some examples.

URANUS IN THE FOURTH HOUSE

Want to see the fourth house? Get a shovel, go out in the backyard, and start digging. That is where it is – basically it is straight down, under the earth. Any planet there is about as invisible as a planet can be. (Technically, it's not "straight" down, but rather opposite the highest point in the sky that the Sun reaches around noon. Unless you are in the Tropics, the Sun is never directly overhead.)

Right there, we have a broad hint about the general meaning of the fourth house: it represents your *inner life,* something about you which no one else can ever see directly.

When Uranus lies in the fourth house, it is similarly hidden. *Everything else being equal, we recognize that the most pivotal venue for the exercise of your personal freedom lies in your own thoughts and meditations.* No one else ever really *needs* to know about them. You may *choose* to share them, and that is fine. But your mantra is "in my soul, I am free."

Implicit in these initial observations is a corollary: with Uranus in the fourth house, you might very well find yourself living a rather normal outer life. For you, there is no pressing Uranian need to swing from public chandeliers dressed in a feather boa. It is the inner life, and not the outer one, in which you are developing your ability to be your natural self. Your thoughts and emotions require more freedom than your outer life.

- I picture a heterosexual man sitting in a topless bar, thinking how strange men are.
- I picture a woman without children reflecting on why so many women feel incomplete without them.

- I picture an American in France feeling amused by the behavior of American tourists.
- I picture an elderly person listening to other elderly people complain about what has happened to their bodies, fascinated by how predictable old people are.

In each of these little vignettes, add a critical ingredient: *a non-judgemental attitude*. In each of these examples, these Uranian characters appear to fit right into the social landscape. And, truly, they *are* fitting in. But they are *thinking thoughts* that no one would suspect them of thinking. The only evidence for that fact is that on their faces, there is the faintest trace of an enigmatic smile.

With Uranus in the fourth house, much of their Uranian learning is purely internal. They are on a path of *spycraft*, in a perfect disguise which allows them to move fluidly through any situation, paying acute attention without triggering any alarms.

Let's take a giant step: the fourth house is also connected to *family*. Naturally that is a huge subject. When Uranus is there, we are looking at the signature of a very particular evolutionary necessity: *rebellion against one's birth family*.

If we took that phrase literally, however, and just ran with it in obvious ways, we would miss the point. Remember what we just learned about this configuration – it does not require dramatic outward expression. What it requires is fundamentally *subjective*, something more in the category of *insight* rather than existential hellfire and brimstone.

Every family system has a style. Every one of them has beliefs about itself and about the nature of reality. We might say that every family has a *myth of itself*. And certainly, every family system is composed of roles, gender assumptions, and sundry psychiatric loose ends.

If you have Uranus in the fourth house, you must learn to *recognize where that myth has taken hold of you*. Your aim is to root it out, and eventually to *form your own family* (in some sense of that word) along lines that are more consistent with the shape of your soul.

Illustration: I sat once with a client who had this fourth house Uranian configuration. As soon as I mentioned that her happiness depended upon ferreting out the baleful influences of her family myth, she laughed out loud. She told me that ever since she was a little girl, she had heard the same thing over and over again from her mother and her aunts. I still remember her exact words: *"All of us Kelly women marry alcoholics. Ho ho ho."*

You probably know the rest of the story. My client had gotten the message. She had found her very own alcoholic and married him. The collapse of that marriage was in fact what brought her to my office.

We can assume that her mother and her aunts did not actually *wish* this same fate upon the little girl. My client had simply overheard these women as they offered each other some camaraderie in the face of their marital challenges. They were giving each other emotional support in the form of shared "gallows humor." It probably eased their burdens a bit.

Still, the family myth sunk deeply into my client. With her Uranus in the fourth house, for her to find happiness, she had to break the stranglehold of that myth upon her imagination.

URANUS IN CAPRICORN

Capricorn is a sign that correlates with monumental acts of sustained self-discipline and focus. At its best, it keeps its eye on the prize – and plods away single-mindedly until it arrives at its goal. Among Capricorn's corollaries are words such as *character* and *morality*.

No one in the history of the world has ever *enjoyed* resisting a temptation – but if you find yourself in a situation where it behooves you to resist one, my hope for you is that you have a planet or two in Capricorn. They help.

If you want to know more about Capricorn, you can read about it in *The Book of Earth*. One point I explore in detail in those pages is that where the devil gets into the Capricorn equations is with collective social assumptions about the *definitions* of right and wrong. The Sea-Goat can climb the wrong mountain just because "it was expected." There are a few eternal truths with which Capricorn – or any other sign – should never quibble: not killing, not stealing, and so forth. But what about more arbitrary moral principles, the ones that come and go as the tides of culture turn? Those are the areas where Uranian individuation becomes critical when that planet finds itself in the sign of the Sea-Goat.

Illustration: when I was young, a man and a woman living together without being married was still socially quite controversial. Older people often viewed such an arrangement as inherently immoral. The phrase "living in sin" was current. Relatively few people think that way today. Many of us have experienced such a living arrangement ourselves. We all know and love people who live that way – and who love each other well and faithfully.

Who would judge them as sinners for "living together" today? Maybe a preacher in Alabama.

With any planet in Capricorn, you have at least one vote in your head for moral strength, along with a capacity for the kind of self-denial that must go along with it. If that planet in Capricorn happens to be Uranus, *be careful what moral map you internalize*. As a result of social conditioning – the way you grew up – you have been given definitions of right and wrong that will not work for you, nor will they feed the evolution of your soul.

Everything else being equal, you are an inherently moral being – but you must redefine the word "morality" in a way that is consistent with the actual voice of your soul rather than with the conditioning that has been pressed upon you. That's not just about your family. That is also about the culture of your high school class, the movies and music you've internalized as part of your generation, and so on: the whole cultural *enchilada*.

With Uranus in Capricorn, you are one of the humans on the Earth today whose task is to redefine the meaning of the words right and wrong for the next century.

By the way, if you were born between 1988 and 1995, I am talking about you. Uranus was in Capricorn during those years – and it will not be back until 2072, so we are counting on you for this redefinition.

EXPECT THE UNEXPECTED

That is one of the standard-issue astrological clichés about Uranus – and for good reason: weird things do happen in Uranian times.

We will take a deeper look at those words when we get to our consideration of Uranian transits and solar arcs in chapter twenty-two. For now, suffice to say that this planet seems to be a lightning rod for highly improbable events. Earthquakes and lightning bolts are phenomena that tend to change the landscape in the blink of an eye. Where Uranus lies in your chart, you are standing on a fault line while pointing a lightning rod at a thunderhead.

Why? Well, because God loves you . . .

And obviously that last line begs for some explanation.

There is nothing easier to get out of than it was to get into in the first place – there's a principle that you can take to the bank. Getting married? Easy! Starting a career? Easy! Deciding to have children! The first steps in that direction are among the easiest ones you have ever taken.

But what if your marriage turns out to be a trap?

What if your career pays you exactly what you need to feed your kids month-by-month – but you realize that it is eating your soul and that you really chose it only to impress your parents fifteen years ago?

What if you were just not cut out for parenthood, or your kid is a junkie, or simply does not like you?

In each of these not-so-unfamiliar situations, we see two sets of fingerprints:

- The classic Uranian scenario, where the outer life has come adrift from the soul's intentions, mostly due to our collective vulnerability to external social conditioning, cultural pressures, and training.
- A very genuine human reality of simply feeling stuck. None of these situations is amenable to easy resolution – at least none that would leave you feeling good about yourself. "Feeling stuck" means that a situation seems irresolvable.

Enter Uranus: sometimes when you have painted yourself into a corner that way, "angels come riding over the horizon to rescue you." Improbable, unpredictable events unfold, giving you a second chance.

This is a common pattern, not a reliable fail-safe principle – but it does happen, and every astrologer should be aware of it.

Before we whoop for joy, let's read the fine print.

This angelic intervention might feel like a direct hit from a lightning bolt. (We are starting with high drama here, by the way – the "angels" can be gentle too.)

I have seen an unexpected, even tragic, death of a partner, parent, or child *set someone free.*

I have seen financial "earthquakes" *destroying a career that was actually killing someone.*

I've seen hit-from-behind, unsuspected infidelities liberating a person from a dead-end marriage.

Just to keep balance here, let me add that I have seen against-the-odds financial windfalls opening doors. I have seen "chance" meetings with the person "who was holding the other half of your deck of cards."

The point is that, if you are inextricably stuck in the mud you have created for yourself, in the part of your chart where Uranus lies, the universe sometimes comes to the rescue.

THE ELEVENTH HOUSE

My favorite book back when I was cutting my astrological teeth was Ronald C. Davison's, *Astrology*. In it, he nicely summarized the meaning of the eleventh house in four dozen words.

"The eleventh house represents the native's ability to stabilize his position in the world and is related to his hopes and wishes. Friends who assist the native to realize his possibilities in this direction and indirectly help to determine his standing are also ruled by the eleventh house."

Very typically, in modern practice, as Davison indicates, the eleventh house is related to the idea of *friendship*. That notion is helpful and accurate, provided that we are thinking of our "five hundred closest friends" rather than our nearest and dearest precious souls. It is really, in other words, more about *group identification* than about intimacy.

More about that in a little while.

Davison also spoke of "hopes and wishes." That is a critical element here, as we will soon see – perhaps the most active piece of the puzzle. His understated, brilliant line, "Friends who assist the native to realize his possibilities in this direction" is what links these two ideas. In choosing our "nearest and dearest," we need to trust our hearts.

But what about how we choose our "five hundred closest friends?"

The phrase – five hundred closest friends – might sound ironical, but I mean nothing cynical or even shallow by it. We all live in a social context.

Here is the whole idea in streamlined form:

If you want to be a musician, hang out with musicians.

Your hopes and wishes must come first, in other words – that is why I called them the most active piece of the puzzle a few seconds ago. *They are what supply the framework of values and long-term purpose that underlie any good choices we might make in forming our broad social network.*

If you want to be a musician, you can learn a lot by playing music with other people. They'll support you, challenge you, inspire you, and criticize you. That human interaction can accelerate your evolution as a player. At a practical level, those other musicians will also email you when there is a sale on guitar strings or when a band you really need to hear is coming to town.

You will do the same for them too, of course. That's what friends are for.

Well, that is *one thing* that friends are for . . . remember: in the eleventh house, we are not talking about intimacy. You might make some intimate friends among those other musicians – but as soon as that any feelings of soul-connection arise, kiss the eleventh house goodbye. You are not there anymore. That friendship has just moved into the domain of the seventh house – the realm of *equality, open-endedness*, and *magic* we explored in the previous chapter.

MY APPRENTICESHIP GROUPS

In the past, I have run various astrological apprenticeship groups on four continents. I am down to just two or three such programs now in order to make time to write this series of books about the astrological elements. I do not miss the traveling, which was becoming exhausting.

But I do miss the people.

In these groups – which are the epitome of the eleventh house – there has always been a feeling of shared "tribal" or "community" experience. We have had dramas. We have had deaths, even a suicide. Marriages have formed and marriages have dissolved. There is a strong sense of "village" connection among us. We are happy to see each other when our meetings come around. People hug each other. There is love in the room that you can feel.

Still, I can honestly say that I don't even *know the names* of all of these people when I see them. At this point, the cumulative roster lies somewhere around two thousand souls – more than I can possibly remember, in other words.

Yet I can sincerely say that I have a feeling of *friendship* towards every one of them.

Let me repeat: I cannot remember all of their names, but I am happy to call them friends.

The part of you that knows what I am talking about is called the eleventh house. We all have one; we all have the psychic circuitry for understanding this particular category of human relationship.

Often, when I am teaching one of these programs and the subject has turned to the eleventh house, I will announce to the class that "we are all friends here." There might be fifty or eighty people in the room. I am sure that, like me, they don't all know each other's names either. But no one argues when I say that we are "all friends." Heads nod agreeably. Then I quickly conjure up the image of a person on one side of the room standing up and pointing to another person, announcing in Inquisitorial fashion, "Actually, I do not like *her* very much."

Everyone laughs, of course. They all understood that when I said that we were all friends, I did not mean that we were all actually *friends* . . .

I was just tempted to write, "perhaps you are beginning to see the dilemma."

But actually, there is no real dilemma. The word "friends" simply has a lot of different legitimate definitions.

My apprentices are all there because they want to learn how to understand this kind of astrology. That desire represents a set of *hopes and wishes that have brought them together for a common purpose.* That is the heart of the eleventh house. I point out that because of life's practical realities, I could not travel so far to teach if there were only two or three students. We need a large group to make it work. I point out that my fee for the teaching is reasonable when it is divided among so many people, but that it would be extremely prohibitive for any one single person to have to cover it. If they didn't have each other, none of them – myself included – could have this valuable experience.

One critical take-away: among my students, *their "hopes and wishes" to learn astrology came first.* Those hopes are the primary *underlying organizing principle* in the social side of their eleventh house experience.

In a nutshell, your hopes and aspirations must define your tribe, not the other way around.

IT'S HARD TO BE A FOOTBALL
PLAYER ALL BY YOURSELF

I mean, how are you going to go out for a pass? Who is going to throw the ball? And if you were to tackle yourself . . . well, somebody's got to say it: you would look like a damned fool.

There is no way anyone can be a football player without a helping hand.

I am no athlete, but I appreciate how playing a team sport could be a personally meaningful experience. But to succeed at it, you are going to need a little help from your friends.

A dear – if utterly Uranian – friendship has formed in my life over the past three years or so. (You might remember my natal Venus-Uranus opposition?) It is with Ricky Williams. His name might ring a bell with any of you readers who happen to also be football fans. Ricky won the Heisman Trophy in college, then went on to play pro football with the New Orleans *Saints*, the Miami *Dolphins*, and the Baltimore *Ravens*. If you Google his name, you will see an eye-popping video of him defying all the laws of physics, flying through the air with the greatest of ease, all the while dodging several 280-pound men seemingly hellbent on murdering him.

Ricky is also a very fine astrologer, and probably "got it" faster than any student I've ever had before.

Once Ricky Williams and I were sitting on the floor in a seedy airport in Tropea, Italy, both of us catching the same morning flight to Rome, then homeward, after a class I had just taught. Ricky is an intelligent, sensitive guy. In conversing with him, I became aware that I was probably carrying a lot of ignorant, groundless generalizations about football players – unfairly thinking that they probably had extra muscles where their brains were supposed to go. After all, there was Ricky himself, defying all of my assumptions.

Football had never had anything to do with my own eleventh house experiences, so I really did not know any players personally except for him.

I asked Ricky a question. I said, "I'm not proud of this – it's pure prejudice – but I am still a little surprised that a big NFL guy like yourself is so interested in astrology. Maybe I've been wrong about football players for all these years. *What percentage of your old teammates would you guess were into astrology, Ricky?*"

Without missing a beat, he said, *"Zero."* .

We both laughed of course.

It turns out that at least some of my "stupid assumptions" were perhaps not quite so "groundless" after all.

Later in a different context, I asked Ricky Williams how he felt about football nowadays. He had a simple, straightforward answer. He said, with feeling, "I still love the game."

Tellingly, Ricky has solitary Saturn in his eleventh house. I think he was lonely a lot during his pro career. But in order to access an experience – professional football – that was critical to his soul's journey, he had to accept being *solitary* (Saturn) *in a crowd* (the eleventh house.) It is too simple to assume that he "had nothing in common with the other players." The reality is that he had one spiritually-critical thing in common with them: *the love of the game of football.*

And for Ricky to gain access to that soul-trigger, that was *enough* common ground.

Intimacy can arise in this "house of friends," but intimacy is not the point. The point is closer to people *being useful* to each other. When intimacy does arise, our attention shifts more in the seventh house direction, and away from the eleventh.

PRIORITIES

To be full of desires is fundamental to the human condition.

Ask the *libido* what it wants, it has a simple, 100% sincere answer: *Everything. Right Now.*

And that is where the negotiations begin.

We have to set *priorities*. Life is too short for us to "have everything." What is the *most important* goal for you? What is your "tenth-most" important goal – and might you be willing to sacrifice it, if pursuing it meant losing out on whatever was third on your list?

These simple insights add another pair of eleventh house words to our vocabulary: *tactics* and *strategy.*

What is the most direct and efficient road to fulfilling your hopes and wishes? Figuring that out starts with editing the list. Maybe wish #10 really does have to be sacrificed. Maybe life is too short to have that dream come true too.

Having "lots of lovers" can be a compelling fantasy for many people – and no judgement is intended there, only one single bit of advice: *ditch that fantasy if you want to have a happy marriage.*

Want to become an astrologer? There are many roads you could follow to that goal. One of them is attending classes. But you might have to divert resources – funds or vacation-time – from that trip you would love to take to Machu Picchu.

Priorities, once again – such a simple, innocent-sounding word. But setting them can be a brutal process. Whatever was number ten on your list of hopes and dreams is going to be hard to abandon.

You might feel Saturn's hands in all of this – and remember: Saturn is every bit as much the natural ruler of the eleventh house as is Uranus. Saturn is the face of the Divine that asks you how *badly* do you want it? What are you willing to *pay?* What are you willing to *sacrifice?*

Ask anyone who has ever written a novel or gotten a PhD or learned to play the piano – no one achieves such goals without wearing blinders at least some of the time. To arrive at such a golden city, you must pay the price. Temptations must be resisted, true enough – but you must also resist some sweet friendships, joyful experiences, and even some authentic spiritual booster shots. The guru is giving a talk, but you've promised yourself to stay home and work.

Never trust anyone who tells you that "you can have it all." That is one of the surest roads to having nothing – or worse, a taste of this, a stab at that, a tee-shirt from this place, a selfie from that place, along with a wistful memory of a half-fulfilled romantic promise with someone who actually forgot about you long ago.

SO WHAT EXACTLY IS YOUR GOAL?

To get the eleventh house right, you have to *make your stand.* Set sail for your soul's destination. Set your priorities, work your strategies, aim for that higher ground. And be willing to pay the Saturnian price.

How do you know what it is? How do you define it?

Start by remembering the other natural ruler of the eleventh house: *Uranus.* In order to recognize that higher ground, you must *individuate.* You must think for yourself. No one else can tell you what it is. No one else's "suggested goal" for you is going to fill you with the sustainable, life-long passion you need if you are going to succeed.

Unless of course that person is an astrologer.

That last line was fun to write, even though I would be the first to admit that it is an exaggeration. I love astrology, but it has its limits. Still, an astrologer can help you define those goals. Perhaps even more valuably, an astrologer can help you – Aquarian fashion – to dump the phony goals that have been foisted upon you ever since you were in diapers.

It is often said that astrology itself is an Aquarian craft. I believe that for one simple reason. That is because astrology and Aquarius share a common goal. The goal is *individuation.*

At its core, a good astrological reading should help you be yourself.

Some astrologers feel that your chart describes *who you are.* There is practical reality in such a statement, but I prefer to phrase it differently. I believe that your chart tells you whom you *could be* – or perhaps we could even say whom you *should* be. It represents the highest intentions of your soul for this lifetime.

And what could be a wiser eleventh house move for anyone than reaching her or his highest soul intentions? That "north star" is revealed not only by the eleventh house, but rather by your chart as a whole. Yet the eleventh house provides a key piece of guidance. *It suggests, across the whole spectrum of our multitudinous goals, which ones we should prioritize.* The eleventh house lights the fuse on the evolutionary rocket fuel. It tells you where to put your foot next.

It helps you *pay attention to who you are in the process of becoming.*

A STRANGE PROPERTY OF PLANETS IN THE ELEVENTH HOUSE

They grow in strength over time.

This is such a simple, even obvious, insight, and yet I do not often hear other astrologers speaking of it. The reasoning behind it is simple: any goal that arises naturally in us automatically gathers momentum and definition as years go by.

You strive; you attain: it is practically a law of the universe.

Whatever energies lie in the eleventh house, you are actively hungry for them. That is what the word "goals" means: those energies are *motivational*. Inevitably, that hunger collides from time to time with opportunity – and before we know it, we have made progress.

Once those positive steps have been taken, nothing can erase them. Then, through further experience and opportunity, we build on the steps we have already made. That is why these planets gather momentum as the years pass. A corollary is that *any planet in the eleventh house tends to become much more dominant in the second half of life.*

Whether that is good news or bad news does not depend on the planet or on any aspects it might make. It depends 100% upon the quality of our response to it.

Let us illustrate this key eleventh house principle with a very human, homespun example. Let us imagine that Santa Claus, in response to your fervent desires, brought you a set of electric trains when you were a child. You played with them avidly for three or four years, then set them aside. But an interest in model railroading had been kindled in you.

Maybe your family moved, and "by chance" you found yourself living near an actual railroad. You would play near the tracks, watching the trains go by. Maybe you even flattened a few pennies.

Synchronicity struck, in other words. For some mysterious reason, the universe wanted you *paying attention to trains*. That is why your family "happened to" move to a house by a railroad.

Years later, you find yourself sitting in a dentist's office. In the pile of magazines is a copy of *Model Railroader*. You pick it up and thumb through it, feeling fascinated by those little toy villages where the trains always run on time.

Next June, you vacation in Switzerland: *trains again*.

You become friends with a coworker. He invites you to a party at his house one Saturday evening. With a goofy grin, he proudly shows you the elaborate layout of electric trains in his basement. Model railroading is his hobby; he has been working on it for years. You think his electric train layout is the coolest thing you have seen in a long while – and he is delighted that you don't poke fun at him for it the way his wife and the rest of his friends do.

Your budding friendship with the co-worker prompts you to get back into the hobby. You absorb the inevitable jibes from your own partner and your other friends, and just enjoy your electric trains, Aquarian-fashion. Let them laugh if they want, in other words. Pretty soon you've got a three-year subscription to *Model Railroader* yourself.

By the time you are retired, your own basement railroad is twice the size of your friend's layout. And *Model Railroader* has done a feature story on you.

You get the picture. *Time has done its work.* You may laugh at yourself, but trains have been an ongoing developmental theme in your life.

Why? Who knows? But you have aimed some of your passion, time, and intelligence in that direction. Inevitably, that focus has led to systematic evolution over time.

When it comes to electric trains, everyone now thinks of you as the local expert.

There is a reason that I have chosen this particular example. Playing with electric trains is the kind of hobby that, if you are older than twelve, you are surely going to get some teasing. It is Uranian in that "everyone knows" they are silly, *yet you enjoy it anyway.* And you may very well have Uranus in your eleventh house. You have indeed "become more peculiar" with the passage of time. Your willingness to overcome your monkey-need for other people's approval is a real spiritual accomplishment. *Your electric trains are simply a method for getting there.*

Let's add that you *needed your co-worker and your fellow model railroaders in order to accomplish it.* And those relationships are part of the eleventh house process too.

In this tale, in other words, we see friendship, synchronicity, development over time, and sustained progress toward a goal: the whole eleventh house *smorgasbord.*

A FEW IMAGES

- Maybe you loved treacly pop music when you were a kid. You listened to it carefully. Your passions, while unsophisticated, are stirred. Building on that love of music, what kind of music are you listening to when you are in your thirties? What about when you are sixty-five? How have your tastes evolved? (And maybe Venus lies in the eleventh house.)

- A sixteen-year-old sits meditating – and we commend him or her. But what will such a person's meditations be like at age ninety, assuming discipline and continuity in spiritual practice over all those years? (And maybe Neptune is in the eleventh house.)
- Two people in their early twenties love each other. Thirty years later, they still love each other, and their children and their grandchildren – how has their love deepened and changed over time? (And maybe the Moon lies in each of their eleventh houses.)

All along, we have been building on three essential points about the eleventh house. Let's quickly reiterate them:

- Priorities must be set and followed in a spirit of *discipline* – that's the Saturn connection.
- Those priorities must be set in strict fidelity to our *individuality* – they are naturally our own business, *and we need to remember that.* We need no one else's approval. There's the Uranian signature.
- You cannot succeed at the eleventh house alone. The experiences are personally meaningful, but they can only be accessed collectively. Perhaps they involve ongoing *group activities*, or perhaps they only need a *social trigger*. In either case, the eleventh house is not a door you can unlock alone.

READY OR NOT, I'M COMING

In working with the notion of an eleventh house planet developing over time, it is pivotal to leave room for freedom, choice, and imagination.

Or for the lack of them.

The height of astrological folly here would be to assume that if you had "bad planets" – usually taken to be Mars, Saturn, and Pluto – in the eleventh house, your life would be destined to become worse and worse over time.

The core of that mistake would be *believing* in the idea of "bad planets" in the first place. There are none.

The penultimate folly would be looking at Jupiter and Venus in the eleventh house, and imagining that, with those "lucky" planets on your side, all you had to do was sit back and everything would come your way.

What might actually come your way could be runaway weight gain, along with a series of bad relationships based on nothing but romantic projections.

As with everything else in astrology, *conscious intentions* must interact with these eleventh house configurations in order for any good results to arise from them. They represent evolutionary goals to which the soul needs to be committed. Time – and effort – are what actually open the flower.

AND A FEW MORE IMAGES

Peppered throughout the pages of this four volume series on the elements, you will find detailed cookbook analyses of the role that each planet plays when it finds itself in the eleventh house.

Right now, let's get a taste of how it all works with three more quick illustrations.

- Jupiter in the eleventh house? Here is the real question: what is the meaning of success for you? If you take the answer to be as simple as "power and money," you may have some hard lessons ahead. How "individuated" do those answers sound? Are there any sad people with power and money in this world? What definition of "success" will actually lead you to fulfillment?

- Saturn in the eleventh house? Your goal is to become an *elder* – and here is a critical hint: that does not simply mean getting old. *Elders are surrounded by younger people who want to be there.* How do you become that man or woman?

- Mercury in the eleventh house? You *find your voice* later in life – provided you spent the first half of your life actually looking for it.

These are just quick thumbnail sketches, nothing more. Adding the planet's sign to the mixture further clarifies and specifies the evolutionary goal. Aspects and the larger context of the chart as a whole make it fully human.

The underlying idea is that your eleventh house planet is gaining momentum in a way that suggests the operation of a purely *mechanical* law.

Consciousness is the ingredient that you need to add. You need to surf the wave of that evolutionary curve, forming a partnership with that planet – and supporting it with some broader human alliances as well. If you want to be an artist, hang out with artists. If you want to be an adventurer, interact with mountain climbers and saltwater sailors. If you want to be happily married, hang out with happy couples.

SOCIAL OVER-EXTENSION

In the eleventh house, we can fairly say that we are looking for "people we can use." Those words are true, but obviously problematic. The trouble is that talking about "using people" sounds hardhearted, almost Machiavellian. Such coldness has no place in real intimacy – no place in the *seventh* house, in other words. But in thinking specifically about the eleventh house, always remember to keep the cart behind the horse. The "horse" in this case is your personal aspirations, goals, and priorities. They have to come first – only then do you seek alliances and networks, and only the ones that support your progress in those established directions.

Even though the phrase "people we can use" sounds icy, the simple reality is that such people are in fact quite useful to you. Some Libran balance enters the equations when we realize that we ourselves are probably useful to them as well. In the orchestra, the violinist is "using" the cellist, but the "cellist" is also using the violinist. They may not even like each other. It might never cross either of their minds to have dinner together, for example. *But when that orchestra is soaring, each one of them is having an ecstatically meaningful personal experience.*

To put it mildly, each one of them is useful to the other.

A few lines ago, we mentioned the basic astrological principle that nothing in your chart can ever simply go away. Everything in it will manifest somehow – and if it does not manifest well, it will surely manifest poorly.

What if you have a planet in the eleventh house, but you have no clear direction in life? You have failed to let the energizes of that planet orient you. Then there is *no overriding organizing principle* giving meaning and direction to the shape of your eleventh house experience, and that includes your communal life. *The inevitable result is that a scattered, aimless vector of social energy enters your biography*. Simply said, you are pulled in many directions by many different people. The shape of your life is then to a significant degree determined by their whimsies, their natures, and their values rather than by your own.

Meaningless *social overextension* is the result. Another weekend, another party. You don't really want to go, but what would people think if you did not show up? And what would you do anyway? Stay home?

You might as well go.

We can take this eleventh house analysis one step further. Even if you are making an unconscious response to an eleventh house planet, it still leaves fingerprints on your social life anyway. You cannot escape that planet, in other words. If, for example, you have Jupiter there, you may find yourself surrounded by *pompous egomaniacs*. Saturn? *Boring people* who think of nothing but work and about what is wrong with everything and everyone. Neptune might attract *drunkards*, while the Moon might attract *whiners, hypochondriacs*, or *people who never individuated from their families of origin*.

Your own weak response to the eleventh house planet is simply mirrored in the nature of the crowd in which you find yourself.

Contemplating the shadow is always a miserable experience. These last few paragraphs have not been fun to read, nor were they fun to write. To be a good astrologer, however, one must be alert to the dark side of life.

Knowledge of it is the best preventative medicine that I know.

BACK TO THE GRAND SCHEME

In this chapter, we have dived deeply into Aquarius and the eleventh house, as well as the two planets which share rulership over them. As we have seen, there are many details and subtleties in these meditations. It takes a while to spell everything out. Inevitably, as we make a careful study of the trees, we might lose sight of the forest. The "forest," in this case, is of course all ten words in the vocabulary of the entire Air Family.

Now that we have a more profound grasp upon the meaning of Gemini, Libra, and Aquarius, let's stand back and marvel appreciatively at the elegant, integrated reality of this third astrological Element.

I've added a few tweaks, but you have seen the next few lines before, earlier in this book. I am hoping that, now that you have come this far in *The Book of Air*, the words will sink a little more deeply into your bones.

This is "the grand scheme" of the three Air signs. This is their essential interdependency. These simple, core ideas carry us miles beyond the simplistic notion of Gemini, Libra, and Aquarius being "harmonious." The three Air signs might very well in fact "like each other," but it is far closer to the mark to affirm that they *need* each other. They form an interdependent whole.

The Air element is what allows consciousness to interface with experience – and without experience, there can be no evolution. Experience is the fuel we are burning on our journeys. To avoid a grievous waste of our lives, we all need to master the skill of truly *paying attention*. How often do we go through life mechanically, our senses dulled to the mysterious wonder of it all by familiarity? If we could for one overwhelmingly psychedelic moment *see what is actually before our eyes,* might we reach the highest spiritual goal? That insight is what brings us back to the heart of the grand Air scheme.

To pay attention effectively . . .
- We need to start with Geminian *curiosity* and *open-mindedness*, taking a wide-open, fresh look at everything that arises on our path. We must cultivate a "beginner's mind," free of the traps created by our own self-perceived expertise. We must listen. We must ask questions – and realize that every good answer must quickly metamorphose into another question. Our mantra must always be, *whatever I see, the truth is more than that.* We celebrate life as a long, fascinating conversation, both with people and with experience itself. We revel in endless learning, forever.
- Then, we need to take a breath and let it out again. Only in serenity can wisdom arise in an integrated way. Only in serenity can it settle into our hearts. We have to shake off the Geminian chaos and integrate what we have experienced. And when such serene wisdom arises, if it is real, *it is also beautiful.* Going further, in order to purify ourselves of error, in a spirit of *cooperation, openness,* and *humility,* we need to compare notes, Libra-fashion, with a few, consciously-chosen soul-friends who are our worthy companions – and, sometimes even our adversaries. Who among them will ask

us *exactly the right questions?* Who among them *sees what we are missing?* Through these human connections, we learn to live with *paradox* and *ambiguity*. We learn that they are inherent to the actual fabric of reality. We learn to expect them – and to mistrust as "too simple" any perception that does not contain them.

• Finally, having observed life for ourselves (Gemini) and then having availed ourselves of the alien wisdom of trusted others and taken time to integrate (Libra), we come to Aquarius. That is to say, we come *independently, honestly,* and *bravely* to our own personal conclusions, even if they run counter to what everyone else is thinking. We make our stand. We see what we see, not what we have been told is there. We embrace our personal *genius.* With maximal efficiency, we claim the experiences which feed our souls. We navigate our lives according to the truths that have been revealed to us, even if the social price is high. We can love – but *we renounce the pitiful need for the approval of other people.* We resolve to use every minute of our lives as consciously and intentionally as possible, with nothing wasted on acting out some socially-conditioned "mistaken identity."

And that is the Grand Scheme. That is the whole system. That is how the Air Element works to support your evolutionary journey. Just remember to flesh out those three paragraphs with the associated signs and ruling planets, and you have mastered one quarter of the whole sacred edifice we call astrology.

6

THE HANDOUT

In November 2015, I presented a four-day seminar on the Air Family to my southern California astrological apprenticeship program. I called it "The Shock of the Senses." In presenting that material, I laid much of the foundation for this book, even though in these pages we are taking the material down many different pathways.

For that "Shock of the Senses" program, I prepared a one-page handout. I want to share it here, with only a few minor modifications. I anticipate that it will serve the same purpose in these pages as I hope it served in that class: simply as an aid-to-memory. A single page cannot substitute for a book or a class – but for someone who has actually read the book or attended the class, perhaps a word or a phrase might resonate with slippery memory, bringing some of it back to the surface.

THE DAZZLERS: EXPLORING THE AIR FAMILY

Everybody's got a "theory of the universe," which may or may not have much to do with reality. Everybody likes being proven right – and no one enjoys being proven wrong. So we walk around with these ideas, opinions, and interpretations in our heads, hell-bent on defending them. Sometimes we are even successful. The Grand Prize? We die just as dumb as we were on the day we were born.

Somehow the larger world in all its shocking mystery needs to get through to us. That is how we evolve. We need to learn. We need to listen. We need to let reality get past the barriers of our beliefs.

Turning our opinions into a Holy Sacrament gets us nowhere.

Introversion is a natural evolutionary path for many people, but it can become too auto-referential – down that road, "agreeing with ourselves" is always easy, especially if no one else is listening or in a position to offer alternative explanations. Our wide-open, innocent – more "extroverted" – self has a place in our evolutionary journeys too. Taking in "dazzling data" that way is the task of the ever-curious Air Family of astrological symbols – Gemini, Libra, and Aquarius, along with their associated houses, and the planets that rule them. These symbols correlate with everything that supports the survival of wonder and amazement in our lives.

To Boldly Learn . . .

GEMINI AND MERCURY

Antagonist: Boredom. Intellectual arrogance. Being an "expert." That which would lull you into inertness and predictability.

Key Concepts: Curiosity. Open-mindedness. That which fascinates you. Learning. Books. Listening. Talking. Conversation. Writing. Reading. Media. Intellectual excitement. Beginner's Mind. Trusting the senses. Believing your own eyes. Shock. Surprise. Wonder. Miracles. Reading signs and omens. Free association. The poem is wiser than the poet. What a fool believes, he sees.

> *Not just any talk is conversation; not just any talk raises consciousness. Good conversation has an edge: it opens your eyes to something, quickens your ears.*
>
> – James Hillman

To Let Yourself Be Affected, Changed and Comforted . . .

LIBRA AND VENUS

Antagonists: Isolation. Brutal ugliness. Tension and nerves. Anxiety. Insensitivity. Selfishness. That which hardens your heart. Resistance. Worry. Egocentricity. Fearing Love. Coldness.

Key Concepts: The catalytic impact of partnership. Love itself. That human masterpiece: friendship. Letting another person touch you. Rivals and enemies. Hugs. Two minds are greater than one. Art. Aesthetic rapture. Serenity. Restoration of equilibrium. Stop and smell the roses. Creativity. Beauty is truth, truth beauty. The Reconciliation of Opposites. Paradox. Irony. Holding two opposing thoughts at once.

Part of you pours out of me in these lines from time to time.

– Joni Mitchell

To Think for Yourself No Matter What Others Think of You . . .

AQUARIUS AND SATURN/URANUS

Antagonist: Conformity. Consensual reality. A pitiful desperation for approval. Social conditioning. Fear of judgement or of being left out. Dissociation. Unresolved Trauma.

Key Concepts: Individuation. Thinking outside the box. Tolerance for solitude and being misunderstood. The hard work of independence. The price we pay for "belonging". Questioning authority. Recognizing erroneous underlying assumptions. Trauma; traumatically-induced dissociation. Perils of socialization. Acceptance of disapproval—and "failure." The price of freedom.

Talent hits a target no one else can hit; Genius hits a target no one else can see.

– Arthur Schopenhauer

PART TWO

MASTERING THE ALCHEMICAL MARRIAGE OF SIGN, HOUSE, AND PLANET

Archetypes such as the ones we have been exploring here are impressive structures. They are ancient beyond imagining – in fact, even that point doesn't express it strongly enough. Archetypes are beyond time itself. We astrologers can spend a lifetime studying them and still be shocked by how much more there is to learn – and hopefully we have enough pure archetypal Mercury in ourselves to enjoy the surprise.

Still, we need to keep perspective. There is an even greater miracle, one that is even more complex than any archetype: that miracle is you yourself. Everyone is composed of an ironical, ambiguous synthesis of all of the astrological archetypes. What varies – and what makes us different from each other – is simply their ratios and roles in the mixture.

Further complicating the picture, an archetype such as Venus or Uranus never exists alone, at least not in the human world. Each one of them draws its character from a sign and a house, along with a set of aspectual relationships with the rest of the planets.

Learning to place the individual members of the Air Family in their astro-logical context is the aim of the next couple of chapters.

What we have learned so far in these pages can be seen as the bricks and mortar of astrological theory.

Let's start thinking about architecture.

7

SYNTHESIS I: PUTTING AN
AIR PLANET IN A SIGN

We might offer an authoritative, helpful talk at an astrological con-
ference about the significance of the planet Uranus. *But the actual
meaning of that planet for individuals is potentially so variable that claiming
we know anything at all about it puts us on shaky ground.* The supernaturally
brilliant actor, Meryl Streep, for one example, is about as "Uranian" as a
person can possibly be – she has the planet only one minute of arc from
a perfect conjunction with her natal Sun. But both bodies lie in Cancer,
aligned with her twelfth house cusp, underscoring a far more subtle, internalized expression of that normally rather zany planet.

Who is Meryl Streep as a person? I have no idea – and if I were to
have dinner with her, I would be "surprised if I weren't surprised." With
that twelfth house Sun, ego in the conventional sense simply never fully
formed in her. At the risk of a slight over-statement, *Meryl Streep can be
anybody she wants to be.* One sees that quality expressed so clearly in her
astonishingly fluid acting. Again, ego simply does not automatically define
her behavior the same way it does in most of us. That's her twelfth house
energy in action.

Add Uranus to the twelfth house, and you have a formula that marries
two words: *actor* and *genius*.

Add the more retiring energies of Cancer to the mix, and another
thing we learn is that she is probably *not all that eager to meet me for dinner.*

After all, I am a total stranger.

Another widely recognized genius – Walt Disney – had a Sun-Uranus conjunction too, but his conjunction fell in groundbreaking, colorful Sagittarius and in the media-oriented third house. Not to rob Walt Disney of his human complexity, but I think it is fair to say that meeting him would be far less of a "discovery mission" than meeting Meryl Streep. Those Sagittarian and third house energies are more straightforward and upfront. Walt Disney would be more like a friendly dog than Meryl's cautious Cancer cat.

This all brings us back to our initial question: *what exactly does Uranus mean?*

Walt and Meryl, taken together, should help us answer that question. After all, they are both highly Uranian. *But they are utterly different human beings.* If Uranus is supposed to correlate with certain specific personality traits, we are standing on shaky ground.

Both of them are widely recognized as *geniuses* – perhaps that's the jackpot. And genius and Uranus are indeed paired in astrological theory.

But here's another Sun-Uranus conjunction for you: Peter Sutcliffe, the infamous Yorkshire Ripper, who murdered at least thirteen women. A genius? There is no way to make that case without bending over backwards. He was a *pathological criminal*, clearly – and "criminal" is another classic Uranian word. With a bow toward modern psychological perspectives, we might add that he was *alienated* and very probably suffering from some kind of *dissociative disorder* – and that too is Uranian language.

Sutcliffe's Sun-Uranus conjunction was in Gemini and in his seventh house. Forgetting his actual story and just reading the symbolism from an evolutionary perspective, we can say that his soul was seeking a *diversity of experiences* (Gemini) in the *relationship category* (seventh house) and that these experiences had to unfold *outside the context of consensual, conventional, socially-approved reality* (Uranus).

Sometimes I get chills writing this stuff.

My point in comparing the very Uranian charts of Meryl Syreep, Walt Disney, and the Yorkshire Ripper is that *claiming that we know very much at all about Uranus seems to verge on pure hubris.* Its meaning is demonstrably quite fluid.

This is one of the reasons, by the way, that a scientifically-convincing "proof of astrology" has been elusive: our variables are simply "too variable." Pinning anything down in a satisfyingly "this means that" kind of way has proven nearly impossible.

Here is the heart of the matter – or really, the twin hearts of the matter.

- The actual meaning of any planet is enormously impacted by the sign and house it occupies, as well as by the larger astrological context in which it finds itself.

- An individual's *level of response* to a planet – the reality of human freedom, in a nutshell – is also pivotal. And it is unpredictable via any internal astrological measurement. You cannot see how a person will use his or her freedom anywhere in the chart itself.

Put Uranus on the Sun in Cancer and the twelfth house, and you get Meryl Streep – or perhaps you might get a maudlin whiner with a string of arrests for Driving Under the Influence.

There but for grace goes Meryl . . .

Put Uranus on the Sun in Sagittarius in the third house, and you get Walt Disney – or a contrarian blowhard with a windy, self-righteous argument belittling anything you happen to say.

There but for grace goes Walt . . .

Put Uranus on the Sun in Gemini and the seventh house, and you get the Yorkshire Ripper – or a fascinating, funny lover, who is an excellent listener and who has boldly made a faithful commitment to someone "born on the wrong side of the tracks."

Uranus, in other words, is only an abstraction. It is these *triads* of planet, sign, and house, flavored by an array of aspects, that are actually the fundamental *quantum units* of astrological reality. That is how we experience the *human* face of the planets.

It is those triads that we must learn to understand if we are to give – or receive – helpful astrological counsel.

And even with exactly the same planet at the center, these triads differ from each other profoundly.

HOW SIGNS INTERACT WITH PLANETS

We have looked at the distinctions among signs, planets, and houses in the previous two volumes of this series. In case you are only joining us now, let's very briefly recap that planet-sign ground again here.

In the next chapter, we will do the same for planets in houses.

If you've been a faithful reader, please pardon the repetition, but this understanding is so mission-critical that I want to make sure no late-comers are left out. Maintaining an awareness of the distinctions among astrology's three main systems of symbols is essential to interpretive success.

The best way I know to understand the meaning of the twelve astrological *signs* is to think of them as *motivational agendas* – the goals, attitudes, interests,orientations, and values which animate our behavior and give direction.

Illustration: here is a chance to swim in freezing cold water with Great White sharks. Don't worry – you will be protected inside a cage, and they *probably* won't be able to get you.

Well, if you are a mild, psychologically-oriented bookworm, you probably blanched as you read those words.

On the other hand, if you are a lion tamer who once climbed the Matterhorn naked, the prospect of getting up close and personal with those Great White sharks probably tempted you.

Being a mild, psychologically-oriented bookworm is not a psychiatric disorder. Being a courageous lion tamer is not inherently virtuous. They are just different ways of being human.

Again, different values. Different motivational agendas. *As such, they reflect the nature of the astrological signs.*

It is essential to avoid value judgments here. Beyond the core principles of natural law – don't kill, don't steal, protect the children – there are countless perfectly fine ways of living. Each sign ultimately represents a legitimate evolutionary path, and in each one there are instinctual values that arise to support it.

In a nutshell, the twelve signs of the zodiac are *what make the planets human*, giving them character, engaging them with life's possibilities – and life's hard choices. Otherwise planets remain in the abstract, Platonic realm we call the Heavens. We saw that with Uranus. We see it with the rest of them too.

WHERE WE ARE ON THE MAP OF THE WORLD

In the rest of this chapter, my plan is to explore in some depth a single example of each one of our Air planets as they are conditioned by a particular sign. My main aim in doing that is to give you a general feeling for how the planet-sign synthesis works in practice – how to go about considering it, in other words. The underlying principles are what count here, not really the four specific descriptions that follow.

Later on in the book, we will explore the same planet-in-a-sign material in shorter form, looking at the meaning of each Air planet in each one of the twelve signs. Those "cookbook" vignettes can be helpful so long as you don't get addicted to them. They offer a starting point. They are my attempt to "telegraph" some core ideas about each of these sign-planet dyads. Another way to say it is that they represent the first thoughts in my head whenever I see any one of the 144 possible planet-sign-house triads.

My hope is that some of the deeper interpretive processes we are about to consider in this present chapter breathe life into those thumbnail descriptions you will be seeing later in the book. Use them – but remember that learning to "think astrologically" is always the best goal. That's what I want to demonstrate here. While cookbook paragraphs can be useful as interpretive starting points, if you are not careful, they can also make you look like you wanted to be an artist, but you never got past your coloring book and your crayons.

MERCURY IN SAGITTARIUS

Mercury rules Gemini – and thus Sagittarius, being the opposite sign, is said to be an unfortunate placement for the planet. The traditional term is that Mercury is "in detriment" there – that is the word for any planet occupying the sign opposite one it rules.

From a counseling perspective, the term "detriment" is a total trainwreck. How do your poor clients feel when they hear that something in their chart is in detriment? No way that can be good news, right? The word "detriment" really sends the wrong message. That is not because astrologers need to "put on a happy face" all the time. The reason is that a planet in detriment is far from a hopeless case. In fact, as we will see, it has many evolutionary advantages over a "well-placed" planet.

Still, there is a certain sense of crossed purposes when Mercury and Sagittarius try to form a partnership. They do have some fundamentally opposite aims and values.

Think of detriment as you might think about friendship. You may have friends who support you and agree with you no matter what. But maybe you have one friend who is so precious, trusted, and intimate that she can *disagree* with you. She can tell you when you seem to be off base about a situation or another person. You do not always like what you hear from her – but if you are wise, you value her counsel above gold and silver. That is how it is with a planet "in detriment." That is how it is with Mercury in Sagittarius.

As we learned in *The Book of Fire,* Sagittarius *seeks meaning* in life. It is the *philosopher.* Traditionally, it was correlated with *religion* – and that connection still holds for many people. Sagittarius connects the dots, sees the underlying patterns that unite the disjointed details of our daily experience. Without Sagittarius, our existence would have no evident purpose at all.

And of course Sagittarius has a dark side. All the astrological symbols do. In its zeal to find patterns of meaning, Sagittarius can be too quick to connect the dots. It can jump to conclusions. A *veil of opinion* can prevent anything unexpected ever arising in one's mind. There's the trap. There's the soul-cage.

Mercury, on the other hand, is *endlessly curious.* Its greatest virtue is a voracious willingness to learn. It delights in surprise.

We get into a lot of trouble with the phrase "there are two kinds of people in this world." Let me risk it anyway. *There are two kinds of people in this world – ones who love to have their minds changed and ones who find it threatening and offensive.*

In simple terms, Mercury is the former and Sagittarius is the latter. There's the so-called "detriment"...

- Whenever Sagittarius "has everything figured out," along comes Mercury with a pesky fact or a loose end.
- Whenever Mercury heaps distraction upon distraction, getting lost in a chaotic maze of disjointed experience, along comes Sagittarius, wondering *what is our real purpose here . . .*

I have enough Sagittarius in me to issue an opinion of my own: in my view, there are two kinds of astrologers in this world – ones who think it is bad for Mercury to be in Sagittarius, and smart ones.

Sagittarius is the *sign* – thus it animates and directs Mercury with a specific set of goals, attitudes, interests, orientations, and values.

Mercury is the *planet* – thus it represents a specific "circuit board" in the human psyche or a specific modality of perception. In Mercury's case, we spotlight the hunger for perception, which feeds thought, and leads to communication.

There is much that we can potentially perceive in this universe. Life is too short for us to look at everything. *So Sagittarian values can give direction to Mercury's curiosity.* The evolutionary intent here orients the mind to focus on the big picture: what does life mean, what is right and wrong, why are we here. If you have Mercury in Sagittarius, that is the right path for you.

Synchronicity will support you in those inquiries too – you will meet the right teachers, hit upon the right books and conversations.

Note, by the way, that while there is something descriptive of your character in what I am writing here, there is also much that is in the category of suggestion or advice. *Conventional astrology describes, while evolutionary astrology prescribes.* Those words are a bit of a bumper sticker, but they do make the point.

Let's delve more deeply. Sagittarius is the traveler or the voyager. It has a fascination with whatever lies over the far horizon, geographically or culturally. Those same values now animate the Mercurial curiosity as well.

"Ever been to Tierra del Fuego?"

"No . . . when should we go?"

Religion has always been concerned with right and wrong. So has Law; in fact, most legal systems are typically an attempt to concretize the moral tenets of religion. Thus does "Thou shalt not kill" metamorphose into Murder One, Manslaughter, Justifiable Homicide, and Euthanasia. This is why Sagittarius is linked to the legal profession as well as to religion and philosophy.

Mercury in Sagittarius? *You could have been a lawyer* – and even if you are not, you can certainly think as if you were one. Equally, you could have been a preacher – or a lama, a rabbi, or a mullah. Or a professor of philosophy.

We could go on with Sagittarius, but you get the picture. The values of that sign orient Mercury's curiosity in a way that is good for your soul. Those interests arise naturally in you; those intellectual reflexes serve your evolutionary needs. If you get this path right, then as you follow up on these particular fascinations, you encounter shock and surprise: *learning opportunities*, in other words. That is Mercury's fingerprint.

What if you make a mess out of Mercury in Sagittarius? You will spend a lot of time feeling angry because reality does not conform to your theories, and that anger will come out as a tendency to get up on your high horse and issue proclamations. Deep down, you really want everything in life to make sense. You put together a version of reality, and instead of letting it grow, you set about defending it. But it is under constant attack by the *contrary, complicating facts of life*. You are constantly playing *Whack-A-Mole*, as Lord Mercury attacks your Sagittarian certainties. That is why you are so angry.

Maybe you are politically conservative. You meet someone with Mercury in Sagittarius who agrees with you about everything – fiscal caution, traditional values, personal responsibility, limited government. *But he or she seems to feel the need to preach to you anyway*. After a while, you are doing everything you can short of murder one, manslaughter, justifiable homicide, or euthanasia *just to get that person to shut up*. He or she has managed to turn you into an antagonist even though you were in agreement.

Such people have "outpictured" their own internal conflict between Mercury and Sagittarius. Their inner argument has now put your own day "in detriment."

Detriment? It can indeed be that way – that is what we just explored.

But Mercury in Sagittarius can be better than that too. Like any other astrological configuration, it can serve a positive purpose. It can be a path. That is what we explored at the outset, and it deserves to be in first place.

VENUS IN LIBRA

With Mercury in Sagittarius, we were looking at a situation of so-called detriment. Let's turn it around and look at the opposite situation: a planet occupying the sign that it rules. Allegedly, this takes us from bad to good – at least that is what old-fashioned astrologers would say. I think it is more accurate to say that rulership takes us from *complicated and paradoxical* to *simple and straightforward.*

We might accurately say that rulership presents us with a situation of *planetary strength.* We just have to be careful not to confuse strength and virtue. Arsenic is strong, but you do not necessarily want it among your morning vitamins.

In this example, we have a double whammy: Venus and Libra are inherently agreeable symbols, and in this case, because of rulership, their agreement is natural and spontaneous. The symbols like each other. They mean very similar things. We use similar language in characterizing either one of them. Unlike Mercury in Sagittarius, neither has the slightest impulse to correct the other.

And that might not be ultimately to the advantage of either one of them.

As I've indicated, there is such a tendency among astrologers to think of the planet in detriment as an unfortunate placement, while having a planet in the sign that it rules is treated like winning a contest. I have to be careful of making the same mistake myself, only backwards: worrying about a planet that is in its own sign, while celebrating one that is in the opposite situation. The reality is that, in either case, we simply have a tool that the soul is using. I think it is safe to say that the universe never makes any mistakes in any of this. The chart you have is the tool that you need.

And like any tool, you can build something with it or you can use it to hurt yourself.

As we learned in chapter four, one basic impulse of Venus is to *establish and maintain a bridge of rapport* with another person. Similarly, one of the goals or values which animate Libra is the drive to establish *cooperative partnerships.* There is therefore no conflict between them; they share an identical understanding of the purpose of life. To both Venus and Libra, the purpose of life is to love.

And what is not to like about that?

Everyone has Venus in his or her chart. Everyone needs some degree of connection and meaningful interaction with other people. We like to pay them attention, and have them pay attention to us. That is true even for the yogi who has been alone in the Himalayan cave for the past decade. Someone showed him the cave. Someone transmitted *dharma* to him. Even the solitary yogi has been impacted by relationships.

Still, I would imagine that anyone who willingly spent ten years alone in a cave would display only a small signature from the Libra Clan of the Air Family. Such a person's path through life is not so constantly animated by meetings with impactful people. Just as in the sky above, some of us are meant to be "single stars" rather than ones in binary systems.

Anyone with Venus in Libra immediately emerges as a person in the polar opposite situation – more likely to be found at a social gathering than in a cave, in other words. With Venus strong, we know that such an individual simply *cannot do what she was born to do without the catalytic effect of other people upon her.* As we learned in chapter four, she is learning *who to trust* and *how to trust.* And no one can learn very much at all about trust or love without some help.

PLEASURES AND PERILS OF ATTRACTIVENESS

With Venus in Libra, everything else being equal, people tend to be *attractive.* In using that word, while I want to include the notion of physical appeal, I also mean an array of *attractive personal qualities*: natural courtesy, respect and interest displayed towards other people, warmth and charm.

In normal social situations, anyone with those qualities will be complimented on them. That is fine, they deserve the praise. But our purpose here is deeper: we recognize that this quality of attractiveness is simply *a tool that the soul is using.* If we cannot learn what we have come here to learn without the catalytic impact of others upon us, we obviously need to be able to attract them in the first place. It would be an evolutionary catastrophe for us to be viewed as repellent – then everyone we meet is full of suggestions about Himalayan caves we might enjoy, elsewhere..

Can being "pretty" trick a person into trouble? That is an easy question. Being physically attractive can often get us off the hook when it comes to attempting to be anything more than that. Beauty can open easy, lazy paths of least resistance. It can lead to *vanity.* It can attract people to us who do not have the faintest idea of who we actually are, nor do they care. Pretty people – of any gender or orientation – generally have no trouble "having a date on Saturday night." But do they experience depth and quality in their intimate lives? Are there no lonely, pretty people in the world?

Again, these are all easy questions.

There is nothing wrong with being attractive. We just have to recognize that certain pitfalls go along with it. No law of the universe pronounces that a person with Venus in Libra will necessarily fall into those traps. Still, the laws of the universe do in fact guarantee that such pitfalls are likely to present themselves.

Resisting them requires character.

It would be too rigid to assume, as I have perhaps unwittingly implied here, that literally *everyone* with Venus in Libra is physically lovely. That is often true, but again it is not a law of the universe. Closer to an actual law is that there is something magnetic and appealing about such people, regardless of their physical appearance.

Such qualities of magnetism and appeal can also get us into similar soul cages. For example . . .

CODEPENDENCY

As we have seen, both Venus and Libra place great value on the *maintenance of rappor*t. In any partnership, they seek balance, fairness, and the middle ground. Stable, ongoing love between adults always requires some degree of *diplomacy*. The Libra clan excels at those diplomatic skills. It can find the place where "lead and gold dust" balance each other, with the scale not tipping too far in either direction. An ability to see the other person's point of view is a precious treasure when it comes to making love work. For Libra and Venus, there is not only an abundance of skill in those areas – there is genuine joy in it.

These Libra-clan energies are essentially *romantic*, and a little romance has never hurt a marriage.

Tools for the job, once again.

And any tool can be misused, or used in a way that hurts the user. *Might I be so motivated to maintain our relationship that I lose sight of who I am?* Might I compromise so far in your direction that I become *spiritually and psychologically compromised?* Might I slip into the trap of *trying to be whoever you want me to be?*

With Venus in Libra, I certainly have the "skills" needed for making exactly these kinds of mistakes. How can I avoid them?

Let us begin by affirming loudly and clearly that you are fully capable of not falling into those kinds of traps. *But to avoid them, your Libran qualities are going to need the support of their two eternal comrades: Gemini and Aquarius.*

Remember our grand scheme? The three Air signs may not always be in harmony, but they do need each other.

With Venus in Libra, you run the risk of getting along with people who are not good for you. Some penetrating *Geminian* questions and conversations can help there – especially if you practice that classic Mercury skill: keeping your eyes open for unexpected information. If someone comes into your life as a potential partner, try for a while to overcome your natural tendency to build bridges. Instead, see if you can simply *observe* that person in the spirit of neutrality, almost as if he or she were a science project. Do not even wrestle with the question of relationship – not yet at least. Keep your eyes open, listen, gather data about this person's nature. Don't adapt yourself to it; just try to discern it clearly, without judgement.

Next, consult your ancient ally, *Aquarius.* How might your *spontaneous, natural, uncompromised nature* impact this person? If you were *simply yourself,* how would this relationship unfold? How would it go if, instead of doing three-quarters of the work of maintaining the bond, you only did your half of it?

With those Geminian and Aquarian energies helping you, your Venus in Libra will do just fine.

GIVE PEACE A CHANCE

In introducing the Libran clan in chapter four, we gave priority to the *goddess of peace.* We focused heavily on achieving serenity of spirit. In doing that, we honored the role of *art* and *aesthetic experience* as methods for soothing our jangled nerves. We appreciated how tolerating life's paradoxes helps us avoid internalizing shock. We looked at several subjects, in other words, that had nothing at all to do with human love.

With Venus in Libra, all of those issues and pathways connected to serenity move towards center stage. Remember to breathe. Tolerate ambiguity. Take time to immerse your senses in beauty, no matter whether it is the beauty of nature or the beauty that humans create.

Venus in Libra is a sensitive configuration and *sensitivity requires maintenance*, lest it become frazzled. Much that we explored in general in that earlier chapter has relevance here.

Still, when it comes to serenity of spirit, there is no treasure more valuable than the comfort of meaningful human love. And there is nothing so upsetting as misbegotten, impossible intimacy – trying to make a relationship work that simply cannot work.

For these reasons, in speaking of Venus in Libra, I have prioritized the evolutionary dynamics of partnership. With Venus in the sign that it rules, that issue is "strong" with you. That does not mean that you are "lucky" there, nor does it mean that you are unlucky. It only tells us that you have come to a place in the evolutionary journey where these are the lessons that you are learning. And you *can* learn them. You can get them right.

The only question is, will you?

And we have one more hint: you cannot fully learn these lessons alone. You need a little help from people who care about you and about whom you care. That shared vulnerability and mutual support is evolutionary protein for you.

SATURN IN LIBRA

... is explored in detail in the "Synthesis I" chapter of *The Book of Earth*. I refer you there for our Saturn-rules-Aquarius example.

We do take that Saturn rulership every bit as seriously as the Uranian rulership, but since our overriding aim in this chapter is really to demonstrate how signs and planets interact, I want to use our time and space efficiently, just referring you back to *The Book of Earth* for how Saturn interacts with a sign, while instead diving into the less familiar territories of the planet Uranus which we are meeting for the first time here in *The Book of Air*.

URANUS IN PISCES

With its eighty-four year orbit, Uranus passed through the sign of the fishes from 2003 through 2009. As I write these words in 2019, some of our Uranus-in-Pisces early birds are just now awakening into the early stages of adult consciousness.

I welcome them; they are going to have a lot to teach us.

Some familiar words: Pisces is the *sign* – thus it animates and directs Uranus with a specific set of goals, attitudes, interests, orientations, and values.

Uranus is the *planet* – thus it represents a specific "circuit board" in the human psyche or a specific modality of perception. In this case, we spotlight the potential ability to sort out who we really are from all that we have been trained to believe about ourselves. We are looking at the actual mechanisms of the process of individuation. Wherever Uranus lies, there is a wild hair in us. There is resistance to being told what to do – and an itchy trigger finger when it comes to anyone presuming to claim any authority over our personal decisions.

If the Uranian and Aquarian energies are prominent in us, those rebellious qualities are likely to be very obvious in our behavior.

If those energies play a more subtle role in our chart, the first point to remember is that they are still there. Everyone has the planet Uranus somewhere in his or her chart. It may however be "the case of the reluctant revolutionary." And that situation can go down a couple of different roads. One of them is a slow, patient burn, followed by an explosion. The other is a gradual descent into *not caring at all* – into a dissociative condition, in other words.

In all cases, the planet Uranus is at least attempting to be the *guardian of your true self.* It constantly whispers in your ear that you do not need anyone's approval – that you are what you are, and no one has any legitimate business telling you otherwise.

Pisces, meanwhile, represents a set of energies that are in many ways diametrically opposed to the spirit of the planet Uranus. To do well with Uranian questions requires – not egocentricity – but genuine *ego strength.* How else can we stand up for ourselves? As Tom Petty sung, "everybody's got to fight to be free."

Pisces, meanwhile, is very much about exploring those dimensions of consciousness that have nothing whatsoever to do with the ego. It is about acceptance and surrender.

Among contemporary astrologers, there has been no tendency to describe the planet Uranus as being in "detriment" or "fall" when it lies in Pisces. The two are not enemies. For an inimical relationship to exist between two symbols, they need to share some contested common ground. Uranus and Pisces are no more enemies than are a sparrow and a great whale.

So what happens when an essentially mystical set of values (*Pisces*) animates one's search for his or her true individuality (*Uranus*)? There's our question.

With anything at all in the sign Pisces, there is very likely to be some detectable pattern of *inexplicable experience* in a person's life – experiences of a psychic nature: knowing things without any logical way of knowing them. Dreams that come true. Weird feelings in rooms where someone has recently died. Precognitions.

Imagine presenting such an experience to some conventional figure of religious authority, and asking for perspective and explanation. Ask the priest, the lama, the rabbi, the minister, the imam . . . ask whoever you want, and two points are absolutely certain. First, you will receive a definitive answer couched in the terms of that person's religion. And secondly, these various explanations are very likely to disagree with each other. Jesus did it. It was your karma. It was the Will of Allah.

In many cases, we could add a third point: that figure of religious authority might very well posit dire metaphysical consequences for you if you were to doubt the explanation he or she has given.

What is the free-thinking planet Uranus to do when faced with that kind of mind control?

Actually, if Uranus could speak, it might very well say, "Let the games begin . . ."

Certainly it will not *kow-tow* to anyone just because he or she "wears the funny hat" that signifies religious authority.

Certainly it will question whatever answers are given.

Put all these observations together, and we can draw a conclusion: *among those people born between 2003 and 2009 are a few who will revolutionize human spirituality.* They are the *rebel mystics.*

- They are too "scientific" to accept the mythologies and platitudes of conventional religion.
- Simultaneously, they are too "mystical" to accept the blindly materialistic *denial of the transcendent* that is characteristic of conventional science and much of modern culture.

That is what I meant a few lines ago when I said that these Uranus in Pisces people have a lot to teach us. Personally, I am excited about the contribution they are about to make to evolutionary astrology. That is just one territory they will touch, but for me – and maybe for you too – it is an evocative one.

Pisces is not simply about spirituality. It is also about *visionary experience* in general – something every creative person has experienced. Uranus in Pisces is not just for artists, writers, and musicians. James Watson, for example, is the co-discoverer of the structure of DNA. He reported stumbling upon its famous "double helix" form through literally dreaming of a spiral staircase. *Where did that dream come from?* How does any dream – or any flash of creative inspiration, for that matter – arise? Not even James Watson could answer those questions. Their very existence constitutes positive proof of the existence of some larger framework of consciousness upon which our normal awareness floats like a cork on an ocean.

Another name for that larger framework is Pisces.

And another word for Uranus is "genius."

Float Uranian genius on a Piscean sea of inspiration, and we soon have another reason to imagine that these people born between 2003 and 2009 have "a lot to teach us." There will be a disproportionate number of inspired geniuses among them.

Tellingly, many of them will not really be able to explain the source of their genius.

Naturally it would be a silly mistake to assume that this whole cohort of people will be packed solidly with geniuses. Most will not be geniuses at all, of course. But in every one of them, there is an extra dose of creativity, capacity for fantasy, and for breaking new ground playfully and whimsically. Furthermore, for these people, the *path of individuation* is inseparable from cultivating those exact skills. They will find themselves as they wander the corridors of their dream lives.

Conscious parents today will recognize all of this and support it in their Uranus-in-Pisces children. Hopefully, they will set an example of *intentional* – and wide-open *tolerant* – *spiritual commitment*. They will cultivate an alertness to *trance states* in their children, and never interfere with those states – if Johnny is alone and quiet in his bedroom, *leave him alone unless the house catches fire,* in other words. They will support any imaginative or creative enterprise that arises in their offspring, honoring it and showing interest in it.

THE RISKS OF SENSITIVITY

To be psychically sensitized is a mixed blessing. There is so much harshness in the world. It is bad enough to watch it unfold on the nightly news. To be attuned to such suffering, anger, and fear at the soul-level can truly become a burden. The existence of any Piscean energy in people puts them that wavelength. Depending on the rest of their astrological details – their ego strength, for example – this potential source of hurt may or may not be a critical issue for them. Still, with Uranus in Pisces – even with nothing else there, and Neptune hiding out in a corner, and nothing in the twelfth house – there is still at least a minor leak in the dam between the individual and the larger matrix of the ambient psychic energy. The bad *ju-ju* of the world can get through.

This leak leads directly to pain, and pain often leads to a *desire for numbness*. Thus we see the fabled – and often valid – connection between Pisces and various forms of *escapism*.

We have spoken of Uranus as the "patron saint of geniuses, revolutionaries, and criminals." All three of those archetypes can interact in potentially diabolical fashion with this particular dark side of Pisces: the urge to numb oneself, to turn off the world. In this cohort of people, we see *geniuses of escapism* – people who create radical new ways to leave the planet without leaving the body. We see *revolutionaries of escapism* as well – people who change the customs, cultural values, and social interpretations of such behavior. And we will see *criminals of escapism* – people so dissociated from natural human instinct that they are willing to break the laws of nature and spirit for even one moment of sweet oblivion.

Down that road lies the realm of the shadow. With Uranus in Pisces, how do we avoid falling into its dark grasp?

We have already seen the answer in earlier paragraphs. The path to success always boils down to the same formula: *if you do not want to get it wrong, then get it right*. There is only so much energy in any sign-planet dyad. Aim it at the higher ground and there is not a single volt left to get you into trouble.

8

SYNTHESIS II:
PUTTING AN AIR PLANET
IN A HOUSE

*S*o, a pig and a political speechwriter walked into a topless bar . . .
. . . and you can take it from there.

I just made that up, Gemini-fashion. I have no idea where it would
go if we ran with it. But we *could* run with it, and that's the point. We have
two characters – a pig and a speechwriter. Adding the topless bar provides
a scene. We now have a situation.

The *plot* thickens . . .

I italicize the word *plot*, because, with the astrological houses, that is
what we are getting at: a storyline. Something is bound to *happen* with that
pig and the speechwriter. And it would be different than if they had instead walked into a church – or stumbled into a party of hungry cannibals.

Characters alone cannot tell a tale – for anything to happen, we have
to put them together in the context of some existential latitude and lon-
gitude. We have to place them in space and time. *That is exactly what the
astrological houses do.* They are quite literally about space and time. They are
the *behavioral arenas* of life. They are where plots "happen" – which is to
say, where we wrestle with the concrete choices that ultimately define the
stories of our lives.

Space and time – in order to grasp houses, they are the literal, astronomical part of what we need to understand. A baby with the Sun in Aries is born at dawn. So the *sign* Aries was literally dawning at that moment too, along with that sunrise.

That baby is then an Aries with Aries rising.

Two hours later, another baby is born in the same hospital – she is still "an Aries," of course – the Sun has only moved about five minutes of arc in that time. But now the sign Aries has finished rising. In this case, the Sun still marks the position of Aries in the sky. But it is now mid-morning, so the Sun is halfway up in the east. That marks the position of Aries as well – so now it is the next sign's turn to be rising. We now have a Taurus Ascendant.

That, in a nutshell, is why the time of birth is so critical in astrology. The rising sign – the astrological Ascendant – is time-sensitive. And as we all know, it plays a pivotal role in everyone's chart. It is the cusp of the first house, and its position also determines which sign falls on the cusps of the rest of the houses.

That's how time fits into the picture.

Let's look at space.

Back to that Aries child, born at dawn – but now we add another child *born at exactly the same instant of time, but on the other side of the Earth.* There, it is not dawn. More likely, halfway around the world, the Sun is setting. Instead of going up, it is going down. That Aries Sun now marks the *Descendant* rather than the Ascendant. That child, born at the same instant as the first one, will have Libra rising, not Aries.

That is how the astrological houses mark space. That is how they put our transcendent souls *in the scene.* Our inner pig and our inner political speechwriter must now figure out what comes next. Being "in the scene" – dealing with time-bound, three-dimensional reality – involves a long series of often-excruciating choices. Do we have a child or not? Do we live here or there? Houses embody the necessity of making those choices. They are where we make our stand in the world.

Try the seventh house – this is one of our Air houses, and of course it is the classic house of marriage.

So, to how many people can you be married at a given moment?

The obvious social consensus is "one," despite much zealous experimentation. But in all honesty, *how many people have you met in your life to whom, if the stars had been aligned differently, you might have made such a commitment?* Even if you are now happy in a relationship – or happily single – the thought of those "roads not taken" is inevitably a bit wistful.

Still, in the realm of marriage, if you cannot "choose one," you are very likely going to be miserable – and probably you will make some other people miserable too.

All the houses are like that. They "suggest" that we make a certain, particular stand – and turn away from other, almost equally worthy ones. The problem is that the soul can soar imaginatively over enough possibilities to fill 10,000 years of life. But the flesh-and-blood part of you does not last long enough to travel down all those roads.

So which road do you choose?

We used the seventh house as an example, but the same principles apply to the rest of the houses too.

Tenth house: how many careers can you have going at the same time and *still expect to give any one of them everything you've got?*

Fourth house: how many homes can you have and still have any single one of them actually *feel like home?*

Ninth house: try being a Buddhist, an Existentialist, a Christian, a Muslim, and a Cynic *all at the same time.*

Third house: you are in the middle of an intense, important conversation, and your telephone rings and your email pings just as someone knocks on the door . . .

Houses are hard that way. But there is a way to get them right, a way to make your best choice among many others that are quite possibly good choices too.

The sign and planets in each of your houses give you the roadmap.

THE MOON IN THE THIRD HOUSE

In the last chapter, we learned about how a sign animates a planet, giving it attitude, values, and direction. Now let's talk about how a planet interacts with a house, operating like a stern guru there, advising you about how to best *behave* in the context of that theater of life.

There are three "Air houses" – the third, the seventh, and the eleventh. (Astrologers generally do not say "Air"houses" because it would get confusing – but they would know what you meant.)

Let's use them as examples, starting with the third house.

As we learned earlier, the root idea in the third house is *perception*. Perception leads to *thought*, and thought leads to *speech*. That is our third house holy trinity.

Say you have the Moon in the third house. The third house is about *thinking* – but the Moon isn't. The Moon's job is to *feel*, to *intuit*, to simply *know things* without reason or logic. The Moon is your heart and soul.

Luna is a major astrological force in anyone's chart, so our example illustrates a person with a major third house focus. To be *happy* – and taking care of the Moon is the secret of happiness – he needs to *act* (houses in general!) in a way that satisfies his *curiosity* (the third house in particular.)

But what is he curious about?

To say "everything" is probably not too far off the mark – but remember another basic point about houses: *life is too short for us to do everything*. This fellow is at his happiest when he is acting on his curiosity about *lunar subjects*. Feelings. Psychological perspectives. Creativity. Imagination. Whimsy. Domestic and familial issues. Homes. Things that grow – children, gardens, trees. Everything that slips through the nets of rational analysis: love, meaning, magic, miracles. With the Moon in the third house, the *behavior of perception* is most happily conditioned by these kinds of lunar concerns.

In following that impulse, our protagonist experiences a sense of well-being. That is accurate – but let's express it more deeply: *these kinds of lunar perceptions represent his optimal evolutionary path*. Gathering those kinds of perceptions is the best use of his limited time on Earth. These are the perceptions that trigger maximum soul growth for him.

And, with the Moon in the third house, that spells happiness.

Going further, our hero naturally *looks at the world through the lens of the Moon*. We speak of people who "look at the world through rose-colored glasses." He is looking at the world through Moon-colored glasses. That perceptual orientation arises naturally in him. *As evolutionary astrologers, we also suggest, support, and encourage it.* The Moon is the *Great Mother*. With the Moon in the third house, in a sense this man is looking at the world through Her eyes. The Great Mother is always particularly alert to the needs and the suffering of Her children – and so, with the Moon here, *we see someone who sees everything as a Healer might,* attuned to hurt and need and longing in other beings.

How does *speech* fit into the picture? The third house is about communication, after all. First, this person is very likely someone who simply *likes to talk.* That is a straightforward observation, easily verified by experience – just please remember our eternal *caveat:* "everything else in the chart being equal." If this gentleman has a Sun-Saturn conjunction in Capricorn in the twelfth house, he might be less chatty than if he were a solar Gemini.

Still, the archetypes of *Teacher* and *Storyteller* are strong in him. His destiny is tied to language – but more specifically, to the kinds of *lunar language* we have been discussing.

The Moon shines by the reflected light of the Sun. In a sense, it is passive and reactive, playing *Yin* to the Sun's *Yang.* I don't want to take that notion too far, but here is why I bring it up at all: a better word for the third house than speech is *communication.* And true communication is always a two-way street. It is as much about listening as it is about talking.

With the "passive" Moon in the third house, we can say that, even though this person probably does in fact like to talk, he is also very likely *a good listener.* What makes him happy is a *fascinating conversation.*

He looks at the world through the eyes of a Healer. How often has someone helped your own heart to heal simply by listening to you?

The dark side of the Moon in the third house? Every front has a back, of course. Feelings are fine, but so is dealing with objective reality in a rational way. You may not feel like stopping for fuel, but if the needle is nearing "E" and you have a hundred miles of empty desert ahead of you, *stop for gas* – even if you are "not in the mood" to do it. That example is pretty obvious, but it still makes the point. With emotions and needs looming so large in the perceptual field, we do need to make an effort to "keep a grip" on the non-negotiable demands of reality.

A very lunar friend of mine was once droning on about some difficulty in her life. Suddenly she broke her own hypnotic trance, met my eyes, and asked, "Steve, do you think I am being too attentive to my own issues?"

It was an endearing moment, typical of why she was in fact my friend. I told her "yes."

A third house Moon can whine and whinge, seeing everything through the lens of its own needs, desires, and self-preserving concerns.

That shadow-piece leads us to our final insight. I think it is a very beautiful one too. To "look at the world through the eyes of the Great Mother" is to perceive hurt and need and suffering in all God's creatures – *including oneself.* Attention to others and their needs balances our attention to our own needs.

The possible "whining and whinging" of a third house Moon arises when that Libran equilibrium is lost. Instead of balancing our "attentiveness to our own issues" with at least an equal commitment to offering words of kindness, insight, and comfort to other people, the sweet lunar energy degenerates into navel-gazing self-pity.

JUPITER IN THE SEVENTH HOUSE

Of all the different people with whom you might conceivably spend your life, who is the right one? As we saw a few pages ago, making such a choice can be poignant, mostly because of the ones we have to turn away. Here, we are not simply talking about how to weed out intimate catastrophes – *Mr. or Ms. Wrong* – before they can sink their teeth into our hearts.

(Astrology can indeed be profoundly helpful in that department; it excels at delineating the characteristics of a good partner for you, while warning you about seductive emotional sinkholes. That is one of its precious gifts to us, but not quite what I am talking about here.)

What I am talking about probably concerns only a handful of people you have met in the course of your years. These are individuals with whom you had a genuine soul connection, but with whom for some reason the relationship never came into full bloom. Maybe the time was wrong. Maybe practical circumstances intervened. Maybe one of you was already committed to someone else. Maybe there was sexual expression; maybe not – with what we are talking about, that doesn't even matter so much.

As we observed earlier, these "roads not taken" are a wistful subject for most of us.

- In the language of astrology, the part of your psyche that is symbolized by *planets in signs* could actually have committed happily to a few of those people.

- But the part of you that is symbolized by *planets in houses* – the part of you that has to make the hard choices in our short lives in this three-dimensional, time-bound world – did not go down that good road with her or him.

And that may very well have been the right choice. The vast majority of us can only share that kind of committed, life-long, pair-bonded intimacy with a very small number of people, one at a time. (The days when I might have written "with one other person" are long-gone at this point in our cultural history, but I do want to at least bow once in the direction of life-long commitment.)

That the seventh house is about radically *accepting* another person into your heart is fairly obvious. Less obvious is that the mechanism of selecting such a partner is primarily one of *rejection*.

Not you, not you, not you . . . *you?* . . . hmmmm . . . no, not you after all . . . not you, not you . . . Ah! *You!*

And hidden in that giggly sequence of words is the eternal law of the seventh house. A process of choosing, done wisely, is above all a process of *discernment*.

People make dumb intimate choices. Learning to avoid them can be understood as "high school" when it comes to the seventh house. To get to "college," we need to weed out some of our possible good choices too. That can be even more difficult. The heart of the seventh house lies in surrendering your heart to another person – but the road there is paved with experiences of rejection, both coming and going.

In a nutshell, most of us tend to kiss a lot more people than we marry.

So what does all this mean if you have Jupiter in the seventh house? As ever, we encounter both light and shadows as we explore this configuration.

Here is the short version: your natural soul-partner is a healthy Jupiter type – while certain "eaters-of-souls" whom you are *also destined to encounter* and to whom you may fall prey if you are not sufficiently discerning will embody the seductive face of dark Jupiter.

Let's explore both possibilities, starting with the happy ones.

To the Romans, Jupiter was the king of the gods. Historically, kings have come in a lot of different flavors, ranging from Vlad the Impaler through noble King Arthur and up to Good King Wenceslas of Christmas

Carol fame. While we are exploring the happy side of our equations, we will think of Jupiter as the *good king* – and while we are invoking Christmas, let's add another positive expression of the Jupiter archetype: *Santa Claus* himself.

Jupiter in your seventh house? Are you destined to marry Santa Claus? In a sense, yes – we just have to do some translation to make the metaphor work.

Ask any child raised in nominally Christian culture: the most fundamental attribute of Santa Claus is his *generosity*. Santa Claus brings us what we want. Similarly, with Jupiter in the seventh house, your natural partner is a *generous soul*. By that behavioral sign, you will recognize him or her.

Often when we hear the word generosity, we think of *material* generosity. That quality is likely to be part of the picture – anyone worthy of your love takes joy in abundantly meeting your material needs and desires, pushing the limits of his or her own wealth in order to do that.

And that is true even if that person doesn't have a lot of money.

"You will marry a rich person" – faced with Jupiter in the seventh house, that might be the fortune-teller's prediction. It is worth noting that marrying into wealth is a somewhat heightened possibility here, but that is miles from the point.

The point is generosity itself.

Who is more generous, the billionaire who gives you a hundred dollars – or the starving refugee who gives you half an apple?

Again, all of this so far is about material generosity – and that is indeed an attribute of the kind of person with whom you could share life in meaningful fashion. No tightwads need apply, in other words.

Far more significant than mere material generosity is *generosity of spirit*. Your natural partner genuinely celebrates your victories. Your natural partner is never threatened by your successes, never needs to stay ahead of you or to dominate you in any way.

Your natural partner believes in you more than you believe in yourself.

Again, by such signs will you recognize this soul.

Here is a famous quote from Santa Claus: *ho ho ho*. Santa – who is simply another incarnation of the ancient Jupiter archetype – laughs from his belly. Similarly, of all the people to whom you might be attracted in life, one criterion for choosing the right one is that he or she *laughs easily*.

He or she probably tells better jokes than you do.

This is the kind of person who laughs at other people's jokes even if they are not particularly funny. He or she does that for two reasons: first, it simply *feels good to laugh*. And secondly, Jupiter people have generous spirits – and *it would be incredibly cheap to not laugh at this poor person's failed joke.*

Again, it is by reading these kinds of big-hearted *behavioral* signs that you recognize your deepest and most evolutionarily-necessary human connections.

If I had to reduce Jupiter to one single question, here is the one I would choose: *how have you been underestimating yourself?* We explored that aspect of Jupiter deeply in *The Book of Fire.* If you need a refresher, you might go back and have a look at that material.

Applying this exact question to the seventh house carries us miles beyond the shaky astrological notion that you will be "lucky in love" – a line often repeated by more deterministic astrologers about a seventh house Jupiter.

The "exceptions to that rule" are approximately equal to the population of India.

Here is the actual heart of the matter: in a nutshell, if you want to be lucky in love, *you must first stop underestimating yourself.*

Another way to say it is that *in order to recognize your natural partner, you first need to recognize the Jupiter archetype in your own psyche.* That is to say, you must embrace your inner King or Queen.

Imagine a heterosexual woman born with Jupiter in her seventh house. She is single and she would rather not be. She has had relationships with men who failed her. Because of those heartbreaks, she is tempted to *lose faith in love* – and with Jupiter, ever to lose faith is the cardinal error.

A new student arrives at a yoga class she attends. She is attracted to his jovial spirit; he laughs a lot – and his laughter seems to be contagious: others laugh a lot around him too. He seems, not "full of himself," but still a little "bigger than life." She knows nothing about him personally, but he seems to have a certain *star quality* – and, delightfully, he seems quite unaware of his own charisma.

He embodies all the Jupiter signatures, in other words. Could he be her natural mate?

Our protagonist in this tale is clearly attracted to this man. Who could blame her for that? He seems quite wonderful. But she also notices that she is far from being alone in this sentiment: many of the other women in the yoga class are signaling a similar attraction to him. Our hero feels outgunned by some of these other females, feeling that they are prettier, smarter, perhaps even more spiritual, than she is.

Why would he ever be attracted to me when so many others are available?

Meanwhile, Mr. Jupiter has noticed our protagonist. He likes her. He is attracted to her. He senses some of that ancient, mysterious gender-chemistry bubbling between them. But he is, in fact, a lot more shy than most people would think in looking at him.

And he senses her turning away from him, seeming to avoid him.

He thinks he knows what those signals mean. She's not that into him.

This is where our story arrives at the fork in the evolutionary road.

Remember our Jupiter questions: how have you been underestimating yourself? How have you settled for too little? For our protagonist with natal Jupiter in her seventh house, her soul is, hopefully, learning how to avoid those traps of self-doubt *specifically in the realm of intimacy.* Since we are looking at a house, it is *actual behavior* – not simply attitude – that makes the difference for her. With all of the astrological houses, actual behavior is where the rubber meets the road.

Maybe she chooses the fork in the evolutionary road that leads to the higher ground. She takes a risk. She draws strength and inspiration from my favorite Jupiter mantra: *Om – roll the dice . . .* Audaciously, with her heart pounding in her chest, she approaches our shy Mr. Jupiter and invites him to have a cup of coffee with her after class.

Cutting to the chase: *. . . and they lived happily ever after.*

What about the other fork in the road, the one that leads to the lower ground? Simple: *nothing happens.* She continues in the erroneous, self-defeating, belittling belief that this man would never have any romantic interest in her.

Sadly, the fact that nothing happens is taken as confirmation of her belief. The groove of self-doubt – of underestimating herself – is now worn a little deeper in her. She comes a little bit closer to losing faith in the possibility of love.

We humans might plausibly say that "nothing happened."

That is not what her guardian angels say.
They are too busy weeping to speak at all.

At the opening of this section, we explored the qualities that distinguish a positive expression of Jupiter energy. If you have Jupiter in the seventh house, your natural partner would fit that profile. As we have seen, it is by those signs, signals, and omens that you can recognize such a person.

Meanwhile, in the foregoing tale of romance in the yoga class, we saw another face of Jupiter: the more internal, evolutionary one. There we were concerned with certain soul-lessons that must be learned in order for love to flourish.

We have one more step to take: *what about dark Jupiter people?* If you take birth with Jupiter in the seventh house, you will always be attracted to people marked by Jupiter energy. That includes the good, the bad, and the ugly. You came into this world *pre-loaded* to be vulnerable to Jupiter-types, across their whole moral spectrum. That can work out fine; all you have to do is supply the brains. All you have to do is to supply discernment, self-awareness, and a healthy dose of valuing yourself.

Dark Jupiter is the dark king – or dark queen. He or she may not be "Vlad the Impaler" – even dark Jupiter does not tend particularly towards violence or sadism. Rather, the negative expressions of this planet look more like *hubris, arrogance, presumption, self-importance, pomposity, vanity*, and *entitlement*, along with *an absolute inability to resist any temptation*. Let's add *self-centeredness* and an *inflated sense of one's significance* in the universal scheme of things.

Other than those issues, dark Jupiter is a real sweetie pie.

Hormones have an incredible capacity to cancel higher brain functions. Once they start flowing, it is hard to stop them. One out of every twelve of you reading these pages has Jupiter in the seventh house. My prayer for you is that, if you are single, the next time you find yourself drawn to someone, you remember this list of "the ten deadly sins of dark Jupiter." Engage your intuition as you contemplate the energy of the person sitting across the table from you. Does the shoe fit?

If so, run away.

And next time be more careful not to underestimate yourself. Don't settle for the kind of man or woman who is simply not worthy of your love.

URANUS IN THE ELEVENTH HOUSE

Uranus is the "weird" planet – and if we simply stop for a moment and reflect upon the impact of that single word, we gain some very fundamental insights into its action and nature.

Think about what happens if someone you love tells you to "stop being so weird." The order may be delivered casually, but the term is still loaded. How do you react? Maybe you get angry – and even though that might not sound like the best response, it is certainly not the worst one.

The worst one, at least from the Uranian point of view, is to allow another person's opinion to alter your nature or your behavior.

Weirdness is very much in the eye of the beholder. Perhaps your "weird behavior" was honest, authentic, and sincere – and just a few standard deviations away from people's "average" behavior. And yet as soon as you are labeled that way, you are under pressure to conform – perhaps even at the price of substituting your healthy, authentic behavior for a phony one that the other person simply prefers to see.

Why on God's green earth would you do something like that to yourself?

Here's the answer: we humans like to be loved. We like approval and respect. We love to be taken seriously. We feel insecure whenever any primary relationship seems to be even slightly in doubt.

There is nothing inherently wrong with any of those needs. We only cross the line into error when we are willing to become a dancing monkey in order to meet them.

An eleventh house Uranus alone is not sufficient to define a person as "Uranian," at least not to a marked degree. For a person to emerge as a particularly Uranian type, the planet must make some significant aspects – it might be linked, for example, to the Sun, Moon, or Ascendant. We might also see significant influences from the sign Aquarius, which would have a similar impact. But with Uranus in the eleventh house, one point is sure: as the years go by, that Uranian energy will become increasingly pressing as a psychological force. Anything in the eleventh house simply gains power as time passes, for better or for worse.

Which form will it take – individuation or alienation?

That is what the choice looks like when we boil an eleventh house Uranus down to its bones.

A baby is born. Immediately its senses go into overload. Noise, smells, blinding lights – it must be overwhelming. No wonder the vast majority of us have no direct memory at all of being born or of infancy. Here's how we survive it. Quickly a kind of cultural screen, like a window blind, is pulled down to protect us. People start "explaining reality" to us. Instead of all that kaleidoscopic chaos, there is now a simplified schematic drawing of what we first saw.

Initially, this simplification offers welcome relief. Shortly, however, a certain suspicion arises in us – maybe this schematic drawing is *too* simple. *Wasn't there something big over there on the left only a moment ago?*

Our imaginary child, just a little bit older now, waits for a moment alone – then pokes a sharpened pencil through the screen and peers through the hole. Sure enough, there *was* something big there on the left – something not included in the social description of reality.

And that of course is the nature of the screen: it is the *cultural agreement* about the nature of the world. It is *consensual reality* – something we begin teaching children in their infancy. In every culture, adherence to this description of reality is defined as *common sense* or even as *sanity*. Those who diverge from it are called "weird" – and as we have seen, that word can work manipulative magic on almost anyone.

Suspicion grows in our child; perhaps he or she pokes yet another hole in the screen. Again, what is actually out there is different from what has been represented.

With Uranus in the eleventh house, by the time you come to midlife, the screen is hanging in rags before your eyes.

Experience has taught you that the collective understanding of life as it is defined by your society is hopelessly flawed. At that point you have that choice we mentioned – *individuation* or *alienation*. You can "fake normal" for the rest of your days, and reap the benefits of having a relatively secure, respected place in your community. The price you pay, however, is exorbitant: your life becomes meaningless to you. Or you can bravely trust what experience has actually been teaching you. You can set out on the road less traveled, being true to yourself and not looking back.

The eleventh house has to do with groups of people. It is about *tribal* or *collective* experience: organizations, movements, classes, congregations, teams. As we saw earlier in these pages, the eleventh house refers to experiences which are personally meaningful to us, *but which can only be accessed in the context of a group.* Playing third violin in a fine orchestra is an effective illustration. So is being on a baseball team or being a member of a meditation group.

To get the eleventh house right, *goals and priorities must come first.* Once we have them figured out, then we can choose *appropriate alliances* to help us reach them.

With Uranus here, the overriding goal is *to be true to oneself,* no matter what anyone else thinks of it. Part of the archetypal Uranian package is that in being true to oneself, a certain degree of social judgment or disapproval is likely to arise.

Who can help you endure that pressure? What kinds of allies can help you keep faith in the integrity of what you are becoming? Who can stand by your side while others vilify you, or pity you, or laugh in your face?

The answer is "other weirdos," just like yourself.

They are your natural tribe. They are your people.

Writing the word "weirdos" was fun, and the word does convey significant information. We just have to be careful of the load of judgement built into it. These *natural allies* are people who, like yourself, have seen consensual reality unraveling before their own eyes. That is one reason why they know that you are not crazy. Their faith gives you faith – and your faith gives the same gift back to them. *You are far stronger together than you could ever be alone.* We are looking at a *symbiosis of souls* – and that is one of the most powerful medicines that humanity has ever created.

Down the dark road with Uranus in the eleventh house, we find the classic Uranian or Aquarian spiritual disorder: *a gradual separation of the nature of the soul from the outward biographical realities of life.* It is like paint peeling from a wall. At first, you probably don't notice it happening.

A style of living – work, relationships, social activities – that might be meaningful and healthy for one person is potentially empty and pointless for another. There are no obvious moral questions here, in other words. We cannot judge these things by appearances. In fact, for most of us, a person effectively *faking normalcy* looks fine to us. That is the nature of consensual reality – few people would imagine that such a person would be anything but happy and fulfilled.

"Anyone would be happy" to be in his or her shoes.

"Everyone knows" such a life should only fill a man or a woman with gratitude.

The trouble is, this is not "anyone." This is an *increasingly* Uranian individual – remember: Uranus is in the eleventh house, so it is growing in strength – who has allowed himself or herself to be steam-rollered by social and tribal expectations. The things that "everyone knows" are not necessarily true for "everyone" – and especially not for Uranians.

PART THREE

MERCURY, VENUS, SATURN, AND URANUS IN THE TWELVE SIGNS AND HOUSES

Roll the Astrodice – each one of these four "Air" planets can find itself in any combination of the twelve signs and twelve houses. In each case, the intrinsic nature of the planet takes on unique coloration and style of expression. Venus, for example, symbolizes the near-universal human need to exchange love with other beings. If you give Venus the cautious motivations of Capricorn and place it in the domestic framework of the fourth house – well, you are not likely to see that person dancing the tango at 2:00 AM in a gay bar dressed only in a feather boa.

If that tango is what you would like to see, you had better look instead for someone with Venus in Sagittarius in the fifth house.

These examples are only cartoons, but you get the point: Venus can manifest in a lot of ways and still be Venus. Its sign and house go a long way to determining which of its faces you are likely to see.

Four "Air" planets, twelve signs, and twelve houses – that is a total of ninety-six possibilities. In the previous chapters, I have tried to illuminate the intuitive, integrative, and essentially creative process that underlies tying a planet to a sign or a house. In the next few chapters, I am hoping to catalyze that process in you by spelling out, one by one, the core ideas that underlie each one of these ninety-six configurations. My prayer is that these paragraphs provide you with a jump-start, rather than short-circuiting your own creativity.

Much of the material in the next six chapters appeared in exactly the same form in The Book of Earth. *That is simply because Mercury, Venus, and Saturn each rule an Earth sign as well as the Air signs we are exploring in this volume. What I wrote in the previous book about, say, Mercury in Pisces, remains just as true and relevant in the present volume. I feel badly "making you buy the same pages twice" – but I am also loathe to leave* The Book of Air *incomplete, especially since I am quite aware that there are likely to be some Geminis, Librans, and Aquarians who did not feel they needed to buy "no steenking book about Earth signs . . ."*

Chapters eleven and fourteen contain fresh, never-before-seen material about the natal placement of Uranus in each house and sign.

9

MERCURY IN
THE TWELVE SIGNS

MERCURY IN ARIES

Cognitive Rocket Fuel: To stay mentally engaged and alive, I must expose my intelligence to edgy, fresh, groundbreaking information. I celebrate debate and disagreement, so long as people are still listening to each other and responding cogently. Ideas grow stronger and perceptions clearer when they are met with challenges.

Learning Strategy: I seek conversations with people who offer constructive arguments and who are not afraid of my passions or my opinions. I avoid those who require me to "walk on eggshells" around them, and require me not to upset them or ever challenge their assumptions. When it comes to ideas, "blow it up and start all over again" often works fine for me.

Natural Style of Communication: Listening and speaking is most effective and comfortable for me when everyone, myself included, can just speak their minds in straightforward, spontaneous, direct fashion. "Just say it!" Just give me honesty and the truth as you see it, and we will take it from there. Sometimes I float a point just to see if it stands up or collapses. I don't necessarily even agree with myself sometimes. When I like people, I often tease them.

My Best Teachers: Those who can most effectively help me learn what I need to learn in this life are not afraid to confront my defenses and opinions directly. They do not hide behind diplomacy. They are not afraid of me, nor do they need to be. When my skull is thick, they know how to penetrate it.

Perceptual Bias: Because of my tendency to focus on the creative tensions generated by opposing ideas, I can see conflict where none is necessary or present. Thinking that "I am only having a conversation," I can miss the fact that I am actually triggering fear or defensiveness in another person without my knowing or intending it. My intensity can sometimes eclipse what I am actually trying to get across.

Defensive Strategy: When I am reflexively shutting myself down to a necessary but threatening perception, I can argue like a crooked attorney. I can win arguments even when I am wrong – and when deep down inside, I even know that myself. I can win arguments by exhausting the listener to the point that he or she simply gives up – then I can take that surrender as agreement. Using this defensive method, I am capable of learning nothing at all.

MERCURY IN TAURUS

Cognitive Rocket Fuel: To stay mentally engaged and alive, I must expose my intelligence to the natural world – and to "natural" people. Tying myself in intellectual knots gets me nowhere. There are complex truths and there are simple truths; for me, it is often the simple ones that get me to the heart of what I need to understand. Silence is my greatest teacher.

Learning Strategy: I seek the simple essence of things. I trust my instincts and my first impressions. I cultivate calm and quiet within my own mind by seeking the same things in my outward experiences. It is in that tranquil condition that I see things most clearly. Understanding requires patience and direct engagement. I find the words later.

Natural Style of Communication: Listening and speaking is most effective and comfortable for me when conversations happen patiently, with the heart of the matter stated clearly, punctuated with reflective silences. Interruption rarely adds to mutual comprehension; I appreciate it when people let me finish a sentence or a paragraph, then let me do the same for them. The best conversations are the ones in which it is safe to take a breath without fear of the other person launching in a different direction.

Best Teachers: Those who can most effectively help me learn what I need to learn in this life are earthy and grounded, full of "chicken soup" wisdom and practical understanding. They use language effectively, even beautifully – but underlying what they say is their appreciation of the fact that words and reality are not the same thing. They convey a lot with their silences.

Perceptual Bias: Because of my tendency to focus on the "grounded" and "the tried and true," I might miss the possibility of radical innovation. The unexpected can sneak up on me – or bypass my attention completely. I can resist change and fight new ideas, even if they could potentially be of benefit to me.

Defensive Strategy: When I am reflexively shutting down to a necessary but threatening perception, I can be stubborn. I can refuse to think outside the box or to question my own assumptions. I can withdraw into silence. I can say, "I don't want to talk about it" and withdraw from meaningful engagement.

MERCURY IN GEMINI

Cognitive Rocket Fuel: To stay mentally engaged and alive, I must expose my intelligence to an endless diet of wonder and amazement. Boredom is anathema to me. I trust my curiosity – and I try to keep it hungry, not by starving it, but by cultivating its bottomless appetite. Fresh wording of old truths can trigger breakthroughs for me.

Learning Strategy: I constantly seek new ideas and fresh perceptions. I read. I listen. I commit to lifelong learning. I question my own beliefs and assumptions, always entertaining perspectives which challenge them. My mantra is, whatever I see, the truth is more than that.

Natural Style of Communication: Listening and speaking is most effective and comfortable for me when two people in conversation can ramble and free-associate, and thus share a mutual process of discovery. I learn almost nothing from communication that happens without joy and spontaneity. I delight in opportunities to say, "I didn't know that I knew that . . ."

My Best Teachers: Those who can most effectively help me learn what I need to learn in this life are articulate. They beguile me with their eloquence as well as by piquing my curiosity with fresh ideas or at least new ways of phrasing older ones. They celebrate language. Typically, they speak rapidly. Underlying their most effective lessons is one foundational concept: *"There might be an entirely different way of looking at this . . ."*

Perceptual Bias: Because of my tendency to focus on words and ideas, I might miss cautionary messages arising in my own physical body – having "a bad feeling in my bones" about a person or suggestion, for example. Thinking and talking are only one way of engaging with reality; I must be careful not to ignore instinct, intuition, or the voice of angels whispering in my ear.

Defensive Strategy: When I am reflexively shutting down to a necessary but threatening perception, I can hide behind a wall of words. I can chatter, and thus prevent another person from speaking or from getting through to me. Even when no one is around, I can endlessly loop a false or limited version of reality in my head until I have totally convinced myself of its truth, even if it is a lie.

MERCURY IN CANCER

Cognitive Rocket Fuel: To stay mentally engaged and alive, I must expose my intelligence to the reality of human needs and human woundedness – both my own and that of other people. I am learning to look at the world through the eyes of the Great Mother, which is to say, with compassion and forgiveness. I see the frightened child in everyone. I think psychologically.

Learning Strategy: I seek insight into the way people are motivated by their often-unconscious emotional needs or by the "wounded child" within them. I look beneath the surface of human behavior in a spirit of gentleness and humility. In the face of the universal, unspoken realities of the human condition, I seek opportunities to be of genuine comfort to other people, knowing that the ones who need it the most are often the ones who deny it.

Natural Style of Communication: Listening and speaking is most effective and comfortable for me when people are gentle and patient with each other, when they take time to genuinely listen and to speak softly from their hearts in a spirit of trust. Psychological language comes naturally to me, as we speak unguardedly of our needs and fears.

My Best Teachers: Those who can most effectively help me learn what I need to learn in this life are people who have made progress healing from their own wounds. My best teachers are kind, gentle, and patient with me. They support me and have an uncanny sense of when I need to be pushed and when I need to go at my own pace. They feel like family to me.

Perceptual Bias: Because of my tendency to focus on what other people need, I can find myself coddling them, perhaps to a point where I become insensitive to two important realities: their innate resilience and my own needs.

Defensive Strategy: When I am reflexively shutting down to a necessary but threatening perception, I can hide inside my shell indefinitely. It is as if I have closed my eyes tightly and put my fingers in my ears. I can also trick people into turning their scrutiny away from my own wounds or needs by focusing helpfully on theirs. In doing this, I may look like a saint, but the reality is that I have isolated my own heart.

MERCURY IN LEO

Cognitive Rocket Fuel: To stay mentally engaged and alive, I must expose my intelligence to the risk of self-expression. I must be vulnerable. I must put my thoughts and ideas out on the stage of the world – hoping for applause, but taking the chance of criticism and rejection. Performance and creativity, in some sense, trigger my rapid evolution.

Learning Strategy: I seek avenues in which I can manifest my imagination and my ideas. I open my mouth and speak; I step out on the stage, perhaps appearing to be fearless, even if I am inwardly quaking. I find my audience and I face it in a spirit of vulnerability and sincerity, whether it is one other person or a crowd. I learn by doing.

Natural Style of Communication: Listening and speaking is most effective and comfortable for me when both people are given a lot of space and support to shine. They take turns being on stage. If I need three or four paragraphs to make a point, I appreciate someone listening attentively until I am finished. I am then happy to do the same for other people, and to enjoy their time in the spotlight. Making room for some style, some sense of "theater," enlivens and supports my unselfconscious spontaneity. I appreciate speaking with anyone who really takes joy in language itself.

My Best Teachers: Those who can most effectively help me learn what I need to learn in this life are masters of stagecraft – even if the stage is a quiet conversation between two people in a café. They know how to reach the heart; they do not hide in some dry intellectual ivory tower. Their personalities themselves are half of the message they bring.

Perceptual Bias: Because of my tendency to focus on presentation and style, I can undervalue the ideas offered by mild or introverted people. I can also be beguiled or even deceived by polished surfaces behind which there is little substantial content. I can become so enamored of my own viewpoint that I blind myself to the useful perspectives of people who disagree with me.

Defensive Strategy: When I am reflexively shutting down to a necessary but threatening perception, I can defend myself behind a brick wall of stubborn opinion. I can override and interrupt another person, perhaps without even knowing that I am doing it. I may even win arguments that it would benefit me enormously to lose.

MERCURY IN VIRGO

Cognitive Rocket Fuel: To stay mentally engaged and alive, I must expose my intelligence to methodology, technique, and craft. I must roll up my sleeves and actually learn how to do things, and to do them in a spirit of pursuing excellence. I seek to approach perfection in my work and in the execution of my responsibilities. I open like a flower in the presence of worthy teachers – masters of whatever field I am seeking to learn.

Learning Strategy: I seek teachers who embody the excellence and skill to which I aspire. I apprentice myself to them in a spirit of gratitude and humility. I burn the midnight oil; I study in a spirit of self-discipline and focused attention. I am not afraid to "read the manual," whatever form it might take.

Natural Style of Communication: Listening and speaking is most effective and comfortable for me when the presentation of ideas is orderly, logical, and detailed. I appreciate competence in anyone offering me information; I also appreciate anyone sufficiently interested in what I am saying to listen in detail. Grounded, rational criticism, coming and going, is a valued treasure in any conversation which I am likely to remember positively.

My Best Teachers: Those who can most effectively help me learn what I need to learn in this life are masters in their fields. The bottom line is that they actually "deliver" in the areas in which they claim competence. My best teachers have had teachers themselves; from time to time, they mention them respectfully and warmly.

Perceptual Bias: Because of my tendency to focus on details, I can lose perspective on the big picture. I can waste time perfecting something that will later be eliminated, rejected, or edited. My critical faculty can blind me to the reality that something, although flawed, is in fact already good enough. I can create in my mind a state of constant worry and doubt, never relaxing enough to accept things the way they actually are.

Defensive Strategy: When I am reflexively shutting down to a necessary but threatening perception, I can nitpick over trivial details and minor quibbles, rejecting a larger perspective that would in fact be useful to me. When self-doubt is making me afraid to go forward, I can defend myself against acknowledging that fact by taking refuge in endless preparation.

MERCURY IN LIBRA

Cognitive Rocket Fuel: To stay mentally engaged and alive, I must expose my intelligence to questions involving a complex balancing act: the tension between valid opposites. I revel in paradox – that humans need both love and freedom, for example. My growth is accelerated as I learn to listen to people who see things differently than I do. Nothing expands my cognitive bandwidth faster than exposure to beauty: poetics, the arts, music, and the beauty of nature itself.

Learning Strategy: I seek aesthetic experience; I immerse my senses in it regularly. I look for people who hold "the other half of the truth" – and recognize that I may have mistaken my own half-truth for the whole thing. Whenever I have a strong opinion, I discipline myself to consider the opposite perspective. I am relentlessly suspicious of any kind of fanaticism.

Natural Style of Communication: Listening and speaking is most effective and comfortable for me when people are sincerely respectful, even courteous, regarding their differences. I appreciate interpersonal grace and I attempt to practice it in all of my communications. I expect the same. Truly listening is a basic courtesy.

My Best Teachers: Those who can most effectively help me learn what I need to learn in this life radiate openness and respect towards me, even when they are offering me corrective suggestions. They are graceful people who present themselves well in terms of their behavior and their appearance. They can always see the opposite point of view. They are blessed with the ability to get along with a very wide spectrum of human types.

Perceptual Bias: Because of my tendency to focus on the creation of harmony and agreement, I can unconsciously find myself avoiding necessary – and potentially creative – conflict. My diplomacy can get in the way of the expression of necessary truths. I can feel I have stated them clearly, but the other person might have no idea of what I intended to convey.

Defensive Strategy: When I am reflexively shutting down to a necessary but threatening perception, I can be very slippery. I can dance away from a discussion, skillfully and smoothly changing the subject in such a way that the person holding the mirror before me has no idea until later about the stunt I just pulled. Maybe I use flattery; maybe I employed the bait of a fascinating diversion; maybe I simply "appeared" to agree. In any case, I can always turn attention away from myself and aim it back at the other person.

MERCURY IN SCORPIO

Cognitive Rocket Fuel: To stay mentally engaged and alive, I must expose my intelligence to the digestion of the raw and difficult truths of life. I think about realities that other people are often afraid to consider. I am exploring beyond the boundaries of customary social taboos, wrestling with subjects that are too emotionally charged for the majority of the human race to face.

Learning Strategy: I seek to unravel my own rationalizations and mechanisms of defense, both the ones I learned as a child and the ones which arise in me as an individual. I am resolved to "think anything," no matter how edgy or extreme the thought might be. From a moral perspective, I edit my behavior, but I never edit my own mind. I cannot imagine any kind of accurate thinking separate from psychoanalytical self-investigation.

Natural Style of Communication: Listening and speaking is most effective and comfortable for me when politeness and conventional customs do not inhibit the direct expression of each person's thoughts and feelings. I appreciate intensity; I am not unduly frightened by it. I am far from humorless – but my sense of humor might be a bit dark for some individuals. I am a good person to talk to when people are faced with difficult situations, but when I am faced with cocktail party chit chat, I need to monitor and restrain my own tendency towards honesty or I will just make trouble for myself and everyone else.

My Best Teachers: Those who can most effectively help me learn what I need to learn in this life look me directly in the eye and speak from their hearts, even when their hearts have a message which I am not eager to hear. They are psychologically-savvy people; many of them have a serious respect for life's darkness, having faced it directly themselves. Their words sink into my soul like a stone. I feel their truth viscerally.

Perceptual Bias: Because of my tendency to focus on charged and taboo psychological material, I may miss the lighter, happier perspectives which contribute so strongly to our ability to continue living in this crazy world. Following my own intellectual instincts, I can get deeper at a pace which is faster than I can handle, and thus sink myself into a brooding, isolated state.

Defensive Strategy: When I am reflexively shutting down to a necessary but threatening perception – which does not happen very often – I can wound people who are only trying to help me. I know where to stick the psychological dagger in anyone's psyche.

MERCURY IN SAGITTARIUS

Cognitive Rocket Fuel: To stay mentally engaged and alive, I must expose my intelligence to influences and perspectives which lie beyond my familiar horizons. In whatever level of society I was born, there are certain assumptions and behaviors which are held as obvious and right; I must break free of them. I am on an intellectual quest which will carry me into a wider world, one beyond the boundaries of the culture of my birth. The holy grail I seek is a sense of the meaning of life. It is out there in the world, waiting for me to find it.

Learning Strategy: I seek everything that is foreign or alien, everything that challenges my assumptions. I embrace the possibility of travel and encounters with people from different societies or ethnicities. I revel in education, whether it is formal or simply experiential. I try to figure out the mysterious underlying laws by which the universe operates, and arrange my moral compass in harmony with them. I seek to align my behavior with cosmic principles.

Natural Style of Communication: Listening and speaking is most effective and comfortable for me when people are obviously engaged in a passionate way with what they are saying. I do not want to listen to people who are bored with their own lectures, nor would I willingly subject anyone else to listening to me were I myself in that pitiful condition. I like speaking about principles and the underlying patterns of life; I am a "big picture" person and I am happiest in conversation with similar people, even if their version of the big picture is different from my own.

My Best Teachers: Those who can most effectively help me learn what I need to learn in this life often come from a different culture or at least a different walk of life than me. They are philosophical people, but they are not sitting alone in some tower, afraid of life. They have lived their passions and learned from their own mistakes. They have a sense of humor about themselves, but they keep their eye on the true prize, which is how to live a life that is ultimately meaningful.

Perceptual Bias: Because of my tendency to focus on the big picture, I might miss details that are important – especially details which might run counter to my own assumptions. This creates a vulnerability in me simply to jumping to conclusions. I am skillful at recognizing patterns; I can connect the dots. The danger is that I might connect two or three dots and come up with what I take for a complete cosmology.

Defensive Strategy: When I am reflexively shutting down to a necessary but threatening perception, I can rationalize any position I might take. I excel at convincing myself that I am correct, even that God is on my side. I can find a moral, even self-righteous, argument for anything I want to do, however crazy or hurtful it might be.

MERCURY IN CAPRICORN

Cognitive Rocket Fuel: To stay mentally engaged and alive, I must expose my intelligence to projects that are worthy of me and which excite my soul. I need challenges that can only be conquered with self-discipline, concentration, and persistence over time – but I have to truly want them in my heart. My mind must engage with great works – prodigious efforts of learning, and perhaps of teaching. As a metaphor, my "writing a book" serves as a fine illustration, although my great work might take many other forms.

Learning Strategy: I seek a mental mountain worth climbing. I survey my heart, asking myself where I feel like making a massive, perhaps lifelong, investment of time and energy. Only then can I commit to the process, radically and without distraction.

Natural Style of Communication: Listening and speaking is most effective and comfortable for me when people present their ideas with sequential logic and demonstrable evidence. Such communication requires patience and careful listening. I do not need to hold forth endlessly, but I do like to have the chance to complete the expression of an idea. In other words, I communicate best with people who tend not to interrupt each other. If something is worth saying, it is worth saying well and clearly.

My Best Teachers: Those who can most effectively help me learn what I need to learn in this life demonstrate their mastery concretely. Many will have already accomplished monumental works of persistence and self-discipline. Many will be elders, at least relative to me. Many fine teachers are young – but give them a few years, and they will become even better. Those are the teachers I seek.

Perceptual Bias: Because of my tendency to focus my total attention upon the project at hand, it is as if I am wearing blinders. I can miss important, unexpected, even disruptive, information emerging from the left or the right. I can also discipline myself to the point of exhaustion, allowing errors and inefficiencies to creep into my work.

Defensive Strategy: When I am reflexively shutting down to a necessary but threatening perception, I can be rigid, inappropriately authoritative, and judging. I can make the other person wrong. I can fool myself by taking refuge in impatience and a hurried resentment of "the distraction."

MERCURY IN AQUARIUS

Cognitive Rocket Fuel: To stay mentally engaged and alive, I must expose my intelligence to ideas and perceptions of a radical or at least unconventional nature. I am stimulated by thinking outside the box. Without getting an inflated head about it, I acknowledge and celebrate my own genius. My intelligence reaches orbital velocity when I recognize the blinding assumptions by which more conventional people paint themselves into corners, and I challenge them.

Learning Strategy: I seek that which has more to do with the human future then it has to do with human history. I am drawn to those who break the rules, or who at least are breaking new ground in their fields. I am willing to consider what others might view as "crazy ideas." I am wisely nervous when anyone begins a sentence with the words, "Everybody knows . . ."

Natural Style of Communication: Listening and speaking is most effective and comfortable for me when everyone is willing to float speculative ideas and to treat them with an open mind, no matter how unusual they might sound. Instinctively, I seek out people's underlying assumptions; I like to bring them out into the light and question them. Those with whom I communicate most easily enjoy this process; they are not offended or threatened by it. They grasp the fact that all human understanding is an eternal work-in-progress.

My Best Teachers: Those who can most effectively help me learn what I need to learn in this life are rebels, revolutionaries, geniuses, and troublemakers. Their favorite sound is the sound of rules breaking. They have probably been in trouble with figures of authority in whatever field of thought they are pursuing.

Perceptual Bias: Because of my tendency to focus on questioning and doubting, I am at risk of undervaluing the gifts our ancestors have provided for us. That which is new is not always better; in overthrowing the past, we may throw the baby out with the bath water. I am in danger of re-inventing the wheel, perhaps in hexagonal form.

Defensive Strategy: When I am reflexively shutting down to a necessary but threatening perception, I can detach emotionally and simply play an intellectual or verbal chess game. I can take on a superior, know-it-all posture. Regardless of my age, I can defend myself against wisdom by acting like a teenager with a bad attitude.

MERCURY IN PISCES

Cognitive Rocket Fuel: To stay mentally engaged and alive, I must expose my intelligence to non-ordinary perceptual states. Staring into space, waiting for the light bulb to light over my head leads me to many an insight I might not otherwise reach. I seek to enter into cognitive rapport with that which has been variously called the soul, God, or the unconscious mind. I am cultivating intuition, even the development of my psychic faculties. Trance states – of which meditation is perhaps the most obvious illustration – are powerful triggers for my evolution.

Learning Strategy: I seek direct experience of the larger framework of consciousness. I aim to empty my mind in order that something transcendent might enter it. I immerse myself appreciatively in the instructions kindly left for us by spiritual and visionary masters who have gone before us. Among them, there are some who speak to my heart. I trust my intuition to discern who is who. I celebrate my creative imagination.

Natural Style of Communication: Listening and speaking is most effective and comfortable for me when images, metaphors, and intuitive expressions are plentiful and welcome. Rigid, focused mental discipline only stifles me; I lose my spontaneity and my capacity for receiving inspiration. The poem is often wiser than the poet.

My Best Teachers: Those who can most effectively help me learn what I need to learn in this life are people of genuine spiritual accomplishment. They are not pretentious about it; generally, they are humble – thus demonstrating the actual reality of not being so identified with their egos. Not all of them can easily be packaged in "religious" terms – many are creative people: artists, musicians, storytellers.

Perceptual Bias: Because of my tendency to focus on receiving messages from my deeper self, I can lose my grip on this three-dimensional human reality. In extreme form, that could make me look crazy. In less dramatic fashion, that loss of groundedness in the common version of reality would simply make it hard for other people to follow what I was saying. The overlay of the psychic realms upon the world of conventional human perception can create a perceptual bias which has the effect of isolating me from other people.

Defensive Strategy: When I am reflexively shutting down to a necessary but threatening perception, I can "abuse transcendence." By that, I mean hiding from human feelings and the gritty work of personal growth by taking refuge in false or premature forgiveness, metaphysical interpretations, or "rising above" everything – just spacing out, in other words.

10

VENUS IN THE TWELVE SIGNS

VENUS IN ARIES

Underlying Intimate Agenda: I resolve to overcome any fears that stand between me and genuine intimacy. I will be direct; I will ask for what I want. When I see something limiting going on between myself and another person, I will bring it up. I will tell the truth; I expect the same. I offer my loyalty; and, again, I expect the same.

Essential Qualities in a Natural Partner: The courage to be authentic. Honesty. Directness. Fierce loyalty. Passion in the context of fidelity.

Strategy: When I am feeling an unmet need or discomfort in a relationship, I express it quickly and cleanly. I do not let bad feelings fester. I do not insist that all my needs be met – but I do insist on the right to express them clearly and to have them taken seriously.

Tools: A passionate nature, inclined to forging ahead in intimacy, taking the risks inherent in keeping love active and alive in the present tense. An ability to be clear.

Returning to Equilibrium: Above all, I benefit from the company of friends and partners as we have just described them. Vigorous exercise. Letting off steam. Dance. Passionate music played loudly. Blowing out the cobwebs. Adventures.

Dealing With The Shadow: I am aware that I might over-dramatize a point of contention. I will not let self-righteous anger limit my ability to see the other person's point of view. I cultivate forgiveness. I let the past be the past. I do not hold a grudge or seek revenge.

VENUS IN TAURUS

Underlying Intimate Agenda: In thinking about dear friends or partners, I keep my eye on the real prize for me: serenity of spirit. I want to feel genuine ease and comfort in my relationships. I am not afraid of working on a relationship, but I never want to force anything to work. I prize naturalness; I trust my instincts. I am looking for someone who helps me feel saner and more peaceful rather than crazier.

Essential Qualities in a Natural Partner: Groundedness. Reasonableness. One who prizes peace, and takes no perverse joy in intimate drama. One who "smells right." The kind of person cats, dogs, and horses seem to like.

Strategy: I make a great effort to sort out the deep passion of a true soul-bond from the hormone-addled, histrionic psychodramas which masquerade as "purple passion." I look for someone whom I simply like, with whom I can be quiet, with whom I sleep easily.

Tools: My body is a powerful sensing instrument when it comes to finding natural partners. I always consult my "inner animal" before I commit to trusting someone. My mind can fool me, but my body never will.

Returning to Equilibrium: Above all, I benefit from the company of friends and partners as we have just described them. Silence is precious. Time spent in the natural world. Yoga. Massage. Hugs. Cuddles. The quiet company of animals with whom I feel a soul-bond.

Dealing With The Shadow: I accept that intimacy sometimes involves hard work. I recognize that my own dark side will certainly be revealed to my partners. I resolve that I will learn to see it clearly too, and to take responsibility for it. I avoid taking anyone for granted. I avoid deadening intimate ruts.

VENUS IN GEMINI

Underlying Intimate Agenda: Excellent communication is critical to my experience of intimacy. The clear translation of soul-states into vocabulary and syntax is always challenging; I resolve to master that skill, both in terms of my own self-expression and in terms of my ability to listen deeply to another person without being blinded by my own preconceptions. I do not do well when I am bored; I resolve to do my part to keep all my relationships interesting, growing, and changing.

Essential Qualities in a Natural Partner: Open-mindedness. Curiosity. An eagerness for new experiences and for opportunities to learn. Listening skills. Articulateness – or at least willing verbal self-expression. A natural predilection for conversation. A willingness to discuss anything.

Strategy: I commit to two resolutions: to listen to any partner carefully and to respond clearly and forthrightly from my own heart. I do my part in keeping a relationship interesting: I suggest travel, I read books and talk about what I have learned, I dynamite deadening intimate routines for the sheer joy of seeing something different. I ask questions.

Tools: I like to talk and I like to listen, at least in intimate situations with people I love. I am naturally interested in many things. I am genuinely curious about the perspectives of others, especially those with whom I am sharing my life.

Returning to Equilibrium: Above all, I benefit from the company of friends and partners as we have just described them. Exposure to anything new, fresh, and enlivening. Quiet time with a book or an interesting program in any medium of communication. Sensory exposure to beauty.

Dealing With The Shadow: there are many interesting and attractive people in the world, but once I am committed to a particular relationship, I am careful not to be distracted by other people. I will use language as a way of building bridges to people about whom I care; I will zealously monitor myself regarding my tendency to hide my heart behind words and elaborate rationalizations.

VENUS IN CANCER

Underlying Intimate Agenda: The formation of strong, long-lasting, committed bonds with other human beings. Stability and longevity in relationship are not the only point – the deeper point is the creation of an intimate environment in which the most vulnerable parts of my being feel safe enough to be revealed. At the heart level, I am seeking home and a feeling of family in some sense of the word.

Essential Qualities in a Natural Partner: A willingness to be radically committed to me. Faithfulness, reliability, and loyalty. One who is not unduly afraid of a powerful word such as "forever." An urge to nurture – whether that nurturing is of children, pets, a garden, or the relationship itself.

Strategy: I must maintain a creative tension between, on one hand, my natural caution about getting hurt and, on the other hand, volunteering to take the risk of opening my heart. I will not be so cautious as to be unreachable.

Tools: A deep and fundamental capacity to love another human being in a spirit of familial devotion and lifelong commitment. A nearly infinite ability simply to care for another person. A natural internal marriage of sexuality with emotions of simple affection.

Returning to Equilibrium: Above all, I benefit from the company of friends and partners as we have just described them. Quiet time at home. Familiar routines: a cup of tea in a comfortable chair that has taken the shape of my own body. Time in bed, even if I am not sleepy. A distinct reduction in the level of external stimuli.

Dealing With The Shadow: I resolve to be aware of my potential for excessive caution and self protection. I will not hide my true feelings or needs behind the "parental" mask of caregiving.

VENUS IN LEO

Underlying Intimate Agenda: I resolve to not settle for anything less in my intimate life than the feeling of being cherished by someone whom I myself treasure. No one has to be perfect. The agenda here is to be perfectly loving – to celebrate each other, stand up for each other, and to consistently prioritize the relationship over other concerns.

Essential Qualities in a Natural Partner: Expressiveness. An affectionate, demonstrative nature. Supportiveness. The ability to say I love you. Attentiveness and a natural fluency in offering compliments. Self-respect – and respect for me – as demonstrated by a willingness to look and behave his or her best.

Strategy: First and foremost, I resolve never to settle for a partner whom I do not genuinely cherish. I would rather be alone than to abase myself that way. Once having found such a person, I actively commit to a lifelong path dedicated to preserving and nurturing the romance of our bond.

Tools: I have a certain flair for style and colorful self-expression. An ability to say what I feel in an impactful way, so it is heard deeply. A degree of healthy pride, self-respect, and dignity – all of which support me in not settling for too little in any of my relationships.

Returning to Equilibrium: Above all, I benefit from the company of friends and partners as we have just described them. My creative outlets soothe me; I cultivate some form of artistic or aesthetic self-expression. I know that it helps me feel good inwardly to look my best outwardly; when I am upset, I groom myself. I dress attractively. Perhaps I shop. Perhaps I try on a new look.

Dealing With The Shadow: I remind myself that no one's life needs to revolve around mine. In a healthy relationship, we are like a double star orbiting a common center of gravity which we have created together. I express my own needs forthrightly – but I also make space to hear the needs and celebrate the victories of my friends and my partners.

VENUS IN VIRGO

Underlying Intimate Agenda: I resolve never to accept a relationship with anyone who is irresponsible or unreliable. Grown-ups only need apply. Groundedness, maturity, and reasonableness are critical ingredients if I am going to trust another person. We accept imperfections in each other and in the relationship, but at the same time, we resolve endlessly to chip away at them, making things better over time.

Essential Qualities in a Natural Partner: A hard working, responsible willingness to behave in an adult fashion. Competence. One "who has a life" in terms of having found meaningful work and responsibilities. An ability to communicate; an astute awareness of human flaws, along with a commitment to self-improvement – and enough of a sense of humor about the whole thing to survive the intensity of the process.

Strategy: I resolve to be cautious in offering my heart to anyone. My aims here are discrimination and discernment; I do not condemn anyone because he or she fails to meet my needs or standards. At the same time, I am resolved never to enter into a relationship which, deep down inside, I know in advance could never satisfy me.

Tools: I have an analytic mind, even in affairs of the heart. When emotions are involved, people often do not think clearly. I am not immune to falling into that trap – but I am more skilled at avoiding it than are most people. Once committed, I am capable of working on myself and working on the relationship, fashioning it into something which we both treasure.

Returning to Equilibrium: Above all, I benefit from the company of friends and partners as we have just described them. Work and routine have soothing effects upon me. So does the practice of any craft, from astrology to bead work. It calms me to do things with my hands. Pleasurable concentration distracts me from worry and relieves tension.

Dealing With The Shadow: I resolve to cultivate an expansive, forgiving view of human nature, my own or that of my friends or partners. I will not nitpick. Even in love, I will recognize the eternal truth that "perfect" is the enemy of "good enough." I will recognize moments when a relaxed acceptance of flawed reality is the highest course.

VENUS IN LIBRA

Underlying Intimate Agenda: To aim for a "perfect relationship" might seem like a quixotic goal, but that is truly the intimate agenda here. To bring this idea down to earth, I recognize that my agenda lies in committing to a process of development, rather than looking for a bond that works automatically, without effort, right from the beginning. Here are the qualities I seek: deep, three-dimensional *attention* to each other. Fairness in all things. The cultivation of grace and serenity. And a lifelong romantic appreciation of each other.

Essential Qualities in a Natural Partner: A civilized quality of grace and courtesy, even elegance. Politeness and evidence of respect for me, even if we are angry. A willingness to take in my point of view even if he or she sees things differently. Aesthetic sensitivities. An instinct for fairness.

Strategy: Cultivating the ability to see other people as they are – which is to say, an appreciation of the fact that they are different from me. A spirit of mutual inquiry. Genuine listening. Peacekeeping skills – but in which such skills are never employed to avoid necessary, difficult negotiations.

Tools: I was born with an affable quality of natural charm; an ability to get along with other people, to build bridges even across wide chasms of human difference. An instinct for understanding another person's point of view. A knack for diplomacy – how to express potentially difficult things in ways that diffuse a situation rather than escalating it.

Returning to Equilibrium: Above all, I benefit from the company of friends and partners as we have just described them. Immersion of my senses in beauty, whether it is the beauty of nature or the beauty created by human artistry. Civilized pleasures. Experiences of elegance, grace, and quality.

Dealing With The Shadow: I resolve never to employ my diplomatic skills in order to paper over hurt or genuine intimate challenges. I put truth on the table first, and only then do I deploy my capacity for respectful negotiation.

VENUS IN SCORPIO

Underlying Intimate Agenda: A radical commitment to honesty. And an equally radical commitment to living truthfully, forgivingly, and humbly with both my own Shadow and the Shadow of my partner. A relationship between the wholenesses of two psyches – including the unconscious minds – rather than simply between two conscious, "virtuous" personalities. Truth above all.

Essential Qualities in a Natural Partner: Psychological savvy, even if the person is not formally educated in that way. A desire to pursue the truth. A commitment never to punish me for pointing out the truth as I see it, no matter how uncomfortable that might be. A willingness to look me directly in the eye.

Strategy: The cultivation of a level of trust sufficient to support true emotional nakedness. The cultivation of the habit of honesty and the establishment of a pattern of mutual acceptance, no matter what. Permission to think anything, with the only restrictions being those placed on behavior itself.

Tools: I have a great innate intensity of being. A capacity to deal acceptingly with emotionally challenging material. A willingness to break the mental taboos imposed by society. An unashamed sense of the power of sexuality to maintain, and even to restore, a sense of bondedness between two human beings.

Returning to Equilibrium: Above all, I benefit from the company of friends and partners as we have just described them. Serious talks with dear friends about charged subjects, such as mortality, aging, and disease. Realness. The antithesis of cocktail party chatter. Humor – often of the "gallows" fashion – plays a pivotal role in the restoration of my serenity.

Dealing With The Shadow: I resolve to learn to recognize the moment when intense emotion or need begins to distort my ability to think clearly. Similarly, I cultivate sensitivity to the signs that someone I love has reached that same point of distortion. I recognize the power of the Shadow, and respect it. Sometimes I need to step back and de-escalate a situation. I learn to let things go. I learn the fine arts of patience and timing when it comes to deep psychological work.

VENUS IN SAGITTARIUS

Underlying Intimate Agenda: The integration of that infamous polarity: love and freedom. I resolve to learn how to love voluntarily, free of the deadening hand of any oppressive sense of duty. Simultaneously, I celebrate the freedom and autonomy of those whom I love. Together, we create more of a sense of the possibility of adventure in our lives than we could ever create alone.

Essential Qualities in a Natural Partner: Independence; a high degree of self-sufficiency. A taste for the open road. A philosophical, principled nature. A powerful motivation to learn and to grow. A willingness to let me be who I am.

Strategy: Experience leads to wisdom in terms of mate selection; I am not afraid to explore intimacy and to learn from diverse experiences there. Before I grant myself love, I must grant myself freedom. I might have to "kiss a few frogs" in order to find my prince or my princess. I keep it honest, keep it loving, and then I let no one shame me for any of it.

Tools: I have a curious, resilient, energetic heart. An ability to build bridges across cultural or social divides. An emotional resilience; the ability to recover rapidly from heartbreak. Faith in life, even when individuals may have failed me.

Returning to Equilibrium: Above all, I benefit from the company of friends and partners as we have just described them. Seeing new places refreshes me. I heed the call of the open road or the far horizon. Uplifting aesthetic experiences – glorious natural scenes, heroic or anthemic music, ambitious films – all of them help me to restore and uplift my soul after some shock.

Dealing With The Shadow: I resolve to actually *find* what I am seeking; I will not hide from the real world of maturity behind the veil of an endless tragic-romantic search for someone who does not exist. I will not take cheap refuge in my incredible capacity for rationalization and explaining myself.

VENUS IN CAPRICORN

Underlying Intimate Agenda: In relationship, my aim is nothing less than a masterpiece and I know that masterpieces take time. I want to create a bond with another human being of which I am truly proud. I seek the ancient vow of a lifelong commitment – a commitment not simply to passing of years together, but rather to the kind of love that might arise between two true elders in the real world, regardless of our actual ages.

Essential Qualities in a Natural Partner: A willingness to make and keep promises. A capacity for seriousness when seriousness is appropriate. One whose already-existing history suggests that he or she places a great value upon integrity. Character is high on such a person's list of attractive qualities, never eclipsed by more transitory charms.

Strategy: Commitment over the long term is fundamental here. But such commitment is not entered spontaneously or frivolously; we earn each other's faith through a gradual, patient process. I am capable of commitment, but I do not offer it lightly.

Tools: An elevated capacity for self-discipline, maturity, and delayed gratification. I, more than most people can actually keep the intimate promises that I make. In times of difficulty, I keep my eye on the prize, which is weathering the storm, and learning from it. That which does not destroy us only makes us stronger.

Returning to Equilibrium: Above all, I benefit from the company of friends and partners as we have just described them. Paradoxically, relaxation comes most easily to me when I am engaged in some focused effort. Ambitious projects are good for me. I might work as hard at my hobbies as other people work at their jobs. I do not let anyone criticize me for that – I know that it is a reliable method for restoring my serenity of spirit after some trying or stressful experience.

Dealing With The Shadow: I resolve always to remember to be tender with myself. That resolution takes several forms. One is that I commit to expressing my needs. I am not ashamed to ask a friend or partner for help, support, or a hug. Love is a joy, not a task. I resolve to remember that – and if love does in fact become a task, I give myself gentle permission to reconsider my promises.

VENUS IN AQUARIUS

Underlying Intimate Agenda: I resolve that all of my intimate choices will be made in a spirit of self-awareness, self-possession, and on a completely voluntary basis. I will not be told what to do, intimately or sexually, by anyone. I am the ultimate authority in my own intimate life. Every community and every ethnic group always has a pre-written script for love, friendship, and sexuality; I reject the script. My choices are my own.

Essential Qualities in a Natural Partner: An unquestioning respect for my own freedom and individuality. An independence of nature, and a corresponding appreciation of my own independence. One who questions authority. A true, one-of-a-kind individual. One who is following his or her own path through life. One who loves me more than he or she needs me.

Strategy: First and foremost, I commit to sorting out my own needs and my own identity before I confuse my own path by trying to accommodate it to someone else's path. In every culture, there is a rule book of customs and assumptions about human intimacy. I toss it out; I am writing my own rule book. Nothing is required of me in any relationship I choose to be part of except honesty.

Tools: I was born with a capacity to think outside the framework of the conventionalities other people typically accept without thinking. I am tolerant of human diversity; I do not need my friends or partners to think the same way I do, or to agree with me about everything. Live and let live – that ideal comes quite naturally to me. I can respond creatively and originally to any intimate dilemma.

Returning to Equilibrium: Above all, I benefit from the company of friends and partners as we have just described them. I am friendly, but often when I am upset, the best way I can regain my serenity of spirit is just to be left alone for a while, not needing to explain myself to anyone. In terms of the arts, my tastes might seem weird to some people – but exposure to art helps me find my balance again. What works for me works for me and I do not need to explain it.

Dealing With The Shadow: I resolve, when someone has earned my trust, that I will struggle sincerely to open my vulnerable heart to that person. I will not hide behind distance, "weirdness," or detachment; I resolve to let myself be truly touched.

VENUS IN PISCES

Underlying Intimate Agenda: I resolve that I will settle for nothing less in this lifetime than relationships that have a genuinely, consciously spiritual basis. This does not mean that we must share a religion or even a philosophy; it means that we can sit together in silent communion. It means that sometimes words are not necessary to bridge the space between us. It means that we can gaze unguardedly and openly into each other's eyes.

Essential Qualities in a Natural Partner: I know that anyone who lacks an active, conscious spiritual life will only fill my heart with loneliness in the long run. The reason is simple: such a person, who may have many virtues, simply cannot grasp a very large part of what I am. My natural partner is, in some sense, a mystic. Under that banner, I include visionaries, creative people, and people of imagination. They may not be churchy, but there is strong evidence in their lives and speech of their communion with something vaster than themselves.

Strategy: I know that the quality and happiness of my intimate life is directly linked to the depth of my own personal spiritual practice. The deeper I go, the deeper my relationships are likely to be – and the deeper are the people whom I attract into my life. As I think about the pressing importance of my spiritual practice, it is helpful to recognize that art and creativity can be quite central to it.

Tools: A capacity for decoupling my consciousness from my personality arises naturally in me. Love helps me with that; so does losing myself in aesthetic rapture – listening to music, gazing at beautiful scenes, and so on. I sense that there is a wider world deep down in my psyche – and that the more I embrace it through those methods, the more my Venus will magnetize the right people into my life.

Returning to Equilibrium: Above all, I benefit from the company of friends and partners as we have just described them. I need a certain amount of time, hopefully each day, to simply sit in silence and release the day's entanglements. Listening to music, gazing at flowers or beautiful paintings, making sure that I don't miss the sunset or the moonrise – all of these experiences of aesthetic trends help to restore my lost tranquility.

Dealing With The Shadow: I resolve not to become a ghost in my own relationships. There are some things I do not need to accept in another person. I need to be clear about those boundaries – and to leave any relationship that is not serving my higher spiritual purposes. I affirm that I have the right to do exactly that. I reject the drunken torpor and toxic stability of bad love.

11

SATURN AND URANUS IN THE TWELVE SIGNS

SATURN IN ARIES

The Worthy Work: I resolve that reflected in the mirror of my outward biographical life, I will eventually see a concrete manifestation of my own courage. I accept that the pioneering evolutionary work I am here on earth to accomplish will attract resistance and challenges, perhaps even enemies. I will not let any of that stop me. I ride out and meet them, undaunted. I am becoming a true spiritual warrior, brave, steadfast, and committed.

Effective Strategy: In relentlessly disciplined fashion, I establish in myself the habit of never, ever giving up. Still, I recognize that in order to win the war, one must strategically accept that some battles must be lost. I compete fairly and I maintain my integrity, but I constantly keep my eye on the prize, while unashamedly valuing honest victory.

Unbreakable Moral Commitment: In this one way above all others, I will never fail myself: fear will never make any of my final decisions.

Natural Resources: In support of my Great Work, I came into this world with tenacity, doggedness, as well as a strong sense of timing. I can think strategically. I can pull victory out of the jaws of defeat. I have a sense of the heroic potential of the human spirit. I will live up to it.

The Blockage: I humbly acknowledge and resolve to get past my blockage in the area of the distortions of awareness and perspective that arise from my passions – anger, resentment, fear, and desire. I will not let them rule my life.

The Shape of the Shadow: Were I to betray my path, I recognize that my life would be fraught with an underlying sense of failure. Bitterness and an unfocused attitude of resentment and acrimony would leave scars on my soul.

SATURN IN TAURUS

The Worthy Work: I resolve that reflected in the mirror of the physical world, I will eventually see a concrete manifestation of my own commitment to building a solid foundation for peace in my own life. My aim, above all, is to provide myself with an effective basis for serenity of spirit – a safe harbor amid the chaos of human existence, a situation in which I can attune myself to the things that are truly important in life, free from petty distractions and temptations.

Effective Strategy: In relentlessly disciplined fashion, I establish in myself the habit of prioritizing my peace of mind above everything else. To that end, I will create physical and financial security for myself – but I will keep perspective, realizing that maintaining stable, loving human connections are part of my strategy too, as is taking care of my health and my soul. I cultivate a closeness to nature, knowing that it stabilizes me.

Unbreakable Moral Commitment: In this one way above all others, I will never fail myself: I resolve to discern sources of chaos and tension from afar and to avoid them, no matter how clever and tempting their disguise.

Natural Resources: In support of my Great Work, I came into this world with common sense and reason. I have an appreciation for simplicity. I can see through pretenses. I can recognize a scoundrel. I am not easily distracted. I can tolerate silence.

The Blockage: I humbly acknowledge and resolve to get past my blockage in the area of being flexible – that means an acceptance of the fact that life involves endless change. I can adjust; I can let go of people and situations which have outlived their usefulness.

The Shape of the Shadow: Were I to betray my path, I recognize that my life would reflect a stodgy, fear-driven commitment to what amounts to endless boredom. While I need material stability in order to fulfill my evolutionary work, I recognize that I can give too much power to money and security.

SATURN IN GEMINI

The Worthy Work: I resolve that reflected in the mirror of my outward biographical life, I will eventually see a concrete manifestation of my own true voice. I will find it and I will reveal it. I will be *heard* in this lifetime. My ideas will be taken seriously. I recognize that in order to attain that goal I must create a voice that is worthy of being heard.

Effective Strategy: In relentlessly disciplined fashion, I establish in myself the habit of endlessly educating myself deeply in anything that attracts my interest. I ask the hard questions and I embrace the complex answers which follow. I will speak up whenever an opportunity to be heard presents itself. I will improve my diction, delivery, and vocabulary. I will become a master of concentration. I will learn to speak with a voice of authority.

Unbreakable Moral Commitment: In this one way above all others, I will never fail myself: when I have something worth saying, no person and no circumstance will ever silence me through intimidation.

Natural Resources: In support of my Great Work, I came into this world with a serious mind capable of sustained, monumental feats of self-education and verbal self-expression.

The Blockage: I humbly acknowledge and resolve to get past my blockage in the area of having full confidence in my own voice.

The Shape of the Shadow: Were I to betray my path, I recognize that my life would reflect a sad pattern of having allowed myself to be chronically distracted from my own true goals. I would recognize that I had thereby silenced myself, and that what I came into this world to say had been left unsaid.

SATURN IN CANCER

The Worthy Work: I resolve that reflected in the mirror of my outward biographical life, I will eventually see a concrete manifestation of my commitment to living a life of kindness. I will become a shining example of that quality to my community. I will know in my heart that I have touched the lives of other people in a healing way. I will also have established a "family" in some sense of the word – a family of which I am proud and one which cherishes and appreciates me.

Effective Strategy: In relentlessly disciplined fashion, I establish in myself the habit of paying attention to my own needs. I will be kind to myself, oriented to healing myself. I understand that this self-care is the necessary foundation for my ability to effectively care for anyone else.

Unbreakable Moral Commitment: In this one way above all others, I will never fail myself: I will find the elusive balance point between caring for myself and caring for other people. Neither one will ever eclipse the other.

Natural Resources: In support of my Great Work, I came into this world with a practical sense of how the wounds of the soul reveal themselves behaviorally and how they might be healed. I am wise and patient in the face of these slow processes. I have a gift when it comes to guiding others in the process of their own self-healing.

The Blockage: I humbly acknowledge and resolve to get past my blockage in the area of trusting the fact that life does not want to hurt me. I appreciate feeling safe, but I will not allow that need to stand between me and honest, two-way street communion with the people with whom I am sharing my life.

The Shape of the Shadow: Were I to betray my path, I recognize that my life would reflect an obsessive and excessive level of self-protection. I would be lonely, even if I were surrounded by people who depended upon me. That loneliness would arise because no one had ever been allowed to see my soul.

SATURN IN LEO

The Worthy Work: I resolve that reflected in the mirror of my outward biographical life, I will eventually see a concrete manifestation of my own genuine, authentic, and original creativity. I will leave in the hands of the world some evidence of my inner life: what I valued, what I held sacred, what I found beautiful. I resolve to be brave enough to stand naked and vulnerable, with my soul exposed to other human beings.

Effective Strategy: In relentlessly disciplined fashion, I establish in myself the habit of developing my self-expressive skills. I will find a concrete outlet – perhaps an art form – for the contents of my psyche, and I will polish it until it provides a transparent window between my soul and the community around me.

Unbreakable Moral Commitment: In this one way above all others, I will never fail myself: I will leave something of myself in the hands of the world. I will gift the world with a treasure that was forged in the cauldron of my experiences.

Natural Resources: In support of my Great Work, I came into this world with the seed of a genuine self-expressive talent. As I identify it and nourish it over time, the seed blossoms.

The Blockage: I humbly acknowledge and resolve to get past my blockage in the area of performance, "stage-fright," and emotionally risky self-revelation. I must face the perils of stepping out on the stage of life.

The Shape of the Shadow: Were I to betray my path, I recognize that my life would reflect the feeling of being a flower that never opened. I would suffer from a sense of having held back something that I was supposed to give – something which other people actually needed.

SATURN IN VIRGO

The Worthy Work: I resolve that reflected in the mirror of my outward biographical life, I will eventually see a concrete manifestation of my own practical ability to make a real difference in the lives of other people. I will become truly "good at something." I will be seen as a valued master of a craft which is of genuine service to my community. I will have done work that I know truly mattered.

Effective Strategy: In relentlessly disciplined fashion, I establish in myself the habits of focus, purposefulness, and hard work. I commit to endless improvement, both in myself and in my craft. I accept that this commitment implies a constant diet of constructive self-criticism. Each day, I will become a little bit better at what I do. I will seek the presence and support of masters who have gone before me; I will learn from them in a spirit of humility.

Unbreakable Moral Commitment: In this one way above all others, I will never fail myself: I will always, without fail, strive to do my best work. Nothing less will ever be acceptable to me.

Natural Resources: In support of my Great Work, I came into this world with a capacity for concentration, an appetite for sustained effort, and a humble ability to assess myself honestly. Through sheer relentless-ness, I can come out ahead of people who may have been born with more natural skill than I have.

The Blockage: I humbly acknowledge and resolve to get past my blockage in the area of self-confidence. I can cripple myself with self-criticism, perhaps slipping into a pattern of defending myself against success through the device of endless preparation. Self-doubt can leave me in a limbo of scut-work.

The Shape of the Shadow: Were I to betray my path, I recognize that my life would reflect a kind of volunteered slavery. I could exhaust myself "putting things in alphabetical order" for people I deemed (incorrectly) to be superior to myself. I could descend into a lather of fuss and worry.

SATURN IN LIBRA

The Worthy Work: I resolve that reflected in the mirror of my outward biographical life, I will eventually see the concrete flowering of three visions: my own aesthetics and taste, something approaching an ideal human partnership, and a style of life characterized by grace, taste, and serenity.

Effective Strategy: In relentlessly disciplined fashion, I establish in myself the habit of seeking balance in all things. I follow the middle path. I resolve to accept that paradox is fundamental to life, and I will not be troubled by a need to "take sides." In the words of the Navajo elders, I resolve to "walk in beauty." I seek friends and partners who don't make me crazy – mature people, capable of commitment and of reason.

Unbreakable Moral Commitment: In this one way above all others, I will never fail myself: I will live in the presence of paradox, knowing that every story has two sides. I will never fall into the illusions created by dogmatism or extremism in any form.

Natural Resources: In support of my Great Work, I came into this world with a strong sense of balance and fairness. I have an ability to endlessly deepen my appreciation of beauty. I naturally tolerate human differences. All of these qualities are supportive of my real goal: the development of inner peace.

The Blockage: I humbly acknowledge and resolve to get past my blockage in the area of facing conflict squarely and honestly. When intimacy is challenging that way, I will not take refuge in hiding my feelings. I will not let secret solitude lurk behind an appearance of acquiescence.

The Shape of the Shadow: Were I to betray my path, I recognize that my life would reflect the triumph of formality and diplomacy over genuine soul-transparency. I would simply be lonely.

SATURN IN SCORPIO

The Worthy Work: I resolve that reflected in the mirror of my outward biographical life, I will eventually see the concrete results of my own commitment to hard inner psychological and spiritual growth. I pursue truth, fearlessly. Specifically, I will be recognized – at least by some people – as a wise elder to whom they can turn confidently when nothing less than the truth will serve their evolutionary purposes.

Effective Strategy: In relentlessly disciplined fashion, I establish in myself the habit of squarely facing every emotional glitch in my life, no matter how threatening it might feel. Patiently, I sort through my emotions and my experiences, seeking what lies hidden behind them. I seek the counsel of a few other brave souls with similar dispositions, and cherish them.

Unbreakable Moral Commitment: In this one way above all others, I will never fail myself: I will never, ever, take refuge in comforting lies. Denial, rationalization, and defensiveness are anathema to me. I resolve to do my best to always recognize them in myself as quickly as possible and to dispel them.

Natural Resources: In support of my Great Work, I came into this world with an innate instinct for psychological work. I can hold steady in the face of strong emotions and situations which other people might find to be overwhelming. I can face anything and still have strength left for those who need me.

The Blockage: I humbly acknowledge and resolve to get past my blockage in the area of simply lightening up. Life is serious – but it is funny too. I will not forget to laugh and thus to maintain a degree of humorous perspective on my own psychological intensity.

The Shape of the Shadow: Were I to betray my path, I recognize that my life would reflect an exaggeratedly gloomy and suspicious view of human existence. I would become isolated, dark, and withdrawn, unable to tap into the deep well of energy that comes from shared human playfulness.

SATURN IN SAGITTARIUS

The Worthy Work: I resolve that reflected in the mirror of my outward bi-ography, I will eventually see a concrete manifestation of everything in which I believe. I will align my life with my understanding of the meaning of life. I will, in other words, walk my talk. Fundamental to my "talk" is the idea that life must be embraced and lived as a spiritual adventure. I will always put morals and principles ahead of practical concerns – and one of my most fundamental principles is that no one gets out of here alive, so let's all seize the day and live each day as if it were a precious evolutionary opportunity.

Effective Strategy: In relentlessly disciplined fashion, I establish in myself the habit of stretching my horizons, both intellectually and experi-entially. I commit to a life of endless learning. I will travel, as opportunities present themselves. I will seek the meaning of life by pursuing teachers and teachings, and by studying philosophy and metaphysics. I will wrestle with the fundamental questions of human existence. I will not be distracted by petty concerns.

Unbreakable Moral Commitment: In this one way above all others, I will never fail myself: I will live in absolute accord with my principles no matter what material costs and practical indignities might arise as a result.

Natural Resources: In support of my Great Work, I came into this world with a firm faith in the fundamental meaningfulness of life. Come thick or thin, I trust in the potential purposefulness of all experience. I am resilient; I can bounce back from losses and hurtful episodes. I am philo-sophical – but I am always willing to subject my beliefs to practical tests.

The Blockage: I humbly acknowledge and resolve to get past my block-age in the area of exaggerated caution. I recognize that life, despite any fears to the contrary, can sometimes go smoothly. Murphy's Law – the idea that anything that can possibly go wrong will go wrong – is a tempting dis-tortion of the truth of life for me. I will not succumb to it. I will not "count on luck" to bail me out – but I will also expect the occasional miracle.

The Shape of the Shadow: Were I to betray my path, I recognize that my life would reflect the reality of my fears smothering my growth and evolu-tion. Caution could triumph over adventure. Vaguely, I would sense that there had been the potential of a vibrant life out there for me – one that I somehow missed living because I was afraid to take any risks.

SATURN IN CAPRICORN

The Worthy Work: I resolve that reflected in the mirror of my outward biographical life, I will eventually see a concrete manifestation of my own commitment to excellence, my capacity for inexorable focus and patience, and my highest ambitions. I will manifest a serious, impressive accomplishment, one that reveals something of my great soul to the world. In some area of life, I will aim for nothing less than perfection. I know I will never fully attain it, but my dignity and my self-respect will thrive on the persistent effort.

Effective Strategy: In relentlessly disciplined fashion, I establish in myself the habit of not allowing myself to be daunted by any difficulty. I keep going, no matter what. I intentionally undertake tasks that intimidate me. In pursuit of great works, I accept that imbalances and sacrifices will be required of me. I acknowledge that I am not here to live a balanced life. That is the price of excellence in any one area.

Unbreakable Moral Commitment: In this one way above all others, I will never fail myself: my higher intentions will always have dominion over my weaknesses, my appetites, and any temptations that might arise.

Natural Resources: In support of my Great Work, I came into this world with an elevated capacity for focus and for keeping my eye on the prize. Sustained determination arises naturally in me. I can keep pounding away when others have given up.

The Blockage: I humbly acknowledge and resolve to get past my blockage in the area of mindful self-monitoring. I will learn to be kinder to myself. Specifically, I resolve to be attentive to bodily signals of tiredness, discomfort, or hunger. I will listen to the non-rational parts of myself, such as instinct and intuition. I give them a voice in my decisions.

The Shape of the Shadow: Were I to betray my path, I recognize that my life would reflect a kind of wasted self-discipline. I would work hard at things that meant nothing to me. I would expend an enormous amount of energy getting to the top of the wrong mountain. I would realize that I had let other people eclipse my own soul's dream, replacing that dream with their own.

SATURN IN AQUARIUS

The Worthy Work: I resolve that reflected in the mirror of my outward bio-graphical life, I will eventually see a concrete manifestation of my own genius – which is to say that I would create something that revealed my unique understanding of life, my unconventional purpose in the world, and the values which animate it. I will put my genius into my life, becoming the practical architect of my liberation from the tyranny of the normal. I will create something that has never before been seen by anyone.

Effective Strategy: In relentlessly disciplined fashion, I establish in myself the habit of always questioning authority. I will never believe any-thing simply because I have been told that it was true; instead, I commit to discerning people's underlying assumptions and to testing them against the backdrop of more creative, iconoclastic possibilities. I resolve to build a practical foundation which allows me to live life with more freedom and fewer conventional strictures.

Unbreakable Moral Commitment: In this one way above all others, I will never fail myself: I will never allow my behavior to be shaped by the need for anyone else's approval.

Natural Resources: In support of my Great Work, I came into this world with a willingness to ask questions. I was born with at least one strand of "genius" DNA – which is to say, an instinctive rebellion against reflexively believing what "everybody knows." I can quietly and practically build a workable escape hatch from the oppressions of conventionality.

The Blockage: I humbly acknowledge and resolve to get past my ten-dency to isolate myself emotionally. I do not give up on entertaining the possibility that I *can* be understood, even loved and appreciated, by at least a few people. I am not afraid to feel or to connect with others.

The Shape of the Shadow: Were I to betray my path, I recognize that my life would reflect a kind of chilly emotional dissociation, as if I had given up on tenderness. I will not allow my objectivity and independence from the crowd to degenerate into simple coldness.

SATURN IN PISCES

The Worthy Work: I resolve that reflected in the mirror of my outward bi-ographical life, I will eventually see concrete manifestations of my own commitment to real spiritual and psychic progress. I will achieve verifiable results in those areas of development. For that reason, many of my most fundamental successes in this lifetime will be invisible to the world at large; my greatest work is inner work. The treasures I create in this lifetime will remain with me for eternity.

Effective Strategy: In relentlessly disciplined fashion, I establish in myself the habit of regularity in meditation and spiritual self-care, along with a commitment to acts of kindness, humility, and charity in the world. Using these ancient methods, each day I chip away at ego-clinging and delusion.

Unbreakable Moral Commitment: In this one way above all others, I will never fail myself: I will always remember that this life is a short dream from which I will soon awaken.

Natural Resources: In support of my Great Work, I came into this world with a precious seed in my consciousness: the capacity eventually to become a *spiritual elder* in my community. I have an instinct for spiritual practice; I hold it precious; I will explore it. I will fulfill my full evolutionary potential in this lifetime.

The Blockage: I humbly acknowledge and resolve to get past my blockage in the area of trusting my own psychic and intuitive impressions. I welcome them into my consciousness and I am willing to act on them. I will not lose heart even though I have come to a steep place on the spiritual mountain.

The Shape of the Shadow: Were I to betray my path, I recognize that my life would reflect the fact that I had come adrift spiritually, having missed an opportunity to make a major step forward – all because I gave too much power to doubt, the illusions and temptations of this world, or perhaps even to simple spiritual laziness.

Uranus Through The Signs

URANUS IN ARIES

What qualities, above all, does it take for me to find my own right path in life? The courage to stand my ground no matter how powerful or intimidating the opposition I face might be. A willingness to be disobedient no matter the consequences. Speedy, bold, and decisive reaction times.

What tools has the universe given me? Righteous anger, if I need it. A love of truth expressed directly and clearly. *In extremis,* a willingness to die for what I believe. An ability to cut through to the heart of any matter. The ability to spot a bully a mile away and to stand up to him or her. The ability to surprise others with unexpected, bold strategies and tactics.

What happens if I actively misdirect this energy? I experience a wild, ungrounded desire simply to break things. I hurt people. I can become cold, mean, and contrary. I start fights and arguments impulsively even in situations that do not really matter to me, and I have no idea why I am doing it.

How do I look if I descend into a dissociative state? I become passive aggressive. I seethe with suppressed frustration. I become a ticking time-bomb – perhaps one that never actually explodes.

URANUS IN TAURUS

What qualities, above all, does it take for me to find my own right path in life? A willingness to spend time in silence. An affinity for Mother Nature. It is in quiet and in the natural world that I best attune myself to my own soul. An openness to heeding the messages of my physical body – I sense a "feeling in my bones" or an uneasiness in my belly even though logic says "go for it." I commit to trusting those instinctual messages

What tools has the universe given me? An ability to see through pretence and to not ever be seduced by it. An attunement to instinct. An ability to attract animal-friends in whose mirrors I sometimes see myself more clearly than I do in the human world. An idiosyncratic "wise old Navajo" sense of what is truly important and what is not.

What happens if I actively misdirect this energy? I become ridiculously stubborn in defense of things that actually do not matter at all – defending my quirks and idiosyncrasies as if they were issues of integrity or mortal gravity. I fight against change.

How do I look if I descend into a dissociative state? My soul withdraws into silence. I become fixed in my routines and habits. A mechanical quality arises in my daily affairs. I numb myself with food and physical comfort.

URANUS IN GEMINI

What qualities, above all, does it take for me to find my own right path in life? A willingness to believe my own eyes. There is always a tension between what lies before them on one hand, and what everybody else believes to be the case – or needs me to believe – on the other hand. I must learn to have faith in my own thoughts and perceptions. On that basis, I choose to speak with my own unique voice and to ignore "my reviews."

What tools has the universe given me? An ability to think outside the box. An ability to recognize and question the assumptions underlying other people's beliefs. Alertness to previously unconsidered possibilities. An instinctive suspicion of intellectual authorities.

What happens if I actively misdirect this energy? I become a contrarian, arguing by unreflective reflex against anything I am told. I rebel against the possibility of my ever finishing anything, militantly defending my right simply to scatter my energies. I talk too much and I listen without internalizing what I am hearing.

How do I look if I descend into a dissociative state? I become a talking head, living in an arid world composed only of abstract concepts, without any actual human, flesh-and-blood, emotionally-engaged, contact with anyone.

URANUS IN CANCER

What qualities, above all, does it take for me to find my own right path in life? A willingness to distinguish myself from the mythologies and beliefs of my family of origin. I do not need to think negatively about those people, but I do need to become my own person. With that step taken, a second step becomes available: that is to establish my own family (in any sense of that word, however unusual) on a new and completely independent foundation.

What tools has the universe given me? An acute sensitivity when it comes to scoping out psychological issues which have their origins in anyone's childhood assumptions or experiences. A willingness to feel whatever emotions I am actually feeling, and to experience them in their true nature rather than in some "scripted" fashion – that is to say, I might not feel jealous when everyone is assuming that I "must" feel jealous. Ditto for happy, sad, safe or threatened, and so on.

What happens if I actively misdirect this energy? I disappear into some kind of caregiving role which I privately and quietly resent. That might involve kids, parents, dependent friends, pets, or even a partner. Perhaps, if such pressures reach a critical threshold in me, I eventually pop – that is to say, I rebel precipitously against the situation, abandoning those who have come to count on me.

How do I look if I descend into a dissociative state? Very, very quiet. My individuality becomes invisible – undetectable via any of my outward behaviors. My real life, such as I have one at all, unfolds almost completely at an imaginary level of fantasy.

URANUS IN LEO

What qualities, above all, does it take for me to find my own right path in life? A near-absolute invulnerability to embarrassment – that means that I cultivate an ability to express myself nakedly, honestly, even dramatically, in any situation without giving a moment of my time to any fear of judgment. Paradox arises because this "invulnerability to embarrassment" frees me to be utterly vulnerable in all other categories. I resolve to have nothing to hide, ever.

What tools has the universe given me? A colorful, memorable, even zany quality of character. Good performance instincts; an ability to sense the mood of a crowd. Highly original creative capacities. The seeds of skill at some form of art, so long as we define the term "art" broadly enough.

What happens if I actively misdirect this energy? Instead of my soul attracting attention via its legitimate, vulnerable acts of self-expression, my ego attracts attention by giving itself unabashed free rein. What I ultimately display, even though I am likely to be unaware of it, is only my own insecurity and my childish need for attention.

How do I look if I descend into a dissociative state? As if I am only going through the motions of my life. I say all the right things, as if I were a politician running for office; I smile with all the sincerity of a beauty pageant contestant. I impress shallow people, while the deeper ones find me uninspiring.

URANUS IN VIRGO

What qualities, above all, does it take for me to find my own right path in life? Work that really matters to me – and the courage and self-awareness to find it. That is because identifying my natural skills and a meaningful path of service depends on my ability to transcend social conditioning and to be willing to live with criticism, as well as the misinformed "help," and even derision, of people around me. In parallel fashion, I must also strengthen my ability to reject other people's versions of my responsibilities. Paradoxically, to be a truly responsible person, I might have to tolerate being labelled as "irresponsible."

What tools has the universe given me? A sincere desire to be useful to other people in my own unique way. The seeds of an ability to become really good at some meaningful, helpful skill that is at least somewhat outside the realm of the ordinary, the predictable, or the conventional. A capacity to reject other people's projections of guilt onto me. I can feel guilty – but only when I have fallen short of my own guiding principles, not anyone else's.

What happens if I actively misdirect this energy? I accept a "job description" that has no personal, evolutionary meaning for me. My resentment of this situation eventually boils over, taking the form of a "criminal" rebellion against my existing responsibilities.

How do I look if I descend into a dissociative state? Like a drone. Like someone who has volunteered for a life of slavery. Like a bored bureaucrat going through the motions, with "only seventeen more years until retirement . . ."

URANUS IN LIBRA

What qualities, above all, does it take for me to find my own right path in life? A capacity to choose my own friends, lovers, or partner in a spirit of complete, radical autonomy. I cultivate a humbling sensitivity toward the extent to which we are all, myself included, trained to choose our intimate connections from a narrow range of "appropriate" or "natural" possibilities. I recognize that some of my most pivotal partnerships will arise outside of that conventional, "approved" context – and that these relationships themselves are likely to unfold in unusual ways.

What tools has the universe given me? A fascination with people from walks of life other than my own. An ability to get along with people who are different from me. An instinctive tolerance for human diversity, even an appreciation of it. Skills as a negotiator, even as a peacemaker.

What happens if I actively misdirect this energy? I develop a chronic pattern of entering into relationships with people who are simply not right for me, even though by all conventional standards they appear to be right. As these relationships fail, I repeat the same mistake with someone new. Eventually I become numbed to love by these sequential accumulated heartbreaks.

How do I look if I descend into a dissociative state? On the surface, I look open and inviting. I have mastered the "mechanics" of how to get others to interpret me as an attractive, appealing "normal" person. But at second glance, or third, there is an aloof, unavailable quality to me. That quality is simply the outer perimeter of the ring of defenses around my broken, lonely, isolated heart.

URANUS IN SCORPIO

What qualities, above all, does it take for me to find my own right path in life? An intense commitment to being unfailingly honest with myself. Sometimes, when I ask myself what I really want, the answer frightens me. I need to face that fear, and to realize its true nature: it is not a fear of my own soul, but rather a fear of other people's judgments of me that would arise were I to follow its dictates. I then resolve to follow them no matter what. I am all about truth in this life.

What tools has the universe given me? The ability to think and feel anything. A wide open channel between my conscious mind and my instincts, my unconscious, and my soul. A capacity to retain my emotional balance in the face of life's more extreme experiences. A capacity to respond to high-drama realities – death, sex, disease, madness – in independent ways, free of the usual social script.

What happens if I actively misdirect this energy? I become a psychological loose cannon. I spew insights – sometimes even accurate, valid ones – in every direction, without any mitigating awareness of other people's readiness to hear them. My impulse control, especially around instinctual matters – sexual desire, for one example – becomes weak. I misbehave, hurting myself and probably hurting other people too.

How do I look if I descend into a dissociative state? Depressed, bitter, and moody. I seem enigmatic, hard for other people to read, having resigned myself to a state of isolation. I have surrendered hopelessly to loneliness, and to accepting that I will never feel truly known or understood.

URANUS IN SAGITTARIUS

What qualities, above all, does it take for me to find my own right path in life? A kind of wise perspective on the urgency of finding some overriding purpose in life – an urgency which starts with the realization that life is short and that death is the only certainty. Such a perspective leads quickly to the understanding that the usual human preoccupations – making money, losing weight, establishing status and respectability – are laughably meaningless in the long run. The only thing that ultimately matters to me is my quest for the meaning of life. I resolve to live that way. A willingness arises at some point for me to undertake a literal wild quest, leaving my comfort zone and exposing myself to whatever lies beyond the far horizon.

What tools has the universe given me? An innate faith that there is in fact genuine meaning in life – and a balancing suspicion of numbingly "religious" answers. I can think for myself. I can cross the mental boundaries that separate cultures from cultures. I am a good traveler in every sense of the word. I am not afraid to roll the existential dice.

What happens if I actively misdirect this energy? I pontificate. I am psychologically driven in ways I do not understand to oppose whatever beliefs anyone presents to me. My desire to be "right" has become confounded with the need to make sure that everyone else is wrong. I feel alienated from my own culture – and equally alienated in every other one.

How do I look if I descend into a dissociative state? Bored out of my skull and resigned to that state as if it were an inevitable condition of human existence. I recite, without the slightest passion, the "holy writs" of whatever religion I have espoused, be it Methodism, science, conservative or liberal politics, complaints about the young, complaints about the old – whatever the "holy writ" might be. The only ones more bored than myself are the ones with the misfortune of having to listen to me.

URANUS IN CAPRICORN

What qualities, above all, does it take for me to find my own right path in life?
Absolute and total freedom of imagination as I determine which mountain
I choose to climb in this lifetime. Immunity to consensual and social definitions of success. A willingness to devote myself to some great work that
resonates with my soul, even if no one else cares about it at all.

What tools has the universe given me? A high degree of auto-referential
self-sufficiency; a relative lack of the need for other people's approval. A
capacity to work alone. An ability to recognize plausible, potentially fruitful, calculated risks that no one has ever recognized before. The instincts of
a gambler who has carefully computed the odds; and *within that context*, a
tolerance for risk.

What happens if I actively misdirect this energy? I become a trusted "key
man or key woman" in some enterprise which has no personal meaning
for me at all. I am "good at something" about which I simply do not care.
My compelling instinct to do the right thing is in constant tension with
an urge to blow everything up and start all over again. Which one of those
urges wins is a toss-up; in the end, both of them are losses.

How do I look if I descend into a dissociative state? Dutiful. Decent, but
distant and rather dull. Longsuffering. Normalcy punctuated with quirkish-
ness. A stranger – even to those with whom I am ostensibly sharing my life.

URANUS IN AQUARIUS

*What qualities, above all, does it take for me to find my own right path in
life?* A radical willingness to be myself. Freedom from the pitiful need to
grovel and writhe for the approval of other people. The recognition that
I have more to do with the human future than with the past or even the
present. Uranus rules this sign, so its fundamental energies of innovation,
free-thinking, and independence are strong here, resonating through every
category of my existence.

What tools has the universe given me? The ability to look at what everybody else is seeing and to see possibilities in it that no one has ever
seen before. The ability to question the assumptions which other people
have made, typically without even being aware that they have made them.
Innovation; a certain genius, at least in the broad sense of the word. The

capacity to shrug my shoulders and walk away if other people disapprove of me, judge me, or feel the need to "fix" me.

What happens if I actively misdirect this energy? I become reflexively rebellious, simply doing the opposite of whatever is expected of me and mythologizing that contrariness as "true individuality." I resist good advice and helpful education; I therefore run the risk of "reinventing the wheel." Unless I am shocking or dismaying other people, I do not feel that I exist at all.

How do I look if I descend into a dissociative state? Cold. Aloof. Detached. Unemotional. Unavailable. Discontent in a vague, distant, and ill-defined sort of way.

URANUS IN PISCES

What qualities, above all, does it take for me to find my own right path in life? It has been said that religion is the study of other people's spiritual experiences, while spirituality is about one's own direct experiences. I need "spiritual experience" in that direct sense, and I resolve to act accordingly. These experiences must be mine alone – something I have encountered and interpreted in my own way, even if others think I am quirkish or even mad. My methods for getting closer to the Great Mystery are no one's business except my own. In this materialistic, existentialist society, to be a consciously and intentionally spiritual person requires a willingness to look weird to a lot of people. I embrace that path without fear, self-consciousness, or any need to apologize, justify, or explain my spiritual path to anyone.

What tools has the universe given me? Lightning bolts of inexplicable, undeniable mystical experience strike me from time to time. They are pure grace; there is nothing I need to do except exist in order for them to happen. I was born with an ability to accept the intrusion of such trans-rational realities into my life. I resolve to use this tool in a spirit of faith and, above all, of gratitude.

What happens if I actively misdirect this energy? I become attached to extreme psychic states, forgetting that the true heart of spirituality lies in a conscious experience of the ordinary mind in everyday life. I become excitable. If I misdirect my energy, I sacrifice my mental balance in pursuit of mystical fireworks, mistaking them for evidence of my evolution.

How do I look if I descend into a dissociative state? Spaced out, lost in the fog, forgetful, absent-minded – these conditions, while they are more "misdemeanors" than "felonies," actually reflect a frightened urge in me to distance myself from my own sensitivity. Perhaps I become lost in mere fantasy. Perhaps I rebel against the normal adult requirements of life, and instead take refuge in some form of escapism.

12

MERCURY IN THE TWELVE HOUSES

MERCURY IN THE FIRST HOUSE

What actual behaviors expose me to what I really need to learn – and thus help me to find my true voice? Making bold, independent statements, so long as I truly believe them – even statements which might appear to be selfish, presumptuous, or rebellious. Displaying receptivity to intellectual risk. Openness to challenging existing authorities or customs. Taking charge of my own thoughts. Standing up for myself verbally. Opening my mouth and seeing what comes out. Writing. Speaking on the spot in front of an audience. Being willing to lead and to teach.

What is my greatest cognitive strength? The courage and confidence simply to try things out. Innovation. A willingness to be "the first one to say it." The capacity to lead – and thus to attract the helpful energies and ideas of followers. How to learn by teaching. Improvisation; confidence that I can successfully "make it up as I go along." A good ability to express myself in writing.

How does the universe correct me? By giving me a lot of latitude to make interesting, instructive mistakes. By tricking me into opening my mouth before my thoughts are fully baked. By making me listen to my own lectures.

How might I defend myself against growth and learning? By needing to be right all the time. By becoming too enamored of the role of leader or expert – and thus believing flattering delusions which other people hold about me. By mistaking charisma and authority in myself for actual wisdom.

MERCURY IN THE SECOND HOUSE

What actual behaviors expose me to what I really need to learn – and thus help me to find my true voice? Committing to learning things that I am afraid might be too hard for me to learn. Building a foundation of concrete skills and knowledge that lend me a real basis for self-confidence; that might mean mastering tools, techniques, and vocabulary. Proving my own intellectual legitimacy to myself, perhaps by gaining credentials or academic certification. Systematically building the skills, resources, and alliances that empower me with a genuine foundation for self-confidence – qualities which attract people who can help me because they see that I can also help them.

What is my greatest cognitive strength? The potential for dogged intellectual persistence over time. Through sheer determination, I can gain access to the full power of my intelligence. An ability to assess resource-bases, strengthening them where they need to be strengthened, and recognizing their potential weaknesses. Good financial instincts. An ability to assess where talents lie in other people.

How does the universe correct me? It spotlights errors and failures whose origin lie in my under-extending myself, or in excessive hesitation or caution. My painful therapy is to think back on my life in a spirit of analytic honesty, looking for the opportunities that I missed, but should have taken.

How might I defend myself against growth and learning? Endless preparation can be a trick I play on myself in order to avoid actually diving into a subject or an endeavor. Crippling self-doubt which leads to my "not even trying." Failure to acquire the skills and assets which are necessary for my evolutionary work.

MERCURY IN THE THIRD HOUSE

What actual behaviors expose me to what I really need to learn – and thus help me to find my true voice? Exposing myself to educational opportunities is a good start, but there is so much to learn that I need more focused guidance than that. On exactly what should I focus my learning efforts? For me, the guiding star is to trust my curiosity. I go where it leads me; it is wiser than me. As I gain experience, especially experience that surprises me and stretches my horizons, my natural voice arises. That voice is spontaneous, engaging, and clear, and it conveys to people not only information, but also childlike enthusiasm for the information.

What is my greatest cognitive strength? A willingness to be surprised. A willingness to entertain perspectives that I had never before considered, even ones regarding which I might feel resistance. A natural ability to teach. Natural ability as a story-teller; a sense of the enchantment of language. An elevated capacity to translate experience into vocabulary, syntax, and grammar. An ability to explain things clearly. Eloquence and articulation.

How does the universe correct me? By presenting me with cognitive dissonance – things that do not "make sense" because the facts and perspectives run contrary to my blinding assumptions. This cognitive dissonance might arise from books, articles, and conversations which I encounter "by chance." These unexpected synchronicities are my correcting guides, if I can let myself take in their messages.

How might I defend myself against growth and learning? By using language as a wall rather than as a bridge. Simply talking too much, and never letting the other person get a word in – or simply by not listening. Rationalizing. Slippery avoidance through distraction, subject changes, or deflecting subjects through the use of my humor and wit. Giving too much power to my "inner crooked lawyer."

MERCURY IN THE FOURTH HOUSE

What actual behaviors expose me to what I really need to learn – and thus help me to find my true voice? My single most powerful evolutionary tool here lies in my powerful capacity for psychological analysis, both of myself and of others. As I fearlessly explore my own mind in a spirit of openness and curiosity, I discover what I need to know in order to empower and activate my true voice. In second place, and not very far behind, is everything I learn from being attentive to the psychodynamics of my own family, however I might define "family." I resolve to learn about its myths and assumptions – and I prepare myself to be startled by the clarity of the mirror they hold before my own existential assumptions.

What is my greatest cognitive strength? An elevated capacity to understand how the underlying emotions, wounds, and archetypes arising in everyone's unconscious minds shape their unwitting conscious personalities. This strength applies to my own self-analysis, but equally it indicates a powerful ability to understand what makes other people tick. I do not necessarily need to become a psychologist, but it is fair to say that I have the mind of a psychologist.

How does the universe correct me? By poking at me from my unconscious mind; nagging intuitions sneak up on me, giving me a bad feeling about something I may have already decided, but would be wise to reconsider. This correction, if I learn to heed it, can give me almost supernatural wisdom. I am learning to take advantage of the fact that my actual consciousness is much vaster than my normal conscious mind. Cooperation with that larger self is what best corrects me.

How might I defend myself against growth and learning? By withdrawing into my interior world, becoming so subjective that I defend myself against any objective learning or useful external guidance. I can dive so deeply into myself that I close my mind – and my ears – to all counsel. Because of my psychological sensitivity to family dynamics, I could fall into the trap of living the life that my family trained me to live – which may have very little to do with my own natural path.

MERCURY IN THE FIFTH HOUSE

What actual behaviors expose me to what I really need to learn – and thus help me to find my true voice? Above all, my path revolves around creative self-expression. Sometimes I just need to open my mouth and see what comes out. Whether or not I know it, I am energized by an audience – and if I do not know that, I can soon learn it by stepping out onto the stage. I need to speak up. I need to polish my skills of presentation. Writing is good for me; so is storytelling – even telling a joke. Unless I am willing to feel vulnerable in front of others, I will never find my true voice. That audience might be one person or it might fill a theater; it works either way.

What is my greatest cognitive strength? The ability to create vivid metaphors, images, and figures of speech – devices which not only skillfully convey information to other people, but also beguile them into listening, identifying with me, even agreeing with me. The ability to simply enjoy a conversation, and to have that joy be contagious – soon others are enjoying it too, opening up, and revealing themselves.

How does the universe correct me? By getting me to just "put it out there," right or wrong, ugly or beautiful. Perhaps I bluster or rant in ways that vividly reveal my own mistaken ideas. Perhaps people laugh at me or treat me dismissively – and in some cases, that is useful feedback. If I am deathly afraid of ever making a fool of myself, I will learn very little in this lifetime.

How might I defend myself against growth and learning? I can grandstand effectively and thus shut down other people's contrary views or opinions – views or opinions which might actually be very useful for me to hear, were I only to listen to them. I can distract myself from everything important in life via an addiction to trivial amusements. I can "sell ice to Eskimos;" I can defend dumb ideas and win – but is that really winning and what is the prize?

MERCURY IN THE SIXTH HOUSE

What actual behaviors expose me to what I really need to learn – and thus help me to find my true voice? Above all, in order to find my true voice, I must sit at the feet of masters – people who have already found their own voices, and the well of wisdom underlying those voices. In this lifetime, it is fundamental to my spiritual health that I seek mentors. I recognize them by the authenticity and beguiling power of their language. More importantly, I sense that their voices are linked directly to their souls. I humbly discipline myself to absorb these teachings; I recognize that it is my destiny to carry the flame of this teaching forward into future generations. That is how I thank my mentors.

What is my greatest cognitive strength? I have an uncanny ability to absorb knowledge and wisdom directly from people who have already attained them. I have the "receptor cells" for direct transmission from those who are more evolved than myself. I can discipline myself to learn; I keep my eye on the prize: the ultimate purpose of this learning lies in serving those who will eventually receive these teachings from me. My mind is orderly; I have an elevated ability to make sense of complexity and to organize it cogently. My skills grow exponentially when faced with genuine need in another person; I can rise to the occasion, and be more helpful than I might have imagined.

How does the universe correct me? By arranging for me to be in the presence of those who are more evolved than myself. This is a powerful method, but it is tough on my poor ego. Therefore, in order to withstand these corrections, I must concentrate on loving myself. I should never judge myself – intellectually or in any other way – in comparison to my teachers; I should only judge myself by the standard of the intensity of my effort. The universe also helps me by arranging for me to be in the presence of those whose needs are pressing and genuine. My skills rise to such challenges.

How might I defend myself against growth and learning? Above all, I can stymie my evolution by failing to recognize those guides and teachers with whom life presents me. Arrogance – or thinly disguised insecurity masquerading as arrogance – can insulate me from these effective triggers for my own growth. If I slip into the grips of my own dark side, I can value being seen as an expert more than the humble process of actually becoming one.

MERCURY IN THE SEVENTH HOUSE

What actual behaviors expose me to what I really need to learn – and thus help me to find my true voice? I need to learn who to trust and how to trust. Most of what I need to learn in this life, I learn from other people. I must spontaneously express myself to them and learn to listen carefully and attentively to their responses. Those who are worthy of my trust are generally verbal people, curious about life, and eager to compare notes about it. They enjoy conversation. They are quick. They are not preoccupied with "trying to be my teachers;" the flow between us is more balanced and natural than that. But they do have a lot to teach me. One sure sign that I have actually found such people is that I will sometimes remember the exact words they said. Their words, which might've been simple at the time, somehow sunk into me like a stone. Those words will then work like the kernel of an idea around which a great body of wisdom coalesces – and out of the wisdom, my true voice arises.

What is my greatest cognitive strength? The ability to truly listen; a genuine fascination with the minds of certain people with whom I recognize a special cognitive rapport. The ability, through animated conversation, to co-create insights I could never generate alone. I have an ear for dialogue; I have an ear for language – and by that, I do not simply mean foreign languages, although I do have the ability to learn them. What I mean is the ability to really understand another person, to let their wisdom enter me, and *vice versa*.

How does the universe correct me? By sending me trusted people who hold the mirror of truth before me. They catch me in my contradictions and my rationalizations, and they typically accomplish that supportive aim in a spirit of respect, even of friendship. I am beguiled into spontaneous dialogue. As such conversations unfold, my errors are revealed – and very typically so are better answers.

How might I defend myself against growth and learning? By avoiding friendships with people who have anything important to say. By squandering my time in pointless chit chat. By using humor and wit as a way of avoiding authentic mental chemistry. By talking too much and not listening enough. By wasting my time with childish human beings.

MERCURY IN THE EIGHTH HOUSE

What actual behaviors expose me to what I really need to learn – and thus help me to find my true voice? Above all, the behavior that best triggers wisdom in me lies in my willingness to initiate difficult conversations. There are many subjects so charged with strong emotions that they are functionally taboo in human society. Illustrations of those subjects are death, sexuality, aging, and disease, although there are many others. Some are more purely personal. Synchronicity guarantees that I will be presented in this lifetime with a few people who are capable of entering into deep dialogue with me in these kinds of areas. I need to seek them out and, with their help and support, cross these lines of verbal taboo. These are my comrades on the path. One of the greatest gifts I could offer myself in this lifetime is a life-partnership with such a person – one with whom I can talk about anything, one with whom the only taboos are silence and avoidance.

What is my greatest cognitive strength? An ability to steady my mind in the face of strong emotional stimulus. I can look penetratingly at difficult subjects. With the right people, I can also discuss them in a spirit of honesty, directness, and shared mutual vulnerability. I think like a psychoanalyst – or perhaps like a police detective. I have a strong stomach for hard truths. It is difficult for anyone to lie to me; I see through them.

How does the universe correct me? When I am avoiding some unpleasant truth, many signs and omens arise, seemingly doing their best to help me face what I must face. These signs and omens often come in the form of conversations with intimate friends who say things that are meaningful to me in ways that the friends probably do not themselves understand. Just as commonly, these signs and omens might take the form of "books falling off shelves, open to the exact page I need to read." It can get spooky, in other words. It is helpful for me to recognize that, contrary to what I might've learned in high school, this is how the universe actually operates.

How might I defend myself against growth and learning? Much of my learning in this lifetime is connected with evolution that takes place specifically in my emotional body. Feelings typically arise before insights. I can avoid growth through the device of escaping these emotions by living in my head – intellectualizing, arguing, rationalizing. Just imagine someone with a brilliant PhD in psychology who is still actually as crazy as a soup sandwich: there, in a nutshell, is my Shadow.

MERCURY IN THE NINTH HOUSE

What actual behaviors expose me to what I really need to learn – and thus help me to find my true voice? Cross-cultural experience is a pivotal trigger for what I need to learn in this lifetime. Underlying that statement is the realization that I have been blinded by some of the assumptions of my own culture and upbringing. To find my true voice, I must get past that particular myopia. Going further, great minds throughout history have wrestled with life's knottiest questions. Their insights are available in books, via educational experiences, and above all in living lineages – I can, in other words, study with their students, or their students' students. If I do all that and absorb these teachings, I will find the basis for my true voice. These boundary-stretching experiences are the yeast in my bread.

What is my greatest cognitive strength? An ability to recognize patterns. An ability to connect the dots and draw generalizable conclusions. An ability to think in terms of first principles – morals, ethics, metaphysical bedrock. A mind-expanding ability to place myself in cross-cultural frameworks – there are problems a Chinese person might solve more quickly than a French person, and *vice versa*. With cross-cultural experience, I can find both of these people in my own head and make allies of them.

How does the universe correct me? By confronting me with questions that I cannot answer, at least not without questioning my own assumptions. Sometimes I "connect the dots" without realizing that there are other dots that I have ignored. Those "dots" then present themselves to me as loose ends and cognitive dissonance. As I pay attention to that errant data rather than defending my previous position, I allow myself to be corrected.

How might I defend myself against growth and learning? I can play the role of teacher in order to avoid learning; I can preach rather than humbling myself before those whose wisdom is beyond my own. I can perceive new, helpful, and necessary information as heresy against which I must defend my faith. I can place too much value on being right, to the point that I become impervious to actual evolution.

MERCURY IN THE TENTH HOUSE

What actual behaviors expose me to what I really need to learn – and thus help me to find my true voice? My highest mission in this world is to become a pipeline of information into the community – a "teacher," in some sense of the word, although that can take many different forms: novelist, journalist, media work – or simply someone whose voice is heard somehow in the community. As I step up to the plate and make sure that people *whom I do not know personally* are being impacted by my thoughts and my ideas, I gain the confidence, authority, and style that support the development of my true voice. My evolutionary trajectory begins with my being some kind of student and evolves into one in which the fruits of my own mind have nourished the minds of many other people.

What is my greatest cognitive strength? I have an almost supernatural sense of what my community needs to hear. Simultaneously I have a good instinct for how I need to phrase it in order that the message be received clearly – even if it is unexpected or unwelcome. More than most people, I understand how the world works, and how there is nothing more powerful than an idea whose time has come. I can bring such ideas before my community.

How does the universe correct me? Everything I misunderstand and misinterpret will be revealed in my public behavior. When I am wrong, I will speak up, imagining that I am right. There will be no way for me to keep my errors secret. If I persist in them, everyone will know it. The universe allows everyone a certain quotient of secrets; I am allowed fewer of them than most people.

How might I defend myself against growth and learning? I can become very skillful at a profession or some other public role that has no personal meaning for me at all. Perhaps this role garners me respect and stability, even a reputation as a great authority. This is a soul-cage in which I could be trapped, stymieing my evolution.

MERCURY IN THE ELEVENTH HOUSE

What actual behaviors expose me to what I really need to learn – and thus help me to find my true voice? First and foremost, I must devote myself *long-term* to the process of finding my voice. I realize that it is a step-by-step process, unfolding over decades – endlessly, really. I must approach the effort strategically: seeking education or experience of writing and public speaking – knowing that such skills gather momentum over time. I accept the fact that my voice will be heard most widely only in the second half of my journey. I seek association with people who are intelligent and interested in life, willing to learn and to grow in their understanding. Perhaps I meet them in classes or while attending lectures – these natural associates and allies are the kinds of people who would be drawn to such situations.

What is my greatest cognitive strength? I have a good ability to think strategically. I know how to set priorities and how to frame long-term plans for achieving them. I know which battles must be won and which ones can be sacrificed. If we define "politics" as what happens whenever more than three or four people are engaged in the same project, then I have a great strength when it comes to understanding politics. I can negotiate; I can bring people together with my words. I can speak for a group; I can also teach a group about their own internal dynamics.

How does the universe correct me? When I feel flummoxed, as if I have lost my track in life, often the problem lies in my tendency to let other people and the social obligations they create to distract me from my true priorities. In that situation, I find myself busy – and yet I am accomplishing nothing of actual importance. If I notice that uncomfortable reality and make the necessary adjustments to address the problem, the universe, via that feedback, has corrected me.

How might I defend myself against growth and learning? There was a time when everyone agreed that the earth was flat. That belief was prevalent despite great evidence to the contrary. This illustrates the deadening power of collective belief-systems and their ability to control, blind, and seduce the "herd animal" inside all of us. I can cripple my own evolutionary journey by not thinking for myself, instead succumbing to the perspective foisted upon me by the social world around me.

MERCURY IN THE TWELFTH HOUSE

What actual behaviors expose me to what I really need to learn – and thus help me to find my true voice? Above all, I benefit from deeper forms of mind-training. Some of that can be understood as meditation practice. While meditation itself helps, I also need teachers and teachings who correct and improve my understanding of the true nature of the mind. Reading metaphysics is good for me. My understanding of life, consciousness, and the universe is being elevated. There is, in other words, a significant intellectual or cognitive component to my spiritual evolution in this lifetime. Words cannot encompass these ultimate mysteries – but for me, certain words and teachings work as magical catalysts, accelerating my growth dramatically. As that process unfolds and my understanding deepens, the archetype of the spiritual teacher begins to crystallize in me. That archetype is the heart of my true voice.

What is my greatest cognitive strength? We are all acclimated to a three-dimensional "common sense" perception of the universe, but our consciousness actually exists in a far more multidimensional framework. Mystics have always said that; for the last century, the physicists have been in agreement. Intuitively, I grasp this mystery. I have an understanding of the vast psychic realms which lie beyond the narrow boundaries of what other people might call "the obvious facts." I can extend the field of my perceptions beyond the obvious framework of everyday reality.

How does the universe correct me? In the course of this lifetime, I will have many uncanny, inexplicable experiences – things that I just know without having any idea how I know them. Some of these experiences may be shocking or unpleasant, while others are simply impossible to explain. Seeing a ghost would be an example. So would dreaming of someone I haven't seen in years and then running into them the next day. So would knowing in advance about someone's death. Whenever I begin to succumb to "common sense" – which is to say the collective mis-definition of reality – I will receive perceptual corrections of this surprising and very psychic nature.

How might I defend myself against growth and learning? Ultimately the deepest mysteries of the universe can only be witnessed, never understood. When I begin to believe my own sermons, as if I had everything figured out, I become stuck in my own delusional certainties. I have the ability to do the sacred work of a spiritual teacher. I should not turn away from that responsibility toward other humans – but when I teach, I must resolve to be vigilant about those "delusional certainties." Whatever I understand, the truth is always beyond that.

13

VENUS IN
THE TWELVE HOUSES

In the following thumbnail descriptions of the meaning of Venus in each of the astrological houses, I often use the term "soul-partners." Obviously enough, the words convey notions of romance, sexuality, and variations on the theme of marriage. Yes indeed – all of that is a big part of what we are talking about here, maybe even the most central part.

But let's not forget how priceless our deepest friendships can be, or the sweetness of family relationships when they travel down good roads. Those people are "soul-partners" too, and as precious in their own ways as those brave, lucky souls with whom we might share a bed.

VENUS IN THE FIRST HOUSE

For love to thrive, I must behave . . . forthrightly. I am developing the ability to be direct, assertive, and independent. I am learning that I naturally possess "half the rights" in any relationship. Love involves compromise; I know that. But it does not mean kowtowing to anyone. In intimacy, I have a right to say yes – and I have a right to say no. I accept that attending to my personal style and my physical appearance are actually spiritual issues for me. I must carefully scrutinize any unnatural exaggerations – or self-diminishments – in those areas.

Where will I meet my soul-partners? I find them when I am not actually looking for them, but instead when I am simply intent upon following my own whimsies and interests. Bold, unilateral actions of any sort on my part – especially ones consistent with the higher intentions of the astrological sign of my Venus – often lead me to unexpected, evolution-triggering human encounters.

How might I recognize them? They are people who seem to know what they are doing, going about life with the appearance of self-confidence and active, positive engagement. They have created meaningful lives for themselves, effectively defending their autonomy. Their behavior reflects a particularly vivid expression of the nature of my Venus sign.

What actions must I avoid or at least not over-do? I need to be careful of assuming too much control over another person's life, even if my motives are benign. Selfishness – real or perceived – is a danger. Learning to listen carefully, along with forging choices jointly, is more helpful than my simply grabbing the steering wheel.

VENUS IN THE SECOND HOUSE

For love to thrive, I must behave . . . with self-confidence and a sense of my own self-worth. Without descending into arrogance, I need to remind myself that people are fortunate to have me in their lives. I need to invest in my own attractiveness. A new hairdo or wardrobe? Could be – such outward advances in confidence can reflect inward ones. But I must take the word "attractiveness" more widely than that. I am developing the ability to not underestimate my value as a partner – and thus risk settling for someone who is not on my own evolutionary level.

Where will I meet my soul-partners? If I pay close attention, I will see that there is an underlying pattern here: I tend to meet people who are important to me when I am doing something that feels like a personal stretch – betting on myself, taking a chance, in other words, acting as if I truly believe in myself. Bold, even personally scary, actions of any sort on my part, especially ones consistent with the sign of my Venus, often lead to soul-triggering human encounters. In more mundane terms, there is an underscored pattern of meeting people while I am doing anything related to money – that is almost a "fortune-telling" statement, but it often works.

How might I recognize them? Quite possibly, you will meet these people when they are facing some difficulty or challenge, when their self-confidence is under pressure. Their own behavior might reflect a particularly uncertain or tentative expression of the nature of my Venus sign – or perhaps a particularly impressive or accomplished one.

What actions must I avoid or at least not over-do? Generosity is a wonderful, natural expression of affection, but I need to be wary of hiding behind it. Famously, no one can buy love – and that notion goes way beyond money. One can try to "buy love" with supportive actions, compliments, and so on. At some point, I must stand naked and let myself be loved for my soul alone – or be rejected, and thus be free to look elsewhere for the real thing.

VENUS IN THE THIRD HOUSE

For love to thrive, I must behave . . . in a verbally revealing, self-expressive way. If I don't speak up and express myself authentically from my heart, no one will know who I am. How could they? I need to trust my curiosity and follow it down any paths of interest which reveal themselves to me, especially if those particular interests involve art, aesthetics, or the exploration of intimacy. This next point might not sound very sexy, but it works: I am developing the ability to be an active, engaged partner in a process of endless learning. Ask any truly sophisticated person: can we imagine any hope for long-term passion in the absence of meaningful, engaging conversation? Communication is one of love's highest arts. I will master it.

Where will I meet my soul-partners? Specifically, I might meet them while, for example, I am attending classes or lectures. Or in a bookstore. To say it more broadly, I am more likely to encounter these people when I am pursuing mental interests that arise naturally in me. Being out there in the great schoolhouse of the world, trusting my whimsies and my curiosity to guide me – those behaviors come naturally to me. But they also have the side effect of placing me in the orbits of the people with whom I have spiritual business. Educational aspirations on my part, especially ones consistent with the sign of my Venus, often lead to life-triggering human encounters.

How might I recognize them? My natural soul-partners show every indication of simply being interested in life. They read. They learn for the sake of learning. Fresh ideas excite them. They are actively engaged with the world. When I first encounter such people, there is an excellent chance that they simply look busy. Conversation is likely to arise quickly and spontaneously between us. "We were strangers, but we just started talking . . ."

What actions must I avoid or at least not over-do? In conversation, silences allow another person space to reflect and then speak – I must never forget that. It is important that I reveal myself verbally – but it is equally important that I support the other person in a parallel process of self-revelation. I need to remember that some of the deepest forms of communication between souls do not involve words or language at all.

VENUS IN THE FOURTH HOUSE

For love to thrive, I must behave . . . in a way that reflects the kind of person I actually am, which is to say that I am deep and rather psychological by nature. I take intimacy seriously and I understand that when it is real – and real is the only way I want it – both people must take the step-by-step risk of gradually becoming more vulnerable over time. Trust takes time. For that reason, it is only right that we are patient and gentle with each other. We let things unfold at their own pace, without any unnatural rush. I am developing the ability to be a lifelong partner, not a person whose life is a series of brief, passionate encounters, punctuated with heartbreak.

Where will I meet my soul-partners? In quiet places, places where people can relax, communicate deeply, and open up their sensitivities. I might meet these people through family – or through the kinds of friends who feel like family to me. Actions involving home or land, especially ones consistent with the sign of my Venus, often lead to life-triggering human encounters. Illustration: with Venus in Sagittarius, I might meet someone while visiting my ancestral homeland. With Venus in Taurus, such encounters might occur in the countryside, on a farm, or near animals.

How might I recognize them? My soul-partners stand out as pensive, reflective people. They do not put themselves forward loudly, theatrically, or aggressively. They do not seem to be in a hurry to connect with me or anyone else. Sexually they are not in a rush. That does not mean that they seem cold or remote – only patient and perhaps a bit cautious. Their outward behavior reflects a particularly interior or psychological expression of the nature of my Venus sign – for example, if my Venus is in Gemini, these soul-friends might bond with me by talking about the books or films that had the deepest emotional impact on them.

What actions must I avoid or at least not over-do? I do need to make myself emotionally available to people. There is an uncomfortable law of the universe which I must learn to accept: *we all date a lot more people than we marry.* There is eternally a risky dance that people must do when they feel attracted to each other. It is a dance of discovery. Some have called it dating, some have called it courtship. I need to embrace those dance steps. Without putting myself out there and taking that risk, no one will even know that I am here or what treasures I have to offer.

VENUS IN THE FIFTH HOUSE

For love to thrive, I must behave . . . in revealing, colorful ways. I am not afraid to command attention or to take up some space. I act accordingly, even dress accordingly, when I feel like it – not that I "always" feel like it. (I can be quiet too.) Bottom line, I am developing the ability to be spontaneous in my self-expression, comfortable in my body, and confident of my sexuality.

Where will I meet my soul-partners? When I am pursuing my own creativity, doing whatever it takes to feed it, I am likely to meet kindred spirits. Maybe I will meet them in a theater group. Perhaps I encounter them in a club where I have gone to listen to some music. Perhaps I encounter them at art galleries or theaters. Performance-oriented actions of any sort on my part, often lead to life-triggering human encounters – and my "performance" might be as simple as my boldly donning a rakish scarf or sexy jeans. The point is that all the world is a stage, and as I bravely step out on it, I meet the souls I need to meet.

How might I recognize them? That will be easy – they are not hiding. Likely when I first lay eyes on them, they themselves are "performing" somehow – holding forth colorfully, maybe telling a joke or embellishing a tale to everyone's delight. Just possibly, they would actually be on stage in some more literal way. I might even find these soul-friends a bit intimidating or over-the-top at first, but I cannot let that perception daunt me. Their behavior reflects a particularly theatrical expression of the nature of my Venus sign – if it is Scorpio, they are sexy. If it is Gemini, they are witty and good with words. Likely, they seem more extroverted at first than I later find them to be. Performers often look like extroverts, but they aren't quite the same thing.

What actions must I avoid or at least not over-do? Everyone has characteristics which are simply boring, prototypical, predictable – and about as sexy as a dishrag. Sooner or later, in every intimate relationship, those dull dimensions of our humanity must be revealed. When people discover that kind of thing about me, I need to be careful not to let that revelation make me feel insecure or unlovable. All the world might be a stage – but sometimes we all need to take off our brilliant costumes.

VENUS IN THE SIXTH HOUSE

For love to thrive, I must behave . . . in competent, skillful, grown-up ways. There is a craft to making love work. Humans have been trying to relate to each other for millennia. Over those years, our ancestors have learned a trick or two. Much of this boils down to all the familiar "chicken soup" wisdom about marriage, gender, and sexuality. I need those skills. Therefore, I benefit from paying attention to older people in my life – my "aunts and uncles," so to speak. There is much that I can learn from them, both from their wisdom and probably from their mistakes too. I am developing the ability to be humble enough to learn how to love. That process begins as I admit my befuddlement and confusion. This is how I develop the skills and the competence to make my relationships work.

Where will I meet my soul-partners? Circumstantially, I might very well make these soul connections at work or in any other situation in which I have duties and responsibilities. Another strong possibility is that I encounter these people "by chance" when I am actively seeking the guidance of mentors – teachers, role models, even spiritual masters. As I seek such teaching and guidance, I also experience life-triggering human encounters.

How might I recognize soul-partners? They radiate a grounded quality of competence. They impress me with their simple effectiveness whatever they are doing. They are humble and unpretentious, without being obsequious or self-effacing. Regardless of their age, I sense a quality of maturity in them. Their behavior reflects helpfulness, supportiveness, and skill.

What actions must I avoid or at least not over-do? While I am always eager to be helpful and supportive of anyone I love, and while that is a virtue, I must be wary of playing a tedious role of endless responsibility and self-sacrifice in my relationships. I will set myself up for being taken for granted. I need to be emotionally available, not just a practical support. Sometimes I might even need to be demanding – if I need grease, I need to be the squeaky wheel.

VENUS IN THE SEVENTH HOUSE

For love to thrive, I must behave . . . in wide-open, fully invested, undefended ways. I must take the risk of true commitment, putting all my eggs in one basket. For this step to be safe – for it not to be an act of absolute madness, in other words – I need to develop a deeply discriminating instinct for the true, three-dimensional reality of other human beings. I must learn to think like a psychologist, or like a novelist who is terrific with characters. I must withdraw my romantic projections and resolve to see the other person clearly before I commit to the perilous path of ultimate trust. I am developing the ability to find the balance between true romance and clear-eyed perception of another person's actual evolutionary condition.

Where will I meet my soul-partners? The bottom line is that these people will find me rather than the other way around. Learning *who to trust* and *how to trust* is a major piece of my evolutionary work in this lifetime; therefore, the laws of synchronicity guarantee that these encounters will happen. I will surely meet true soul partners – and I will equally surely meet people who offer a subtle education in discrimination: the wise art of thinking twice before I trust another person. I may very well meet people in both of these categories through mutual friends. In general, spontaneous actions of human outreach on my part, especially ones consistent with the sign of my Venus, often lead to life-triggering human encounters.

How might I recognize them? My natural soul-partners are people of natural grace. They may tell a dirty joke or sometimes use the famous f-word, but they are never needlessly crude. Many are artists – or at least avid enthusiasts relative to the arts. They have outstanding "people skills," knowing how to get along diplomatically, perhaps even warmly, with human beings who are different from themselves. They probably dress becomingly, knowing, for one simple example, which colors work with their eyes or the tone of their skin. Their behavior reflects their own version of a particularly charming and engaging expression of the nature of my Venus sign – if my Venus is in Cancer, they anticipate my needs in advance. If it is in Capricorn, they know when I need to be left alone.

What actions must I avoid or at least not over-do? Compromise and meeting-in-the-middle are of course absolutely critical skills in maintaining any kind of grown-up partnership. I need to be careful that I do not locate that "middle" too far in the direction of the other person. Behaviorally, I can create the appearance of getting along with people who in fact are not good for me.

VENUS IN THE EIGHTH HOUSE

For love to thrive, I must behave . . . in psychologically courageous ways. I am developing the ability to be a lot more honest – and thus a lot more truly intimate – than most people can ever imagine. Obviously, I cannot do that alone. One behavior I must master is how to assess, as quickly and as painlessly as possible, whether another person is actually brave enough and sane enough to meet me in that same place of soul nakedness. I accept that this kind of love will naturally be difficult sometimes; it is Shadow work, after all. I resolve never to allow myself to punish another person for being truthful, even if I do not like what I am hearing.

Where will I meet my soul-partners? We might first encounter each other "by chance" in circumstances of genuine drama or emotional intensity – the sorts of raw situations where people's "true colors" show: squabbles, accidents, crisis, even deaths. Even if the scene is not so dramatic, we quickly find ourselves talking deeply about something real: sexuality, aging, disease – any of life's emotionally-charged areas. I improve the odds of encountering these soul-partners whenever I willingly undertake any kind of "self-help." In other words, as I face what is blocking me from full self-actualization, I magnetize these kinds of people into my life.

How might I recognize them? There is a certain reflectiveness and intensity around these soul-partners – qualities which I might interpret as moodiness or perhaps even a tendency toward isolation. At the same time, regardless of their physical appearance, there is an ineffable quality of simple sexiness about them. Their behavior and motivations reflect a particularly psychologically-savvy expression of the nature of my Venus sign – were my Venus in Taurus, they might reveal a real psychic bond with their cat or their dog. Were it in Libra, they might have a taste for serious film.

What actions must I avoid or at least not over-do? Genuine intimacy and deep psychological conversation are inseparable concepts for me. That is fine and natural, but I must be careful not to transgress the limits of human tolerance for inner work. Sometimes I need to simply let go of an issue: forgive and forget. Sometimes I need to just give it a break for a few days.

VENUS IN THE NINTH HOUSE

For love to thrive, I must behave . . . in adventurous, expansive, open-minded ways. Life itself is a quest; I am delighted if someone volunteers to share that quest with me – but I never forget to keep perspective: for me, the point is abundant life-experience, and not just intimacy. In fact, in my mind, those two concepts cannot be separated. Zealously I strive to avoid the claustrophobia and predictability that always threatens the vitality of any long-term committed relationship. We learn together; we travel together; we grow together – or it is just not worth the trouble and the sacrifice. I am developing the ability to pack the experiences of many lifetimes into this one lifetime. Love is one of those experiences, but it is only real if it actually enhances and supports the rest of the package.

Where will I meet my soul-partners? I may meet them on the road – literally when I am traveling. They may be foreigners themselves, or at least have their origins in a different part of the country or a different walk of life. I may meet them as I pursue education. I may meet them as I chase down any fresh or novel experience – swimming with the dolphins or spelunking in some cavern full of stalactites. Wild, adventurous, independent actions of any sort on my part, especially ones consistent with the sign of my Venus, often lead to these kinds of life-triggering human encounters.

How might I recognize them? If I can get my hands on their passports, all I have to do is count the stamps. These are adventurous people; their biographies do not lie about any of that. They may or may not be educated in the formal sense, but they are motivated to learn and often surprise me with the eclectic scope of their knowledge. Here is the biggest test: all I need to do is to just inquire about their opinion of the meaning of life. To pass the test, first, they do not look at me as if that were a dumb or even a surprising question. Second, they have thought about it and they have some kind of answer ready. Third – and in many ways foremost – they are also interested in my own answer. Finally, their philosophy of life reflects a particularly robust expression of the nature of my own Venus sign – in Cancer, it's about kindness; in Scorpio, it's about facing reality.

What actions must I avoid or at least not over-do? The quest for love, in principle, is an idealistic one. Naturally, I think about what kind of partner would be perfect for me – but perfection is not something that humans ever actually find in this world. At some point, I must stop searching and I make my stand with other human beings as imperfect as myself.

VENUS IN THE TENTH HOUSE

For love to thrive, I must behave . . . in ways that might be described as ambitious or career-oriented, even if those are not big motivators for me. More accurately, those behaviors can be framed as my sense of having a mission in this world. Words such as "community" and "social responsibility" are relevant as well. There is a kind of dignity and sense of personal empowerment that comes from touching the lives of people with whom I do not have close personal relationships – and from being appreciated for it. That deeper dignity and sense of empowerment plays a critical role in my ability to find love that works, and is worthy of me. No true soul-friend will ever ask me to choose between love and my mission. Anyone who asks that question has no idea who I am.

Where will I meet my soul-partners? The answer may be as simple as my meeting them at work. Equally, we might encounter each other in some public forum – on a political campaign, as members of the Parent Teacher Organization, or protesting against fracking the local parklands. Professional or public actions of any sort on my part, especially ones consistent with the underlying values of the sign of my Venus, often lead to these life-triggering human encounters. Conversely, if I am not meaningfully engaged with my community, I am not likely to meet the people whom I need to meet.

How might I recognize them? These people are not necessarily prominent or powerful, but they are engaged in activities which have an impact upon the direction of my society – activities in which I myself have a natural interest or investment. These activities reflect a public expression of the values inherent in the nature of my Venus sign – if my Venus is in Leo, we might meet in connection with the performing arts. In Virgo, in connection with the practical mechanics of how societies run. Because of the way these shared values are put to practical work, these people automatically trigger in me a great sense of respect for them.

What actions must I avoid or at least not over-do? There is an eternal tension between, on one hand the demands of public life – one's job, one's mission – and, on the other hand, the legitimate requirements posed by intimacy and domestic life. I need both. The trick – and it will likely be a constant battle – is to make sure that the demands of the public side of my life do not suck the vitality out of my private life.

VENUS IN THE ELEVENTH HOUSE

For love to thrive, I must behave . . . in ways that prioritize reaching my own personal goals. Love is grand, but it can be a distraction; I need to constantly guard against having my own course through life derailed by partners and friends – otherwise resentments creep into my primary relationships. I am developing the ability to keep my eyes on the prize, even when someone else's needs must be factored into the calculations. All that having been said, with Venus in my eleventh house, it is helpful to remember that building a happy, long-term relationship is in fact right near the top of any wise list of my natural aims. If I forget that or undervalue it, I have lost sight of what is truly important to me in the long run. I need to find the balance between human relationship and maintaining a relationship with my own dreams and aspirations.

Where will I meet my soul-partners? I might very well meet them in the context of our shared affiliation with a group or a tribe, whether it is a formal organization or a spontaneous assemblage of friends. Such people might emerge first as a tangential member of "the crowd." Group-related actions of any sort on my part, especially ones consistent with the sign of my Venus, often lead to life-triggering human encounters. In general, Venusian goals are the ones which arise most naturally in me. That might reflect a long-term desire to develop myself artistically. Maybe I aspire to play the violin. And guess who I might find sitting next to me in the orchestra pit?

How might I recognize them? My soul-partners are not necessarily extroverted people, but they are actively engaged in activities that require some kind of group participation. Maybe, for example, they play in a band – or on a softball team. Maybe they're members of a support group for authors or poets. Our shared goals – which have nothing to do with relationships – are what bring us together. In being true to ourselves, we find each other.

What actions must I avoid or at least not over-do? When love works out in a stable, committed way, one of its joys lies in simply planning and dreaming together. There is an uplifting and liberating alchemy that arises when two people jointly conspire to create a future they are both enthusiastic about sharing. That is indeed a gift from the universe – but I must be wary of letting it take us too far away from the present moment. Too much focus on tomorrow can pull our attention away from the here and now – and that is where love makes its moment to moment stand. I must be vigilant about not letting dreams about the future blind us to the slippery, ever-changing, immediate realities generated by two souls in complicated embrace.

VENUS IN THE TWELFTH HOUSE

For love to thrive, I must behave . . . in ways that reflect my most sacred commitment to myself: that I take my own spiritual life seriously. I am a loving person – and love is indeed part of my spiritual life – but I need mindful time alone too. Creativity – and the trance states it engenders in me – may also be a pivotal piece of my inner journey; I need time and support for that part of my life as well. I am developing the ability to fulfill my own half of an ancient bargain: to be part of a truly spiritual partnership. That involves monitoring the collision of two tectonic plates: one is being true to my own separate spiritual needs, while the other is being true to the needs of my relationships. In any case, the only kind of relationships that work well for me in the long run are ones with a basis in shared spirituality.

Where will I meet my soul-partners? Wherever people gather for the sake of their souls, I am likely to meet the sorts of individuals with whom I resonate. Depending upon the specific qualities of my own nature, these places could quite possibly be literal religious institutions – meeting in a church or a temple, for example. Just as easily, I might think of a meditation group, a yoga class, or a presentation by a spiritual teacher. Voluntary actions motivated by my broad interest in the exploration of consciousness – especially ones consistent with the underlying values of the sign of my Venus – often lead to these life-triggering human encounters.

How might I recognize them? Every one of my true soul-partners has an independent, pre-existing spiritual life of his or her own. That is bedrock.

Our theologies may not overlap at all, but we are capable of shared, comfortable silences with each other. Our *souls can communicate*, in other words. As we look into each other's eyes, I experience spaciousness, compassion, and a sense of undefended mutual acceptance. When I mention my spiritual perspectives or my psychic experiences, I am met with unfailing support and the kind of understanding that can only be born in parallel experiences.

What actions must I avoid or at least not over-do? What is the role of ego in human intimacy? For me, that question is the source of deep and fruitful meditation. Too much ego is obviously perilous in any loving relationship – but too little is dangerous too. And that latter pitfall is the one regarding which I must be particularly cautious. Being "agreeable," when carried to an extreme, is equivalent to being invisible. We might say the same for runaway expressions of pliability, conflict avoidance – even of forgiveness. In moderation, these qualities are love's vitamins. In excess, they become toxic conditions, conditions in which we feel like we are living with the ghost or at least someone who is not fully, humanly, present.

14

SATURN AND URANUS IN THE TWELVE HOUSES

SATURN IN THE FIRST HOUSE

The Great Work: Self-respect and dignity earned through success at difficult accomplishments – ones which I have chosen personally, freely and in soul-centered fashion. Attaining a state of self-sufficient, self-directed autonomy. This is not to be confused with lovelessness, isolation, or coldness – only with being free of any driving desperation for others' support or approval.

The Strategy For Achieving It: Single-minded, undistracted focus on the goals that are actually important to me, even if people call them selfish. Relentless effort sustained over time, sometimes without external rewards or attention. Remaining impervious to all external manipulations aimed at distracting me, however cunning and guilt-inducing they might be. Developing the ability to endure disapproval and isolation for the sake of fulfilling a task that is a worthy expression of the best I have to offer. Success is its own reward; anything more is welcome, but not necessary.

The Blockage That Must Be Faced Squarely: The personal insecurity and self-doubt that arise naturally in the face of anything difficult. The fear of loneliness, rejection, or alienation. The fear of failure.

The Price of Failure: A feeling of having "missed the boat" in my life, of being a flower that never opened. Soul-isolation – a condition which may still see me surrounded by people, but ones who have no idea of what my actual potential had been. And that is because I never gave any manifestation to the reality of my true nature; I never revealed myself to the community through my Great Work.

SATURN IN THE SECOND HOUSE

The Great Work: Metaphorically speaking, I must climb an intimidatingly tall mountain in this lifetime. Initially, that Great Work appears to be too much for me. That daunted feeling, by the way, is one of the signs by which I actually recognize my mountain. I must prove myself to myself through this concrete, visible accomplishment. The inward side of the work lies in the development of self-confidence and a sense of my own power – but I can only attain those inward victories through an impressive outward effort of sustained self-discipline aimed at completing a project that is truly worthy of me and expressive of my soul.

The Strategy For Achieving It: I start by realizing that my feelings of insecurity do not have their fundamental origin in my psychological make-up; instead, they derive directly from rational assessments of my own weak points in terms of skills, resources, and necessary alliances. Once I focus on shoring up that base of necessary support, an increasing confidence that I can successfully "climb the mountain" arises naturally in me.

The Blockage That Must Be Faced Squarely: The deep-down fearful feeling that I simply do not "have what it takes." Unaddressed, that attitude could lead me to climb lesser peaks. By way of compensation for this sense of spiritual failure, I could take on time-serving, difficult, undertakings – but ones which serve no true spiritual purpose for me at all. I might spend my life counting beans for other people.

The Price of Failure: Getting to the top of the wrong mountain, and finding that it leaves me empty and unsatisfied. Down that path, I find myself mired in sticky duties and cascading responsibilities which leave me feeling robotic, exhausted – and probably resentful of those whom I am serving.

SATURN IN THE THIRD HOUSE

The Great Work: Bringing forth my true voice, which is the voice of the Elder or the Sage. Developing a style of self-expression that is inherently commanding and authoritative without ever sounding arrogant. Creating, over a long period of time, a body of verbal work – the product of my intellect leavened by all that I have learned in life. That work might be written; it might take the form of teaching; just as easily, it might be a set of helpful ideas and insights which are always ready to roll off my tongue skillfully and compellingly when presented with some genuine human need.

The Strategy For Achieving It: Study is critical here; I must not be afraid to "burn the midnight oil," learning what I need to learn. I must cut through mental laziness or any lack of sustained focus. The discipline of long-term concentration is pivotal to me. Through it, I can outperform people who might be more innately gifted than myself. I celebrate language; I develop my vocabulary and my ability to speak confidently and in complete paragraphs.

The Blockage That Must Be Faced Squarely: Fear and insecurity about my voice and my intelligence can silence me; I am not here on this earth to be silenced. I affirm that I have something important to say, and that I can express it seriously and authoritatively, and thus be taken seriously by others. Whenever I lose sight of those truths, it is a sign that I have succumbed to my area of blockage.

The Price of Failure: Being haunted by the repetitive experience of a feeling that "I should have said that." Knowing that in many situations I had real insights that were never shared – and not because I failed to love other people enough to care about them, but rather because I failed to honor myself and my own wisdom. In extreme form, I might die knowing that "I had a book in me" that I never wrote.

SATURN IN THE FOURTH HOUSE

The Great Work: Building roots; finding and building a true soul-home for myself in this world. That home may very well include a physical house, along with a spiritual relationship with the land on which it sits. Beyond that, certainly such a home includes "family" in some sense of the word – committed relationships with people, and perhaps with animal companions with whom I share my life. Deep inner work aimed at establishing a conscious connection with my vivid inner archetype of the Wise Elder. Eventually I resolve to fulfill the guiding role of "grandmother" or "grandfather," figuratively if not literally.

The Strategy For Achieving It: Sustaining human commitments over long periods of time; doing the necessary maintenance work that nourishes stable, long-term relationships – deep shared processes, including forgiveness and tolerance for differences, along with the work on my own psyche that underlies my own ability to love skillfully in the real world. The long, shared story with other souls. Realizing that romantic love is sweet and real, but that it is ultimately only a bridge I cross to where I will do my real evolutionary work. Building a sense of family. Putting down physical roots; commitment to a community, to a tribe, or to a physical place.

The Blockage That Must Be Faced Squarely: The most frightening words anyone can possibly utter are, "I will never leave you." I recognize that natural fear inside myself; I recognize that it is based on realistic wisdom. But I will never let that fear block me from my evolutionary path, which lies down the road of the long, shared story with a few other human beings. Even in long-term relationships, I will not hide from intimacy behind my psychological walls.

The Price of Failure: A feeling of rootlessness; a feeling that I have no true home in this world, that I have always been a displaced person – an alienated outsider. A pervasive, and rather stoic, mood of unending sadness in my life. Distance from my own heart. My silence may have been mistaken for depth, but I know in my heart that it was truly the face of my fear of being seen or deeply known.

SATURN IN THE FIFTH HOUSE

The Great Work: Giving some concrete outward manifestation to the contents of my inner world. Leaving tangible evidence of my imagination and my values in the hands of my community. My Great Work, in a nutshell, lies in cultivating and expanding my creativity. This creative process may take the form of "art" in the conventional sense of that word – but, just as easily, I might leave the fingerprints of my aspirations, tastes, and my nature upon an institution or an event. Whatever form this creative self-expression takes, I will constantly strive to polish, mature, and improve it.

The Strategy For Achieving It: I commit myself to the discipline of mastering the technical foundations underlying whatever creative field I am drawn to explore. I will learn from those who have gone before me. I respect the tradition in which I practice; I do not seek to copy anyone, but I will humble myself and discipline myself sufficiently to learn what my forebears have learned, and so build upon the solid ground they have shown me.

The Blockage That Must Be Faced Squarely: There is a wild god or goddess behind all creative inspiration. I acknowledge that I fear surrendering to such chaotic forces; I also understand that unless I do, my work will be mechanical and derivative. I resolve to learn the discipline of spontaneity. I resolve to surrender to my muse.

The Price of Failure: Were I to fail to learn how to surf these Dionysian waves of creativity, melancholia would suffuse my life. I would feel bottled up and inhibited when faced with any of life's wild joys. My soul would remain invisible; I would feel as if the best parts of myself were unknown.

SATURN IN THE SIXTH HOUSE

The Great Work: Finding meaningful responsibilities. Finding work that truly matters. I am capable of making enormous, focused effort when presented with a worthy task. I understand that in so doing I will experience exhaustion; I accept that exhaustion. I even celebrate it – but only if the work passes two tests: it expresses my soul and it makes a real difference in someone else's life. Nothing else is worth the monumental efforts of which I am capable.

The Strategy For Achieving It: I will find my true teachers, mentors, and role models no matter how difficult it is to locate them. I accept that part of my Great Work eventually lies in passing on what they have taught me – but first, I must sit at their feet and learn it directly from them. Always, I view the work itself as more important to me than any recognition or appreciation which I might achieve; I want those things too, but they are always secondary. The work comes first.

The Blockage That Must Be Faced Squarely: I am part of a lineage; that means that I am blocked from meaningful progress unless I first humbly recognize my need for the guidance of certain specific teachers. Nothing will stand between me and finding them – not my arrogance, nor any sense of unworthiness or self-doubt. I affirm that, with their triggering help, I am capable of this Great Work – and of passing on the treasure of this knowledge before I leave this world.

The Price of Failure: Slavery, in a nutshell. Some slaves have expensive automobiles and corner offices, but they are still slaves. I will not be one of them. Work exacts a blood-price from anyone's life – so much of our time and energy is absorbed that way; it is only worth that price if the work pays me a lot more than mere money. If I fail on this path, I will pour my life down the rat-hole of meaningless duty and responsibility.

SATURN IN THE SEVENTH HOUSE

The Great Work: Restoring my ability to trust other people – which in turn depends upon deepening my skill when it comes to judging character. I must learn to discern who is worthy of my trust. Having done that, I must take the risk of radical commitment to a few other human beings – ones who have made similar commitments to me. The Great Work manifests as an honorable, life-long vow, kept and cherished. Such vows are not limited to marriage; lasting friendships of great depth are part of them as well.

The Strategy For Achieving It: Learning reliably to sense a quality of trustworthiness in another person. Recognizing and fully appreciating steadiness, maturity, and reasonableness in somebody – and valuing those qualities above more transitory temptations, such as glamour or sexiness. Taking time to build genuine psychological familiarity; patience; not rushing intimacy – and learning to value people who do not rush me into it.

The Blockage That Must Be Faced Squarely: Due to unresolved abandonment or grievous bereavement in a prior lifetime, I was born with a defended heart. There is no shame in this; I came by this blockage honestly, as a result of tragedy. I resolve to heal that wound in this lifetime; I realize that I can only succeed in that process with the consistent help of someone who does not fail me or abandon me.

The Price of Failure: If I fail in this Great Work of recovering my ability to trust, two dark roads lie ahead of me. I will travel down one, or possibly both of them. The first is a life of isolation and loneliness, as I simply defend myself against the possibility of pain by avoiding entanglements. The second lies in choosing people whom it would not be too hard to lose – those who are either unworthy of me or otherwise unreachable. They are the way I keep the stakes low; they are only symbols of my unresolved fear.

SATURN IN THE EIGHTH HOUSE

The Great Work: A focused and disciplined approach to facing certain specific and fundamental wounds in my psyche. It is not that I am more wounded than other people; it is only that I am ready now to face this deep work, while others might not be. I will in this lifetime reestablish my ability to trust existence itself, along with trusting a carefully selected group of humans who are worthy of my love and my fierce honesty.

The Strategy For Achieving It: I commit radically to that honesty. Simultaneously, I commit to what we might call "a lifetime of psychoanalysis," even if that is just a metaphor for an examined life. Perhaps I will do much of that psychoanalytic work all by myself – that is fine and natural. But I resolve in the course of this life to bare my soul to at least one other human being, with nothing hidden and nothing held back. I will choose that person with great care.

The Blockage That Must Be Faced Squarely: Due to painful prior life experiences with human sexuality, I am blocked when it comes to bonding deeply with another human being. Due to a tragic, violent, lingering, or untimely prior life experiences of death, I have fears around my physical mortality in this lifetime. I will face them honestly. (Note that this is not a "fear of death" *per se*; more accurately, it is a fear of *dying* whose origins lie in the deep memory banks of my soul.)

The Price of Failure: A morbid feeling of pessimism and foreboding; an unfocused sense that something dreadful always lies just around the corner. An inability to be wide open and vulnerable to the healing touch of human love. Loneliness. Sexuality suffused with the archetypes of tragic romance – that, or simple asexuality.

SATURN IN THE NINTH HOUSE

The Great Work: Education, in the largest sense of the word. I will exercise and expand my intelligence; I commit to achieving mastery in fields that intimidate me intellectually. I seek only truths which are supported by my own direct experience; if some belief has not worked for me personally, I put it on the back burner. I am never afraid of questions. For me, "faith" is subordinate to the realities of experience. I resolve to expand my understanding of life beyond the horizons of my own culture and training.

The Strategy For Achieving It: Institutions of higher education attract me; that might include universities – but it also applies to less formal paths, so long as they are serious: ongoing classes or training programs count as well. In other words, at least for a while, I am willing to humble myself before experts, to learn what they have to teach. I am eager to travel and to cross cultural boundaries, knowing that my own society has blinded me with its unconscious assumptions and prejudices to some things I must understand.

The Blockage That Must Be Faced Squarely: I like order, coherence, and rationality, but I must remember that the universe operates by more mysterious laws and principles. I resolve to avoid rigidity in my thinking and in my beliefs. I allow space for questions and for that which I do not yet comprehend. I am not offended by loose ends, nor by the irrational, nor by the miraculous.

The Price of Failure: Crippling conservatism in my views; a narrow mind, committed to defending its preexisting beliefs and its own identity as an expert. A lack of imagination. Bad religion. A parochial perspective, unable to escape the narrow bandwidth of "what was good enough for my grandparents."

SATURN IN THE TENTH HOUSE

The Great Work: Finding my true, meaningful mission in the community. Creating a purposeful role for myself in society, one to which I can willingly submit. In some broad sense, this mission will be filed under the archetype of the Elder or the Priest – words which I do not need to take literally since they are only references to a shepherding, guiding role – one which I aspire to be worthy of playing in my community. Through that role, I will touch the lives of people with whom I do not necessarily share personal karma.

The Strategy For Achieving It: I initially affirm that I simply *have* a mission; my sense of having "a Calling" is real and authentic. Part of my evolutionary work in this lifetime lies in turning myself into a worthy gift for my people. I accept that path; I surrender to it. Like a good priest, I recognize that my treasure is not necessarily in this world – it might not, in other words, be about money or prestige. It is the work itself that matters; I recognize that sacrifices will be demanded of me. I accept that part too.

The Blockage That Must Be Faced Squarely: The requirements of my mission daunt me; in order to succeed at it, I must develop skills that do not arise naturally in my personality. Faced with the pathway to my natural work, I am plagued by feelings of insecurity, ineptitude, and illegitimacy. Through sustained discipline, I must face those feelings down. One seductive way my blockages might manifest is by presenting me with "alternative careers" – ones which make practical sense to every part of me except to my own soul.

The Price of Failure: Playing a time-serving, ultimately boring role in the world – one in which my unthinkingly mechanical or automatic skills dominate while my soul hibernates. Looking like a success, while feeling like a failure. Illustrating the old proverb: it's lonely at the top. Actual failure, having never found my path and thus having just given up.

SATURN IN THE ELEVENTH HOUSE

The Great Work: Living a life structured in accord with the actual long-term priorities of my soul. Keeping first things first, regardless of pressures, distractions, or temptations. Setting goals, both spiritually and practically – and keeping my eye on the prize consistently over the decades of my life. A life lived intentionally, navigated by the guiding stars of my soul's inspiration. Seeking the support of a community of people who share these same guiding stars; my helping them – and in turn being helped by them. My aim is that at the end of my life, I will have accomplished something concrete and real of which I am very proud, and of which I may very well have dimly dreamed when I was young.

The Strategy For Achieving It: Even though Saturn is a rational planet, I must first suspend rationality and ask my heart one pressing question: *when I am old, what kind of life do I want to look back upon?* Once I have that answer, I must formulate a practical strategy for embodying such a life over time. I must set fierce and focused priorities – and honor them by avoiding all tempting distractions and side tracks. It is critical that I seek creative, supportive alliances with people who are traveling a similar road.

The Blockage That Must Be Faced Squarely: I acknowledge that I am hesitant about relating to groups of people. I tend to not trust them or feel comfortable in them. I need to overcome this blockage – carefully. The aim is not that I try to transform myself into some kind of extroverted party animal; rather, the aim is that I recognize that certain other people are holding cards that I need, just as I am holding cards which they themselves need. Thus, fruitful alliances can arise – but only if I am first clear about my own direction and what I want to achieve in this lifetime. That knowledge must come first; these alliances are a natural side-effect of this initial self-knowledge. If I want to play third violin, I am going to need an orchestra.

The Price of Failure: A feeling of being lost at sea, without any guiding stars. Directionlessness. A life of tactics, lacking any larger strategy. Coping and reacting rather than keeping my eyes on a defined prize. Squandering my energy with a similarly lost and directionless crowd – or simply feeling a kind of urban anonymity, *ennui*, and Kafka-esque alienation.

SATURN IN THE TWELFTH HOUSE

The Great Work: A profound commitment to a lifetime of practical spiritual progress, based upon effort, self-discipline, and, above all, *consistency* of practice. Strange as this might sound to religious people, in this lifetime I am casting off any need for faith. My "faith" is strong enough just as it is; now what benefits me are *proofs* based on my own inner experience. To find those proofs, I will cultivate direct experience of the Divine. I will undertake certain established spiritual practices in a spirit of regularity; I am not afraid of austerity and self-sacrifice. I know the prize is worth ten times the effort.

The Strategy For Achieving It: Consistency of spiritual effort is critical to my success. I will, for example, meditate not because I want to, but because it is six o'clock in the morning and that is when I have promised myself I will meditate. Fasting might be of benefit to me, as is a periodic vow of silence. My spirituality is supported by times of solitude, away from the buzz of the world. I will not lose sight of compassion for myself – but the bottom line is that I am teaching "my inner monkey" who is the boss.

The Blockage That Must Be Faced Squarely: People often use the metaphor of "climbing a mountain" for the spiritual path. If so, I must recognize that I have come to a steep stage in that ascent. For me, the next steps involve a challenging, but potentially very fruitful battle with my fears, my appetites, and my own laziness. Facing that "steepness" is hard, humbling work – but the good news is, when climbing a steep mountain, a little bit of forward progress puts a person on much higher ground.

The Price of Failure: A feeling of spiritual stagnation, as if my forward progress has been stymied, and my inner psychic experience – whatever level of it I may have attained – has become predictable and routine. At its worst, failure here can lead to a loss of active spiritual engagement – a feeling of having been "abandoned by God." Cynicism might arise in me. A dark night of the soul potentially looms – but only if I lose sight of my Great Work and the strategies I must employ consistently for attaining it.

Uranus Through The Twelve Houses

URANUS IN THE FIRST HOUSE

In what arena of life must I make a radical commitment to thinking and acting for myself? At each one of the fundamental, biography-defining forks-in-the-road of my life – such as decisions about career direction, major relationships, residence – I resolve to practice complete autonomy and self-direction. I recognize that when I am true to myself, my decisions in these root areas of life are likely to trigger worry, criticism, or even manipulative tactics in some of the people around me. My level of comfort in being defined as "unusual" is growing day by day.

What qualities of character support me in fulfilling that intention? My affirmation is that I refuse to be manipulated into being someone other than who I actually am. I celebrate my autonomy and my independence. What others think of me is their business, not mine. Who are they that I should have to falsify myself?

What do I look like when I am getting this right? To those who appreciate me, I look like a self-directed free-thinker. To those who do not, I look odd or even dangerous in some way. Either way, I am what I am. If you like me, that is great – and if you don't, then do us both a favor: go away. Does that attitude look "uncaring" or just "free?" My best answer is that I am not concerned with anyone's answer: either way, it is just someone else's opinion, just dogs barking in the night, and none of my business.

What form does the shadow take? Detachment from human feelings. An unreachable, impossible, or distant quality of personal affect. Transitory social customs aside, there are some laws of behavior that are rooted in nature: not hurting others for joy or gain, coming to the aid of those in

need, for example. When this configuration goes dark, behaviors can arise
that are in violation of these principles.

URANUS IN THE SECOND HOUSE

*In what arena of life must I make a radical commitment to thinking and acting
for myself?* I resolve that my self-confidence and my dignity arise 100% from
my integrity – and 0% from other people's approval. I prove myself to myself by making bold and risky moves in uncharted directions. I do not care
if they impress anyone else; I only need them to impress me. I declare my
independence from the money-myths of this world. I need food and shel-
ter, but I vigorously renounce the need for any ego-boost that comes from
impressing anybody with my financial status. As the brilliant jazz innovator
and mentor, Art Blakey, put it, ""You can't just think about making money.
Because you ain't never going to see an armored car following a hearse."

What qualities of character support me in fulfilling that intention? The
more I distance myself from the need to elicit applause from anyone, the
wiser, happier, and freer I become. I have a strong innate potential for
figuring out a way to be financially self-sustaining – perhaps through an
innovative approach to self-employment or perhaps through paring down
my material needs. Such an independent and individuated relationship to
money would be an enormous support to my fulfilling my evolutionary
intentions; it would free me to reach them.

What do I look like when I am getting this right? Oscar Wilde once said,
"I put all my genius into my life; I put only my talent into my works." If I
get this configuration right, I will be able to say that too.

What form does the shadow take? Perhaps I pay no attention to material things. Maybe that behavior hurts me – or maybe other people have to
take up the slack created by my irresponsibility or indifference. Perhaps I
am drawn to dubious money-making schemes, perhaps even to try crime
in some sense of the word. Or maybe, out of insecurity, I feel compelled
to support myself in such soul-numbing fashion that I shut down my own
heart in order to survive my job.

URANUS IN THE THIRD HOUSE

In what arena of life must I make a radical commitment to thinking and acting for myself? Above all, I am learning how to trust my own senses. People generally see exactly what they are taught to see. I resolve to go beyond that trap in this lifetime, learning to see what is actually before my eyes and to *trust those perceptions*. If I get that part right, I then move to the second developmental stage, which is learning to speak the truth of what I have seen, even if people do not always clap their hands about it.

What qualities of character support me in fulfilling that intention? A capacity for thinking "outside the box." The ability to recognize errors in other people's foundational assumptions. An instinct for asking the right questions. "Lightbulbs light over my head;" I am subject to inexplicable flashes of inspiration and insight.

What do I look like when I am getting this right? I will probably hear the words, "You are a genius" many times. That does not necessarily mean that people will think of me the way they think of Einstein or Mozart, but rather that they will be impressed by my originality, my innovations, and my ability to bring fresh solutions in unexpected ways.

What form does the shadow take? Rather than actually thinking for myself, I might instead take my cues from what everyone else is saying – and then simply contradict them. My ability to shock people can cloak my own cognitive emptiness. I can be cold and mean in my speech and in my evaluations of others.

URANUS IN THE FOURTH HOUSE

In what arena of life must I make a radical commitment to thinking and acting for myself? Family is potentially good for me – but only if I approach such commitments on my own terms and with a willingness to do it my own way. Without unnecessarily criticizing my own family of origin, I realize that what works spiritually for me is very different from what I learned growing up. It is not essential that I live some "alternative lifestyle," but it is truly essential that I find the part of myself that is capable of going down such a free-spirited road if I wanted to.

What qualities of character support me in fulfilling that intention? Life is currently experimenting with new visions of what the word "family" means; I am part of that experiment, blessed with many open-minded, creative instincts and insights in that area. When it comes to grasping "family psychology," I bring fresh eyes to all the questions. There, I toss out all of the rules except for mutual respect.

What do I look like when I am getting this right? I have found a way to honor two human needs that often exist in tension with each other. The first is my need for space simply to be myself, unencumbered by the burden of other people's expectations. The second is my need for a few stable, deeply committed, deeply familiar, relationships in my life – relationships upon which I can fully count, with people who can count on me.

What form does the shadow take? I feel invisible, lost in a tangled web of "ties that bind," always with people who have projected their own needs and expectations onto me without any apparent sense of who I actually am. I feel alienated within my family system, but unable to escape it.

URANUS IN THE FIFTH HOUSE

In what arena of life must I make a radical commitment to thinking and acting for myself? I begin by finding some avenue of self-expression. Perhaps it is an art, perhaps it's a hobby or a sport. I am spontaneous there; I do not care if I look silly. On the foundation of that free flow of child-like vitality, I recover my ability to choose freely and wisely the people who will be my friends and partners in life. By learning to reveal who I really am, I magnetize into my life people who appreciate who I really am – and simultaneously put off the people with whom I have no authentic business anyway.

What qualities of character support me in fulfilling that intention? I have good instincts around "performance" in the larger sense of that word. I can loosen up, be colorful and spontaneous. I can get people to identify with me. I am creative in a very original way. I can choose friends and relationships that lie outside the realm of other people's expectations of me.

What do I look like when I am getting this right? I look like I am *individuating* through my art and my creativity, whatever forms they take. I display a disarming and endearing lack of self-consciousness. The less seriously I seem to take myself, the more seriously people take me. I learn about myself in exactly the same way that a child learns – self-discovery through play.

What form does the shadow take? A lack of boundaries and limits when it comes to any pleasurable activity. A compulsion to shock people. Mean humor; cruel characterizations. Self-destructive behaviors linked to excess and an inability to stop.

URANUS IN THE SIXTH HOUSE

In what arena of life must I make a radical commitment to thinking and acting for myself? I am a responsible person, but I need to be vigilant about how I define my responsibilities or who I allow to define them for me. That process of definition must unfold in a spirit of total independence. I question anyone else's right to "tell me what to do." I find work, skills and responsibilities that truly matter to me personally, free of any need to impress anyone else.

What qualities of character support me in fulfilling that intention? I have a solid instinct for sorting out my true guides and mentors – my spiritual "aunts" and "uncles" – from people who "appoint themselves" to such positions. In spending time with the true ones, I grow freer and stronger. I am born with innate work skills in an area of life that may seem strange to many people, but which can be satisfyingly supportive to a few people who genuinely need me.

What do I look like when I am getting this right? I may very well look "self-employed." That term easily could be literal – but more deeply it means that I have found a craft involving some kind of meaningful service in my life that reflects the values and nature of my own soul. I am a servant, but never a slave. I know the difference between those two words. Others can see the difference clearly for themselves when they look at me.

What form does the shadow take? Alienation and resentment seethe inside of me as I fulfill meaningless responsibilities which others have assigned to me. I feel like a slave, whether I am in some conventional form of employment or "serving a purpose" in a domestic situation. Down that road, odd, undiagnosable physical complaints soon arise in me.

URANUS IN THE SEVENTH HOUSE

In what arena of life must I make a radical commitment to thinking and acting for myself? My ability to recognize those who are my natural partners in life must become fully free, independent, and individuated. I am willing to cross lines of social judgment in order to be with the ones whom I truly love – and who are capable of truly loving me. For me, individuation must precede successful mate selection. I must know myself before I can know anyone else.

What qualities of character support me in fulfilling that intention? People always seem to believe that their relationship choices are their own business. The actual reality is that we are "aimed" at certain kinds of friends and partners by social forces. I am uniquely aware of those pressures; in recognizing them, I am capable of preventing them from grabbing the steering wheel of my life. In matters of the heart, I think for myself. I like people who might seem a little weird to others. In matters of the heart, patience is my finest ally.

What do I look like when I am getting this right? I look happily established in mutually-rewarding human bonds with partners and friends who might seem "wrong for me" or "kind of weird." In my relationships, it is obvious that we have both thrown away the book of rules. It is *our* relationship, and nobody else's.

What form does the shadow take? The standard negative interpretation here is "instability in love." Fair enough – but the source of such instability is actually the impossibility of making any relationship work that is not based on a genuine soul connection. And the potential origin of that problem for me lies in allowing society to choose my partners and friends rather than doing it for myself. Choose the wrong partner, and instability naturally follows.

URANUS IN THE EIGHTH HOUSE

In what arena of life must I make a radical commitment to thinking and acting for myself? There is much overlap here with Uranus in the seventh house, except that we are now more narrowly focused on sexuality and the basis of *lasting* passion. My primary affirmation is that my sexuality is my own business; I make my own decisions there. Shall I be celibate for a while if I so choose? Shall I be promiscuous? Partnered? Single? Something in between? Those are my own choices to make. I need no one's approval; I do not even need anyone to understand.

What qualities of character support me in fulfilling that intention? I have an elevated ability to stand apart from the cultural norms surrounding what subjects are deemed "acceptable." I question the collective, ever-changing definitions of "appropriate behavior," especially in intimacy. I have my own independent sense of what constitutes "attractiveness" – whether it is my own attractiveness or someone else's. I can be alone if I need to be.

What do I look like when I am getting this right? Like a fully adult human being who has made his or her own intimate choices without reference to anyone else's approval or disapproval. I am established in satisfying relationships that very probably have some unusual characteristics. "How can I miss you if you won't go away" is one of my favorite refrains.

What form does the shadow take? An underlying unaddressed dissociative disorder in me leads to various unsatisfying possibilities, such as alienation in partnerships – and that can take the form of instability, or worse, of a "zombie marriage." I might also experience a general distancing from my own intimate drives – I might be physically present, but emotionally unavailable.

URANUS IN THE NINTH HOUSE

In what arena of life must I make a radical commitment to thinking and acting for myself? My fundamental values. What is the meaning and purpose of my life? Every society answers that question with tyrannical authority – and for me personally, most of the answers I was given are wrong. I am on a *quest for true meaning,* and I resolve to accept the fact that my quest will carry me far from my starting point in the values and mythologies of my family and culture of origin. I boldly resolve to explore life, both geographically and philosophically. No question ever scares me – and when answers scare me, I vow to dig more deeply into them.

What qualities of character support me in fulfilling that intention? I was born as "a stranger in a strange land," and I will die that way. I accept that condition, even revel in it for its clarity of perception. That gives me a freedom to roam, to move fluidly through the "worlds" that humans create, and to do so without undue stress or feelings of alienation. Culturally, it "never gets too weird for me." I am drawn to unusual "ways of knowing" – in fact, right at this moment, I am illustrating that point by reading an astrology book.

What do I look like when I am getting this right? One strong possibility is that I simply look like someone who is living a colorful, adventurous life. If my nature is milder or more introverted, then my freedom might be more internal – I might even "look normal," but if people knew what I was thinking, they would either be scandalized or totally baffled. I have chosen my philosophy of life independently, and without the need to convert anyone to my beliefs, I am walking my talk.

What form does the shadow take? I participate with every appearance of normalcy in the customs and probably the religion of my society, without any of it meaning anything at all to me personally. I go through the motions, keeping people happy with me. I am so distant from the raw realities of my own life that I learn very little from my experience in this incarnation.

URANUS IN THE TENTH HOUSE

In what arena of life must I make a radical commitment to thinking and acting for myself? I acknowledge that in this lifetime my soul has taken on a mission – I need to play a catalytic role in my community. It might or might not look like a job, but it will certainly impact the lives of people whom I do not know personally. To be worthy of this mission, I must leave behind most of the conventional social expectations that were pressed on me around issues of career, reputation, and how to attain status. I am a force of change in the world. Some will see me as a revolutionary in some sense; others may use words such as "troublemaker" or even "criminal" if they feel sufficiently threatened by what I represent. *What qualities of character support me in fulfilling that intention?* I have always had an affinity for plucky people who follow their own hearts, make their rules, and stick out their tongues at judgmental figures of authority. As I learn to trust those same qualities in myself, I follow the slender threads in my life that lead me to finding and fulfilling my mission, however unusual it might be. To find my mission, all I must do is become my true self; the universe handles the rest.

What do I look like when I am getting this right? A force for change at some level in my community. A role model for others who might follow in my footsteps. A free spirit. Someone who has done what people always talk about, but are rarely bold enough to accomplish – that is, truly *leading my own life*, trusting the universe.

What form does the shadow take? Alienation within a social role, often a role of some social or professional prominence. "Scandal" or "downfall" are common astrological prophecies; what such astrologers miss is that such apparent reversals are typically last-ditch efforts on the part of the soul to escape final suffocation. Once the prison walls are dynamited however, the question remains: what is next?

URANUS IN THE ELEVENTH HOUSE

In what arena of life must I make a radical commitment to thinking and acting for myself? I resolve not only to accept, but also to revel in the fact that with every breath I take, I move further away from the conventional social descriptions of success, the agreed-upon sources of meaning in life, and interpretations of the nature of reality itself. I was born into this society, but I am cut from different cloth. I also recognize that in following my natural life-path, I need the support of an interdependent alliance with a tribe of fellow questioners and cultural dissidents.

What qualities of character support me in fulfilling that intention? There arises naturally within me a long-term, strategic – even patient – sense of my own evolutionary track. As David Bowie put it, "I think ageing is an extraordinary process whereby you become the person you always should have been." David and I would have understood each other. I have a good instinct for aligning myself with other free-thinking people, and drawing strength, support, and encouragement from them.

What do I look like when I am getting this right? Weirder in the second half of my life than I was in the first half, for sure. My genius blossoms late, but it blossoms powerfully when its moment finally arrives. Even though I am unusual, I have managed to find a community into which I fit comfortably and naturally. With their support, it is easy for me to not really care what the world thinks of me.

What form does the shadow take? I become accustomed, for one illustration, to being the "spy" drinking martinis at the country club bar with no one there having the slightest notion of how crazy and empty I think they all actually are. All my life, my true identity has been a kind of "state secret." The joke is on me; in fact, I have *become* the joke: no one ever had any idea who I actually was; I never gave them a clue.

URANUS IN THE TWELFTH HOUSE

In what arena of life must I make a radical commitment to thinking and acting for myself? I resolve to be absolutely honest with myself about my actual spiritual and psychic experiences, both in terms of what I see and in terms of what I do not see. I will never fake a spiritual perception in order to maintain elevated social status: if the "sacred crystal" feels like a sweaty rock to me, that is what I will say. And if the spirit of Crazy Horse or Zoroaster appeared at the foot of my bed whistling "Dixie," I will say that too. For me, now, at this point in my journey, spirituality is only about the truth and nothing else.

What qualities of character support me in fulfilling that intention? I am subject to "lightning bolt" awakenings – psychic experiences that come at me suddenly and unexpectedly, and which trigger evolutionary break-throughs. My "inner guru" encourages me to be suspicious of gurus in general – and really, of all teachings and teachers except for those which resonate immediately with the realities of my own direct experience. I am deeply aware of the difference between religion and spirituality.

What do I look like when I am getting this right? I look like someone who is not afraid to look strange or even stupid in pursuit of my authentic spiritual path. I am not afraid of looking "too extreme." I am open to un-conventional methods of opening my mind – maybe I lie in a sense depri-vation tank with headphones pumping my brain waves, or maybe I convert to Orthodox Judaism. Whatever I do, it is based on the dictates of my soul, with never a glance at "the judge and jury."

What form does the shadow take? Distancing from psychic experience; intellectualizing it; using cognitive structures as a way of blocking the ul-timate need to simply surrender to the Great Mystery. Resisting such sur-render is like trying to shore up the straining dam – at some point, psychic contents break through in overwhelming fashion, dangerously and sud-denly weakening my grasp on conventional reality.

15

A FRESH LOOK AT THE ASTROLOGICAL ASPECTS: YODS, GRAND CROSSES, AND GRAND TRINES

As I write these words in the summer of the year 2019, two of the brightest planets in the sky – Jupiter and Saturn – are in the same starry neighborhood. They are currently standing about 30° apart. That is nowhere near a conjunction yet, but with every passing week, it becomes clearer that they are on a collision course. There is no danger that they will ever actually collide – Saturn's orbit lies much further out in space. But from the astrological perspective – and from the perspective of visual astronomy – it is clear that these two bright planets have a date with destiny.

In December 2020, Jupiter and Saturn form a conjunction in early Aquarius. It is a big deal astrologically – but my point is broader. First, this alignment has happened, like clockwork, every twenty years throughout recorded history. Humans, no doubt, have been wondering about it ever since they were first aware of it. Somewhere back in time, in the misty dawn of astrological thought, someone had figured out that Saturn correlated with *blockages* and Jupiter with *opportunities*. Normally, the two bodies are in different parts of the sky, which made astrological thinking easy:

here in this area of life where Jupiter is contacting you, you are lucky, but there, where Saturn lies, perhaps not so lucky.

But what could it possibly mean when blockage and opportunity coincide?

Wrestling with slippery questions of *symbolic merger* such as that one led to the doctrine of astrological aspects – and to a profound deepening of astrological thought. Planets, each with a different meaning, would sometimes come together. Our ancestors observed that for a little while, there would be a kind of transitory "meta-planet" in the sky. The phenomenon would not last long – but during that time, astrologers would have to think on their feet, synthesizing complex, ambiguous layers of meaning into some kind of coherent statement.

That kind of thinking arose rather obviously with conjunctions, which were doubtless the first aspect that anyone contemplated. It was not long, however, before astrologers observed that other specific geometrical angles between planets had a similar effect: planetary meanings would merge, forming transitory, complex symbolic structures.

In *The Book of Fire* and *The Book of Earth*, we explored aspects as they operate between planets in the natal chart and also as they operate as triggers via transits, progressions, and solar arcs. Here, in *The Book of Air*, in order to avoid repetition, I want to take us down a different road. More about that in a moment. One point about aspects is so fundamental, however, that it bears repetition here, at least in shortened form ...

ALL ASPECTS ARE ABOUT INTEGRATION

If you forget everything else and simply let that integrative principle guide your thinking, then your work with aspects will be helpful, accurate, and profound. And if you forget that all aspects – even the so-called "bad" ones – are still ultimately about integration, you lapse into a far more limiting form of astrological work, one that is not only less sophisticated, but which is also unnecessarily depressing a lot of the time. Conversely, sometimes it could be unrealistically encouraging.

I emphasize this integrative principle in order to counter the ubiquitous idea that there are "good" aspects and "bad" aspects. It is simply not true. We see this thumbs up, thumbs down, notion everywhere in astrological literature. It has never once helped anyone become wiser or more self-accepting, let alone luckier.

Good and bad aspects are not totally useless concepts, but it is far more accurate – and really just as simple – to instead think of "easy" aspects and "hard" aspects.

The pivotal concept here is not some pop-psychological taboo about using judgmental words or against being negative. It is simply that when two planets are in aspect, the reality is always that *they are somehow trying to figure out a way to work together.* They are trying to *integrate their energies* in service of the evolution of your consciousness.

Your job is to help them do that.

- If two planets are linked by a so-called "bad aspect," that integration is indeed more difficult – but the need is pressingly energized.
- If it is an "easy" aspect linking them, the integration is easier – but there is also a danger of *laziness* or a *lack of that pressing motivation.*

If you are relatively new to astrology and do not yet feel confident about knowing the difference between a quintile and a quincunx, you might want to go back to the aspects chapters in either of the two previous volumes in this series. You will find all the foundational material spelled out there.

Bottom line, my suggestion is that when you are confronted with any astrological aspect, that you organize your thinking in four steps, as follows:

- *Step One:* Start by contemplating the energies the planetary archetypes represent. (Examples: Saturn is *solitude* and Venus is *love*). Realize that if they are linked by any aspect at all, they are trying to cooperate – and your evolutionary success currently depends upon them working together. (Think this way: *solitude and love are not truly opposites*; everyone knows that sometimes "absence makes the heart grow fonder.)
- *Step Two:* Imagine what such an integration might look like if it were successful. (*Two people who guard each other's solitude; lovers with sufficient sexual sophistication that they appreciate the aphrodisiacal qualities of occasionally missing each other.*)
- *Step Three:* Pay attention to what it would look like if the planetary partnership became unhealthy – that is always a possibility too. (*If I am not getting time alone in a healthy, straightforward way, I might cut myself off from you emotionally.*)

(Notice that everything I have said so far is totally independent of exactly what aspect we are talking about—it could be a trine, a square, or a sesquiquadrate. So far, the specific nature of the aspect does not matter. Regardless of the aspect, it is all about integration, always.)

- *Step Four:* Next, for the first time, consider the specific nature of the aspect. Are we talking about *friction* or *complementary tensions* between the two archetypes – hard aspects, in other words? Or are we in the realm of the easy aspects? Are we now talking about *mutual enhancement* and *support* – and the possibility of laziness, a lack of motivation, and dark collusion? *In a nutshell, put the planetary integration first and save the nature of the aspect for last.*

CHART PATTERNS

So far, everything that we have explored about aspects assumes a geometrical angle between a pair of planets. But what if more than two planets are involved? This is a common astrological occurrence. There might, for example, be a conjunction of two planets which makes a trine aspect to a third planet. In that case, I would encourage you to figure out the meaning of the conjunction using the steps we have just outlined, then establish a way that the trining planet might play a supportive role.

The procedure is, in other words, not very different from what we have considered in the two earlier volumes in this series.

Sometimes, however, the geometry among multiple planets takes a more spectacular turn. Crystalline structures begin to emerge in the chart: triangles, boxes, diamonds, stars, even more complex formations. Many were described by astrologer Marc Edmund Jones, who was born back in 1888. In his 1941 book, *Guide to Horoscope Interpretation*, he described the Splay, Splash, Bundle, Bowl, Locomotive, Bucket, Kite and Seesaw patterns. As synchronicity would have it, just yesterday, I wrote an enthusiastic cover endorsement for another book on the same subject – *Discover The Aspect Pattern In Your Birthchart* by Glenn E. Mitchell II. He has added a deep, data-driven update to this whole important area of astrological work.

All of these *macro-aspects* – commonly referred to simply as "chart patterns" – are composed of familiar ingredients, but they do benefit from some special interpretive procedures.

Here, in *The Book of Air*, rather than skimming over the surface of all of these possible configurations, I instead want to explore in some detail three of the more commonly encountered and developmentally pivotal ones.

- The *Grand Trine*, which forms when three planets find themselves approximately 120° from each other, forming an equilateral triangle.
- The *Grand Cross*, which forms when two planets in opposition to each other lie in square aspect to the axis of another two planets in opposition aspect. They make a square box in the chart, in other words.
- The *Yod*, which forms when one planet lies in opposition to the midpoint of two planets in sextile aspect. Another way to say the same thing is that two planets in sextile aspect are both quincunx to the same third "focal" planet.

With all three of these chart patterns, we recognize that any of the four angles – the Ascendant, the Descendant, the Midheaven, as well as the Astrological Nadir – can function as "planets," and thus help form one of these complex structures.

The same might be said for any asteroid, Centaur object, trans-Neptunian object, or the south node of the Moon.

The Moon's *north* node is a special case – a point which we will explore in just a moment.

Whether you employ such secondary bodies in your work is up to you. Keep perspective though: naturally, a Grand Trine involving the Sun, Moon, and Ascendant would be a lot more significant than one built of the Vertex, the south node of Venus, and the asteroid Monty Python (13681) . . .

. . . and yes, it's true: I am not making that last one up. The asteroid Monty Python (13681) was discovered on August 7, 1997 by Milos Tichý and Zdenek Moravec at Klet Observatory near Cesky Budovice, Czech Republic.

Google it if you doubt me!

And what about the Moon's north node? It is certainly a significant point – should we use it in constructing any of these forms? That is a delicate question, and ultimately not one that can be answered definitively via any purely technical astrological method. As we explored in detail in my book *Yesterday's Sky*, the north node boils down to "an excellent suggestion." It is the most effective natural remedy for one's karmic blind spots. But, as with any other good suggestion, we can heed it – or not. That is our own choice.

Have we heeded it? Have we made any progress toward manifesting that north node? The answer to that question does not lie in the chart. It lies in your own hands.

- If a person has made progress toward his or her north node of the Moon, *and thus activated it,* it can indeed play a role in any aspect pattern.
- If, on the other hand, a person has not made such efforts, then the north node lies latently only as a possibility, and would not be sufficiently energized to play a role in any aspects at all.

One obvious point to underline here is that since the south node is *always* activated, it definitely holds its own in any chart pattern. Any planet in aspect to the south node is also of course in aspect to the north node as well – but that south node might not be in the right geometrical position to complete a Grand Trine or a Yod, while only a consciously-activated north node can complete a Grand Cross.

There is another point that pervades our approach to all of these chart patterns: *a full understanding of any one of them requires unpacking a large part of the integrated meaning of an entire chart.* The reason is simple and inescapable – we are always talking about at least three planets. As we have seen earlier in this book, even to understand *one* planet in a sign and a house is a complex interpretive operation. Each such triad is a multidimensional symbol, capable of high and low expressions.

With the Grand Trine or the Yod, we need to understand at least *three* of these triads of planet, sign, and house, along with their interactions – I say "at least" three of them because it is not unusual for there to be conjunctions involved at any one of the three points.

With the Grand Cross, we obviously move up to at least four of these triads.

On many occasions, people have asked me if I might "take a quick look" at their Grand Cross or their Yod. I can only laugh – and either run away, or say the fateful words, "show me your chart."

THE GRAND TRINE

If we take trines to be "good aspects," then wouldn't it be "grand" to have a Grand Trine in your chart? It's a reasonable thought, but as we will see, the truth is more complex. There are some real advantages to having a Grand Trine – but remember: trines are not so much "good" as they are "easy."

It might be tempting to think that easy is the same as good, and that attitude is not always entirely wrong. If you are mowing the lawn, figuring out your taxes, or trying to fly somewhere through the horror-show of modern commercial air travel, then yes indeed: go ahead and draw that equal sign between easy and good. Why look a gift horse in the mouth?

I cannot prove this, but I would bet heavily on the premise that if you have a Grand Trine in your natal chart, over a lifetime of air travel, you and your luggage are more likely to arrive consistently on the same flight.

That is obviously welcome news.

Here are some other things that can happen "easily": getting into a bad relationship, getting hooked on pharmaceuticals, getting fat, disappearing into television or video games, getting into the habit of eating fast food, getting into a safe, but meaningless career, falling in with a bad crowd, getting out of shape . . .

Those "easy" options go along with a Grand Trine too.

As we saw in the previous two volumes of this series, the bad news about "good aspects" is that they lack internal combustion. They do truly represent genuine integrative opportunities, but they can also be lazy and just let those opportunities slip by.

Meanwhile, the good news about "bad aspects" is just the opposite: while they are difficult, they also *hurt* – and hurt can be very motivating.

Taking it a little deeper, we have all been through hard times that taught us valuable lessons and made us stronger and wiser. Hard aspects often correlate with those kinds of events and challenges. We may never want to go through them again, but, at least in retrospect, we are glad that we did go through them.

On the other hand, as you get older, you may barely remember a year of your life that passed by uneventfully a decade or two ago: that looks like easy aspects in action. "Uneventful" times can feel good as you are passing through them. Nothing to regret there – sometimes you just need a rest.

The more deeply we reflect on these kinds of philosophical and experiential perspectives, the weaker and less relevant words such as "good" and "bad" become. And that shift of attitude is guaranteed to make you a better, more accurate astrologer.

A TRUE STORY

As with my story about my Uranian friend "Lily" earlier in this book, ethics once again demand that I invent a name and distort a few facts out of respect for client privacy. Even though in what follows I will twist a few points in order to protect the hapless innocent, not to mention the truly guilty, the essence of the tale I am about to recount is as real as gravity.

Years ago, in a galaxy far, far away, I had a client with a "glorious" Fiery grand trine in his chart involving the Sun, the Moon, and the planet Jupiter in a near-perfect equilateral triangle.

Note: as I recount the story, please keep one question in the back of your mind: *is this a tale of good luck – or of something else entirely?*

My client – and I will call him "Joey" – was married. His wife had a good job, while Joey rarely worked, preferring to live the "life of a gentleman," riding his wife's gravy train. His unemployed condition left him a fair amount of free time, which he filled by entertaining a much younger girlfriend in a city two or three hours from where he lived with his generous, if unsuspecting, wife.

A crisis arose: Joey's girlfriend turned up pregnant and wanted to have the baby. Poor hapless Joey was penniless. His wife soon learned of the affair and the pregnancy, and reacted in understandable fashion. She told Joey to pack his bags.

So that's where destiny left our Joey: separated from his sweet and prosperous wife, homeless, unemployed – and due to become a father in a few months with a much younger woman whom in truth he barely actually knew.

Naturally, we all thought that Joey's footloose karma was finally catching up with him. Most of us who knew him admitted that there was more than a dollop of *schadenfreude* in our attitudes: Joey seemed to be getting what he deserved for his mistreatment of his poor wife. How could he possibly get out of this one?

His Grand Trine to the rescue . . .

Within that short time-frame, Joey's father suddenly and unexpectedly passed away, leaving him six million dollars.

Problem solved.

This really happened almost exactly as I have just recounted it.

Remember the question I posed a moment ago: *is this a tale of good luck – or something else entirely?*

Joey's Grand Trine indeed "rescued him from the brink of catastrophe in the nick of time." If we were doing conventional meat-and-potatoes existentialist astrology, what was there not to like in this story – at least for Joey himself? He got "lucky;" he got off the hook – and ain't that the very definition of good luck?

But that is not the kind of astrology this book is about. We are talking about the evolution of the soul. We are looking at life, not as a random, pointless series of events, but rather as a meaningful opportunity for the growth of conscious self-awareness.

In that philosophical light, how lucky was Joey really?

My point is many miles from saying that a Grand Trine is a bad thing. My point is only that it is complicated. How can we use such a structure intentionally? What is its evolutionary purpose?

And how can we resist the temptations having one affords us?

THE BOTTOM LINE

Familiar words – all aspects are about integration. With trines in general, that integration is easier, but we are less driven to take advantage of the integrative opportunity. To help a Grand Trine serve its true evolutionary purpose, we need to come up with some genuine motivation.

Going further, the action of trines, at least if we are making a vibrant response to them, is that the planets involved *enhance* and *support* each other. They become *allies*, each filling in the blanks in the other one. Think of our "grand scheme" of the Air signs, and how they are *interdependent* more than they are "harmonious." All of the Element families illustrate the principles behind Grand Trines that way. They work together, in other words, like a well-lubricated engine. Such an engine, compared to a clunkier one, is efficient, wasting nothing.

In astrology, the Grand Trine is the Rolls-Royce version of such an engine.

- Get a Grand Trine right and you have multidimensional creativity, an efficient and highly productive use of energy – and all of it supported by that mysterious existential ingredient we call good luck.
- Get a Grand Trine wrong and you have slick, slippery defensiveness, amotivational syndrome – plus a self-contained immunity to reality-checks as "luck" helps you skip evolutionary opportunities.

As with everything else in any kind of mindful astrology, the actual meaning of a configuration arises at the interface of astrological symbolism and a person's own choices. Worrying about whether to call a Grand Trine lucky or not misses the point entirely. It is not the random toss of the coin that answers the question. *You* are what answers the question.

This is a good time to echo another astrological axiom: your chart is perfect for you. It reflects your karmic predicament – *and the path of its resolution* – as clearly as a fine mirror reflects the shape of your face.

If you have a Grand Trine in your chart, you need one.

Lack one? You didn't need it.

We can take our metaphor of a well-lubricated engine a step further. Planets in hard aspect to each other always fight each other to some extent. As we have seen, that is not always a bad thing – as a result of such interplanetary squabbles, both planets might very well grow stronger. Still, some energy is inevitably wasted in internal friction.

With a Grand Trine, especially one involving major features of a person's chart, the planetary energy can manifest with a high degree of efficiency and very little loss. The effect is that as we contemplate such a person, we are often struck by a quality of *radiance*. They can pulse with energy and life-force. They frequently have palpable *charisma* and a quality of *presence*.

Here are some examples, chosen from among singers.

- Bono, of U2 fame, was born with a Grand Trine of Venus, Jupiter, and Pluto in Earth signs.
- Billie Holiday, who changed the face of popular music in more ways than one, had a watery Grand Trine involving her Midheaven, her Neptune, and a Mars-Mercury conjunction.

- Bob Marley, often revered as "The Prophet" by his devoted fans, had an airy Grand Trine involving Neptune, Uranus, and Mercury.
- Bing Crosby, who sold more than 300 million records back in the day, had an airy Grand Trine involving Saturn, Mercury and his Ascendant.
- John Lennon, of Beatles fame, had an earthy Grand Trine composed of Venus, his Midheaven, and his Jupiter-Saturn conjunction.
- Whitney Houston, a mythically tragic figure, had a tight, fiery Grand Trine of Sun, Moon, and Midheaven.
- Bruce Springsteen, with his fanatical following for the past forty years, has an airy Grand Trine composed of his Aquarian Midheaven, his Gemini Ascendant, and his fifth house Libra Moon.
- Finally, the immortal Aretha Franklin became "the queen of soul" singing out of the emotional depths of her watery Grand Trine of Mercury, the Moon, and the Ascendant.

As you reflect on these famous musical names, I would like to direct your attention to a critical perspective. There have been countless famous singers in history, and many do not have Grand Trines. In astrology, one can come up with almost any harebrained theory – one example being that a Grand Trine means that you will become a famous singer – and find a few charts to support it if you hunt long enough.

Not to take anything away from their talent, but we could make a case that each of these artists got a kiss or two from Lady Luck in their lives. That's probably true, but even that is not quite the point that I am making. Most people who get famous owe something to "luck." My point here as you reflect on this list of singers is a little bit more subtle – and a lot more connected with the actual meaning of Grand Trines.

My deeper point is that each one of these singers has invoked extreme devotion and a worshipful attitude in their fans – something that went beyond their musical talent. Each one of them was or is *radiant* at some transcendent level. Each one of them invoked in others an *urge to identify with them.* Energy flows through each one of them with enormous efficiency, just as if they were "well-lubricated engines." People responded to it, and wanted to draw some of that same energy into themselves.

And that is the point with Grand Trines.

That is what magnetizes their famous "luck" into their lives. It is synchronicity. Their inner sense that they were born to face open doors all their lives has its classic effect: *doors open.*

GRAND TRINES BY ELEMENT

The purest and most common form of the Grand Trine involves three planets or points, all in the same element. All planets in Air signs, for example, share a certain interconnectedness, no matter their exact degree positions. They energize each other. We could make a case that anyone with planets in all three Air signs – or in any other single element, for that matter – has a Grand Trine, or at least something very close to one. That would not be a terribly misleading practice.

Personally, I prefer to raise the bar by applying more restrictive aspectual orbs.

This quickly gets into a technical area which we explored in detail in *The Book of Fire* and *The Book of Earth*. Briefly, we can use *whole sign aspects* – that is, we can make a case that a planet in the *first* degree of Aries has a "trine" kind of relationship with any planet in the *last* degree of Leo. I wouldn't argue against any astrologer taking that position – but for my purposes, I prefer to think of those two planets as being related via a quincunx aspect rather than by a trine.

This ambivalence about how exactly to define aspects – by whole sign or by geometrical angle – is quite fundamental to astrological theory, and a source of much debate.

Our core point is that purest, simplest expression of the essential underlying harmony that defines the Grand Trine macro-aspect arises from all three symbols being united by the fact that they share a common element. Sometimes, however, we do encounter an *out-of-quality* Grand Trine, where the angles are right, but the signs are wrong: one planet lies in the first degree of Aries, one lies in the first degree of Leo – and a third one lies, not in the first degree of Sagittarius, but rather in the last degree of Scorpio.

That is a geometrically tight Grand Trine, but weakened in its expression by Water "dousing" some of the Fire.

Note that this is not a "worse" situation – it is just not as pure an example of the Grand Trine. Do we count it as one or not? Again, that is a judgment call. Certainly, many of our ideas here would still apply, but in a significantly more complex form. The core principle – the underlying interconnectedness created by three planets sharing a single element – is now absent ... although we still have an energetic engine at work, just one that requires more mindfulness to operate.

We just have to figure out a way to get that out-of-quality planet to participate in the joint enterprise.

For our purposes here, I want to concentrate on the clearer, and more common, situation where all three symbols are in the same element. To trigger the full, positive flowering of any Grand Trine, we need to exploit the potential for *mutual enhancement* that exists among the three planets *specifically because of* their shared element. In other words, we are looking to encourage an expression of the sort of *interdependent harmony* within an element that we have been calling our "grand scheme" all along. That means harnessing the distinct and *complementary* energies of each of the signs in a specific Triplicity.

To get it right, in other words, we need that one single element "firing on all three cylinders" simultaneously.

- For Fire signs, success requires achieving balance in the arenas of *Courage* (Aries), *Unselfconscious Self-Expression and Creativity* (Leo), and *Questing* (Sagittarius)
- For Earth signs, success requires achieving balance in the arenas of *Resource Management and Attunement to Instinct* (Taurus), *Discrimination, Refinement, and Good Mentoring* (Virgo), and *Self-Disciplined Manifestation* (Capricorn)
- For Air signs, success requires achieving balance in the arenas of *Alertness and Open-Minded Curiosity* (Gemini), *Tolerance for Paradox and Right Partnerships* (Libra), and *Freedom from Consensual Assumptions* (Aquarius)
- For Water signs, success requires achieving balance in the arenas of *Self-Healing* (Cancer), *Psychological Penetration* (Scorpio), and *Mystical, Visionary Union* (Pisces)

As ever, we need to acknowledge that there is a shadow expression potentially available to each kind of Grand Trine. If we do not get them right, we will surely get them wrong. Shadow energy is typically just like the higher ground, only backwards. Ego is served instead of soul. Division defeats unity. Fear conquers love and faith, while grabbing the steering wheel. High and low are different sides of the same coin.

When a Grand Trine in Fire lands ...

Heads up: Charisma; initiative; presence; creativity; leadership.

Tails Up: Amoral egocentricity, selfishness, and emotional violence.

When a Grand Trine in Earth signs lands:

Heads up: Persistence; skilled service; self-discipline; Great Works.

Tails Up: Numb routine plodding as a defence against change and even against feeling anything at all.

When a Grand Trine in Air signs lands:

Heads up: Brilliance; capacity to conceptualize; teaching; learning.

Tails Up: Glib rationalization; smooth lies; living in one's head.

When a Grand Trine in Water signs lands:

Heads up: Imagination; the gift of healing; spiritual illumination and inspiration.

Tails Up: Moody self-containment; escapism; a wall of defensive subjectivity.

THE GRAND CROSS

Is it a cross or is it a box? A Grand Cross can be defined as two oppositions lying crosswise or equally as a simple four-cornered square. Take your pick; either way, it is the same geometry expressed in different language. And either way, a Grand Cross is composed of the two main "bad guys" in the world of conventional aspect theory: squares and oppositions, where evil auguries of blockage, difficulty, and misfortune abound.

Don't believe it – at least not without the proverbial grain of salt. As we will see, having a Grand Cross in your chart is not equivalent to having a terrible jinx on your life.

For one thing, this aspect pattern is highly *motivational* – hard aspects tend to be self-starting, and a Grand Cross is composed of a *smorgasbord* of them. That self-starting quality is there for the same reason that no matter how tired you are from the day's backpacking, if your foot wanders into the campfire, you quickly find the energy to move it.

No one sleeps through hard aspects. We may get them wrong, but we cannot ignore them.

With the Grand Trine, we saw three planets bound together because they shared a common *element*. This can never be the case with a Grand Cross; planets in exact square or opposition to each other are never in the same element family. But they are in fact joined by a different form of astrological kinship, one that is not as inherently harmonious as a shared element, but which is every bit as powerful: *mode*.

CARDINAL, FIXED, AND MUTABLE: ASTROLOGY'S THREE MODES

As we have been seeing through this series of books, each element expresses itself as three signs. Those three signs are the *Cardinal, Fixed*, and *Mutable* expressions of the element. These three astrological *modes* operate very differently from each other. In fact the word "operation" – *their style of action* – is what distinguishes them from each other.

- *Cardinal* energy *starts* things. Its job is to *initiate action*. Its blind spot lies in not following through on what it has started. The four Cardinal signs, sometimes linked in Grand Cross configurations, are Aries, Cancer, Libra, and Capricorn.
- *Fixed* energy *sustains* things. It keeps the engines oiled and running. Its blind spot can lie in stubborn resistance to change. The four Fixed signs, sometimes linked in Grand Cross configurations, are Taurus, Leo, Scorpio, and Aquarius.
- *Mutable* energy *ends* things or *adjusts* them. Its main qualities are responsiveness and an ability to improvise. Its blind spot can lie in fickleness and a tendency toward distraction. The four Mutable signs, sometimes linked in Grand Cross configurations are, Gemini, Virgo, Sagittarius, and Pisces.

As you can see, each mode embraces a Fire sign, an Earth sign, an Air sign, and a Water sign. At the truly primeval level, this three-times-four situation is the core of all astrological theory: three elements expressing themselves in four modes – *voilà:* the twelve signs of the zodiac.

A Grand Cross is composed of four points – *that means four different signs, but each one is in the same mode.* There are Cardinal Grand Crosses, Fixed ones, and Mutable ones. Even though the signs involved are battling it out in squares or oppositions, they do share *modal* common ground. That is not quite the same as elemental harmony, but it does suggest the possibility of *pulling together.*

As we will see, that pulling together is the heart of the matter when it comes to any positive response to a Grand Cross. These are the dray horses of astrology. They can pull a plow through the mud.

A familiar footnote here is that, just as with the Grand Trine, since aspects do not have to be exact in order to work, it is possible to see an *out-of-quality* Grand Cross – that is, one with a planet or two in the "wrong" sign. Once more, in this case, we see a considerably weakened expression of this aspect pattern.

There is something solid about a box. That is probably why it is such a ubiquitous form in architecture. Walls support roofs. Floors support walls. When the "flying buttress" was developed, I suspect that many people thought it was the work of the devil.

Solid strength sounds like a good ally – but strength cannot always be equated with wisdom. One can be both strong and foolish at the same time, and the combination can be deadly. *Each mode can be stubbornly persistent in its attachment to its own style.* And while starting, sustaining, and ending are all essential mechanisms when applied at the right time, they are all potential catastrophes when applied at wrong times or under wrong circumstances or with wrong motivations. Then, lacking the requisite wisdom, they become forms of self-sabotage.

This quality of strength, *in both its positive and negative faces,* is fundamental to our understanding of how the Grand Cross works.

- When the Grand Cross falls in the *Cardinal* Mode, its main strength lies in *boldly initiating action* and in *attracting support,* while the main forms of self-sabotage lie either in starting things that should never have been started in the first place, or in failing to follow through on one's inspired beginnings – the failure to finish what was started.
- When the Grand Cross falls in the *Fixed* Mode, its main strength lies in *sustaining intentions* over time and in the face of whatever resistance arises, while the main form of self-sabotage lies in failing to recognize clear calls to change or adapt, or in ignoring clear signs that "the party is over."

- When the Grand Cross falls in the *Mutable* Mode, one main strength lies in *adaptability, responsiveness,* and in the *ability to "tweak" strategies in the face of shifting realities.* Another strength is the early recognition of the need to let go, to "die" in some sense of the word, and simply to move on. The main form of self-sabotage lies in distraction, scattered energy, loss of focus on one's primary aims, and general discouragement.

When healthy, any Grand Cross is a source of tremendous endurance and tenacity. It can "keep its eye on the prize," manifesting high levels of engagement, focus and determination. The trick lies in choosing the right prize.

When unhealthy, a Grand Cross can correlate with feelings of being *trapped* or *stuck.* (You might feel the vexing hand of squares and oppositions in those words.) This is true even in the mutable situation – for an illustration, ask anyone whose "marriage has been dying for decades."

Those kinds of stuck feelings arise when we have applied this formidable power to the attainment of wrong or unworthy goals. We attain them, all right – and they are harder for us to release than they were to grasp. Stubborn strength and determination become our enemies then. The world appears to be defined by impossibilities and by situations in which we feel as if we are damned if we do and damned if we don't. Naturally, feelings of depression and futility arise.

- In the dark expression of *Cardinal* Grand Cross energy, this sickness manifests as endlessly beginning new projects in a spirit of hope that a new day is dawning, only to lose interest and focus for no obvious reason.
- In the dark expression of *Fixed* Grand Cross energy, this sickness manifests as Einstein's famous definition of madness: constantly repeating the same failed methods in hopes of achieving a different result. Another way to express the same idea is "failure to flow with changing times."
- In the dark expression of *Mutable* Grand Cross energy, this sickness manifests in our remaining locked in "endless endings." The most obvious illustration is one we saw a moment ago – a marriage that ended in every meaningful sense of the word long ago, but still limps ever onward through the unchanging and hopeless fog.

HOW TO TUNE YOUR GRAND CROSS

To properly "tune" a Grand Cross, the analytic key lies in breaking the structure down into the specific dynamics of its two oppositions and its four squares. Some of what follows here may be familiar to you if you have read the previous two volumes in this series, but I repeat it since it is essential to any grasp of how to encourage the healthy expression of a Grand Cross. It boils down to getting squares and oppositions to work for you rather than against you. And remember: those aspects are not bad, they are just hard. There's a difference.

- With *oppositions*, the low response is always *polarization* – the two planets stall each other's growth. You feel stuck in irresolvable situations. The high response to opposition aspects lies in recognizing their *complementarity*. Here, we build on the common ground and healthy interdependency that underlies all of nature's polarities. Examples: kindness and truthfulness, pride and humility, head and heart. Are these all natural antagonists – or potentially friends? Down the friendship road, we see the complementary dimension of how opposition aspects can be made to work.

- With *squares*, the low response is simply the idea of two human drives – a.k.a., "planets" – operating "at crossed purposes." They block and vex each other, each one sabotaging the other one's intentions. In the high response to a square, each planet offers the other one *valued criticism, perspective,* and *correction.* For example, Aries can teach Cancer a lot about the virtues of directness and boldness, while Cancer can teach Aries about self-care, kindness, and good boundaries.

With this understanding of the underlying dynamics of squares and oppositions, we can begin to turn a Grand Cross into a source of strength, self-knowledge, even wisdom. In a moment, we will see how that works in practice, but first: some perspective.

The word "planet" has become a little fuzzy lately with the discovery of the trans-Neptunians, along with Pluto's ambivalent status among the astronomers. Basically, most modern astrologers use a system of ten planets. A Grand Cross involves four of them. What I am about to say is a gross oversimplification since I am leaving out the Angles and the nodes, but to interpret a Grand Cross, you essentially have to interpret "40%" of anyone's chart – a whole lot of it in other words.

It is not enough to say that someone was born with a Grand Cross involving "Neptune square Saturn square Jupiter square Mercury" – even though saying just that much is a mouthful.

But what *signs* are conditioning those four planets? We have learned that, while "Neptune" is a meaningful term, it only takes on human meaning when it is conditioned and motivated by its presence in a specific sign.

And then of course the question of what *house* it occupies comes into play.

Let's say Neptune is in the fourth house in the sign Leo. It squares a sixth house Saturn, retrograde, in Scorpio, while opposing a tenth house Jupiter in Aquarius. Meanwhile, a twelfth house Mercury in Taurus squares the Neptune-Jupiter axis and opposes that sixth house Saturn.

Got all that? It's an even bigger mouthful – and by this point, perhaps you are ready for a . . .

A BRIEF COURSE OF PSYCHOTHERAPY

There is no shame in feeling confused and overwhelmed by all of this! I feel like that for at least a little while every day of my working existence. Life is complicated, and astrology holds a mirror before it. *Astrologers who are never confused are probably not very good astrologers.* Why? Because they are oversimplifying both life and the nature of the psyche.

We have to somehow surf the waves of all this confusion.

How?

Orderly methods help a lot. Maybe you are in despair because you have "a million things to do." *Well, make a list and start at the top.* You feel better already, right? We will do exactly that astrologically in a moment as we sort through this very complex Grand Cross.

Here's another tip: when faced with the overwhelming complexity of any macro-aspect, look for *patterns* in the symbolism. *Is it giving you the same message multiple times?* If so, you have found a *unifying theme*, not to mention a good starting point for your interpretation.

To be a good astrologer, you need a Virgo virtue – attention to detail. But you also need a Sagittarian virtue – the intuitive ability to soar over an ocean of details and grasp the big picture. If either of those virtues is missing, you will be in trouble. Virgo and Sagittarius are square to each other, but remember: all aspects are about integration.

Pull Virgo and Sagittarius together, and you will be eating Grand Crosses for breakfast.

MILES DAVIS

The seminal American jazz musician, Miles Davis, was born on May 26, 1926, at 5:00 in the morning in Alton, Illinois, USA. The chart has a Rodden rating of AA. A full interpretation of his chart is beyond the scope of this book, but he is the person whose Grand Cross I have been describing. He is the man with Neptune in the fourth house in the sign Leo, squaring a sixth house Saturn, retrograde, in Scorpio, while opposing his tenth house Jupiter in Aquarius. And meanwhile, a twelfth house Mercury in Taurus squares the Neptune-Jupiter axis and opposes that sixth house Saturn.

As we just saw, we can avoid becoming overwhelmed by employing an orderly approach. Let's use that strategy as we dive into the Grand Cross that drove this complicated man's transformative genius.

Begin with the recognition that Miles Davis's Grand Cross is in the Fixed mode. As we learned a few pages ago, that tells us that his potential strength lies in *sustaining intentions* over time and in the face of whatever resistance arises, while the main form of self-sabotage lies in failing to recognize clear calls to change or adapt, or in ignoring clear signs that "the party is over."

Miles – and I've never met a jazz fan who called him "Davis" – certainly "sustained his intentions" over time: he got his first trumpet for his thirteenth birthday and basically played until the end of his life.

Self-sabotage? We will find plenty of that in his story, but it did not take the form of a failure to change, at least not in the musical category. Miles' own words: "I want to keep creating, changing. Music isn't about standing still and becoming safe."

Even though his Grand Cross was in Fixed mode, both his Sun and his Ascendant were in Mutable Gemini. That helped! We are forever balancing contradictory testimonies in every chart.

Now let's *look for patterns* in his Grand Cross.

- A sixth house planet and a tenth house planet: *work* and *mission* themes jump out.

- Neptune is part of it, plus there is a twelfth house planet: inner life themes emerge; creative themes; possible escapist themes too. Those are "doubled" here – it's good to notice that pattern.
- The "star-quality" symbolism of the tenth house Jupiter in rebel-Aquarius is juxtaposed against the very "yin," inward qualities of the other three planets in the Cross. The theme of fame – *along with stress and ambivalence over it* – leaps out of the synthesis.

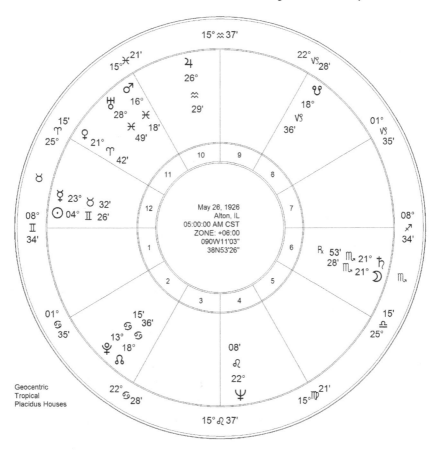

MILES DAVIS

We have already made a good start. Maybe you feel somewhat less overwhelmed than the way you felt when you read, "Neptune is in the fourth house in the sign Leo. It squares a sixth house Saturn, retrograde, in Scorpio, while opposing a tenth house Jupiter in Aquarius. Meanwhile, a twelfth house Mercury in Taurus squares the Neptune-Jupiter axis and opposes that sixth house Saturn."

Again, whenever you are faced with daunting levels of astrological complexity, take refuge in two strategies: an orderly, step-by-step approach and a quest for any underlying themes or patterns in the symbolism.

Let's delve more deeply into Miles Davis's Grand Cross by taking a brief look at these four planets one at a time, starting with Neptune in Leo in the fourth house. With the big patterns clear in our minds, we can risk facing the details without so much fear of getting lost in them.

Miles' *creativity* is obvious and is reflected in the happy marriage of Neptunian *openness to inspiration* working in tandem with the Leo urge to *offer some tangible evidence of his inner life to the larger world.*

There is a darker side to that Neptunian theme. Miles was addicted to heroin, starting in 1949. Quoting from Astrodatabank, "With strong *family support* (the italics are mine) for rehabilitation, he went into rehab to get clean. Though he overcame heroin in the early '50s, he continued to use cocaine until 1981."

I italicized "family support" because of Neptune being in his fourth house. His people were there for him when he finally realized that he needed them.

Miles' music came out of a deep well of spirituality, and like most sensitive souls, his sensitivity overwhelmed him sometimes – hence his escapist tendencies.

He also had another Neptunian fourth house quality: *his mythic, magical relationship with Africa and his Leo pride in his racial heritage* – and note here how Neptune is opposed by that tenth house Jupiter. He integrated these two poles to produce his music. But this same opposition also reflects Miles' antagonist, tense relationship with the dominant culture of his times: "white society," in a nutshell. He was dependent upon it, and he resented it too.

Miles' sixth house Saturn in Scorpio manifested in many ways. That he was both demanding of his "servants" and hard-working himself leaps out. Arguments and splits with other musicians abound in his biography.

There is also the *mentoring* aspect of the sixth house – as a young man, Miles studied music under his teachers at Julliard, burning the midnight oil, learning music theory. And of course his "mentoring" of subsequent generations of jazz players is legendary.

This sixth house Scorpionic Saturn configuration also often suggests that sickness might play a role in a person's life. Quoting again from Astrodatabank, "Plagued by illness much of his life, at various times Davis battled diabetes, pneumonia, a stroke, and hip joint problems caused by sickle cell anemia. He had surgery to remove polyps on his vocal cords in 1956 and broke both legs in an auto accident in 1972. By 1971 he moved into five years of health problems that were so severe that he dropped out of circulation ...Davis died of pneumonia, respiratory failure and a stroke."

That sixth house Scorpionic Saturn manifested in a third way. To support his heroin habit, he became a pimp with a string of seven prostitutes – a professional vector that is also reflected in the "criminal" dimensions of his Aquarian Jupiter.

Jupiter in Aquarius in Miles Davis's tenth house manifested in many clear ways. He was obviously a public figure; he had an experience of fame and success in the world – and his Aquarian energies left their mark on his professional life. He was both a rebel and an innovator.

Beyond the self-evident "fame-and-success" meanings of Jupiter in the tenth, we can also see a broader *call to mission*. And the nature of that mission was that Miles was an embodiment of Jupiter: one who represented *hope, dignity,* and *possibility* to his community in a way that involved the particularly Aquarian quality of challenging the existing *status quo*. There are both musical and racial resonances there, in that he challenged both systems.

Jupiter is also prone to excess, ostentation, and extravagance. Again, we see Miles' public patterns of addiction, sexual extremities, expensive tastes, four divorces, and so on.

Swinging around to *Mercury in Taurus in the twelfth house*, we come to perhaps the most elusive piece of the Grand Cross puzzle. There are some obvious elements here, and we will get to them, but this configuration – along with his prominent Neptune – suggests the richness of his interior life. His music was only the tip of the inner iceberg.

298 THE BOOK OF AIR

Mercury rules both his Ascendant and his Sun, giving it focal centrality here. Yet anything in the twelfth house is only halfway in this physical
world. *From where does such genius as we heard in Miles Davis's work spring?*
Probably not even he could fully answer that question.

Earlier, I made reference to the tension between his extravagant Jupiter on one hand – and everything else in his Grand Cross on the other
hand. Miles was clearly a public figure, with a mission in the world. But the
wellspring of vision which supported that mission arose from the deepest
mysteries of his own consciousness.

In his later years, Miles Davis would often perform with his back to
the audience, *as if he were a priest facing an altar in communion with the gods.*

That last line might seem a bit overwrought – at least until you look
at his Grand Cross.

At a more concrete level, there is another way in which we can see the
signature of Miles' Mercury being in Taurus and the twelfth house – not
to mention being opposed by Saturn and squared by Neptune. He literally had *problems* (Saturn) with his *voice* (Mercury), having had surgery to
remove polyps from his larynx. His physician ordered him not to speak for
ten days. Instead he argued with a member of his band – and permanently
damaged his vocal cords.

He spoke with a raspy voice for the rest of his life.

How do we judge the life of someone like Miles Davis? Why would
we even feel the need to judge it? Our task as astrologers is not to judge,
but rather to help. In reflecting on the four points in Miles' Grand Cross,
and comparing their astrological meanings with the story of his life, we see
a soul struggling with a complex synthesis of energies. He made mistakes;
he hurt himself and he hurt other people.

And, in ways we will never fully understand, he went down, like a
shaman, into his fierce, stormy soul, and came forth wounded, but alive,
bearing gifts that can still lift us up.

Just play *Sketches of Spain* or *Kind of Blue* and you will hear what I
mean.

THE YOD

Two planets, sextile each other, while each one lies in quincunx aspect to a third planet – that is the *Yod*.

We can express that same astrological geometry in another way – one that means exactly the same thing: two planets in sextile aspect, with a third one *opposing their midpoint*.

Either way you express it, in the Yod aspect pattern, we have one of the most energetic structures available in the entire vocabulary of astrology.

Speaking of vocabulary, let's call the sextile planets the *base* of the Yod and the planet to which they both form a quincunx the *focal planet*.

Yod is also the tenth letter of the Hebrew alphabet. There it is pronounced to rhyme with "code," even though the custom in the contemporary world of astrology is to rhyme it with "odd."

I am no scholar of Hebrew, but I gather that there was a historical connection between Yod being the tenth letter of the Hebew alphabet and our having ten fingers. The letter became linked symbolically to human hands, and eventually narrowed down simply to the index finger.

Thus was born a common astrological synonym for the Yod aspect – the *Finger of God*. That is a powerful and, as we will soon see, extremely evocative metaphor for the energy generated by this particular aspect pattern. Getting ahead of myself, can you imagine what it might feel like to be innocently walking down the street one day when suddenly the clouds part, a *basso profundo* voice from the heavens pronounces your name, then the "finger of God" points directly at you?

That's how a Yod feels. God seems to have high expectations of you, and God is quite insistent about them. You are called to serve something bigger than yourself.

To understand how a Yod works, we have to break it down into its components, just as we did with the Grand Trine and the Grand Cross. We have to dissect the Yod, starting with . . .

THE SEXTILE

Two planets, approximately 60° apart – that sextile aspect is the *base* of the Yod and the engine that drives it. The first step in making your Yod dance is to get that sextile tuned up. Let's start by understanding how sextiles work.

When I was a young astrologer, I learned that the sextile was the lesser of the two "good" aspects. The trine was taken as the gold standard and the sextile got the silver medal. The sextile was typically described as being "like a trine, only less powerful."

There is some truth in that, but the deeper reality is that the tonality of a sextile aspect is quite distinct from that of the trine. With trines, I often think of a state of *mutual enhancement* existing between two planets. With sextiles, I think of *stimulus, excitement,* and *a far wilder ride.*

Picture a mature couple thirty years down the road of sharing life. They love each other – *calmly.* Compare their relationship to that of two teenagers who met at a party five days ago and who have been devouring each other in ecstasy ever since.

The first relationship has the spirit of the trine, while the second one is far closer to the feeling of the sextile. In either case, we are looking at something like love. But the nature of the energetic exchange is quite distinct. We respect those young lovers and understand that they are having an important developmental experience. *Still, would you bet your favorite shirt that they would still be in love six weeks from now?* Young love tends to be unstable and unpredictable. Sextiles are like that too. They can start vibrating so hard that the rivets pop out of their wings and they experience a crash landing.

For a sextile aspect to truly *hum* in the psyche, each of the planets needs to mature – again, just like our young lovers.

As we rise toward the higher evolutionary realms presented by each individual planet in the sextile, we tune the engine that drives the Yod. This tuning must always be the first step; if we do not get it right, then we are sitting on the psycho-spiritual equivalent of Chernobyl.

So far, I am speaking in abstractions. We will soon clarify these points with an example. But the sextile is only one part of the Yod. As we continue our dissection of the structure, our attention turns to . . .

THE QUINCUNX

In Latin, *"quinc"* references the number five, while *"unx"* is linked to the number twelve. Thus, "five twelfths" is a good translation of quincunx – and that brings us right to the point. Count five signs forward and you arrive at the quincunx aspect. Call Aries "zero" since it is the starting point, then Taurus becomes one, Gemini two, Cancer three, Leo four – and Virgo is number five. If you have a planet in the middle of Aries and another planet in the middle of Virgo, you are looking at a quincunx.

And if you want to drive an Aries person crazy, all you have to do is lock him in a small room with a Virgo for a few days.

It works the other way around too – you can drive a Virgo crazy with an overdose of Aries energy just as easily.

Aries: Why prepare so much? Why are you always so worried? I'm starting to feel impatient. Don't sweat, we can just make it up as we go along – improvise, you know. It will be okay, don't worry.

Virgo: But this could go wrong and that could go wrong. Can't you see that? We need Plan B and Plan C – and what about equipment? We haven't even *talked about* equipment yet. And what about learning a little bit about the place before we get there?

Aries: Just don't worry.

Virgo: Somebody's obviously got to.

Please note that here in introducing the quincunx aspect, I have been using the *signs*, Aries and Virgo, to illustrate the principles. What *planets* are we talking about? At this point, that does not matter. The fundamental tensions which characterize the quincunx aspect can be understood most clearly simply through the signs involved. Those sign energies are what is motivating each planet, and it is those *motivations* that are "quincunx" to each other. The planets themselves are merely carrying that sign signature.

To really understand the action of a quincunx, we need to stand in the middle, halfway between Aries and Virgo, respecting both of them, seeing the wisdom in each of their positions. For Aries to understand Virgo, or *vice versa*, each one must undertake an *enormous adjustment*.

That *mutual adjustment* is one of the most critical elements in grasping the integrative action of a quincunx, and how to get it right. Without that mutual adjustment, in a quincunx, there is only misunderstanding and a squandering of vital force in endless mutual sabotage.

Here is another critical piece of the quincunx puzzle: *mutual fascination.*

In a healthy quincunx situation, each planet seems to sense – quite correctly – that the other one "understands something that I am missing." Even though there is a strong signature of exasperation and frustration as these two very different sign energies attempt to integrate, a kind of *magnetism* also pulls them together.

It is for this "magnetic" reason that we see a common, if little recognized, astrological phenomenon: *a romantic couple linked by a quincunx aspect.* Barack and Michelle Obama are a fine illustration – he is a Leo and she is a Capricorn. Creative partnerships are common here too. If you are a fan of Led Zeppelin, just think of Jimmy Page and Robert Plant. Again, we have a Leo and a Capricorn with a long history of both prodigious artistic synergy – and driving each other crazy.

Bottom line: a quincunx aspect is difficult and unstable, and yet, with a commitment to cross oceans of difference – a commitment, driven by mutual fascination, to *adjust* to each other for the sake of love – enormous energies can be released. It is like the nuclear fusion that drives the heart of the Sun – and wait a minute: didn't I just use the metaphor of Chernobyl a few lines ago?

That is my second nuclear metaphor in six hundred words.

And that was not an accident. A Yod is explosive.

VOILÀ: THE YOD

To make a Yod, you marry a sextile to a pair of quincunxes. And if you have been paying attention, you probably sense a certain parallel with marrying a detonator to a stick of dynamite. The simile is extreme – but so is the action of a Yod. If you have one, it is as if you suddenly find yourself riding a bucking bronco. You've got to hold on tight and roll with the bounces. Riding it is scary, but falling off is worse.

- In a Yod aspect pattern, the exciting, stimulating energies of the sextile ride up the twin quincunx channels, thereby adding an additional layer of wild energy in the process, and then they jam themselves mercilessly into that focal planet, energizing it to the point of incandescence.

It is as if the *Finger of God* is pointing to that focal planet. And when God calls your name, it is difficult to answer, "No, sorry, I'm already busy that day . . ."

I have never seen a truly reliable astrological indicator of fame. A stellium in the tenth house might do it, but typically it does not. A person with such a tenth house configuration might respond in laudable fashion to it without ever getting on the evening news. Such a stellium is about *relating meaningfully to one's community* – and "community" can mean anything from global notoriety to having an impact on one little town in Iowa.

If the planet Jupiter plays a central role in a person's chart, he or she often displays a certain *star quality* – but, once again, many people with that energetic signature do not become famous, nor do they need to.

If I had to pick one astrological configuration as a predictor of fame, it would not be the tenth house or a big Jupiter. It would be the Yod.

With that said, I still stand by my previous statement that I have never seen a truly reliable astrological indicator of fame. Even a Yod does not necessarily spell a bazillion "Likes" and "followers," nor does it need to. Yods often have other meanings, and we will soon explore them.

Still, in every case, we see extreme developmental pressure on that focal planet.

That makes sense when you remember that the Finger of God has pointed straight at you.

MICHEL GAUEQUELIN

Those who claim that there is "no scientific evidence" for astrology have ignored – or chosen to ignore – the work of Michel Gauquelin. Working with thousands and thousands of hand-calculated charts over six volumes of research, with the help of his partner Francoise, he essentially created a statistical proof that specific planetary placements correlated with success in specific careers.

Gauquelin started his work in 1950. His most influential book, *Cosmic Clocks*, came out in 1967. I'm not going to summarize his work any further here. If you are interested, Google him – or read my book, *The Night Speaks,* where I tell a bit more of his story.

A line might have slipped past you: "Thousands and thousands of charts"... *before home computers.* In the old days when I too had to prepare a chart with my ephemeris, my Table of Houses, a pencil, and patience, setting one up usually took me about fifteen minutes. Gauquelin did "thousands and thousands" of them that way.

You have got to be crazy – or have a Yod in your chart – to work that obsessively. This man was driven.

Michel Gauquelin was born in Paris on November 13, 1928, at 10:15 in the evening. Neptune in Virgo in his first house closely sextiles his Scorpionic Mercury on the astrological nadir. Both are quincunx an Arian Uranus in the ninth house, making Uranus the focal point of a Yod.

Let's start with the base of the Yod. In Michel Gauequelin, spiritual or *metaphysical interests* (Neptune) were motivated by Virgo *skepticism* and a *willingness to question and criticize.* His Neptune expressed itself behaviorally in a highly *autonomous, independent* style – it is there in the "I'm the boss" first house. Curious Mercury was powerfully placed, just a couple of degrees from the midnight point of his chart. It was animated by Scorpionic values – a *probing, psychological* mind, especially fascinated by anything "taboo," and expressing itself in the fourth house realm of *psychology, family, and inner life.*

That Neptune-Mercury sextile was accurate to within two degrees, and with both planets in Angular houses, it was a powerful engine. This enormous sextile energy drove the focal planet hard.

And that focal planet was rebel-Uranus, in battle-hungry Aries, in the crusading ninth house.

No Yod is ever "mellow," but Michel Gauquelin's had Warp Drive and photon torpedoes.

Astrology has come a long way from 1950 in terms of public acceptance. Back then, any interest in the subject was generally taken as good evidence that a person was weak in the head. As Gauquelin's work gained notice, he attracted far worse poisons than mere academic criticism or indifference.

It is a long story. Once again, I tell it in *The Night Speaks* and I am not going to repeat it here. Suffice to say that some of Gauquelin's antagonists actually *doctored research* with an aim to falsify his honest results supporting the basic premises of astrology. One scientist described the way they treated his work as "the biggest scandal in the history of rationalism." That may be a bit hyperbolic, but it does illuminate something of Michel Gauquelin's experience of an Arian Uranus as the focal point of his mighty Yod – he was attacked mercilessly, unfairly, and passionately. He was driven by his principles into a battle that left him scarred.

In so doing, he gave astrology a gift that needs to be more widely recognized.

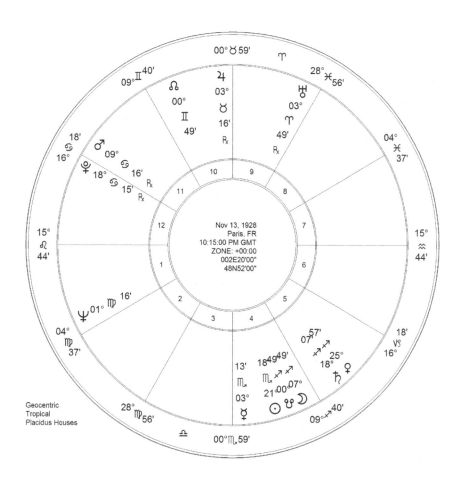

MICHEL GAUQUELIN

I met Michel Gauquelin briefly in New Orleans in 1989. We were both speaking at the United Astrology Congress there. We rode an elevator together, recognized each other, and had a quick conversation. His Sun fell on my Ascendant and his focal-point Uranus was only half a degree from my Moon. There was a kind of instant *simpatico* between us.

That was the only time I ever saw him.

A couple of years later he was dead by his own hand. He burned brightly and he burned too briefly. I honor his memory and I am happy to applaud him here in these pages.

I, ME, MINE

The human ego being the beastie that it is, one's own chart is naturally the most fascinating subject in the world. Balancing the spiritual perils of self-obsession, it is also fair to say that your own chart is the natural laboratory for (potentially) the most honest kind of astrological study. While the ego's fears and wishes are notorious enemies of true self-knowledge, the soul to which we have the most direct access is invariably our own.

In working with the charts of famous people, or even of friends, we see only surfaces – events, situations, patterns of experience. From them, we can conjecture about the inner meaning of outward things. This is not an entirely futile exercise, especially when our perceptual acuity is sharpened by astrology – or by love, for that matter.

Still, the most naked insights arise when we contemplate our own reflection staring back at us in the astrological mirror.

At the risk of being self-indulgent here, I want to say a few words about my own personal experience with a Yod chart pattern that has dominated my own life.

I have a very tight (1°18') Mars-Mercury conjunction on the cusp of my third house. It is a weird one in that Mercury is in the last couple of minutes of Capricorn, while Mars is in early Aquarius.

Right there, you see it. There's my life: when I am not talking, I am writing. Mercury rules the third house, and Mars rules my chart, along with Pluto.

My Moon in early Aries lies in the fourth house, and forms a sextile to that Mars-Mercury conjunction.

Moon in Aries: my hair has been on fire ever since the day I was born. There's another Mars signature.

My natal Saturn lies in Virgo in a nearly precise conjunction with my midheaven. It opposes the midpoint of that sextile and thus operates as the focal point of the Yod. Hardworking Saturn motivated by the hardworking values of Virgo and expressing itself on the hardworking Midheaven.

Perhaps you detect a pattern there?

Now, we punch the accelerator. That hot sextile pumps up Saturn – and it's not just any sextile. This one is made of a combination of a Mercury-third house *thematic pattern* married to a Mars-Aries *thematic pattern*.

None of those suggest a quiet evening sitting in an easy chair.

I am seventy-one years old and I am working harder now than I have ever worked in my life – which is saying something because I have always worked hard. The phrase, "I am not complaining," immediately comes to mind. I love my work and I am genuinely grateful for it. Because of this astrological tiger I have had by the tail for almost sixty years, my life feels meaningful to me. With each passing year, I treasure that feeling of meaningfulness more and more.

But of course I whine constantly.

Saturn in Virgo on the Midheaven? The Moon of a "heroic martyr?" An acerbic Mars-Mercury conjunction? I complain of overwork. I complain of the endless demands of the counseling profession. I complain that I never have time to relax or any time for much self-care.

Do I change anything? No, not really. Bottom line, I love it all.

Given my age, naturally people inquire about my retirement plans. I used to respond, would the Pope retire?

Then, of course, a Pope did.

But not me.

To say that I am having *too much fun* to retire is "truthy" – but not quite right. It is more truthful to say that I am too "driven" to retire – but that makes me sound neurotic. And I do not actually feel neurotic.

To say that I "was born for this mission" is quite accurate, at least subjectively – that is how I feel about it. This work does honestly feel "bigger than me." So long as my body and my wits do not fail me, retirement does not even feel like a *moral* option.

The trouble with talking like that is that it sounds so grandiose and self-important. Libra-paradox fashion, it sits on the other side of the see-saw from my apologetically dismissing myself as "neurotic."

So: onward through the fog.

That is my Yod, which is pretty much the story of my life, minus a few footnotes about romance, cats, bands, sailboats, and hikes.

I am too busy to think about this anymore. I need to finish *The Book of Air*, so I can get to *The Book of Water* . . .

PART FOUR

SEEING FUTURES

For all of us, there is a time when everything depends upon us simply stopping and paying attention. The universe is trying to give us a fresh message. It is time for a realignment of the world you believe that you are living in – the one in your head – and the one that is actually out there. Your map is bad, in other words. It needs to be updated, or you will think you are heading for London, but you've just gotten on the bus for Timbuktu.

No matter your astrological makeup, you will pass through such Air-dominated periods. Navigating them is what this book is all about.

What signals the arrival of such times? And how can we best prepare for them and use them intentionally and consciously?

Against the backdrop of your natal chart, there is a constant tidal flow of moving points: transits, progressions, and solar arcs. They provide the keys to understanding the dynamics of our entire journey through life on a day-by-day, year-by-year basis.

Sometimes these astrological triggers move into Air signs or into the "Air" houses – three, seven, and eleven. Sometimes they form aspects with Mercury, Venus, Saturn, or Uranus.

At such times, the universe is simply inviting us to "listen up." It is saying, "I've got news for you."

Within that broader tidal flow of moving planets we just mentioned, there is another set of motions: those four Air planets themselves moving through your natal chart, hitting sensitive points via their own transits, progressions and solar arcs. They too are begging us to "pay attention."

All or any of these kinds of astrological events mark the outset of Air chapters in your journey. Some are minor, gone in a week. Others will rock your world. These are times when you are invited to go to bed smarter, better informed, and wiser than you were when you got up that morning.

In the pages that follow, we throw away the astrologers' traditional crystal ball. We are not making predictions, at least not in any concrete, deterministic way. We will be using techniques that astrologers have used to "see the future" – but seeing the future is not our aim here. Instead, we use these Airy events to predict the questions that you will face, and to suggest answers – which is to say, conscious choices – that lead you to the higher ground.

You have many possible futures. Astrology can describe them all, along with their consequences. It can help you navigate wisely among them. It hands you the menu, in other words.

What you choose to eat is up to you.

16

THE AIR FAMILY AND ASTROLOGY'S CRYSTAL BALL

Our aim in this chapter is to begin to move toward understanding transits, progressions, and solar arcs connected with the Air Family. Other than the specific focus on the Air Element in these pages, that is exactly the same aim we had in the parallel chapters of *The Book of Fire* and *The Book of Earth*. Compounding the dilemma of repetition is the fact that Venus, Mercury, and Saturn all made their debuts in the previous volume, so that territory is already familiar to readers who have been following the series – and *terra incognita* to readers who have begun reading with this Air volume.

I face the familiar conundrum – do I repeat the previous material or boldly plunge forward, knowing that in doing so I would be leaving some readers to face college without benefit of kindergarten?

What I am going to do is to review the previous material, but in a tightened, shortened, mostly re-written form. I will focus at greater length on adding the new perspectives that are associated with the specific realities of the Air signs and with the planet Uranus, which we are meeting for the first time in this volume.

Some of you will read on and some will skip ahead – and if you fall in the latter camp, please do slow down when you see the words "Air" or "Uranus." That material is fresh, mission-critical, and previously unexplored.

SLOW AND FAST

A transit of Mercury and a transit of Uranus, *while they are actually happening*, are of equal strength. That statement would raise many an astrological eyebrow. "Everyone knows" that a Uranus transit is a bigger deal than a Mercury transit. True, but time is what makes their impact on our lives so different. Time is why, in practical astrological terms, a Uranus transit is a more significant event than a Mercury transit.

It all boils down to how long your consciousness is exposed to the energy.

Still, we should never lose sight of the fact that *while Mercury is passing through a sensitive zone, its impact on your life is every bit as palpable as that of Uranus.* It just doesn't last as long.

Real-life astrology happens at the interface of consciousness and the vast archetypal fields of possibility that the symbols represent. At our human end of the pipeline, it is all about consciousness. And consciousness is swimming in a river of time.

This leads us to a truly elemental principle in developmental astrology: generally the more slowly an astrological event unfolds, the more significant it is. Why? Simply because the slow-moving events have more time to develop depth and complexity of human meaning.

Maybe once you had a romantic fling with someone. Even though you were ships in the night, the memory is sweet, even tender, and the soul-encounter was intense. But it all happened many years ago. It's not forgotten – but months, even years go by when you don't even think of that person.

On the other hand, perhaps you were actually partners with someone for a decade or two – married, or something similar. And perhaps you parted many years ago. As we all know, that kind of partnership is a whole different psychological reality than a fling. That long relationship shaped you in ways that you are probably still figuring out.

Think carefully about the difference between these two scenarios: minute by minute, the experience of the fling was almost certainly far more intense than any random sample of moments from the long partnership.

And yet which sinks more deeply into your bones, a fling or a marriage?

That is exactly why a Uranus transit changes your life, while a Mercury transit typically does not.

SOME QUICK DEFINITIONS

There are many different techniques for moving planets and points against the backdrop of the natal chart. In my own practice, I use three of them: *transits, progressions, and solar arcs.*

- *Transits* are the actual motions of planets in the sky. If, for example, Venus is currently in Pisces by transit, that is true for everyone. Transits, in other words, are *external factors.* They are like weather. Everyone shares them. We just each respond to them in our own way – just like some people find a gray drizzling day gloomy while others may find it poignant and romantic.

- *Progressions* work more like an internal biological clock. They are unique to you; while your Mercury is progressing through Virgo, my Mercury might be progressing through Aries. The theory behind progressions sounds strange, but they work reliably: *days are set symbolically equal to years.* If you want to know the positions of your progressed planets on your fortieth birthday, you find out where those planets were in the sky literally forty *days* after your birth. *Voilà:* those are your progressed planetary positions.

- *Solar arcs* are a subset of progressions. We note the distance in degrees that the Sun has progressed according to the methods we described a moment ago. Then we add exactly that same "arc" to every one of the rest of the planets, equally. All solar arcs move at *exactly the same speed.* With small variations, the Sun progresses approximately 1° for every year of your life, so when you turn thirty, it has moved about 30° ahead of where it was located when you were born. To calculate your solar arcs on your thirtieth birthday, we would then add *that same 30°* to your Moon, your Mercury, your Ascendant, and all the rest.

(One quick technical note: Earth's orbit around the Sun is elliptical. The effect is that we are moving more slowly during the northern hemisphere summer and more quickly six months later. *So if you were born with the Sun in Capricorn, your solar arcs move slightly faster than someone born with the Sun in Cancer.* The idea that Solar arcs move 1° per year is only a useful approximation, in other words. Yours will vary slightly. The average annual motion of the progressed Sun is 59'08".)

Since solar arcs are slaved to the Sun, they reflect the Sun's nature – which is to say they tend, like the Sun, to be more *biographical and outward* in their manifestations.

Meanwhile, progressions are more sensitive to evolutions occurring beyond the boundaries of the human ego and the conscious, rational mind. Most of us have had the mysterious experience of waking up one morning and suddenly everything looks very different to us, even though we cannot put our finger on exactly why. Somehow our attitude has shifted. Progressions are more likely to mirror those kinds of deep psychic events than are solar arcs. They are not, in other words, quite as tied to the reasoning parts of our conscious "solar" minds.

At the same time, let's give your poor ego a break. You need it and it needs you, and solar arcs are its astrological reflecting pool.

THE RHYTHMS OF THE HEAVENS

Throughout the rest of the book, we will attempt to fathom all three of these developmental techniques as they relate to the Air Family. Exploring the enlivening, informing, perspective-shifting effects of the transits, progressions, and solar arcs of Venus, Mercury, Saturn, and Uranus is a big part of it. You will find all of that material spelled out in subsequent chapters. For now, let's consider a general point that applies to the motions of all planets no matter which element they occupy or represent.

- The transits of Sun, Moon, Mercury, Venus, and Mars are quick; they do not have much time to develop "depth and complexity of meaning." Instead, they tend to operate as *precipitating triggers* for events whose deeper significance is reflected in slower-moving cycles.
- All progressions and solar arcs, plus the transits of Jupiter, Saturn, Uranus, Neptune, and Pluto move slowly enough to sink into our bones. They are the basic tools we employ in holding the *thematic* astrological mirror before anyone's life.

VENUS AND MERCURY LIVE DOWNTOWN

Think of an archery target with its familiar concentric rings. Since the Sun lies at the center of the solar system, let's call it the bull's eye. Since Mercury and Venus orbit closer to the Sun than does the Earth, it is as if they are placed on the first and second rings of the target. Meanwhile, we earthlings are standing out on the third ring – while all the Martians occupy the fourth ring, and so on out to the edge of deep space.

Want a peek at Mercury or Venus? *Because their orbits circle inside of ours, to look in their general direction is to look, more or less, in the general direction of the Sun.*

They "live downtown," so to speak.

Just like the rest of the planets, Mercury and Venus can form conjunctions with the Sun – but unlike the rest of the planets, these conjunctions come in two flavors: *inferior* conjunctions and *superior* conjunctions. An inferior conjunction occurs when Mercury or Venus lies directly *between* the Earth and the Sun. A superior conjunction occurs when they are on the *far side* of the Sun. Either way, the planet and the Sun are lined up.

As you might imagine, these two kinds of conjunctions are rather different beasts – a point that will become pivotal in chapter twenty-one when we explore the Venus pentangle.

No other planets besides Mercury and Venus can possibly form inferior conjunctions with the Sun. For the rest of them, their orbits lie far out in space and the only way they can align with the Sun is by being directly opposite us, on the other side of the solar system, on the other side of the Sun – in superior conjunction, in other words.

As we have seen, a practical effect of the "downtown" status of Mercury and Venus is that from our point of view, they can never lie *very far* from the Sun.

- The maximum *elongation* of Mercury from the Sun is 27° – that is as far away as it can ever be from the Sun in any astrological chart.
- For Venus, the figure is 47°.
- One effect of all of this is that the only *major natal* aspect that either Mercury or Venus can ever form with the Sun is the conjunction. No other *natal* aspects are possible – although by transits, progressions, and solar arcs any aspect can form.

SPEED

With planets, speed is everything when it comes to their level of impact on us. Slowness equals power. And Mercury and Venus – at least by transit – are speed demons. They do not have much time to develop the "depth and complexity of meaning" that is characteristic of slower astrological events.

For that reason, neither Venus nor Mercury step full force into the status of true theme-builders until we see them operating by progression or by solar arc.

The solar arcs of Mercury and Venus unfold at the standard pace of about one degree each year. Their progressions, however, are much more complex. As we saw earlier, the actual positions of the planets thirty days after you were born are their progressed positions on your thirtieth birthday. How far have Mercury and Venus moved in the first month of your infancy?

That is a slippery question.

Since Mercury and Venus are slaved to the Sun, their *average* daily motion is exactly the same as that of the Sun – 59'08", or very slightly less than one degree.

What I just wrote is accurate, but it is also wildly misleading. The critical word there was "average." The *actual* daily motions of Mercury and Venus vary enormously. They slow down, even stop – or *make a station*, to use the technical term – as they prepare to turn retrograde. And they do the same thing again when they turn direct. Near stations, their motion is very slow. At stations, they are totally stopped. Midway between these "stations," they can attain impressive speeds.

The actual daily motions of Venus and Mercury are, in other words, all over the map. You really need to look at them case-by-case. That variation is expressed in their progressions as well, but in slow motion. If *progressed* Venus, for example, makes a station during your lifetime, there will be *many years* of your life when it barely moves at all.

Mercury's *maximum* daily motion is 1°40', while that of Venus is 1°22'. That is as fast as they can ever go. Their speeds range downward from there – all the way down to zero if they happen to be making a station.

Those are daily figures. They refer to *transiting* Mercury and Venus, in other words. For progressions, those exact same numbers refer to their *yearly* motions.

- If you happened to be born near a Venus station, the planet might only progress five or six degrees in the first twenty years of your life.

- If you were born during a faster part of its cycle, Venus might make it through *an entire sign* in that same length of time.

Venus is retrograde for roughly forty days out of its 584-day cycle – that is the length of time between its *successive inferior conjunctions*. So, *by progression*, once Venus turns retrograde, it will stay that way for about four decades, or a little longer.

This connection between Venus and the number forty, by the way, is very likely the source of many Biblical references, such as the children of Israel wandering in the wilderness for forty years before entering the Promised Land, or Jesus fasting in the wilderness for forty days – not to mention Noah experiencing some monumentally sour weather for "forty days and forty nights."

That is a big subject, but not one for this book. Bottom line, there is a lot more astrology in the Bible than meets the eye.

That long Venus cycle has some rather amazing features. After five inferior conjunctions, the planet has traced out a nearly perfect five-pointed star – a *pentangle*. It takes almost exactly eight years to do that by transit, providing a powerful, but relatively underutilized Venus cycle.

I am going to save that subject for later. It is rich enough to deserve an entire chapter of its own.

In the sky, Mercury is retrograde for an average of about three weeks. Thus, by progression, it remains retrograde for a bit over two decades – a fascinating period of life that we explored in chapter nineteen of *The Book of Earth*.

I will not repeat that material in this volume.

In summary, we have learned that by transit Mercury and Venus move too quickly to be of very deep evolutionary consequence. In that fashion, they only operate as event-triggers for more important, slower-moving, factors. It is only by progression and by solar arc that these two "downtown" planets really begin to shine.

We have two more Air Family planets to consider: Saturn and Uranus, which jointly rule the sign Aquarius.

SATURN IN MOTION

The further a planet lies from the Sun, the more slowly it moves forward in its orbit. It is not only slower, but its actual trek around the Sun is a lot longer too. The effect is that outer planets take a whole lot longer to move through the twelve signs than do the inner ones. We shift from the realm of months to the realm of decades.

Saturn's distance from the Sun ranges between eight and ten times further out into space than Earth's. The result is that Saturn is a slow boat, taking just a little under three decades to orbit the Sun a single time. The precise figure is 29.457 years. That works out to an average daily motion of 2'01" – only about 1/30 of a degree.

Hopefully, you jumped a little when you read the term *average* daily motion. As we learned with Mercury and Venus, "average" figures can be quite misleading. In common with the rest of the planets, Saturn slows down, makes a station, and slowly takes off in the opposite direction.

If Saturn takes almost thirty years to transit around the zodiac, how long would it take for it to do the same thing by progression? A lot longer! For practical purposes, you can put that one on the back burner. The answer is just under 11,000 years. *By progression Saturn simply doesn't do very much.* Even when it does form an aspect, the event unfolds so slowly that any awareness we might have of it is quite abstract. It might be in effect for half of your life.

I recommend ignoring the progressions of Saturn – and for similar reasons, I would also ignore the progressions of Jupiter, Uranus, Neptune, and Pluto.

Never fear: that leaves two faces of Saturn that are capable of changing the direction of your life – Saturn's transits and its solar arcs.

By transit, as we have seen, Saturn takes about twenty-nine years to get through the twelve signs and averages approximately 2' of motion per day. That languorous motion gives it plenty of time to develop depth and complexity of meaning. We will detail all of that in psychological and evolutionary terms in subsequent chapters.

Watching Saturn night after night against the starry background, we would see it lose speed, stop in its tracks, then loop backwards in retrograde motion for a while before turning around and advancing again. Just like the rest of the planets, it takes two steps forward, then one step back, then two more steps forward, eternally. In approximate terms, *Saturn generally remains in direct motion for about eight months, followed by four or five months of retrograde motion.* The exact figures vary somewhat because of the elliptical nature of its orbit.

Natally, that means that about one out of every three people is born with Saturn retrograde – and of course that also tells us that by transit, Saturn is retrograde about a third of the time.

Be mindful of Saturn's stations. At these times, its energies are particularly focused and intense. Transiting Saturn making a station conjunct your natal Sun is going to hit you a lot harder than Saturn moving pedal-to-the-metal through the same aspect.

URANUS IN MOTION

Uranus takes about eighty-four years to complete a circuit of the Sun. That works out to seven years or so to transit through each sign of the zodiac.

Taking seven years to advance thirty degrees tells us that *Uranus needs about three months to get through a single degree.*

How long do the effects of Uranian transits last? Much depends on how one defines the *orbs* of the aspects. If you use a relatively tight orb of, say, two or three degrees, then Uranus is likely to hang around a sensitive point for something on the order of two and a half years – definitely long enough to develop that famous "depth and complexity of meaning."

As with Saturn, the actual reality of Uranian behavior in the sky is complicated by retrogradation. Uranus advances for about seven months, slows to a station, then retrogrades for about five months before turning around and advancing again – so: seven steps forward and five steps back.

Stations, as always, are times of intensified Uranian expression. Never ignore them! A classic beginner's mistake is to trust the computer screen when it tells you that the last hit of Uranus on your Moon "happens in April" – when actually the following February brings Uranus back to a station only two degrees past your Moon. That might actually be the most intense part of the whole experience.

Never ignore planetary stations! Even if the aspect is off by two or three degrees, they are often the most dramatic moments of the entire passage. Stations really amplify the energy of a transiting planet.

By progression, Uranus, like Saturn, is simply too slow to notice. As of this moment, the oldest living person in the world is claimed to be Kane Tanaka of Japan. She is currently 116 years old. She's a Capricorn, born on January 2, 1903. Her natal Uranus lies in 22°36' of Sagittarius.

Her progressed Uranus, as I write today in August 2019, has made it all the way to 25°19' – 116 years of effort has only yielded 2°43' of "progress."

Such progressions are not meaningless. It's just that their meaning is too subtle for us to notice. Do we notice the galaxy turning? Do we notice mountains turning into flat plains or continents drifting? Do we even notice ourselves growing up?

The solar arcs of Uranus are powerful and obvious in their effects. They of course move at the same speed as all other solar arcs – linked forever to the Sun and moving at about one degree each year.

That is how the Air planets move. Let's talk about what those motions mean.

17

CELESTIAL NAVIGATION I: MERCURY TIMES, GEMINI TIMES

By transit, Mercury's path resembles a drunken mouse on steroids. It zooms along, faster than anything else in the sky except the Moon, then it skids to a halt, goes backwards for three weeks, changes its mind, goes forward . . . hesitantly at first, then faster and faster . . . looping through the sky that way three or even four times each year.

Mercury's motion by progression is cut from the identical pattern, but very much slowed down. Days become years, so watching the whole dance leaves you less dizzy. By progression, Mercury will remain retrograde for over two decades – again, understanding that is an important piece of astrological theory, which we covered in detail in *The Book of Earth*.

By solar arc, Mercury presents the universal, stately, predictable one-degree-per-year march forward, with never a retrograde moment.

In any of these three moving forms, Mercury always presses the same exhortation on us all: *pay attention, there is something right before your eyes that you are missing. Reality is not quite what you think it is . . .*

Above all, Mercury symbolizes that basic vitamin of personal evolution: *learning to see things differently.*

In Mercury times, the "Kingdom of God" is *not* within you – it is out there in that sacred mandala we call the world. That is where the secrets are being revealed – in conversations, in seemingly random bits of information, in events which the laws of synchronicity are staging for your personal benefit, if only you can remember to pay attention.

During Mercury times, the universe interrupts your normal programming for an important message . . .

WOW, I NEVER THOUGHT OF THAT BEFORE!

Back in the days when I did a lot of straightforward counseling, I worked with a young college man who described a breakthrough Mercury-moment that changed his life. This is one of those "you had to be there" stories, but it was powerful for him. One day, out of the blue, he simply realized that *"he was a bohemian."* The thought came into his mind like a bolt of lightning in those exact words – and the insight liberated him in one instant from many conventional familial strictures on his imagination about himself and his life. He immediately changed his major from Business to something more creative – and happily his relationship with his parents survived.

"I am a bohemian." It's just four words, almost trivial, easily forgotten. And yet they marked a turning point in this young man's life.

- Sometimes exactly the right words at exactly the right moment can change everything. Sometimes words are powerful beyond measure.

As this realization was happening, his progressed Mercury was sextile this young man's arty natal Venus. He had never thought of himself "as a bohemian" before. The words – and the fresh, liberating self-imagery underlying them – altered the direction of his life.

Words can change us; words are powerful medicine.
Mercury times are word times.

Speaking of words, I think fondly of J.K.Rowling, who gave us the *Harry Potter* saga. I quote this line straight out of Wikipedia: *"In 1990, while she was on a four-hour-delayed train trip from Manchester to London, the idea for a story of a young boy attending a school of wizardry "came fully formed" into her mind."*

Rowling had "never thought of *that* before" – and in October of that pivotal year in her life, progressed Mercury made a station and turned direct. Once again, never ignore a planetary station; as a planet changes direction, so does your life. If the planet is Mercury, words or ideas may very well wield the magic wand.

It worked for J.K. Rowling and it will work for you too.

In 1968, with Mercury progressing through a trine to her natal Uranus and heading for a sextile to its own position, novelist Ursula K. Le-Guin became haunted by an image of two distant figures making their way across a vast snowfield. She began pulling that imaginative thread – and by following that strange, evocative picture down into her soul, she was led to write her proto-feminist masterpiece, *The Left Hand of Darkness*.

The DNA molecule was discovered way back in 1869, but no one could figure out its structure. James Watson was stumped until one night he dreamed of a spiral staircase – and that was his breakthrough moment. He realized he could explain the chemical behavior of DNA by modeling it as a spiral staircase – the now-famous "double helix" that gives you your mama's nose and your papa's eyes.

Watson's dream happened in late February of 1953. Solar arc Mercury hit his Sun on June 25, 1952 and made a conjunction with his Jupiter on September 18, 1952. (Remember, at one degree per year, both aspects were still very active in early 1953.) Meanwhile, his progressed Mercury was heading for his astrological nadir – the very bottom of his chart, where dreams arise. It arrived there exactly on January 31, 1954 – again, close enough to lie within the orbs of the alignment when his pivotal dream-image came to him: the double helix was a Mercury message from his interior world.

Here's another dream-story – and note how Mercury's messages can come to us in the strange world of dreams. We can *pay attention* there too.

With solar arc Saturn squaring his natal Mercury, while progressed Mercury moved into a trine with his natal Uranus, Elias Howe was inspired by a dream to invent the sewing machine. In his dream, cannibals were preparing to dine on him. As they readied the stew-pot, they merrily danced around the campfire, waving their spears.

Howe *paid attention*; he noticed *a small hole through the shaft at the head of each of those spears.* When he awoke, the up-and-down motion of the spears as the cannibals danced stuck with him – and gave him the mission-critical notion of passing sewing machine thread through the pointy-end of needle instead of in the traditional way at the blunt end.

And that is how Mercury gave us the sewing machine.

Note how in every one of these tales, we encounter the same gold-star Mercury-mantra: *wow, I never thought of that before!*

SIGN AND OMENS

A friend recommends a new film. You nod your head agreeably, not really thinking very much about it. Two days later, a second friend speaks glowingly about the same film. Again, you nod your head. That weekend, you board a transoceanic flight. You brought a book, but it is beginning to bore you. You notice the in-flight movie menu includes the film your two friends have recommended.

You decide to watch it. Somehow it feels as if you are *supposed* to.

That does not sound exactly like a rational statement, but it is a very human one. And if by "rationality," we mean dealing with reality as it actually is, then perhaps trusting such a *synchronistic pattern* might be more rational than our science teachers led us to believe.

Three people you know, independently of each other, mention an opera they are planning to attend this weekend. You wish them well, but you have no taste for opera. Still, it strikes you as "perhaps a sign" that three people have mentioned it . . .

"By chance," a co-worker has a spare ticket to that same opera. His partner has the flu and can't go. He offers it to you at the last minute. *It seems as if the universe is telling you to be there.*

You accept the ticket – and to your surprise, you enjoy the opera.

You are out for a walk in a forest on a cloudy day. You arrive at a fork in the trail and experience a moment of uncertainty about which direction to take. In that moment of indecision, the clouds part and a ray of sunshine falls on the path to the left.

Who would then turn right?

The point of each of these anecdotes is that even though "reading signs and omens" sounds like some exotic anthropological practice, we humans all still do it almost automatically. In fact, it is likely that you yourself have actually had such an experience within the past week or two. You acted on an omen – and barely noticed that you were doing it.

Such *divination* may not be an official part of our culture, but it is hardwired into human nature. That is our critical point here, and it is inextricably bound to the nature of Mercury, the "messenger of the gods".

Carl Jung called this phenomenon *synchronicity*. Historically, that is a relatively new term. But the idea behind it is actually ancient – and it is one of the methods that Mercury uses to get through to us. During Mercury times, *paying attention* to such omens and taking them seriously can save you quite a lot of trouble.

Those messenger-gods are trying to help you, and they know things that you do not know – and that you probably need to know.

SPEAKING AND LISTENING

Mercury is the part of us that knows how to talk. Hopefully, it is the part of us that also knows how to listen. Communication is classic Mercury territory, and that process goes in two directions. Even though it is absolutely central to our understanding of Mercury, language is a subject I have intentionally avoided for the last few paragraphs. I did not want to get bogged down in it right away. The points I have made so far are much closer to the evolutionary heart of Mercury. The essence of the matter is that Mercury offers us a chance to *learn what we do not already know.*

There are many ways to accomplish that aim. High on the list is simply *listening* – and of course, we famously learn a lot more with our mouths closed than we do with our mouths open. During times of Mercury stimulus, *conversations* abound. Texts and emails are thick. You are flooded with data. *And somewhere in that haystack is the needle of something you really need to take in.*

Talking can be part of the Mercury process, provided we do not let it get in the way of listening. In terms of actively talking, Mercury's most powerful tool lies in *asking questions* – sincere questions, questions to which we genuinely do not have prefabricated answers.

Again, with Mercury, everything boils down to getting our own opinions and interpretations out of the way, and thus allowing our minds to be fed by the unexpected, the unanticipated, and the miraculous. A good conversation can do that, provided it is a two-way street and we work as hard at listening as we do at being perceived as wise and witty.

DISTRACTION

Mercury is curious about everything – and "everything" is a very big word. Because of that, during times of heightened Mercury activity, the possibility of *distraction* arises. You are halfway through one project when you get sidetracked by another one . . . which leads to a third sidetrack, and meanwhile number one is forgotten, then the phone rings.

That "project" might be as simple as a sentence you are trying to say, only to change course in the middle. Or we might find an aspiring novelist who has three genuinely compelling book ideas – and makes the mistake of getting three chapters into one, then starting another . . .

One obvious exhortation here is that during a Mercury time, we need to make an effort to *stay focused*. And indeed, if we truly want to learn anything during such a passage, some degree of *sustained mental discipline* is helpful. If we allow ourselves to be distracted by every whimsy, we doom ourselves to perpetual superficiality – which is a classic Mercury trap.

To that caution, we can add a deeper one.

If the laws of synchronicity are guiding you toward learning something *which might threaten your ego's defences*, then "distraction" might take on a darker quality. As you approach a deep insight, you might suddenly be consumed with an urge to Google something – anything, really. What ever happened to your favorite band from high school? Who invented television?

Anything.

Distraction – *changing the subject*, in other words – can be dark Mercury's way of keeping the ego's illusions, defences, and pre-recorded announcements safe.

During a Mercury time, *just as too little mental discipline can be a terrible enemy here, so can too much of it.* Keeping militantly "on the subject" may also be a way of avoiding other, less pleasant realizations. When there is something that we really do not want to know, we can *filibuster* – just keep hammering away verbally at the same familiar themes, maybe add some wit and a few red herrings . . . soon enough, everyone, yourself included, is too exhausted to ask you any hard questions at all.

With all of that spelled out, we come to a classic Libran moment – *on the other hand . . .*

Free-association is sometimes a legitimate and effective Mercury tool. Relaxing mental discipline and just letting one's thoughts drift on their own mysterious currents can lead us to understandings we might not otherwise encounter.

Case in point: J.K. Rowling sat on a delayed train and her thoughts drifted free-associatively to an idea that made her a bazillionaire.

Sorting all this out can be tricky. There is no rigid formula for getting it right. Mercury, like a child, needs both discipline and indulgence. It's a classic air-sign situation: a real tail-twitcher. Castor has to listen to Pollux, and *vice versa*.

As a guideline, when, during a Mercury time, you are dealing with emotionally-charged psychological questions, free association is not likely to produce much genuine insight. That is because the unconscious mind underlies and shapes that "free" association in ways that likely serve its darker, repressive purposes. Something inside of you is doing its level best to *keep* the material unconscious. Guaranteed, if you let your mind drift naturally, it will "drift" away from exactly what you need to know.

On the other hand, when you are faced with creative, scientific, professional, or practical questions, such free association during a Mercury time can be highly productive. "Disciplined" thought often goes down tired, established pathways – and in a Mercury time, you are always looking for serendipity. The unknown, the unexpected, and that which you have never before imagined are what actually feed you.

Put out the welcome mat for them.

At such times, free association, unencumbered by any psychological snakes in your head, can be a terrific tool. *Insight comes wrapped in surprise.* You may dream of natives dancing with their spears – and invent the sewing machine.

ENTERING GEMINI

Sooner or later, planets transit, progress, or solar arc into the sign Gemini. Parallel to the way signs flavor your *natal* planets, when this happens the character of the *moving* planet changes too. Venus is still Venus and Mars remains Mars, but their mood changes. They have different aims and different values than they did while they were passing through the previous sign, Taurus.

Gemini-fashion, they become more lively, curious, and communicative – and probably more easily distracted.

Here is an analogy. Just think back to a visit with your parents. Maybe it was a loving situation, maybe not – but one point is almost universally true: *you are a different person in the presence of your parents than the one you are in the presence of your friends.* We are not necessarily talking about any self-conscious editing of your behavior in order to avoid triggering family psychodrama. Maybe you got lucky, and you do not need to fake anything with your mother and father.

But for pretty much everyone, being with one's parents is a different *psychological context* than what we experience with our peers. Your friends know a different "you" than the one your parents know. There is, in other words, more than one "genuine you." All of them are real; all are sincere.

Similarly, there is more than one Uranus or Jupiter. There is the one in Taurus and there is the one in Gemini. They are equally authentic – but context modifies them significantly, the same way as visiting mom and dad modifies you.

When a planet enters Gemini, it becomes *restless, easily bored, hungry for something to happen.* It glances in every direction, sniffing the air for possibilities. Even if the planet is solitary Saturn, it takes on a somewhat more extroverted flavor. Maybe meeting someone new is no longer exactly the worst case scenario.

Underlying these energetic qualities is the evolutionary substratum. For that planet newly arrived in Gemini effectively to continue its developmental journey, it is going to require *further education.* There is something that it now *needs to learn* – something, by definition, that it does not already know.

Typically, a person is unaware of this evolutionary need, at least in conscious terms. That is not a problem – trusting that restless curiosity will do the trick, even if the person does not understand its purpose. The simple urge to just get out there and experience something fresh is sufficient. The laws of synchronicity take care of the rest. We bump into what we need to learn.

The only question is whether we truly see what is then lying right before our eyes.

SHE'S LEAVING HOME

A father has his natal Venus in the fifth house. He loves his Libran daughter very much. When she is sixteen years old, his Venus – not hers – progresses into Gemini. At the same time, his daughter is verging into womanhood.

Here comes a line that might strike you as silly, but it is actually quite important to the point I am making: *for all her life, the man's daughter has been younger than that.* This means that the entirety of the father's experience of her has been based upon his seeing her – accurately, at the time – as a child.

Now, with his Venus moving into Gemini, the eternal question arises: *can he see what is presently before his eyes?* Or will he see only his preexisting beliefs? Can he register that his beloved daughter is no longer exactly a child, and that she now needs him to treat her differently? What used to work just fine between them will not work anymore.

There are many possible happy endings to this story, and many possible sad ones as well. Either way, we can understand the nature of this very *Geminian evolutionary question* which has arisen in this father's life. His progressed Venus has entered Gemini. His *love* (Venus) must open its eyes to a *new reality* (Gemini). He must *pay attention* to what his daughter has become, and adapt his loving behavior to the fresh circumstances.

"Dad, I'm not a kid anymore." How easily those precious, loaded words could go in one of his ears and out the other. *"Yes, of course, dear. I know that . . ."*

And he knows nothing, sees nothing, hears nothing.

Or, more happily, he hands her the keys to the car he just bought for her, then he winks and says, "Don't do anything I wouldn't do."

And she winks back.

Thirty years later, they are still best friends.

THE SLOOP JOHN B

In the chart of a saltwater sailor who has been boat-bumming around the Caribbean for several years, Mars has just transited into Gemini, where it is squaring his natal Pisces Moon – an aspect sometimes ominous of accidents.

His little sloop, the *John B*, has served him well, but now it is time for him to serve the vessel equally well. *Does he see that?* Rot has started under a chainplate; in a hard blow, beating to windward, its connection to the hull might give way. The shroud would then come loose and the mast would come tumbling down.

Is our sailor vigilant enough to notice the potentially catastrophic problem? With transiting Mars in Gemini, *does he inspect his vessel?* Does he pay attention in a Mars way – which is to say, with a healthy dose of *life-preserving paranoia?*

Why might he fail to do that? Well, that sloop has *always* been reliable and that mast has been *standing for years* with no problem at all . . .

It is always the same question when a planet enters Gemini: *do we see reality, or do we see the preexisting contents of our own minds and mistake them for current reality?*

MAKING MILLIONS

Many years ago, Jupiter entered Gemini by solar arc in the tenth house of a high-powered executive in the telecommunications industry. She noticed that cell phones were starting to get very common – and she realized what that meant for the future of landline telephones.

How much money was that timely perception worth?

A DIVORCE AVERTED

Mars enters Gemini by progression in the eighth house of a married woman. *Paying attention* to her husband, she notices that he seems a little distracted lately. The truth is that he has become attracted to another woman, even though "nothing has happened." The wife does not know that – but she does sense that something is wrong. She moves preemptively and wisely. She lights candles, puts on a sexy nightgown, looks him in the eye and asks him how he is doing – and, by *paying attention* to her husband's fresh signals, she saves her marriage, and helps to save her husband from a karmic pratfall.

A FEW MORE . . .

Saturn solar arcs into Gemini; a young woman destined to become one of the voices of her generation begins work on her first novel.

The Sun progresses into Gemini; a middle-aged man leaves his job in a small town in Oklahoma and moves to Zurich to study Jungian psychology. Ten years later, he has a successful practice in Glasgow, Scotland, where he is happily married to a woman from Bangladesh.

The Moon progresses into Gemini in a man's eleventh house. Out shopping one day, he notices a flyer on the bulletin board of the health food grocery store. A guru from India is offering a lecture and workshop in town in two weeks' time. Our protagonist *pays attention*, looking carefully at the poster, resting his eyes on the eyes of the guru. He has a good feeling about the man and decides to attend the lecture.

Three years later, with his Moon now progressing into the first house, he experiences a new beginning: he quits his job and moves to India to handle social media for his beloved teacher.

Seven happy stories, mostly made-up – but in each one of them, we see the same fingerprints: as a planet enters Gemini, *attention is paid*, synchronicity strikes, and doors open.

18

MERCURY TIMES, GEMINI TIMES: THE BUILDING BLOCKS

As Mercury jitterbugs around your chart by transit or waltzes in more stately fashion by solar arc or progression, it forms a predictable series of aspects with the planets and sensitive points.

Each one of those natal planets and points symbolizes a lofty evolutionary intention. And at such a time, each one of them can benefit enormously from a visit by "the messenger of the gods." Mercury always offers liberating insight or at least some helpful news – but only if we are willing to listen.

What stops us from getting the message? Ignorance is a possibility – but Mercury is a skillful teacher, adept at dispelling ignorance.

More often, what blocks us is simply pride. We all love to be "right." We are all attached to a carefully-constructed – and usually at least somewhat defensive – narrative about who we are and how we came to this point in our lives. That narrative is inevitably fraught with distortions, rationalizations, lies we have been told, and laced with blame, misperceptions, accusations, judgements, and so on.

Along comes Mercury inviting us to clear away all that detritus and breathe the clean, fresh air of truth.

All we have to do is pay attention.

In the pages that follow, we consider the effects of Mercury as it moves through any kind of aspect to any one of the rest of the natal planets. That is potentially an overwhelming undertaking since there are a vast number of possible combinations. For example, solar arc Mercury in Gemini in the fourth house might form a quincunx aspect to your Jupiter-Neptune conjunction in Scorpio and the ninth house.

Switch any single one of those ten variables and you are in a different astrological situation.

There would be no way to cover each one of the possible variants on all of these Air configurations individually – at least not without writing the fattest book in the history of human literature. We have to approach the subject more systematically, trying to fathom the core principles that unlock the individual configurations.

Let's start by reiterating that all aspects are about integration, no matter whether we are talking about soft ones or hard ones. So, as a starting point in our attempt to keep our subject manageable, we will ignore the very real distinctions between a quincunx and a quintile, focusing instead upon the *core integration* that any such aspect represents. In the following pages, we focus only on the essential elements of the various *integrative processes* as Mercury dances with the Sun, the Moon, and the rest of the planets.

Again, the same basic synthesis of two archetypes is always present regardless of which technical aspect is in play. The aspect only serves to describe the *nature of the negotiations* that can lead to the helpful, temporary merger of the two planets. Again, it is not that the specific nature of the aspect is unimportant. Once you have grasped the core synthesis of the two archetypes, you will need to add whether it is happening via a square or a sextile to the mix on your own.

Once we are done with Mercury's aspects to the other planets, we will look in similarly cookbook fashion at what to expect when any of them enter the sign Gemini.

What follows here in terms of moving Mercury's aspects to each of the other planets appears exactly, word for word, as it appeared in *The Book of Earth*. My apologies, but there is no way around that dilemma. Mercury contacting natal Venus has the same meaning no matter which element we are exploring.

Let me quickly add that if that natal Venus were in an Earth sign, that is a different situation than if it were in an Air sign – but parsing out those kinds of distinctions would require a few hundred more pages.

Later in this chapter, where we reflect systematically on the meaning of any planet entering Gemini, we are in brand new territory. None of that writing has appeared anywhere before.

MERCURY CONTACTING THE SUN

What I Need to Learn: How to speak up and let people know who I am. How to step up to the plate verbally. How to express my values and opinions clearly and forthrightly. How to command attention without being seen as strident or pushy. How to think critically. How to defend a point. In doing all of this, I must pay attention to my impact on other people – I have something new to learn about how they are reading me.

Potential Blindspot: Mistaking my opinions for reality. Mistaking subjectivity for objectivity. Not realizing that I have said too much or spoken too long. My mouth might be revealing my ego.

Omens and Synchronicities: The world is my mirror now; I see myself reflected in it. It is time to look for feedback about how I appear to other people. Surprises, signs, and omens arise – I notice them, and I interpret them as clues to something I need to learn.

How to Recognize Your Teachers: They express themselves with natural authority. People want to listen to them. They can use themselves as examples without seeming egocentric. Their own story is a teaching device. They are notably articulate.

Squandered: Compulsive nervous chatter. Distraction standing in the way of actual accomplishment. Mental fugues in my head; rationalization. "Convincing others" as a way of trying to convince myself.

MERCURY CONTACTING THE MOON

What I Need to Learn: How to speak straight from my heart. How to accurately articulate the precise nature of my needs so others can grasp them clearly. How to effectively translate my feelings into words. How to verbally express tenderness and vulnerability. How to think about what I feel before I blurt out statements that only create confusion and misunderstanding.

Potential Blindspot: Emotions clouding reason. Strong feelings distorting my sense of reality. Mood and attitude poisoning communication. My own needs blinding me to the legitimate needs and perspectives of other people.

Omens and Synchronicities: Heart to heart conversations leading to revelations and fresh understanding. Emotional outbursts in myself or other people which offer clues as to the nature of energies moving in either of our unconscious minds. Messages from family. Insights which arise in candlelight, moonlight, or twilight.

How to Recognize Your Teachers: They are emotionally present. They express themselves fluently with immediacy and vulnerability. Even upon my first meeting them, they feel familiar – as if they were already family. Literal family members may have much to teach me now.

Squandered: Talk can build bridges between two hearts, but it can also build walls. If there is something that I am afraid to feel now, nervousness arises in me and I release it in compulsive chatter. I am being more defensive than I realize.

MERCURY CONTACTING MERCURY

What I Need to Learn: I am ready to take a great leap forward in terms of my skill and confidence as a speaker, a teacher, or a writer. I resolve to say exactly what I mean, taking as much time as I need to express myself clearly. I enunciate my words; I am articulate. I speak in complete sentences; I am interesting. I am always willing to learn something new. I am not afraid to use my full vocabulary.

Potential Blindspot: Compulsively describing reality does not change reality at all. I resolve to be wary of my own defense mechanisms as they reveal themselves in a need to argue or to convince other people of my version of things. I take note of my present tendency to be distracted; I use it as a clue to help me understand what I am avoiding knowing.

Omens and Synchronicities: Signs and synchronicities are abundant now. I resolve to be alert to the messages inherent in patterns of "coincidence." I note carefully the correlation between thoughts arising in my mind and external changes in the light, the wind, and the flights of birds. I realize and appreciate that I am being actively guided now. I am grateful for these signs and I acknowledge their Source.

How to Recognize Your Teachers: They trigger fresh thoughts and fresh understandings in you. They may say things that you already know – but they say them in such an unexpected way that you hear them as if it were the first time. They are masters of language – articulate, engaging, and fascinating. They themselves are curious, always willing to learn. They may, for example, display genuine interest and excitement about something that you can teach them.

Squandered: Talk that has nothing to do with communication. Empty conversation with no one really listening. Distraction; running around in circles. The heart eclipsed by the mind; the heart drowning in a sea of meaningless words.

MERCURY CONTACTING VENUS

What I Need to Learn: How to use language to build genuine bridges to other people – and that is at least as much about listening and responding as it is about talking. How to say I love you. How to listen well and help others feel that I have actually heard them and understood them. How to be more eloquent and graceful in my speech. How to express myself without profanity, if that is what I choose. How to pay constant attention to my listeners, monitoring their level of engagement with what I am saying.

Potential Blindspot: Talking "at" others rather than "speaking with" them. Becoming narcissistically enamored of my own eloquence. Concentrating so much on reaching the other person and eliciting his or her agreement that I have lost my moorings in my own feelings about reality. Diplomacy eclipsing truth.

Omens and Synchronicities: I resolve to pay close attention to messages coming to me from people whom I love. I will not let my familiarity with them blind me to the fact that they have something new and important to say to me. Messages come to me woven into art – films, novels, music – which I "happen" to encounter now.

How to Recognize Your Teachers: They immediately elicit strong feelings of affection and affinity in me towards them. They may be artists. They are "beautiful" in some sense of that very multidimensional word. They are easy with other people, getting along with them even if they are very different. Love is more important to them than insight.

Squandered: Papering over genuine differences with empty, agreeable words. Wasting time with forgettable chit-chat. "Preaching to the choir" – that is, endlessly reiterating that which is already obvious to everyone. Telling people what they want to hear rather than what actually feels true.

MERCURY CONTACTING MARS

What I Need to Learn: How to express opinions which I hold passionately in an engaging, effective way – that is to say, in a way that intrigues and convinces other people rather than triggering their defensive reflexes. How to argue effectively. How to express anger without seeming strident, out of control, or merely silly.

Potential Blindspot: Not seeing how my edgy style of verbal delivery can create resistance in other people to hearing what I am actually saying. My own passion can create a blockage to mutual understanding and the effective resolution of conflict.

Omens and Synchronicities: Annoying circumstances arise which potentially trigger shoot-from-the-hip reactions in myself or in other people. Stressful messages appear unexpectedly. Trivial conflicts burst on the scene; by not reacting reflexively in anger to them I can follow them down to the roots of the real issue.

How to Recognize Your Teachers: They may make you angry. They may appear as rivals or competitors, even as enemies. In argument or disagreement, they are your worthy opponents, compelling you to clarify your own thoughts and to express your views effectively.

Squandered: Fights, disagreements, or tiffs whose apparent content is actually unrelated to the true, underlying issues. Displacement; misdirection. Example: arguing about politics because you are angry about sex. Blowing off steam. Saying things we later wish that we could unsay.

MERCURY CONTACTING JUPITER

What I Need to Learn: That I have something significant to say. That I have underestimated my persuasiveness and my natural authority. That without seeming arrogant, I can speak with the voice of a king or a queen. That an attitude of generosity and positiveness towards other people can open their minds to me. That humor often builds bridges of heart-to-heart communication. That I am worthy of further education.

Potential Blindspot: Blustering. Taking up more than my fair share of people's time or attention. Flogging a point that has already been expressed and understood. Overestimating my knowledge, authority, or entertainment value.

Omens and Synchronicities: Messages arrive opening doors for me. These messages might be obvious, such as a phone call offering me a better job. They might be more subtle, such as reading an article about an emerging technology – and suddenly realizing that it is the missing ingredient in a creative idea I have been entertaining. The message could take the form of a hopeful, open glance from someone in whom I am interested. Always, the key to success here lies in acting boldly and audaciously upon the opportunity of the moment.

How to Recognize Your Teachers: They display a certain "star quality" without seeming arrogant about it. Their natures are generous and expansive. They radiate contagious optimism and faith in future possibilities – and probably faith in me as well. They tell better jokes than I do.

Squandered: Talking an idea to death. Alienating potential support through an appearance of arrogance or self-importance. Reaching for that which is truly impossible or unreachable. Jumping to conclusions, then using those shaky conclusions as the foundation of strategy.

MERCURY CONTACTING SATURN

What I Need to Learn: That this is a time in my life when the only true way forward lies in a sustained, disciplined effort to master new information and new skills. Education opens doors for me now. Knowledge – especially knowledge not easily won – is power. In terms of my speech, I need to move forward to my next natural stage of verbal maturation. At some level, my style of self-expression must become more "adult" – that is to say, more authoritative, clear, and confident. It is time for my intelligence to manifest some kind of Great Work.

Potential Blindspot: Any hesitation I might feel in regard to monumental intellectual effort can cripple me now. Insecurity and fear can distort my sense of the nature of the road ahead. Laziness – especially mental laziness – is catastrophic at this point. I might not see that the perceived immaturity of my voice is having a negative impact upon people's perceptions of me.

Omens and Synchronicities: Situations arise indicating that my own ignorance or lack of necessary skill is blocking my evolution. The purpose of these signals is not to discourage me; it is to steel my resolve to dispel the ignorance and to develop the skills I need. Opportunities to do exactly that materialize before me. Attention turns to me; chances to speak up with greater quiet authority than ever before arise.

How to Recognize Your Teachers: They are serious people, probably enough older than myself that I notice the age difference. They may be true elders. They may have a "wizardly" quality. They may or may not be "intellectuals" in the academic sense, but they radiate high intelligence.

Squandered: Missing a real chance to arm myself with missing knowledge or valuable education. Indulging in mental laziness. Believing that what worked for me last year will work for me next year. Failure to speak up. Masking intellectual insecurity behind silence. The single most fatal line at such a time is, "I don't want to talk about it."

MERCURY CONTACTING URANUS

What I Need to Learn: That my truth is my truth even if others disagree with me. I appreciate their support, but I do not need it. I have a natural right to my own understanding of things, and I have a right to express it – even if it does not elicit applause. I am currently experiencing a genuine "genius" stage in my development, which means that some very original and unprecedented insights are arising in me. I may not be right about everything, but I need to trust these insights and follow them to the natural conclusions.

Potential Blindspot: Am I mistaking mere contrariness for genuine intellectual independence? I might come across to other people now as simply cranky, stubborn, and opinionated, thereby creating an emotional reaction in them of negativity towards me – a reaction which might eclipse the potential of their actual agreeing with me, or learning anything from me.

Omens and Synchronicities: Patterns of weird coincidence arise now, conveying important messages and guidance to me. For example, in the same week three different people happen to mention Papua, New Guinea. That means that maybe it is time for me to go there. During this time, the universe labels all of its pivotal communications with me in the same way: they all have the fingerprints of the weird, the unlikely, and the improbable on them.

How to Recognize Your Teachers: They dance to the beat of a different drummer. It is not that they do not care about other people; it is only that they will not modify their behavior or their understanding of life in order to win the approval of others. They think outside the box. Some might call them weird or peculiar.

Squandered: Reflexive contrariness. Wasting time trying to garner the approval and support of other people. Equally, wasting time by trying to trigger a reaction of shock or judgment in others. Either way, I have enslaved myself to other people's reactions to me. I have turned my back on true freedom.

MERCURY CONTACTING NEPTUNE

What I Need to Learn: That reality is far more complex than common sense would indicate. That psychic phenomena are real. That there are other dimensions folded into the three dimensions that we can see; that those dimensions contain unimaginable energies, wellsprings of information – and even inhabitants with whom I can interact. I am presently receiving an accelerated spiritual or metaphysical education. It may come to me through books or teachers; it will certainly come to me now via direct, mysterious, inexplicable experience.

Potential Blindspot: Not trusting the reality of my own senses or my own actual experience; instead, pasting consensual reality over them, fearing that the place where my own soul is trying to lead me is madness rather than a higher state of evolution. Alternatively, escaping reality through fanciful, ungrounded "spiritual" ideas – taking a "flight into light," in which comforting delusions prevent me from facing reality head on.

Omens and Synchronicities: Look for "impossible" experiences. Knowing a twelve will come up on the dice just before I toss them. Knowing who is on the phone just before I answer it. Seeing light around the head of a lecturer. "Thinking" I saw something moving in the corner of my eye. Try trusting these perceptions; they are now leading you deeper into the mystery. Teachers and teachings appear abundantly.

How to Recognize Your Teachers: They are classic mystics – sensitive people, with a dreamlike quality about them. They may be psychic; they are certainly compassionate. They are warm when they meet me, but they seem to need a lot of time alone as well. I feel protective towards them, even though they actually seem to be doing fine without my help.

Squandered: Getting lost in an endless, ever-expanding labyrinth of delusion and misperception. Substituting comfortable fantasy for genuine spiritual experience and authentic learning. Becoming hypnotized by mere ideas; confusing thinking with actual meditation.

MERCURY CONTACTING PLUTO

What I Need to Learn: How to speak difficult truths in ways that can actually be heard and received. That my understanding of my own life has been flawed and incomplete; that I am now ready to see myself and my personal history more deeply and more honestly than ever before. That sometimes "the truth will set you free, but first it will make you miserable." That I do not need to be afraid of reality as it actually is; that I am now strong enough to deal with it.

Potential Blindspot: As this psycho-spiritual development begins to unfold, there is something fundamental which I am not allowing myself to see. That is my blindspot, and it is always present at the outset of such events for everyone. There is no shame in that – but it would indeed be a shame if I were still maintaining that same blindness by the end of this contact.

Omens and Synchronicities: Hidden or buried truths emerge; lies and rationalizations are revealed in their true natures. Pivotal conversations occur. Pieces of the puzzle come together. Old letters, emails, photographs, and fragments of memory are shared, triggering revelation.

How to Recognize Your Teachers: I feel that I can say anything to them and that, so long as I am honest, I will not be judged. They are not so much "good" as they are "real." They look me directly in the eye. There is a certain intensity around them; they are too much for some people. They have made some instructive mistakes in their lives – and learned from them. They have not been afraid of their own passions.

Squandered: Enormous creative energy can be wasted now in maintaining lies and creating new ones. "Pride" – which is really only enslavement to the need for other people's approval – attempts to sustain a false narrative of my life. It may succeed; then my ego survives behind a lonely wall of disinformation and delusion. In an effort to defend myself, my words and my insights can become offensive weapons, doing hurtful damage to the souls of anyone who gets near enough to me to begin to get the scent of my buried truths.

ENTERING GEMINI

Sooner or later, one way or another, everything passes through Gemini. With the transiting Moon, you never have to wait more than a month. With transiting Pluto, the fun begins next on June 15, 2127. By progression, it depends on where things were originally in your natal chart. The wait could take millennia.

What goes up must come down, the planets orbit until the Sun goes poof – and that means that everything, eventually, enters Gemini.

When it does, the itchy, curious, experimental tonality of that sign animates the planet in a fresh way. It gets a little more nervous, looks a little bit younger. It wakes up and smells coffee, its eyes get wider – and it starts to *pay closer attention . . .*

At least that is what is supposed to happen. There is also a chance that the planet just begins to talk and never shuts up. There is a chance it starts frantically running around in circles.

Gemini is a wild horse and, if we are going to ride it – rather than the other way around – we have to learn how to work the reins.

In the pages that follow, we look at each planet as it crosses into Gemini. As ever, in doing this, we are only looking at the bare bones of an interaction between two broad archetypes. Saying "here is what happens when Venus enters Gemini" can only offer us an approximation at best. Even if we understand those principles with great clarity, there is inevitably much that we are leaving out. In what house is that transit or progression happening? What aspects are involved?

More fundamentally, what role does the Air Family play in this person's life? Maybe his south node is in Gemini, and he needs to be particularly wary of the Geminian shadow. Maybe her *north* node is there, and she just needs to dive in, and not be too worried about mistakes.

Astrology is complicated, and we cannot simplify it too much without losing its ability to hold its uncanny mirror before our lives.

Still, in broad terms, there are real, observable, and helpful things that we can say about Venus – or any planet – entering Gemini. My hope is that the seeds that follow provide you with a starting point. I also hope that it is not your "finishing point" as well.

Let's think about Venus entering Gemini by transit. As I write these words, the next time that happens, Venus will remain in the sign for four months. That is a relatively long time. The next time after that, it will take less than a month to pass through the sign. Venus's transits through a sign are wildly variable in length, in other words. All we know for sure, until we look it up, is that they are always too short to develop much depth and complexity of meaning.

On the other hand, by solar arc, Venus will always remain in Gemini for about three decades. With progressions, because they reflect Venus's transits during your infancy, we are back to "wildly variable" – but they are always lengthy, plenty long enough to have real, life-altering psychic momentum.

Below you will find a section simply labeled "Venus Entering Gemini."
• If you are reflecting on a transit, lighten the words up.
• If you are reflecting on a progression or a solar arc, cue some dramatic music, the march of the elephants, and the Aurora Borealis.

Again, all of these sections in this entire Elements Series are your starter kit, that's all. You've got to supply context – and some soul.

FROM TAURUS TO GEMINI

One thing is certain, or nearly so: a planet entering Gemini has recently been enjoying the hospitality of Taurus. My "nearly so" caveat is in there only because sometimes a planet in Cancer happens to turn retrograde and enter Gemini through the back door.

As we learned in *The Book of Earth*, Taurus is all about quieting down and hearing the instinctual voice of the wise animal inside of you, as it tells you who "smells right," what path ahead has real heart. These are instinctual truths – ones we can best access only if we are quiet. Audio engineers talk about the signal-to-noise ratio; in Taurus, to get the signal, we really need to cut out as much of the noise as possible. In a Taurus time, you benefit more from a quiet hour in a garden than you do from channel-surfing.

Entering Gemini? *Start channel-surfing.*

It is difficult to read a line like that without it sounding trite – or as if I am making Taurus sound a lot more lofty than Gemini. To be sure, Gemini cannot simply be equated with channel-surfing. It is bigger and deeper than that, as I hope you've already seen in the foregoing pages.

Still, punching that "forward" button does actually provide a good Gemini metaphor.

The conventional understanding would be that anyone "channel surf-ing" is randomly flipping through TV programs in hope of finding some-thing engaging. *But what if, in a Gemini time, the universe works far more magically than that?* What if synchronicity is a reality, as I believe it is? What if, during a Gemini time, you just "happen" to channel-surf yourself directly into the path of information that will change your life?

That is how the Gemininian archetypal field actually works. It is about being open to all avenues of learning and information, especially the ones you have never before considered. One trick is simply to *have faith that you are being guided.* That magical expectation alone boosts your desire to pay attention. What if "angels are whispering in your ears?" Books fall off shelves and land on your feet – and three friends mention the same opera before a fourth one offers you that spare ticket.

In a Gemini time, the universe is trying to tell you something. As we saw earlier, it needs to interrupt your normal programming for an impor-tant message.

THE SUN ENTERING GEMINI

What part of my life is currently hobbled developmentally by bad information? Fundamentally, the answer is "every part of it." My entire self-image is ready for an update. The values by which I have been navigating my life are outdated. I am defined by bad data. Behaviors that used to work or which used to energize me are now failing. The evidence is right there before my eyes, if only I can get my stubborn pride out of the way and look.

How can I actively learn what I need to learn? Above all, I need to listen. People are giving me life-changing feedback, which might go in one of my ears and out the other if I am not attentive and humble enough to hear it. There is more than one way to connect the dots that are there before my eyes. The way I have been connecting them is plausible and convincing – and mostly wrong.

What kinds of synchronicities arise now to support me? My own ego-driven craziness, delusions and blindspots are manifesting outwardly now in the form of people I meet or characters I see in films, books, or the news. If I pay attention, I see myself – and where I need to open up – mirrored in the world around me. Surprises abound. I resolve not to miss any of them by being blinded by my own erroneous certainties.

If I resist learning and changing, what happens? Bottom line, I remain just as ignorant when this passage is over as I was when it began. The only difference is that I am more tired. I have talked and talked rather than listened. Some of that talk was only in my own head as I compulsively tried to hold onto an outdated description of my life and my goals. The rest of it was me boring everyone around me with my long-winded soliloquies.

THE MOON ENTERING GEMINI

What part of my life is currently hobbled developmentally by bad information? People often believe that truly to feel with the innermost heart, I should just close my eyes and let waves of unfiltered emotion pass over me. Not true, not now. For me in this moment, I need my eyes open. I need to get my heart into alignment with emerging, changing realities. I'm scared, annoyed, or worried about realities that are no longer out there. Out of habit and repetition, I have memorized an outdated description of what is in my own heart. Bad information leads to emotions and attitudes that tie me up in knots, and which are dangerously disconnected from what is actually, currently, arising on my path.

How can I actively learn what I need to learn? I must become more aware of my own emotional scripts. I may, for example, say that "I have always hated zucchini" – but, if I let myself actually taste it, I will realize that I have changed; it tastes better to me now. Similarly, all my emotional position papers are up for renewal: I love my job, I am angry at my father, I am happy in my relationship . . . every emotion needs to breathe the fresh air of emerging, immediate reality. That is how I learn what I need to learn.

What kinds of synchronicities arise now to support me? Conversations, stories, and films hold a mirror before my heart. Situations and circumstances appear that are custom-designed to press my emotional buttons in ways that I label "pleasant" and "unpleasant." Do I reflexively stick to my old interpretations or do I flow into feeling what I actually feel in the radical present tense?

If I resist learning and changing, what happens? I feel compelled to describe my feelings, needs, gripes, or worries, both out loud and silently in my own mind, and to do so repetitively. What is really going on is that I am clinging to an old emotional reality rather than surrendering to the process of discovering the true new one.

MERCURY ENTERING GEMINI

What part of my life is currently hobbled developmentally by bad information? Words either bridge me to the world or stand between me and the world. My language itself – both spoken and in my head – needs to be updated. This is not just about improving my vocabulary or impressing anyone – this is about how words define the way I experience reality. There is, for one example, a big difference between saying, "My mother was judgemental" and "my mother projected her own shame onto me." It is time for greater precision – and deeper truth – in the language I use to explain myself to myself.

How can I actively learn what I need to learn? By reading. By listening carefully to people whose language I find compelling and articulate. By listening to my own words and asking myself these questions: am I expressing something that way because I have always expressed it that way? Given who I have become today, is that the clearest, most precise – most ultimately honest – language I can find? Am I truly speaking for myself – or just echoing expressions I have heard from others?

What kinds of synchronicities arise now to support me? I am currently bombarded by words, and hypnotized by them. I smile at a witty phrase or a trenchant insight I hear on the street or on television. Is there actually more skillful speech out there, or am I just noticing it more? Either way, the world is guiding me into learning my new vocabulary and mastering my emerging, updated style of more sophisticated self-expression.

If I resist learning and changing, what happens? I fret and I worry. I talk my head off, saying very little. Chatter and nervousness dissipate my energies. I learn nothing; no new information or perspective can blast through the walls of compulsive fugues of repetition in my head. If I keep repeating a falsehood, maybe it will turn into a reality – I may not admit it, but that is exactly what I am doing.

VENUS ENTERING GEMINI

What part of my life is currently hobbled developmentally by bad information? How clearly am I seeing the people I love? How have habit and familiarity blinded me to who they have actually become? When I meet new people, I am actively engaged in discovering who they are – but what about the ones I think I already know? Additionally, I am ready for some "art education." My serenity of spirit is supported by aesthetic experience, but "my favorite band from my high school days" might not move me as much today as it once did. Can I notice that my tastes have changed?

How can I actively learn what I need to learn? Listening carefully and freshly to the people with whom I share my life is the heart of the matter. I also need to encourage them to open their hearts – something I can accomplish by conveying genuine interest in them. I prime the pump by asking questions – and for every bit of advice I offer, I take in at least three new facts about the people in my life. Aesthetically, I willingly try new experiences with an open-mind: if I have "always hated" hip hop or opera or jazz, I make a point of listening to some.

What kinds of synchronicities arise now to support me? I meet new people. More importantly, I find myself in new, emergent, or unusual situations with people I already know. The fresh context brings out fresh mutual perceptions. Opportunities for long conversations come up – long car trips, for example, or delays in waiting rooms.

If I resist learning and changing, what happens? Boredom nibbles away at love. "Yes, dear" replaces valid listening. Without knowing that I am doing it, I fail to respond to the content of what family, friends, or partners are saying. I talk in order to herd people into familiar patterns and behavioral boxes.

MARS ENTERING GEMINI

What part of my life is currently hobbled developmentally by bad information? There are questions I am afraid to ask because I am afraid of the answers. I may not realize that fact consciously – but with just a little effort I can grasp it. This is a time for me to develop *the courage to know.* I have distortions in my thinking around how ready people around me are to hear what I have to say; they are more ready than I imagine; I am unnecessarily hobbled and constrained in my speech.

How can I actively learn what I need to learn? I speak up and say what is on my mind, and I deal with the social or interpersonal consequences. I am bold in my questions – and I resolve never to punish anyone for giving me a truthful answer, even if it is not what I wanted to hear. Argument can be a form of communication; I resolve to argue skillfully, to listen well, to aim for true resolutions and reasonable compromises – but to hold very little back regarding my own views and opinions.

What kinds of synchronicities arise now to support me? Verbal conflict or sparring is likely to arise suddenly and unexpectedly. Someone – possibly myself – "says the wrong thing," and before I know it, we are knee-deep in an edgy conversation. Here is my chance to remember that the wise warrior always uses precisely enough force, but never any more than that. I want resolution, not bloodshed – or revenge.

If I resist learning and changing, what happens? One possibility is silly, embarrassing fights that resolve nothing, go nowhere, and only damage our ability to trust each other in the long run. I get up on my high horse about subjects that do not really matter that much to me – my real issues have been sublimated down dead end roads, and so really I am only blowing off steam. Alternatively, if I lack boldness, I find myself chronically beating myself up, thinking, "I should have said that . . ."

JUPITER ENTERING GEMINI

What part of my life is currently hobbled developmentally by bad information? Happy new possibilities have arisen in my life. The question is, am I aware of them – or are old habits blinding me? It may be as simple as this: circumstances have changed and doors are open that once were closed. Will I *pay attention* and notice that they have opened – or will I go on thinking habitually and blindly that "those doors are *always* closed?" Another possibility is that, while nothing has changed in the world, I myself have grown stronger and more capable. Pathways forward that were once beyond me are now within my grasp.

How can I actively learn what I need to learn? Are there any questions that a King or a Queen would be afraid to ask or requests that he or she would fear making? I need to knock on doors. I need to seek – and maybe pay for – expert advice, skillful support, and the maps that show the way to the treasure. I affirm that I am sufficiently intelligent to learn whatever I need to learn in order to light the fuse of a dream.

What kinds of synchronicities arise now to support me? Opportunities to learn present themselves. The timely appearance of teachers, books, and classes is indicated. Doorways to knowledge and critical information open. Snatches of overheard conversation, throwaway lines uttered by strangers, magazines opened by chance – all point the way.

If I resist learning and changing, what happens? I may dissipate this energy in mere fantasy. I may put all the Jupiter-juice into daydreaming about "what I would do with a billion dollars" – all the while a chance to actually make a million dollars slips unnoticed through my fingers. Rather than actually improving myself, I attempt to aggrandize myself. I am not as funny, compelling, or engaging as I imagine myself to be – and if I would only pay attention to people's faces, I would probably figure that out.

SATURN ENTERING GEMINI

What part of my life is currently hobbled developmentally by bad information? I would be truly astonished if I knew how thin an eggshell of ignorance stood between me and my ability to accomplish something great. A little bit of information, education, or attitudinal reorientation can trigger the opening of a path to success at something of which I would be proud for the rest of my life. Getting that information may not be easy, but it is worth the effort. That knowledge and those skills will put what previously seemed impossible within my reach.

How can I actively learn what I need to learn? Intellectual discipline is required now. I resolve to burn the midnight oil, focusing my concentration in a sustained way on one subject until I have mastered it. I will not allow myself to be distracted, nor will I give any power to mental laziness. I will ask the right questions of the right, worthy teachers. I am not afraid of undertaking daunting feats of memorization. I accept that some boring rote learning can light the fuse for later creativity – and that someone who cannot paint a table shouldn't try to paint an *abstract* table.

What kinds of synchronicities arise now to support me? Teachers appear. The right, necessary information appears. I recognize them both by their signature: nothing they offer is easy to learn. Learning what I need to learn here will take everything I have got.

If I resist learning and changing, what happens? I stagnate mentally. I begin telling the same old stories over and over again. I am afraid to learn anything new; I only do what I have succeeded at doing in the past. I become tedious, over-explaining things that everyone either knows already or about which they do not really care.

URANUS ENTERING GEMINI

What part of my life is currently hobbled developmentally by bad information? To say that "I have no idea who I am" is too extreme, but it gets me thinking in the right direction. It is more accurate to say that *in certain areas of my life*, I am navigating by the stars of a false identity – and the proof of that condition is that I sometimes "get what I want" and it turns to sawdust in my mouth. The part of me that had that desire has been bamboozled into having it. My soul never wanted it in the first place.

How can I actively learn what I need to learn? I must pay attention to certain gaps that arise between what I say and what I actually feel. My "speech-body" still reflects habitual patterns and social-conditioning, even though my deeper self has already moved in a more authentic direction. As I generate mindfulness about that disconnection, I learn what I need to learn about who I truly have become.

What kinds of synchronicities arise now to support me? Two kinds of conversations arise in which this "gap" issue is vividly evident to me. In one kind, I emphatically state a value or an opinion, and immediately I realize that I do not actually feel that way. In the second kind of conversation, I spontaneously make a statement that a) feels totally true, b) shocks me, and c) shocks everyone else too. Question: where did *that* come from? Answer: my newly-assertive true self.

If I resist learning and changing, what happens? I increasingly feel like a store mannequin or a robot pre-programmed with little speeches that make me feel silly, hypocritical, or simply dismissible whenever I reflexively spout them.

NEPTUNE ENTERING GEMINI

What part of my life is currently hobbled developmentally by bad information? Nobody, including myself, has everything all figured out. Nowhere is that so true as in the areas of spirituality and the meaning of life. Philosophical preconceptions get in the way of clear present-tense psychic perception. Religion itself can get in the way. My spiritual growth is currently hampered by wrong assumptions about consciousness, meditation, and the Great Mystery itself. I am praying to the wrong gods.

How can I actively learn what I need to learn? For my journey to continue, I need to simply open my inner eye to the reality of my actual psychic experience. My "ordinary mind" can reveal itself in extraordinary ways, if only I let go of my need to feel correct about everything. An effective method now is to expose myself to teachings and teachers from alien traditions – if I am Buddhist, I need to listen to gospel music, for example. If I am Muslim, I need to participate in a pagan drumming circle.

What kinds of synchronicities arise now to support me? Little miracles abound – and the most valuable ones to me are the ones I might not even notice unless I am paying close attention. I meet teachers from alien paths who glow in the dark with the power of their experience. A metaphysical book "I know I lost many years ago" mysteriously appears on my bookshelf – it must be time to read it again. A fresh spiritual insight arises – and in that exact moment, the Moon peeks out from behind the clouds.

If I resist learning and changing, what happens? I become a dreary "expert" in all matters philosophical or spiritual. I parrot ideas that may be valid, and may even be helpful to others, but which have lost their ability to truly impact or engage my own soul. I experience a bad case of *preacher's malaise.* For lack of anything fresh to say, I fail in upholding my end of my endless conversation with the Divine. Meanwhile, the Divine sits back silently and waits to see if I ever become more interesting.

PLUTO ENTERING GEMINI

What part of my life is currently hobbled developmentally by bad information? I am actually crazier than I believe myself to be. To state that point more precisely, I am crazy in ways that I do not understand. By "crazy," I mean that unresolved hurts and wounds in my psyche are distorting the perceptions which I now need to experience in clear form in order for my journey to continue. These hurts and wounds may have been echoed in my childhood – but they are almost certainly also rooted in prior-life experiences as well.

How can I actively learn what I need to learn? I affirm that at this point my spiritual journey is inseparable from my successfully doing inner work of a fundamentally psychological nature. Conversations with people of grounded wisdom and trenchant insight are invaluable now. They do not have to be "mental health professionals" in any narrow sense, but they do need to speak that kind of language. With them, I hear myself spontaneously saying exactly the words that I need to hear.

What kinds of synchronicities arise now to support me? Miscommunications arise. I say things I wish I could somehow take back. Now that they are said, maybe I can learn something from them. Mysterious passions exaggerate my language. Bottom line: my wounds take over my tongue. It is awkward and embarrassing – but in those moments, the truths I now need to see about myself are revealed.

If I resist learning and changing, what happens? Two possibilities: an extroverted one and an introverted one. In the extroverted version, I become *mean*. I don't know why, but I hurt people – or just put them off with my edgy cynicism, sarcasm, or bitterness. In the introverted version, all that bile is internalized. I become isolated, in that what is in my heart is never uttered or known by any other human being.

19

CELESTIAL NAVIGATION II: VENUS TIMES, LIBRA TIMES

Never in all my years in the field of astrology have I seen a significant relationship start unheralded by the heavens themselves.

That line might sound hyperventilated, but it is the truth: relationship-oriented transits, progressions, or solar arcs are invariably activated when loving partnership gets started, at least one that has any kind of lasting significance.

How could it possibly be otherwise? Your chart is the mirror of your soul's evolution. *And is there any single category of experience more relevant to your spiritual journey than the dance you do with your soulmates?* Naturally, your chart reflects the timing – and the meaning – of such encounters.

Always. Every time.

The progressions and solar arcs of Venus are one possibility for that kind of astrological signal. We will be talking a lot about them in this chapter and the next one. Let's be quick to include some other possibilities as well. While significant relationships never begin without accompanying astrological symbolism, it does not always take the form of the progressions or solar arcs of Venus. Just as commonly, such signals might appear in the form of a major stimulus of the natal position of Venus: the progressed Sun conjuncting it, for example. From there we would need to range further – perhaps we meet lasting love when the Moon progresses into our seventh house or when our natal Saturn in the eighth house is trined by solar arc Jupiter.

Love is a big part of life, obviously enough. And astrology's love symbolism is multi-dimensional. It is never *only* about Venus.

But here, in this chapter, Venus is our subject – at least initially. In a few pages, we will also explore the meaning of planets entering Libra and the seventh house.

They are part of the spectrum of intimate symbolism too.

TRANSITING VENUS

I have mentioned progressed and solar arc Venus, but not transiting Venus. That is because it operates in a different, and ultimately more minor, category. To say that such transits are "not as important" gets us looking in the right direction. Perhaps it would be more accurate to say that transiting Venus is important in a different way. Being a fast-moving point, it does not have sufficient time to develop much depth and complexity of meaning. Instead it operates as a *trigger*, precipitating more fundamental astrological themes into active development. Quick inner planet transits play a role in *tactical* astrology, rather than being part of the bigger strategic picture.

For example, Saturn *(the need for solitude)* might be transiting into your seventh house. That is a big, slow theme-builder. You have a partner whom you love, but right now you need some space. Saturn *("The Elder")* might also suggest that you need the relationship to *mature* – in other words, there is an increasing risk of you two simply *outgrowing each other*. It is time to update your intimate contract.

Those can be delicate subjects to negotiate. When do you "have the conversation?" Perhaps it is "triggered" when *transiting* Venus aligns with your Sun – and trines your partner's Moon. And perhaps, as a result of that quick boost of Venusian love and diplomacy, that conversation goes very well.

Here is another spin on that same story: if you are a counseling astrologer working with a client, you might *actively suggest* that this upcoming minor Venus transit could be a good time to initiate a critical intimate talk.

Based on intuition alone, we can all potentially live in harmony with the natural rhythms of the universe, not knowing anything about astrology

– but knowing about it helps most of us do a better job of living. Without astrology, for example, it might be possible that a Mars transit could trigger that critical conversation, but for the wrong reasons – your anger and frustration just boiled over. "Tactical" astrology can caution us about those kinds of badly-timed moves.

Our practical bottom line here is that the *transits* of Venus draw their meaning from the bigger picture.

Meanwhile, its progression*s* and solar arcs *are* the bigger picture.

PREPARING FOR LOVE

To be in love, or not to be. To take the plunge or not to take the plunge ... those are serious questions. No one ever has to take such risks. No one is ever required to put her or his heart on the chopping block. Without a doubt, the leading cause of heartbreak is falling in love in the first place. If we avoid that eventuality, we have perfect immunity – no one will ever find us drinking whiskey alone in a dive-bar at four o'clock in the afternoon, listening to doleful Country and Western tunes about cheatin' hearts or fish that got away.

Venus is hard to resist, though. Even if we have made passionate, brokenhearted speeches about how "we will never love again," along comes the right person and we are pulled back helplessly into the ancient vortex.

Of course, we can also say exactly the same thing with only one modification and the words remain just as true: along comes the *wrong* person and we are pulled into that ancient vortex.

How can we distinguish these two situations?

That is a complex question, involving many factors in the natal chart – and going beyond the natal chart as well into the realm of transits, progressions, and arcs. The birth-position of Venus is one thread in the greater symbolic tapestry. In our earlier chapters about the Libra Clan, we covered a lot of that natal Venusian material – how your chart reflects your particular intimate needs and style.

The larger point – which I still find totally, amazingly mind-blowing – is that your chart also provides a detailed portrait of your natural partner, *even if he or she has not yet been born.* I mean, maybe you are a baby, just a week old. We look at your chart, and there he or she is, jumping out of the symbolism – even though that person will not be born for another three years.

All of this precious anti-heartbreak medicine is there to be read in anyone's natal chart. It requires some astrological skill to interpret it – but it requires an even more impressive trick actually to *remember it* when you find yourself pulled into that ancient vortex that we were just discussing.

Hormones are famously blinding.

Will you remember it? When Venus comes along by progression or by solar arc, you will learn the answer. Those times are the tests – and, as with any test, it is a good idea to prepare. Astrology can supply helpful intellectual support. At a simple cognitive level, knowing the general qualities of your natural mate as he or she is revealed in the birthchart can help you weed out obvious catastrophes in advance – but again, only if you can *remember* ... only if you can retain mindfulness in the face of an onslaught of truly primeval compulsions.

Having that kind of astrological knowledge is a powerful form of preparation. But there are other forms too, and they are all very much in the domain of Venus.

The strange thing is that these forms of preparation do not seem to have very much to do with love at all.

BREATHE

Venus and Libra, as we learned in earlier chapters, are both about *balance*. They are both about *maintaining serenity of spirit*. Perhaps more than in any other way, these *calming strategies* help us prepare for Venusian tests.

Simple chicken soup advice: before you fall in love, take a breath, let it out. Get quiet. Get centered. As everyone knows, those are good ways to listen to your heart.

Falling in love is exciting; it sweeps us along, maybe faster than anyone should be swept, considering how high the stakes are. Mother Nature is famously skillful at tricking heterosexual people into making babies.

Take a breath first. What is the rush?

A major Venus event typically unfolds over a year or two. With astrology on your side, you can see it coming. Even apart from any issues of human intimacy, such a time is a call to *calm down* – and to do it early. To make the right intimate choices, you must first get in touch with your instinctual side. That process is all centered on Venus – but it particularly relates to the planet's *Taurean* dimension. In *The Book of Earth*, we saw what a primary role that "wise Taurean animal" inside of you plays in all of the important choices of your life, perhaps most especially the ones about mating and bonding.

With Venus knocking on your front door, you need that wise inner animal on your side. You need to pay attention to it.

Exactly *how* do we calm down? How do we find that peace? We learned some good answers back in chapter four. We repeat them here in short form because they are excellent preliminary practices whenever Venus is approaching a sensitive zone. They remind you of your wise instinctual foundation. They help you answer those two classic Venusian questions: *who to trust* and *how to trust?*

Look for opportunities to move in the directions we list here. Because of synchronicity, they are likely to be abundant.

- Expose yourself to the calming, stress-releasing, soul-attuning impact of *art*, both by appreciating it and possibly by creating it.
- Expose yourself to the peace and beauty of *nature*.
- Find *silence*; hunt for it if you have to. Time spent in outward silence creates space for inward silence. And "peace-and-quiet" is almost one single word, and for good reason.
- Listen to your *body's messages*.
- Sit in a garden.
- Cultivate a *tolerance for paradox* and ambiguity; you do not need to have an opinion about everything.
- Invite *touch*; ask for a hug.

Practicing each of these methods is its own reward – serenity of spirit is a treasure beyond measure. But they also help to bring you to a place where you can better trust your own judgment when it comes to deciding whether to leap into that ancient Venusian vortex – or to resist its massive gravitational field, saving your love for another day and perhaps for a more worthy person.

I have often seen, during a long Venusian period, someone who wisely says "no" to one intimate possibility, wisely choosing solitude over bad love – only to have another, better-suited person show up not long afterwards.

Remember: Venus periods last a year or two. That is a lot of time.

I have also seen affairs that ended badly or painfully – but whose lessons led a person to making a better relationship choice later on, during the same progressed or solar arc Venus event, or even a later one.

Then, on the sad side of the equations, I have also seen affairs that end painfully, then trigger another classic Venus trap: falling in love "on the rebound" with the next convenient and reasonably "decorative" person who happens by.

That is not love, that is "pain medication."

FRIENDSHIP

In thinking about Venus, the human mind naturally gravitates towards questions of romantic and sexual intimacy. Those are always compelling subjects, and rightly so: arguably no single area of life experience so effectively reveals the true nature of our actual evolutionary state.

Still, where would we be without friendship? And how powerful a role does that kind of non-erotic intimacy play in our spiritual journeys? Those are Venusian realities too.

We cannot understand the progressions and solar arcs of Venus in any kind of full-spectrum fashion without including friendship in our calculations. I believe that is always true for everyone – and increasingly true as we move on into the second half of life, becoming more aware of worlds of sweet connection that lie beyond the veil of youth's blinding sexual fires.

When I use the word *soulmates*, it is natural that we think of couples. But I do like to employ the term in a more inclusive way – in my way of thinking, anyone with whom we have "soul business" is a soulmate, and that includes anyone who has a catalytic effect upon our consciousness or on our biography. Our encounters with such people are also often synchronized with Venusian events. We are better astrologers if we include them in our consultations too. Maybe a guy goes through a romantic dry spell while progressed Venus is making a trine to his Saturn. Maybe that dry spell is actually good for him, giving him a chance to take a more mature view of what he might want his intimate life to look like in the long run.

During that period, he meets a man who becomes like a brother to him for the next forty years.

As astrologers, let's not miss the importance of that friendship.

Throughout the four volumes of this Elements Series, we have had countless occasions to refer to the phenomenon of *synchronicity*. The term was coined when the seminal psychologist Carl Jung had a fertile meeting of minds with Wolfgang Pauli, the seminal physicist. The two men met for the first time in January, 1932. Pauli was relatively unknown at the time, while Jung, twenty-six years his senior, was the toast of four or five continents. Pauli arrived in a state of psychological crisis, looking for professional help, but their work soon blossomed into an avalanche of mutual creativity.

The meeting of Carl Jung and Wolfgang Pauli beautifully illustrates the fertile possibilities of a Mercury-Gemini shockwave of new, unexpected ideas – but for our purposes here, it also illustrates the impact of the non-sexual dimensions of Venus. Specifically, when Jung met Pauli, Jung's *solar arc Pluto had conjuncted his natal Venus* only six months earlier – it still fell within an orb of only half a degree, in other words. Meanwhile, in the exact month of their first meeting, transiting Jupiter was in a sextile aspect to Pauli's natal Venus.

Beatle Paul McCartney was born with a telling Mars-Pluto conjunction in Leo in his tenth house – a sign that he would leave a mark on the world, or at least upon his community. When he first met bandmate John Lennon, McCartney's solar arc Venus was making a sextile to both of those natal planets. Meanwhile, solar arc Pluto was squaring his natal Venus.

McCartney's story also provides an Illustration of the triggering effects of *transiting* Venus – moving quickly, it had made a conjunction to his Mars-Pluto alignment just three or four days before his fateful first contact with John Lennon.

At the same time, Venus was also busy in John Lennon's chart. Just seven weeks after he first met McCartney, Lennon's progressed Moon made a conjunction to his natal Venus. That means that it was only a couple of degrees from his Venus when they first met – well within the effective orbs of interaction. Even more tellingly, less than four months later, Lennon's progressed (and solar arc!) Sun made a sextile to Venus. It was time for him to meet some soulmates.

It is helpful for us to remember that in addition to this being a significant *partnership* and *friendship* experience for both Lennon and McCartney, it was also Venusian in another sense: the Beatles soon emerged, which changed their lives *artistically* as well as intimately.

The moral of all of these tales: never neglect friendship when you are looking at Venusian events.

VENUS RETROGRADE BY PROGRESSION

There is a cycle of 584 days between successive *inferior conjunctions* of Venus with the Sun – and just in case you need a reminder, the inferior conjunction is the one in which Venus lines up with the Sun because it is directly between Earth and the Sun. (In the *superior conjunction*, Venus is also lined up with the Sun, but far away on the other side of its orbit, with Sun in between.)

For between forty and forty-two days centered on that inferior conjunction, Venus is in *retrograde motion*, going backwards through the signs and degrees of the zodiac. In fact, that is the only way to tell from the ephemeris – or your computer screen – which kind of Sun-Venus conjunction you are seeing. *If Venus is retrograde, it is an inferior conjunction and if Venus is direct, it is a superior conjunction, 100% of the time.*

This 584-day cycle of transiting Venus is so fascinating and full of meaning that it merits its own chapter – number twenty-one, coming up soon. There, we will reflect on the elegant pentangle its inferior conjunctions trace in the sky. We will also think about the difference between Venus playing the role of the Morning Star versus the Evening Star – *Venus Lucifer* and *Venus Hesperus*. Those are classical Roman designations for these two faces of Venus, terms which astrologer Dane Rudhyar popularized a few generations ago.

Here in this chapter, let's reflect on Venus being retrograde by *progression* rather than by transit. As you might imagine, progression slows everything down dramatically. In fact, a complete progressed Venus cycle would require almost six centuries to unfold.

If you want to experience one, stay away from fast food.

That approximately forty day *transiting* retrograde period is more tractable, however – in progressions, that translates to forty years, or perhaps a little longer. That is obviously a big chunk of a person's life, but it is short enough that we can make some human sense of it.

We will return to that progressed retrograde cycle in a moment.

A BRIEF MATHEMATICAL INTERLUDE . . .

Venus is retrograde, more or less, for forty out of every 584 days. Forty is 0.0684931 of 584, so that boils down to Venus being in retrograde motion about 7% of the time.

Voilà: only about seven out of every one hundred people are born with Venus retrograde.

For those seven people, it is guaranteed that sometime within the first forty years of their lives, progressed Venus will make a station and turn direct – and that it will remain direct for the rest of their lives.

Maybe someone is born ten days *before* transiting Venus turns retrograde. Then when that person is ten years old, *progressed* Venus stations – and remains retrograde until he or she is about age fifty or fifty-two.

Maybe someone is born *seventy* days before Venus turns retrograde. When he or she is about seventy, progressed Venus stations and *continues retrograde for another four decades* – for the rest of that person's life, in other words.

Maybe someone is born on the *very day* that transiting Venus turns direct. That individual will *never* experience a progressed Venus station. It will remain in direct progressed motion for another six centuries.

Arbitrarily assuming that humans live for eighty years, most people born any time during the final eighty days of Venus's long direct period will experience Venus turning retrograde by progression before they die. And when it does turn retrograde, it will not go direct again in their lifetimes.

Let's take one more step with the numbers. All of this tells us that there is a period averaging around 464 days out of the entire 584-day Venus cycle in which no one born is ever going to have to worry about Venus being retrograde by progression.

That tells us that about 80% of the human population is completely immune to everything I am about to write about progressed Venus in retrograde motion.

PROGRESSED VENUS STATIONS

With transits, progressions, and solar arcs, *slow means strong* – that is a principle that we have already seen in action many times. Nothing can possibly be slower than stopped – and that, basically, is what happens when a planet makes a station. We could quibble and point out the planets are never actually fully stopped in their tracks. True enough – but for practical purposes they are not moving in a perceptible way.

The result is that they then become extremely powerful.

This observation is true regardless of whether the planet is turning retrograde or turning direct. Either way, it is a planetary station and it will knock your socks off.

In the night sky, a planet making a station can be seen to be standing still relative to the background stars for several days. "Several days" is a vague term, but it puts us in the right territory: exactly when we decide to announce that the planet is officially moving again is very much an arbitrary question.

Of course, with progressions, those "several days" become "several years." And during that whole time, the energies of that planet leave a dramatic mark upon one's life and experience. Again, that is because stationary planets always pack a punch. In the case of progressed Venus, that "punch" can last for a long time. And during that whole period, everything in the archetypal realm of Venus makes itself felt vividly.

Here is an example.

(PERHAPS I CAN GET SOME) SATISFACTION

Mick Jagger of Rolling Stones fame experienced his progressed Venus making a station and turning retrograde on March 25, 1964. It froze in its forward track at precisely 20° 33' of the sign Virgo – and on that day, it began to fall backwards for the next four decades of his life.

That is an astrological fact – but as we will see, fussing about the exact date of Mick Jagger's Venus station is sheer folly. A progressed Venusian stationary period lasts a long time. The planet is barely moving – and thus very strong – for a number of years on either side of the station. Fully five years earlier, for example, Jagger's progressed Venus was at 20° 4' of Virgo – that is only half a degree away from where it would eventually stop.

Five years after the station, Venus had retrograded a similar half-a-degree distance, lying then at 20° 3' of Virgo.

In the ten years centered on 1964, in other words, Mick Jagger's progressed Venus barely moved. Those were ten big years for him, as any fan would tell you. The Rolling Stones formed in 1962 and had their first international Number One hit, *(I Can't Get No) Satisfaction,* in summer 1965. By the time Venus was moving again, the band had established its indelible place in rock'n'roll history.

Note that all Jagger's biography so far is about that classic Venusian territory: *art*. Even using a narrow one-half degree orb for that progressed Venus station, we are looking at the period from 1959 through 1969. During that time, Mick Jagger's progressed Venus station *defined and established his identity as an artist*.

What about love and partnership? What about sexuality?

In terms of *relationship*, defined broadly, it is fair to say that, without the rest of the Rolling Stones, a critical element of artistic chemistry would have been missing from Mick's make-up. So the *partnership* dimensions of Venus are quite active during this time as well – and they provide us with yet another caution about how critically important it is to remember to think outside the sexual box during Venusian times.

Even though the Rolling Stones always cultivated a "bad boy" reputation, I've often gotten a smile out of realizing that one of the most successful – and *enduring* – "marriages" of my generation is the creative bond between Mick Jagger and Keith Richards.

Not to be sidetracked here, but the Rolling Stones formed in 1962, the same year that Richard's progressed Moon entered his seventh house – and in that observation, we get another reminder that human partnership, from an astrological perspective, is not only about Venus.

But what about romance? While it is a big mistake to limit our attention to it in Venusian times, we certainly should never ignore it.

Sexually, Mick Jagger has always been famously enthusiastic, but the long period of his Venus station stands out in that regard. From 1966 to 1970, he had a romantic bond with singer Marianne Faithfull.

He pursued a serious connection with another singer, Marsha Hunt, in 1969 – which ended in June 1970, with her pregnant with his first child.

In 1970, he also met Bianca De Macias. He married her – and this was his only actual marriage – on May 12, 1971. On that day, Jagger's progressed Venus had retrograded back to 19°33' of Virgo – only 1° from where it had made its station seven years earlier.

So Mick Jagger "married during his Venus station."

An astrologer might argue, saying that my statement is actually off by seven years. I would counter that argument by saying yes – but that I am happy to use a 1° orb in defining a planetary station.

Who is right? At least with Mick Jagger, the facts are on my side.

Bottom line, while not very many people experience Venus stations in their lifetimes, when they happen, it helps to look at them broadly and inclusively. They are operative for a long time, as befits any astrological event of such monumental significance – a significance we can only fully appreciate by delving more deeply into the meaning of the *full four decades* of your entire progressed Venus retrograde period.

That is our next subject.

THE MEANING OF PROGRESSED VENUS RETROGRADE

Planets are the active ingredients in astrology. They are the spark plugs, making things happen in our lives. This active quality is reflected in the fact that most of the time they are moving *forward* through the zodiac – in direct, rather than in retrograde motion, in other words. That means "forward into life" too.

- Direct motion is *extroverted*, engaging with people and circumstances. Its orientation is *outward, vital,* tending towards *obvious manifestation.*
- Turn those words on their heads and you have a good working definition of what it means for a planet to be retrograde. In that mode, the planet is *looking inward.* It is *introverted,* far less inclined to engage with people or with external circumstances – and much more attracted to our inner worlds. Instead of tending toward the obvious, *a retrograde planet tends towards the subtle.*

Astrologers who imply that there is something wrong with a planet in retrograde motion are the same kinds of people who believe that all introverts and loners have psychiatric issues. Give us a break, in other words. For the world to keep on going 'round and 'round, it takes both kinds of people.

Retrograde periods are as necessary as sleep, and necessary for similar reasons: they are times of *reflection*, closer to our dream-bodies than to our "beta brain waves" of waking cognition and normal daily functioning.

When a planet turns retrograde, it tends to become quieter. It follows that when Venus goes retrograde by progression, a person tends to become *less motivated to meet people.* How do you imagine, for example, that even that consummate Leo, Mick Jagger, would have felt about a chance to sit down with dozens of his adoring – and actively projecting – fans in 1970? I suspect that he soon began to feel a much stronger impulse of social withdrawal, setting boundaries around his private life. Famous people often have to do that for obvious reasons. It is the same with anyone experiencing progressed Venus beginning to accelerate in retrograde motion, even if the outward reasons for their withdrawal are less immediately evident.

As always in astrology, we must integrate this retrograde factor into the larger context of the symbolism. A fifth house Sagittarian with Leo rising and Jupiter conjunct the Ascendant Is not going to become a shy hermit living in a cave just because his or her Venus has turned retrograde. We can safely say however that compared to who he or she was in the past, the trend is now flowing in a softer, more inward, less socially-motivated direction.

- One might say that a retrograde planet is *quieter* – and with progressed Venus retrograde our tastes run towards interaction with quieter people.
- One might say that a retrograde planet is *deeper* – and with progressed Venus retrograde, we are drawn towards deeper, more psychologically-oriented people.
- One might say that a retrograde planet is *less social* – and with progressed Venus retrograde, we are more inclined toward deep, one-on-one conversations than to loud parties and chances to interact with strangers.

Ultimately everything that happens in your chart reflects *evolutionary necessity.* It needs to happen, in other words. There is no guarantee that you will get it right – but there is an ironclad guarantee that it is *possible* for you to get it right. *With Venus retrograde by progression, what we need in intimacy is now something deeper than we have ever known.*

As we look more deeply into ourselves, two fresh needs arise:

One need is for the validation that comes from feeling that another person is acknowledging our depth simply by seeing it.

The second need is for intimacy with someone as deep as ourselves.

Not everyone experiencing progressed Venus retrograde will think in these exact terms, but they are terms which explain and underlie what is happening – or at least what is trying to happen.

In any weak response to Venus retrograde, a person simply becomes withdrawn, alienated, and insecure. Still, because of synchronicity, the help we need to resolve those issues is out there waiting for us. The only question is whether we see that help and open our hearts to it – whether or not we *pay attention* to it.

GETTING ON WITH THE PAST

People often say, "you can't go home again." I thought it was an old proverb, but it was actually the title of a Thomas Wolfe book from 1940. It is a catchy phrase, but of course it is not really correct – you very probably *can* go home again if you feel like it. The point of the saying is that the home you remember is not the home you will see when you return. You are seeing it now through different eyes, and – just maybe – those eyes have grown clearer with the passage of time.

When a planet is retrograde, in a sense it is "going home again." It is literally returning to degrees of the zodiac through which it has already passed. But those degrees will look different now. A new perspective has arisen. That's true with all retrogradation. With Venus, that sense of "review" takes on its own unique tonality.

A man's face lights up in a used book store. He has found a dog-eared copy of his favorite book from back when he was twelve years old. It is a tale of derring-do. In it, a child runs away from home and winds up having a grand adventure among pirates, pyramids, and desert caravans. When our protagonist was a kid, he avidly read that book five times. He was obsessed with it. He read it under his covers at night with a flashlight.

Feeling the nostalgic gravity of that long-ago pleasure, he eagerly buys the book, takes it home, and begins reading it again that evening.

This time, *reading the book as a man rather than as a boy*, turning those pages gives him chills. He now understands the story in an entirely different way. The child in the story escaped an abusive home. With goose-bumps, our reader begins to realize *why he was so identified with the runaway*. He too was abused, but the abuse he experienced was more subtle, more psychological than physical.

When he was a child, he did not even think of it as abuse. Like most abused kids, he simply thought of it as reality.

Our protagonist now finds himself understanding his childhood in a new way. The experience of re-reading that book represents an "evolutionary necessity" for him. He too "can't go home" to that same book again, at least not exactly. He is not that boy anymore. It is the same book; it is a different book. Both statements are true.

Reading that book triggers an important realization: he now understands his relationship with his psychologically abusive family from a fresh perspective.

He now understands what it actually felt like to be himself when he was ten years old.

It is a short step from there to another lightbulb lighting in his head: for seven years, he was married to a woman who constantly shamed him until she finally betrayed him with another man.

Just as with the rest of us, the wounds of his childhood were carried forward into his adult life.

The astrology underlying a story such as this one can take many forms. It could be a Pluto transit, for example, or some major event in the eighth house. Those kinds of events often correspond to uncomfortable, but helpful, realizations. We will explore that territory thoroughly in *The Book of Water*.

Our point here is that these events could also be connected with progressed Venus retrograde. That is because this man is going into his *past relationship history* and *seeing it in a new way*. Specifically, in Venusian fashion, he is learning something about the source of repeating patterns of dysfunction in his *intimate life*.

Icing the cake, our anecdote here turns upon him "happening" to find a copy of that old novel in the used book store. Novels are an *art form* and so there again we see the broad archetypal Venus fingerprint – and of course ever-present the invisible hand that we call synchronicity.

His progressed Venus remains retrograde for four decades. During that time, perhaps along comes a big Pluto transit, and it unfolds while something else is triggering his eighth house Moon – and on the day he finds the book, transiting Mercury has hit his natal Venus.

That is how astrology really works. It is always multifactorial. Progressed Venus retrograde is like an underlying current in the ocean. Storms may churn the surface waves and high pressure cells may turn the water blue and beautiful. But that current is always down there, pushing.

DEEPER INTO THE PAST

Most of us have had the experience of meeting someone for the first time who seems inexplicably familiar. We might even say, "I feel like I have known you before."

And maybe we actually have.

Reincarnation is quite fundamental to the cosmology that underlies evolutionary astrology – that's a subject I explore in detail in my book *Yesterday's Sky* and, really, in almost all of my work outside of these four volumes, which are more focused on astrology's psychological and existential dimensions.

No one needs to believe in past lives for astrology to work helpfully, however. The last thing I would ever want to do is to try to force such a belief on anyone.

In thinking about progressed Venus retrograde, my own mind points directly to the idea of it signalling periods of reconnection with people whom we have known in prior lifetimes.

You can take that notion literally, as I do, or you can take it as a metaphor. Either way, it rings the right bells in the heart. I will go ahead and use that language. Translate it into whatever terms work for you, Aquarian fashion, if you will – with my blessings.

Broadly, I believe it is accurate to say that from a karmic perspective, humans rarely enter into deep or complex intimacy with people who are total strangers to them. That is to say, it rarely happens with people with whom they have never before interacted in prior lifetimes. The lovers today, for example, may have been parent and child in a prior lifetime, or even bitter rivals. The roles we play in relation to each other change – but the process of "truly getting to know each other" takes a lot longer than our brief mortal eyes are likely to see.

In my view, the belief I just expressed is true of everyone all the time – and that is the case regardless of the direction in which Venus is progressing.

So, metaphysically, what distinguishes a retrograde progressed Venus?

The bottom line can be expressed in two words: *unfinished business*.

During any retrograde period, involving any planet, there is always an element of *going back into the past*. That is simply by definition with retrogradation – the planet is literally returning to places where it has recently been. *That means that something from long ago needs to be understood in a clearer way.* If we can attain that clarity, then our present-tense existences can be liberated from repeating dead-end patterns from the past.

When Venus is retrograde, that unfinished business is interpersonal. *Those ghosts from the past tend to be humans in the present.*

And we recognize them.

Maybe you simply longed for someone romantically in a prior life. Maybe she or he was unavailable. That longing is now an *unresolved energy* between you. It will surely bring you together again.

What happens next? We are now in the present – the realm of magic, free-will, and possibility.

We have no idea what will happen next.

But we do know the nature of the starting line: it is your own *feelings of longing projected onto that person* – along with whatever feelings, if any, the other person had towards you.

Desire is a powerful force, in other words. It sets wheels turning between souls – wheels that can turn for centuries.

Maybe it is not about love. Venus, as we have seen, refers to all sorts of human relationships. Maybe you stole money from someone. Maybe that theft gave you pleasure; maybe in order to live with your crime, you diminished that person in your own mind. Or maybe you felt guilty about it – but you never made it right.

You will meet again.

You will pick up that drama where you both left off. Will you steal again? Will you feel "inexplicably" compelled to offer that person something in recompense?

Perhaps you and another person were simply *loyal companions* in times of difficulty. Simple love – with no rusty razor blades in the mix at all – still binds you together. Obviously no one would call that bad karma, but the attachment is still unfinished business. You still love each other; you are still there for each other.

You too are very likely to meet again.

For reasons we learned a few pages ago, most of us never experience progressed Venus retrograde. We do need to keep that perspective. This is a special case – *one that underscores the critical role that this kind of mutual release from karmic patterns is trying to play in the lives of both people.*

When we do experience such a retrogradation, during that extended period of our lives, much of our evolution revolves around *learning to love as unconditionally as possible.* Those words can sound like generic spiritual advice, but they take on a very specific, precisely-defined relevance if you personally are experiencing a lifetime in which progressed Venus is retrograde. That is because these times are about *releasing* other people – not to mention releasing ourselves – from compulsive karmic patterns of projection and expectation.

In a word, they are about *forgiveness.*

Every one of us, regardless of our charts, has unfinished business with other souls. The difference here with progressed Venus retrograde, is that the karma has now ripened. We are ready to deal with it.

Again, by all the laws of the universe, we will meet once more in this lifetime.

As so often happens with astrology, in looking through the lens of Venus retrograde, we briefly part the curtain that separates this world from a higher one. We get a glimpse of a contract that binds one soul to another – *a contract that may be fulfilled, or broken, or even renewed, depending on our ability to pay attention to what we have each become, rather than yet again "getting on with the past".*

20

VENUS TIMES, LIBRA TIMES: THE BUILDING BLOCKS

When *transiting* Venus contacts your natal Mars, you may have a heated exchange with a friend or partner. That heat may take the form of anger or, if the gods are smiling on you, it may take the form of passionate sexual expression. Either way, unless this transiting Venus event is part of some larger pattern, the situation quickly fades into the past. Before long it is completely forgotten.

When, on the other hand, Venus contacts your natal Mars via *progression* or *solar arc*, that is a major event. Your intimate life needs to take a critical evolutionary step forward. Maybe a truly fundamental difference of viewpoints and values arises between you and someone you love. Negotiations are critical and necessary now – and they can be successful. That big, slow-moving Venus event signals this particular kind of evolutionary necessity. During such a time, the emotional stakes are high, and so *passions* (Mars) are likely to arise. The couple cannot pretend that these feelings are not there – that would be dishonest, and only lead to permanent estrangement. But they also have to be careful that those passions do not take over the conversation. When Venus contacts Mars, people can say things in the heat of the moment that they later wish they could take back.

Is there actually a way for this relationship to move forward? Will our partnership survive this process? *Should it?* Perhaps we both desire that outcome – but there is only one way to reach an authentic answer: *that is going bravely forward into the questions,* wherever they might lead us.

If we can resolve the situation, the battle – for all its exhausting difficulty – *was worth it.* The prize might very well be a renaissance in terms of our deeper soul-passion for each other. If we cannot resolve the dilemma – but we have tried bravely and honorably to do so and we each respect that virtue in each other – even our goodbyes might have a sweet sexual component.

My adding that last bit of sexuality to the interpretation is not gratuitous, by the way. When Venus and Mars come together, if we are not willing to speak frankly about sexuality, we are simply being prim. "Goodbye sex" – I have also heard it called "break-up sex" – is simply a human reality.

And anything in human reality can be portrayed by astrological symbolism.

In our words so far we have been speaking of *progressions* or *solar arcs* of Venus as examples of these larger developmental patterns. That is quite accurate; such astrological events are reliable signals of intimate evolution. But they are not the only ones. In this chapter, we will also consider two other possibilities.
- The first is the entry of any major moving astrological factor into the seventh house.
- The second, which is less reliable, has to do with any progression, solar arc, or significant transit as it enters the sign Libra.

In common with the structure of these "Building Blocks" chapters throughout this series of books, what I offer here are a few *seed ideas* to get you started on thinking more deeply and individually about each possible moving planetary configuration in the broad Libran family.

We will look at Venus-in-motion making an aspect to each one of the other planets individually. What I write is intended only as a starting point; it is up to you to make it three-dimensional by integrating the messages of the signs and houses involved, and also about exactly which aspectual processes are impacting the configuration.

Similarly, I will look at each planet as it enters the seventh house – but I will do that as if there were no difference between Taurus and Aquarius. In a counseling session, that would be a huge blunder. In a book of any reasonable length, it is an unfortunate necessity.

You get the picture: think of the paragraphs that follow as a launching pad for your deeper astrological skills. You need to supply the rocket fuel.

What follows here in terms of Venus's aspects to each of the other planets is repeated word-for-word from *The Book of Earth*. Once again, while I apologize for the repetition, for the sake of there not being an echoing vacuum in *The Book of Air*, including this material a second time seems like a wiser choice than leaving it out.

Later in this chapter, we reflect systematically on the meaning of any planet entering Libra or the seventh house. There, we are in brand new territory. None of that writing has appeared anywhere before.

VENUS CONTACTING THE SUN

How Best to Reduce Your Stress Load: Stand up for yourself. Ask for what you want. Insist on having your critical needs met. Look your best. Dress as if you are proud of yourself – it affects how people see you. Hold your head high. Expect to be taken seriously – and to be liked. Do something creative – and make sure that at least a few people know about it. Reach out to someone; make yourself available and obvious.

Most Beneficial Aesthetic Input: Anything big and bright. Spectacles; heroism; drama. Anything noble, reflecting high aspirations and the basis for human dignity. Anything that dramatizes someone prevailing against the odds, injustice, or resistance.

What You Need To Learn About Love and Trust: That you are still worthy of love even when you are up front about your needs. Ditto, when you are clear about what is not acceptable to you. That you must put yourself forward if there is to be any chance of your being seen and appreciated. That it is not fair of you to expect that others will understand your needs via some supernatural power of perception. Speak up and be straightforward.

How to Identify Your Soul-Helpers: They are colorful and direct. You know exactly where you stand with them. They can "perform," even when you are the only one in the audience – and they clap generously for your performances too. They are spontaneous; they seem to move comfortably and without self-consciousness through the social world. They have a certain animal magnetism, *gravitas*, or charisma.

What Happens If You Squander the Opportunity: A tense feeling arises, as if you needed some release that never came. Insecurity triggers outward displays which others read as vanity. You feel caught in "playing a part," perhaps representing a character whom you do not like very much.

VENUS CONTACTING THE MOON

How Best To Reduce Your Stress Load: Spend time at home, if your home is peaceful – and if it's not peaceful, move if you can! Be self-indulgent. Be kind to yourself. Listen to your body. Sleep a lot – dreams are restorative, and sleep is how to have them. Eat well. Go see your soul-family, even if they live far away.

Most Beneficial Aesthetic Input: Soft light: candlelight, firelight, literal moonlight. Silence. Trancing out to beautiful music. Being near bodies of water. Spending time outside at night. Fine fabrics; quilts; comforters. Romantic films and literature, especially familiar ones.

What You Need To Learn About Love and Trust: That real trust comes slowly and is earned over time. That there is no one as precious as an old friend, tried and true. That you need family – and that the meaning of the word "family" might be different for you from what is written in the dictionary. That the ultimate expression of love and trust is shared vulnerability in a spirit of long-term commitment.

How to Identify Your Soul-Helpers: They are comfortable expressing emotions of tenderness and vulnerability. They are comfortable when you do the same thing; they make that kind of sharing easy for you. They have a personal history of long-term relationships. There is a good chance that they love their families and are involved with them in ongoing ways. They are not afraid of commitment.

What Happens If You Squander the Opportunity: A spirit of lassitude arises – not quite depression – rather something more like just not caring very much. Temptations become harder to resist; it is as if your defenses against your own runaway appetites has collapsed. You make self-destructive intimate choices as laziness and emotionality eclipse your ability to make sober assessments of reality.

VENUS CONTACTING MERCURY

How Best To Reduce Your Stress Load: Deep, open-ended conversation with someone you love and whose company you enjoy. Arrange a situation in which you are confident that you are truly being heard by someone who cares about you. You need to engage your mind and your senses with a fresh face of the world. Get out and do things that expose you to new ideas and new experiences, especially ones with significant aesthetic dimensions.

Most Beneficial Aesthetic Input: Read poetry. Read literary novels. Watch films made for grown-ups. Travel to beautiful places. Pick up the house, make it pretty. Go to museums. Visit a planetarium. Look through a telescope at the heavens. Gaze at anything beautiful.

What You Need To Learn About Love and Trust: That love and trust thrive on a diet of patient, respectful communication conducted in a spirit of genuine mutual interest and inquiry. That being heard – and your words being remembered – builds a bond of trust between people. That feeling ignored, dismissed, taken for granted – or simply not heard at all – erode the bridge of affection.

How to Identify Your Soul-Helpers: Words come easily to them; they can express themselves fluently and clearly. They display a vibration of mental quickness. They listen well too. They are probably witty; they make you laugh – and to think in new ways.

What Happens If You Squander the Opportunity: Your words begin to feel scripted and phony, as if you are simply saying your lines in a play of manners. Talk, talk, talk – and it is all forgotten by the next day. The triumph of propriety over honesty; the triumph of diplomatic stability over genuine process. Polite words building a wall between souls.

VENUS CONTACTING VENUS

How Best To Reduce Your Stress Load: Say "I love you" to someone who deserves to hear it. Hear the same words yourself – and believe them. Take the risk of making genuine heart-contact with someone whom you hold in affection; blow out the walls of deadening habit; freshen your love. Meet new people, but only if they really interest you. Trust any instinctual feelings of fondness that arise in you toward anyone. Pretty yourself up and look approvingly at yourself in the mirror.

Most Beneficial Aesthetic Input: Anything that makes you sigh when you hear it, see it, feel it, or smell it. Shared aesthetic experiences are more effective than solo ones – attend a concert with a friend whose company gives you pleasure, for example. Go to art galleries. Enjoy something expensive; share it, if possible.

What You Need To Learn About Love and Trust: That courtship, displays of respect, and simple courtesy nurture love and trust. That when people love each other they savor their hours together; they are patient; they take time with each other. In the kind of sexuality that is meaningful and lasting, the eyes are more important than the genitals.

How to Identify Your Soul-Helpers: They are naturally courteous and comfortable to be around – polite without being formal or stiff about it. They move fluidly through varying social landscapes; they seem to know how to get along with different kinds of people. They present themselves well and gracefully; their grooming and clothing reflect mindfulness and taste without pretense.

What Happens If You Squander the Opportunity: Your life devolves into something resembling a boring cocktail party, full of empty chit-chat and obligatory social interactions. Your appetites loom pressingly in exaggerated fashion, promising relief, as a kind of low-level social anxiety takes its subliminal toll on you.

VENUS CONTACTING MARS

How Best To Reduce Your Stress Load: Get all sweaty. Exercise. Dance. Enthusiastic, uninhibited sexual expression works magic. Walk on the wild side. Have an adventure. Break up your intimate routines; do something different – or, if you are doing something familiar, do it in a different place. Above all, if an issue has been festering in any of your primary relationships, now is the time to put it on the table and deal with it.

Most Beneficial Aesthetic Input: Passionate, loud music – whether it is Beethoven, hip hop, or rock 'n roll, *turn it up* and move your body to it. Anger crystallized in art; bright colors, bold contrasts. Novels and films portraying courage, heroic scenes, and grand adventures. Tales of conflict, especially ones where the good guys win in the end.

What You Need To Learn About Love and Trust: That love and anger are not opposites, but rather a complementary pair. Without the healthy expression of anger and resentment, love and trust are diminished. If you are in a sexual partnership, you are invited to participate in an ancient mystery: that humans can literally *make* love – that is, enhance and deepen their sense of connection – in sexual union.

How to Identify Your Soul-Helpers: They are direct and honest with you. They have presence and intensity. Often, no matter their physical appearance, they possess an ineffable quality of sexiness. You know where you stand with them. They are fiercely loyal – but if you do something which displeases them, you will quickly hear about it.

What Happens If You Squander the Opportunity: Pointless conflicts arise. People blow off steam – which is to say, squabbles arise which have little to do with any of the actual issues underlying the tensions: arguments about money that are sublimated arguments about sex or family dynamics. Alternatively, necessary negotiations are entirely avoided, leading to a mood of frustration and unspoken resentment.

VENUS CONTACTING JUPITER

How Best To Reduce Your Stress Load: Be your own Santa Claus. Give yourself a gift; spend some money on yourself; blow off responsibilities and have some fun. Dress in bright colors. Take center stage, at least in front of your friends – tell a joke. Tell a mostly-true story about yourself, one that puts you in a good light, and do not be afraid to embellish it a bit for effect.

Most Beneficial Aesthetic Input: Something "above your pay grade" in any category: buy a beautiful painting, upgrade your sound system, go shopping and purchase something personal of impressive quality that you can barely afford. Buy yourself expensive tickets to a performance that attracts you. Dress up when you attend it. Do everything you can to like what you see when you look in the mirror.

What You Need To Learn About Love and Trust: That generosity of spirit is precious and essential to the maintenance of an attitude of love and trust. By generosity of spirit, we mean a supportive attitude, a spirit of forgiveness and radical acceptance, and the expression of sincere joy at the other person's victories. You must both offer and receive this kind of affirmation. Now is the time to assure that it is flowing. Shared laughter builds love and trust; make time for some giggles.

How to Identify Your Soul-Helpers: They are big-hearted, generous spirits. They laugh easily. Look carefully and you will also detect a hint of *star quality* in them, as if in a parallel universe, they could be in the film industry. They *believe in you,* perhaps even more than you believe in yourself. Their presence lifts your spirits; when they walk into the room, your reflex is to smile.

What Happens If You Squander the Opportunity: You overreach in a relationship, making unconsciously-selfish assumptions about another person's generosity – or level of duty – toward you. You lord it over someone, creating a reaction of resentment in them. Without realizing it, you make yourself look silly, "entitled," or foolish.

VENUS CONTACTING SATURN

How Best To Reduce Your Stress Load: Even if you are in happy, satisfying relationships, you might simply need some time to yourself. Do not let a misguided sense of duty or responsibility prevent you from asking for it. Laughter and fun feed the life-force – but so does seriousness. You need some of that seriousness with your partner or your friends right now. What is the *next developmental stage* in these intimacies? It is time to take those steps together. That may not be easy – but the thus-far unmet need to take those steps is the source of the underlying tension that you are feeling.

Most Beneficial Aesthetic Input: Some artists in every discipline have functioned almost like a priesthood, mediating between human beings and the enormity of life's real issues: love's difficulties, the reality of loss and defeat, mortality. Exposure to such serious art is helpful to you now; mere entertainment will seem hopelessly trivial. Listening carefully and deeply to a symphony utilizes a different part of your consciousness than does tapping your feet to a pop song; that "symphonic" place is the part of your consciousness which needs to be fed at this juncture of your life.

What You Need To Learn About Love and Trust: That loyalty, reliability, and commitment are essential to the maintenance of love and trust. That people need to keep their word. That vows and promises kept and honored are the life-blood of any lasting human bond in the adult world. That relationships, just like people, need to grow up – and that the process never ends. What worked just fine in a high school fling no longer works in our forties or our fifties.

How to Identify Your Soul-Helpers: They radiate competence. You can trust them – not only to have good intentions, but also to execute those intentions effectively. They are good at what they do. They show up on time. They can laugh – but they can also be serious. They do not hide from life behind humor. They will never make a joke out of your attempts to be serious.

What Happens If You Squander the Opportunity: Loneliness arises. That word might have its usual, straightforward meaning: you might find yourself isolated or alone. What you are not recognizing, if that is the case, is the evolutionary necessity of some solitude now. Try to appreciate it. Alternatively, loneliness can arise within a relationship or a crowd. That happens when we are still interacting with people whom we have outgrown, or when we have failed to do the hard work of actually growing the relationship.

VENUS CONTACTING URANUS

How Best To Reduce Your Stress Load: Break out of the tyranny of your own routines and habits. You are at risk of becoming a victim of your own predictability. Deep down, you are sick and tired of it. Trust those feelings. You need change in terms of your circumstances, your memorized daily patterns, and above all, your attitude. You need more of a sense of freedom in your life, and you need to be its author or it will not happen. This edgy feeling is most pressing in your primary relationships. Astrologers often use these aspects to predict breakups; here, we are turning it around, talking about how to *avoid* breakups.

Most Beneficial Aesthetic Input: Your tastes are at risk of becoming jaded. It is time to stretch your aesthetic horizons. You need fresh input – something that perks up your ears or your eyes, something new. If you like pop music, try listening to an opera. If you like modern abstract painting, make a study of Rembrandt, Velasquez or Delacroix.

What You Need To Learn About Love and Trust: Nothing sustains a relationship more effectively than blessing our partners' natural right to follow their evolutionary threads wherever they lead. As the U2 song says, "We are one, but we are not the same." Love and trust should enhance our freedom rather than diminishing it. Change is equivalent to being fully alive; partners celebrate that aliveness in each other: they support each others' changes.

How to Identify Your Soul-Helpers: They hear a different drummer and dance to a different tune than most people. From the conventional point of view, they are probably at least a little bit strange. They regale you with unexpected perspectives and unusual understandings. They may seem "not to be your type," although the opposite is the actual truth.

What Happens If You Squander the Opportunity: Your relationships move in the direction of becoming stale and predictable. Perhaps consciously, perhaps subliminally, you begin to lose interest in each other. People do drift apart, and sometimes that is what this aspect indicates. But it can also be something darker: a failure to do the work of keeping up with each other's changes. Then a love that does not need to die, dies.

VENUS CONTACTING NEPTUNE

How Best To Reduce Your Stress Load: Meditation – especially meditation upon serenity – is the sovereign remedy. Similarly effective is sitting quietly in a garden or watching as a beautiful sunset slowly unfolds. Those are "meditations" too, just not so formal. The aim is to empty your mind. A Buddhist metaphor comes to mind: let a glass full of turbid water sit for an hour. Watch it become clear as gravity settles the suspended particles of dirt to the bottom. The same thing will happen to your mind if you sit for an hour. Try gazing at a flower or a beautiful stone – that will make the sustained focus easier to maintain.

Most Beneficial Aesthetic Input: Romantic, idealistic art that uplifts your spirits. Art that elevates your consciousness. There are worlds beyond this physical one; visionary artists since the beginning of time have attempted to represent those worlds in imagery, poetic language, and sound. Turn your attention now to those artists. You are ready to understand and appreciate them – and to be helped toward serenity by them.

What You Need To Learn About Love and Trust: That love, for you, must have a spiritual basis – that is to say, two spirits must experience a sense of psychic connection. This does not imply mental telepathy or shared religion; those things are neither here nor there. It does imply easy shared silence. It implies an underlying sense of resonance and empathy linking the two partners, one that does not require discussion or physical contact.

How to Identify Your Soul-Helpers: They are sensitive souls, perhaps a bit otherworldly at times. They respond knowingly and avidly if you bring up metaphysical topics: psychic phenomena, life after death, seeing ghosts. They have vivid dreams and vivid imaginations. They often have a faraway look in their eyes; they often seem to return from "elsewhere" when you call their names.

What Happens If You Squander the Opportunity: You might find yourself falling in love with an illusion – that is to say, a person whom you are misreading or one who is not what he or she seems to be. You might "hang on the cross" of loneliness feeling sorry for yourself, all the while not making any practical attempt to reach out and connect with anyone. You might experience an exaggeration of any of your innate tendencies towards escapism.

VENUS CONTACTING PLUTO

How Best To Reduce Your Stress Load: There is a paradox here: in order to reduce the level of stress you are carrying, you will probably first have to increase it. Psychological realizations – some of them difficult – are pressing at you from the unconscious. They are most likely uncomfortable insights into issues underlying your primary relationships. Some of these insights are about you; some are about people whom you love. You ultimately reduce your stress load through the often-stressful process of facing these emerging truths squarely.

Most Beneficial Aesthetic Input: Everything you are facing has been faced by other people before you. Some of them have been successful, some have failed. And some have turned their experiences into art: serious books and films, for example. You benefit from exposure to those art-forms; you may even create some yourself now. Humor plays a very helpful role here as well. At first, that sounds like a very different notion, but actually, humor is one of the most effective art forms humans have ever created for dealing with subjects which make them nervous or uncomfortable. You may find humor very helpful at this point in your journey.

What You Need To Learn About Love and Trust: That without honesty, there is no such thing as trust. Love may exist without it, but only in the form of kindness. Right now, you need the whole package: love – but also enough honesty that you can trust what you are hearing. This is a two-way street: you must speak the truth that is actually in your heart, but you must also strive to become the kind of person who can hear truth without punishing the person who is telling it.

How to Identify Your Soul-Helpers: They look you directly in the eye. They are not trying to win a staring contest with you, but they are trying to make sure that you are linked by an authentic soul-to-soul connection. They tell you things you might not want to hear. They can keep your secrets; they offer you some secrets of their own. Whether or not they are formally educated, they have a natural ability to speak in psychological terms.

What Happens If You Squander the Opportunity: Relationships rot because of festering issues left unaddressed. Suspicions grow; people begin to generate "psychiatric" interpretations of each other, generally characterized by a sense of hopelessness or resignation about the other person ever improving. We fail to look at ourselves; we imagine the issue to have its sole origin in the other person's intransigence.

PLANETS ENTERING THE SEVENTH HOUSE

When a planet enters the seventh house, people enter our lives. Remember: houses are very much oriented to events. The seventh house is, above all, about *trust* – and no one learns much about trust all by themselves. We need help in accomplishing that aim, and the laws of synchronicity assure us that when a planet is entering the seventh house, some kind of help is in fact on the way.

Keep in mind, however, that the seventh house is not just about romance and coupling – it is about friendship as well. Sometimes it even signals the arrival of rivals or opponents – we can learn a lot about ourselves in those kinds of "intimate" situations as well.

In other words, if you work with astrological clients, always protect yourself against them coming back a year later demanding a refund because "Prince or Princess Charming" failed to ride over the horizon on a white stallion "like you predicted."

And if you did predict that, then give them their money back – they deserve it.

Contemplating the seventh house experience from a structural perspective, we can make three fundamental points about it.
* First, a planet entering the seventh house describes the *nature of the evolutionary lesson* that your soul needs to learn – and the dark side of that planet paints a picture of the cost of failure.

- Second, a planet entering the seventh house describes the *nature of the person* who will help you learn that lesson. The symbolism may refer to someone new, or it may underscore the nature of developments within an existing relationship *with that type of person*.
- Third, a planet entering the seventh house warns you about the nature of people who, through their own madness or malice, can be dangerous to you. *They might have the keys to your locks, but they do not deserve entry into your heart*.

A MOMENT OF REFLECTION

One of the most poignant experiences available to us on this Earth is to meet a genuine soulmate who, through a series of bad choices, has gone down a dark road. They arrive on our door steps, and we are primed to trust them and to do the work that we made a soul-contract to do together.

But they have become human wreckage; they cannot hold up their end of the bargain.

In that kind of situation, you are holding a ticket to a First Class cabin on the *Titanic*. My advice: tear it up and stay safe and dry in Ireland.

How can we spot these dangerous people? It is not difficult, provided you use your Air wisdom, some astrological insight, and you *pay attention*. What planet is interacting with your seventh house? *What is the dark or weak expression of that planet?* Have a deeper look at this attractive stranger, and be clinically honest with yourself – does he or she fit that profile?

This is not about being judgemental; it is about being *discerning*. There is a difference. Remember: people often find themselves in messy evolutionary predicaments without having arrived there out of evil intent. Think of any kind of addict, for example – the condition is sad and tragic, but not necessarily reflective of malice in the person. We can have compassion. Maybe we can even help.

But never lose sight of the fact that, for you, this seventh house transit or progression is about a chance for you to learn something about trust. You have a right to try to learn that from a *trustworthy* person – and you would be a fool to try to learn how to trust with someone unworthy of your trust or incapable of coming through for you.

Again, with planets entering the seventh house, it is the slow-moving ones that tell the deeper story. As you read through the sections about the Sun, Moon, Mercury, Venus, and Mars below, take the words more seriously if you are looking at progressions or solar arcs. These planets work by transit too – but those kinds of "transitory" events are less central to your soul's journey. They probably refer more precisely to events happening in the context of existing relationships than to the profiles of emerging soulmates.

THE SUN ENTERING THE SEVENTH HOUSE

What am I learning now about love and partnership? How to be forthright, direct, and free of self-consciousness in my relationships. How to assure that my own needs take up a rightful amount of space . . . not too much – but definitely not too little. How to insist that my needs, intentions, and desires are understood unequivocally. How to stand up for myself. How to avoid codependent behaviors. How to relax and spontaneously be myself, assuming that I will be loved.

Who can help me learn it? People who are naturally direct. People with a lot of presence. People with strong (not "big") ego-structures – they can "take it." They can stand up for themselves when they need to without feeling that they need to constantly prove that they can. People who attract attention or who have "star quality" or who are "natural leaders."

Whom should I avoid? Narcissists and egomaniacs, above all. People who cannot see past themselves enough to actually love me or anyone else. People who always need to be at the center of attention. People who say "I, me, or mine" too often. People who do not remember what I tell them.

What happens if I get this wrong? I become a doormat. I slip into enabling and codependent styles of interactive behavior. I feel like I am playing second fiddle to a buzz saw. My life goes into orbit around someone else's dreams, needs – or craziness.

THE MOON ENTERING THE SEVENTH HOUSE

What am I learning now about love and partnership? How to trust deeply with all my heart. How to reveal myself. How to be emotionally vulnerable. How to nurture another person and how to ask for nurture myself. How to feel loved for simply being myself. How to experience a sense of being *safe* in intimacy, with no fear of abandonment. How to create family-feeling.

Who can help me learn it? People who are not unduly afraid of words such as "always" and "forever." Emotional, even sentimental, people. Kindness and caring radiate from them. Animals like them. Children like them. People who enjoy homelife and know how to make a house into a home. Often they can cook. Many times they are gardeners or have success with houseplants – that is because they are drawn to helping things grow.

Whom should I avoid? Childish people who chronically allow their feelings to eclipse any perspective on mature, adult responsibility. Self-indulgent people whose needs and demands are always front and center, leaving little room for my own needs. Hypochondriacs. People who whine. People who make a religion out of their moods.

What happens if I get this wrong? I become enmeshed in emotionally-draining dramas characterized ultimately by impossibility. I lose the thread of my own natural path through life, having been pulled into someone else's framework. I disappear into a relationship. I fall in love with someone who sucks the life out of me.

MERCURY ENTERING THE SEVENTH HOUSE

What am I learning now about love and partnership? How to speak up. How to express myself clearly and effectively. How to reach people about whom I care with words – the point being not so much that I feel loved, but rather that I feel genuinely *heard*. The time has come for the kinds of intimate talks which update my loved ones about who I am, what interests me, and what I am thinking. I am learning how to be a better listener, how to hold up my end of true two-way communication.

Who can help me learn it? People who listen well – and who prove it to me by responding to the actual content of what I say. People who show evidence that they enjoy the process of learning. People who are both interesting themselves and who convey their genuine interest in me, in my thoughts, and in what is behind my opinions. People who make me laugh. People who surprise me and make me think.

Whom should I avoid? Motor-mouth individuals who never make space for me to say much of anything. People who always interrupt. People whose presence makes me feel nervous or jumpy. Immature, distractible people who are always changing their minds or their direction in life.

What happens if I get this wrong? Instead of genuine relationship, I become entangled in an endless two-person "discussion group about our relationship." Talk, talk, talk – and no real feeling of connection. It feels like two video screens are facing each other, each one with the volume up – and no one actually in the room.

VENUS ENTERING THE SEVENTH HOUSE

What am I learning now about love and partnership? How to enhance and preserve romantic feelings in existing relationships. How to initiate intimacy and connection in new ones. How I might convey openness and receptivity to an exchange of affection. How to invite love into my life. How to add more grace to the tone of my connections. How to present myself appealingly. How to negotiate satisfactory compromises.

Who can help me learn it? Warm-hearted individuals who make me feel as if I am the only person in the room – that I "count" for them. People with natural grace. People who have integrated diplomacy with genuine sincerity. Artists – or people who respond to the arts. People who present themselves attractively in terms of dress and social style.

Whom should I avoid? Narcissists. Vain people. Skillful manipulators. People who cannot walk past a mirror without glancing at their own reflection. Lazy people. People who seem compelled to numb themselves in various ways. People who are "too good to be true." Seducers. Silver-tongued devils. Con artists.

What happens if I get this wrong? I become enmeshed in a relationship that is like a sugar-diet: sweet, but not nourishing. Some critical, funky ingredient of raw humanity is missing from the mix. Conflict-avoidance allows issues to fester beneath the surface – issues which will eventually leach the vitality and passion out of the bond.

MARS ENTERING THE SEVENTH HOUSE

What am I learning now about love and partnership? How effectively handling natural conflicts that arise in intimacy is the key to keeping passion alive – and how not being honest and direct about such issues eventually sucks life out of any human bond. I am learning how to make sure that my own needs are met, starting with deepening my ability to be forthright and clear about them.

Who can help me learn it? People who know that love is not really the opposite of anger and resentment – that love has to be big enough sometimes to include them. People who can be direct. People who do not shame my intensity, passion, or anger in an attempt to control it or to silence me. People whose loyalty and commitment to me is not contingent on my "being nice" all the time.

Whom should I avoid? Two kinds of dysfunctional people are dangerous for me now. The first are people who respond to any complaints or criticism with nuclear retaliation; they make my being honest so costly emotionally that I risk squelching it simply in order to avoid the drama it triggers. The second type of dysfunctional person for me to avoid is one who is so intimidated by my anger that he or she dissembles, offering terrified, insincere apologies and *mea culpas*, mostly to mollify me.

What happens if I get this wrong? I become difficult. I breathe fire and stomp my feet, but nothing comes of it except the kind of conflict that leads nowhere. Meanness and sarcasm become costly ways of blowing off steam. All that – or I paste a smiling face over interpersonal situations that really need to be addressed, allowing the unexpressed resentments to gather interest, just delaying the inevitable detonation.

JUPITER ENTERING THE SEVENTH HOUSE

What am I learning now about love and partnership? How to never settle for less in my relationships than what I naturally deserve. How to ask for more of what I need or want. How to make a good relationship *even* better – and possibly how to exit an unredeemably bad one. Generosity of spirit, both towards my partners and toward myself.

Who can help me learn it? People who believe in me and who encourage me. Big-hearted people who make me laugh a lot. People with charisma and presence. People who are generous, perhaps materially, but above all in terms of celebrating my good qualities, while not putting my flaws or failures under a microscope.

Whom should I avoid? Anyone showing signs of self-importance or pomposity. People who "know everything." People who are so blinded by pride that they are incapable of laughing at themselves. Inflated egos. People who never offer me a compliment. Anyone who chronically tries to draw other people's attention away from me and back onto himself or herself.

What happens if I get this wrong? I become the vassal of a self-appointed King or Queen. I become the loyal secretary of his or her fan club. I am eclipsed by someone else's monumental, insatiable ego. I spend my life in her or his shadow.

SATURN ENTERING THE SEVENTH HOUSE

What am I learning now about love and partnership? How to evaluate another person's character dispassionately. How to be almost clinically discerning. How to determine who is worthy of my trust before I offer it. How to walk away if that is the wisest choice; how to be self-sufficient if I need to be. How to recognize that any long-term partnership must continuously mature, reflecting the maturation of the individuals who compose it. How to do the maintenance work that keeps love alive. I am learning about my own blockages and fears around trust. I have an opportunity now to recover from damage in those areas.

Who can help me learn it? People of honor and integrity. People with a high degree of maturity – which might possibly mean people who are older than me. People whose "word" means a lot to them. They are reliable, reasonable – and very probably punctual. "I'll meet you at 7:00" means 7:00, not 7:15 – a small thing, but one that reveals much about their characters.

Whom should I avoid? Withholding people. Those who are emotionally restrained to the point of being unavailable. Perpetual loners. People who offer too much unsolicited, unnecessary advice. Distant people. Never mistake silence for emotional depth or strength.

What happens if I get this wrong? I become lonely, either because I was afraid to take the inevitable risks of love, or because I have allowed myself to become involved with someone who cannot love me – or probably anyone else either.

URANUS ENTERING THE SEVENTH HOUSE

What am I learning now about love and partnership? How to feel free, spontaneous, and independent within the context of my human relationships. How to find that elusive balance point between intimacy and individuality. How to make sure that people in my life are updated about who I have actually become, as opposed to them seeing me through the lens of their memories of me as I was in the past.

Who can help me learn it? People who value their own freedom and exercise it regularly. They can love, but they are also pointedly wary of the way love so often leads to perilous compromises of one's individuality. They "hear a different drummer" – which is to say they might seem eccentric or peculiar to others. That is why they will support my own "eccentricities" or "peculiarities" as well.

Whom should I avoid? Anyone who is emotionally detached on a chronic basis. This may be part of their natural make-up, but people who are estranged from their own hearts will surely never touch mine. People who are so traumatized by past events that they may have become psychologically dissociated. People whose "weirdness" does not arise from their own natures, but rather from a desire to create reactions in other people. People who *intend* to shock. Anyone trying to be seen as "cool."

What happens if I get this wrong? Perhaps I become compulsively and precipitously independent, suddenly leaving relationships that could be made to work if I only made the effort to be clear about my own changes and growth. Instead of being revised and re-written, intimate contracts are simply torn up. Alternatively, I go through old motions, keeping moribund relationships propped up via endless enslavement to worn-out patterns of behavior.

NEPTUNE ENTERING THE SEVENTH HOUSE

What am I learning now about love and partnership? How to find higher spiritual ground in my intimate life. That without a sense of *spiritual relationship*, I have very little sense of relationship at all. I am learning that, in order to keep my own inner life vibrant, I benefit enormously from sharing it. I need to look into someone else's eyes and see soul there, while I know that he or she is having the same experience looking back into my eyes.

Who can help me learn it? Only people with active inner lives can help me – or even understand who I am and what I have come to value most. These people very likely are open to the idea of psychic phenomena; they have probably experienced such things themselves. Compassionate people. They may or may not be religious, but they comfortably self-identify as "spiritual." They are interested in dreams. I can speak to them of the continuity of consciousness after death and they nod their heads in understanding and tacit agreement.

Whom should I avoid? First and foremost, escapists of all sorts: drunkards, addicts, compulsive shoppers, compulsive gamers – anyone who is "medicating" his or her own sensitivities. Flaky people whose lives are defined by the kinds of mistakes that arise from simply not paying attention. Delusional people; people with serious mental health problems – I may be able to help them, but I think twice before putting my heart in their shaky hands.

What happens if I get this wrong? I become disillusioned by love – and for that disaster to have happened, I first had to become "illusioned." I fell in love with a projection out of my own fantasy life. Because of my compelling hunger for spiritual connection, I saw a crystalline soul in another person. Perhaps I saw it correctly – but I failed to see the flaws in his or her worldly personality even though they were staring me in the face.

PLUTO ENTERING THE SEVENTH HOUSE

What am I learning now about love and partnership? How to insist upon transparent truthfulness in a few critical partnerships. That means truthfulness in how I express myself. It also means my insisting on the same transparency from the other person. I am currently confronting my own core wounds when it comes to fully trusting anyone. In this lifetime or in previous ones, I have been grievously lied to. I resolve to do my part in seeing that such betrayal does not happen again. I am careful only to choose honest people.

Who can help me learn it? People who are real. People who have done hard work on themselves. People who look me directly in the eye. People with whom I can talk about anything, no matter how charged or taboo the subject may be. People with a natural orientation to psychology, whether or not they are formally educated in it. People who give me insights into myself which I could never generate on my own. People who have been to hell and found their way back.

Whom should I avoid? This is an excellent time to be wary of scoundrels – liars, manipulators, con artists, seducers, and users. How? Some of them are very slick, so I ask hard questions, and I listen carefully and critically to the answers. Above all, I am wary of people who can offer me truly brilliant, trenchant insights into myself – but *who cannot receive such insights about themselves coming from me.* Beware of "psychologists" who have never made their own personal relationships work.

What happens if I get this wrong? I blunder into relationships with people who can truly do serious damage to my soul. I allow myself to be manipulated and used; I allow myself to be shamed – or perhaps I even shame myself. I believe lies. I am pulled down into a darker world than the one in which I actually want to live.

PLANETS ENTERING LIBRA

Sooner or later, in the course of a lifetime, most of the planets will enter Libra via transits, progressions, or by solar arc. There are exceptions, but not many. For example of an exception, someone born in 1957 with natal Neptune right at the beginning of Scorpio would have to live to be well over three hundred years old before the planet entered Libra by solar arc.

Prospects for that person experiencing *transiting* Neptune's entrance into Libra are slightly more encouraging, but only by comparison. Neptune enters Libra for us all for the next time on November 21, 2105. Our friend born in 1957 will have just celebrated her 148th birthday. That's a lot of "days" from now – and remember, with progressions, days become years.

So let's not even think of her Neptune *progressing* into Libra.

Meanwhile, some of you older readers were born with Neptune in Virgo, so Neptune's solar arc into Libra is a reality for you in this lifetime, albeit in the past tense.

In what follows, we will look briefly at the meaning of each planet entering Libra. As that happens, the basic nature of the planet becomes charged with a new set of interests, motivations, and values. Mercury in Libra, for example, is a different creature than Mercury in Virgo – less hungry for facts and techniques, more hungry for aesthetic and interpersonal experience.

As we just saw, planets entering the *seventh house* have a reliable correlation with significant meetings. That is less true with planets entering Libra, where the motivational orientation covers a wider range of possibilities. As ever, houses can be relied on to manifest in concrete events far more than can any of the signs. There, we are looking more at attitudes and drives. At the highest level, as we have seen earlier in this volume, all of those Libran attitudes and drives converge on simply *calming down* – and calming down helps us make better intimate choices, among other things.

Again, just as we saw with planets entering the seventh house, it is the slow-moving ones entering Libra that tell the important tales. As you read through the sections that follow about the Sun, Moon, Mercury, Venus, and Mars, take the words more seriously if you are looking at progressions or solar arcs. They operate by transit too, but those kinds of passing astrological events are less central to your deep psyche.

THE SUN ENTERING LIBRA

What part of me needs to stop and take a deep breath? My basic values and orientation to life are ready for an update based on a more accurate appraisal of who I have actually become. Peace is more important to me than it once was. The quality of my relationships has always been a significant motivator for me, but its centrality is increasing. Balancing that and opening up space for it, I am not so driven by work, duty, and responsibility anymore.

Where might I need to be more open to paradox and ambiguity? There needs to be more openness in my definition of my responsibilities and the values that underlie them. Sometimes my not doing "what I am supposed to do" creates real evolutionary opportunity, both for myself and for other people as well. Tension always exists between loving oneself and loving others – I will not make the mistake of falling into either extreme, and instead I resolve to live this question day to day in a fresh, open-minded way.

Where do I need some help? Really in most areas of my life, I could use some assistance and supportive insight now. Probably all I have to do is to ask for it. The point of it all is simply that I need more of my twin resources of time and energy to be directed at restoring me to a state of inner ease rather than in chasing the chimerical goals of success in this world..

What happens if I muscle through this period of time rather than surrendering to it? Stress accumulates in me, perhaps to a dangerous point. I interfere with the evolution of other people by doing for them what they should be learning to do for themselves. In the name of helping people, I hinder them – and I hinder myself in the process.

THE MOON ENTERING LIBRA

What part of me needs to stop and take a deep breath? Functioning as an adult in the world often requires that we keep our emotions in check and make rational, principled choices – for example, we have an angry impulse to hit someone, but we refrain from doing it. I have gotten a little "too good for my own good" at that kind of self-control. At this point in my journey, I need to relax and let myself feel. I have become "too adult," which is to say, too mechanical. I may need to cry for no reason. I may need to ask for a hug.

Where might I need to be more open to paradox and ambiguity? My feelings do not make sense, and that is fine with me. I let myself simultaneously love people and want to avoid them too. As I open my mind to the idea of opposite emotions existing in myself, I allow myself to feel what I am really feeling instead of repressing half of it.

Where do I need some help? I discover the messages of my own heart in intimate conversation. I see my needs reflected in the mirror of a friend's eyes. As I extend myself to another person, offering counsel and support, I counsel and support myself.

What happens if I muscle through this period of time rather than surrendering to it? Simply said, I become unhappy. The secret of happiness lies in our lives being aligned with our own hearts – which is to say, with our Moons. Right now, I need to relax into letting myself feel simply in order to allow that alignment to emerge and to heal.

MERCURY ENTERING LIBRA

What part of me needs to stop and take a deep breath? My nervous, chattering mind – which is constantly "explaining everything" to me, and is often wrong about it all too. Some simple silence between my ears would do me a world of good.

Where might I need to be more open to paradox and ambiguity? In my explanation of my own life. In my rationalizations. In the narrative I have invented to explain myself to myself.

Where do I need some help? As I listen to people I like and trust, I see everything through their fresh eyes rather than through my own jaded ones – but that only works if I truly listen.

What happens if I muscle through this period of time rather than surrendering to it? I remain actually a lot more confused than I believe myself to be. The parts of reality that I refused to acknowledge sneak up on me and undo my efforts. I am ambushed by the ignorance I chose to protect.

VENUS ENTERING LIBRA

What part of me needs to stop and take a deep breath? My loving heart needs to be paid some attention and shown some appreciation. The idea that "I can be happy on my own" has value sometimes in life, but not now, not really, not for me. I need contact. I need a feeling of connection. I need some support. I need to be touched and to feel cherished.

Where might I need to be more open to paradox and ambiguity? In my perceptions of my partners and friends. Their reality is more complex than the images of them that I am carrying in my mind. As I release those images, these people "stop making sense" to me – and that is when I truly begin to see them as they are: paradoxical, ambiguous, and always changing – just as I am.

Where do I need some help? I need the people with whom I share my life to sit with me and open up about who they are and who they have become – their dreams, their worries, their fantasies. I need to prime the pump in that regard by showing interest in them, by asking them questions, and by making time for intimate processes to unfold at their own natural pace.

What happens if I muscle through this period of time rather than surrendering to it? My primary relationships start running on auto-pilot. Souls drift apart, while our "previously scripted lines" remain unchanged.

MARS ENTERING LIBRA

What part of me needs to stop and take a deep breath? A tense stew of fiery energies have accumulated in my mind and in my body. I need to release them before they damage me. This "stew" has many components: anger, stress, resentments, pent-up sexual energy, frustrations. I do not need to sort it all out psychologically – instead, I just need to *breathe* it out.

Where might I need to be more open to paradox and ambiguity? It helps me to try to see the viewpoints of people whose actions or attitudes have vexed me. Live and let live. I do not need to understand anyone else in order to accept that people have a right to make their own choices. They have a right to swing their fists – but that right comes to a boundary just before their fist reaches my nose.

Where do I need some help? People can often negotiate their differences if they are willing to talk and listen to each other. Will I get that kind of goodwill and cooperation? I don't know.

What I do know is that I can ask for it, take advantage of it if it is offered – and be open to radical alternatives if it is not..

What happens if I muscle through this period of time rather than surrendering to it? A chance to release accumulated tensions passes me by. I pay the price of holding onto them. I set the stage for intimate ugliness down the road.

JUPITER ENTERING LIBRA

What part of me needs to stop and take a deep breath? Jupiter times always hold the potential for improving some part of our lives, but *what part exactly?* For me now, I might need to tune into the potential of my expanding my creativity. Or enhancing the beauty of my home. Or improving my physical appearance. Above all, I need to address ways of deepening and updating my connections with my friends and partners.

Where might I need to be more open to paradox and ambiguity? There is a silly saying: "whoever dies with the most toys wins." Obviously that does not reflect the wisdom of the ages, but it is helpful to me now to find the kernel of wisdom in those words. My inner child and the mature, responsible adult in me need to find a better way of living together.

Where do I need some help? A joy shared is a joy doubled for both people. I resolve, for one example, to invite graceful, funny friends to enjoy an elegant dinner at my expense. In the broader sense, I take the initiative on sharing life's pleasures with people I love and whose company uplifts me.

What happens if I muscle through this period of time rather than surrendering to it? I become too mechanical and predictable. I resign myself to living in the gray middle of muddling through daily life. I miss a chance to put some sparkle back in my eyes.

SATURN ENTERING LIBRA

What part of me needs to stop and take a deep breath? Every day I plod through long lists of "things I must do." If I stop and take a breath, I will realize that some of those tasks can be deleted. I am working too hard. Unnecessary, exaggerated duties are taxing me more than I should be taxed. It does not have to be that way.

Where might I need to be more open to paradox and ambiguity? I always try to do the right thing. That is a commendable attitude – but there is now room for some fundamental re-interpretation of my "alleged" duties and responsibilities. There is more than one way of looking at them. I am now ready to see that.

Where do I need some help? Another set of eyes looking at the weight I am carrying can support my understanding and my necessary re-interpretations of it. I might simply say to a friend, "I am tired" – and thereby open a floodgate of helpful suggestions.

What happens if I muscle through this period of time rather than surrendering to it? I am caught in an outdated past, discharging an outdated, unnecessary set of duties – and too exhausted to even think about changing anything.

URANUS ENTERING LIBRA

What part of me needs to stop and take a deep breath? The part of me that does not want to be told what to do. That feisty inner rebel needs to be honored and heard – but also to be better informed about its current nature. As I stop and take a breath, I realize that I am no longer who I thought I was. New directions open up for me – and I simply walk away from some old battles that no longer interest or compel me. I don't need to win them. Not every relationship needs to be saved either.

Where might I need to be more open to paradox and ambiguity? I am a walking paradox, half of me is my actual self and the other half is what I have been tricked into believing about myself. That simple realization triggers an avalanche of insight and change, especially in my relationships.

Where do I need some help? I am in desperate need of some "bad influences" – the term is fun and it strikes the right naughty note, but what it really means is that I need some colorful people in my life who support my breaking out of conventional, expected patterns of behavior. Others may call them "bad influences." I call them my friends.

What happens if I muscle through this period of time rather than surrendering to it? I never stopped and took that deep breath, so I never realized who I had become. The result: nothing happened. I stayed the same when I needed to change. I become dull.

NEPTUNE ENTERING LIBRA

What part of me needs to stop and take a deep breath? Spirituality has many faces, ranging across the spectrum from mind-boggling insight through ecstasies and psychic phenomena. For me, at this crossroads, the face of spirituality that most profits my soul is simply attaining deeper *serenity*. Literally taking a deep breath and letting it out is perhaps the most ancient doorway to that kind of inner peace.

Where might I need to be more open to paradox and ambiguity? My ordinary mind, right now, as it actually exists, has in its nature the quality of enlightenment. I meditate deeply on that paradox.

Where do I need some help? Spiritual friends are a precious treasure. I seek them now – and the laws of synchronicity assure me that they are available. The emphasis here is not upon finding spiritual masters, although they might show up too. The emphasis is on finding my spiritual *peers*. We can support and comfort each other.

What happens if I muscle through this period of time rather than surrendering to it? My inner life remains cluttered and stressed. My spiritual aims, if I have any, are distorted with various delusions that overly complicate everything. I missed a simple, precious clue on my soul's journey.

PLUTO ENTERING LIBRA

What part of me needs to stop and take a deep breath? I am always generating psychological insights into myself. I am pretty good at doing that. Such insights inevitably come packaged with a certain emotional intensity. That is stressful. Right now, that load of stress is what is blocking me. At this point, I need a release of tension more than I need another insight.

Where might I need to be more open to paradox and ambiguity? I am sane enough to know how crazy I am. Another way to express it is that I am crazy enough to imagine myself to be sane. The part of me that can sit comfortably with those paradoxical statements is right now exactly on the cutting edge of my personal evolution.

Where do I need some help? I can do inner work on my own, but at this moment, insights generated by trusted friends and counsellors can trigger rapid growth in me. One of the most effective insights they can offer me now is connected to how I can work myself up into a psychiatric lather of self-criticism or of second-guessing myself – and how I do not need to do that.

What happens if I muscle through this period of time rather than surrendering to it? I overload my psyche with thought, worry, and even genuine insight, when what I really needed was to find a few pockets of peace.

21

THE VENUSIAN
PENTANGLE

Back in chapter sixteen, we described how Venus "lives downtown," which is a way of saying that its orbital path lies inside of our own. (The same is true of Mercury as well, but that is not the focus of this chapter.) That means that when we look for Venus in the sky, it can never be very far away from the Sun. That is why, if you want to see it, you always have to look for it near sunset or sunrise.

That leads to a second insight: that Venus, unlike the rest of the planets except for Mercury, can form two different kinds of conjunctions with the Sun – one where they are lined up with the Sun because Venus lies *between* us and the Sun, and the other because the planet is on the *other side* of the Sun, as far away from Earth as it can possibly get. As we learned earlier, the close one is called an *inferior conjunction*, while the far one is called a *superior conjunction*.

Either way, most astrologers just call it a conjunction. Both kinds look the same on your computer screen or your ephemeris – with one critical distinction. In inferior conjunction, Venus is always retrograde. In superior conjunction, it is always direct.

Inferior Sun-Venus conjunctions occur like clockwork every 584 days, which is just a little over nineteen months.

As I write these words in summer 2019, here is a list of upcoming inferior conjunctions of Venus and the Sun:

- June 3, 2020 in 13°36' of Gemini
- January 8, 2022 in 18°43' of Capricorn . . . *which is an advance of about 215°*
- August 13, 2023 in 20°28' of Leo . . . *which is an advance of about 212°*
- March 22, 2025 in 2°39' of Aries. . . *which is an advance of about 222°*
- October 23, 2026 in 0°45' of Scorpio . . . *which is an advance of about 208°*
- June 1, 2028 in 11°26' of Gemini. . . *which is an advance of about 221°*
- January 6, 2030 in 16°16' of Capricorn. . . *which is an advance of about 215°*

Hidden inside these numbers, believe it or not, is one of the most elegant mysteries of our solar system.

First, note that the inferior conjunctions of 2022 and 2030 occur very close together in the zodiac. They both happen in the middle of Capricorn, their positions separated by only 2° 27'.

They also occur almost exactly eight years apart.

If you were to print out centuries of these inferior conjunctions, you would see that same pattern repeating reliably and consistently.

- Every eight years the Venus-Sun inferior conjunction returns to approximately the same point in the zodiac and starts the cycle over again.

Stating it more precisely, every 7.997 years – eight years, minus about one day – the inferior conjunction returns to a point two or three degrees earlier in the zodiac. We see the pattern clearly in the list of dates above: January 8, 2022 to January 6, 2030 is a couple of days short of eight years and the conjunction-points are separated only by 2°27'.

We are talking about *transiting* Venus here, of course – the actual Venus in the sky. Earlier in this book, we underscored the point that Venus transits generally unfold too quickly to develop much psychic momentum. For our deeper purposes, we pay more attention to the progressions and solar arcs of the planet.

Here we have uncovered *an eight-year cycle of transiting Venus* – something slow enough to develop true depth and complexity of meaning.

This Venus cycle is one of the basic rhythms of the solar system. It seems as if it must be meaningful. But how can we use it in practical terms? It presents us with many technical problems. For one, the Venus cycle doesn't form aspects in the usual way. You can't say that "the eight-year Venusian cycle is conjuncting my Sun this April."

You can't even use it personally, like a Saturn return which happens for everyone on a unique date.

With this Venus cycle, for everyone on the planet, we are looking at exactly the same dates and degrees. The Venus cycle doesn't seem to relate to you *as an individual* . . .

More about that problem later . . . First, there is another mystery to discover.

THE PENTANGLE

Arbitrarily, let's call the inferior conjunction of January 2022 the starting point. (You could pick any one of these conjunctions, and see the same "return" eight years later.) Then the inferior conjunction of August 2023 would be *repetition number one. Number two* happens in March 2025, while *number three* happens in October 2026. We come to the *fourth one* in June 2028. And then the cycle completes itself with the *fifth repetition* on January 6, 2030, when the conjunction returns to the middle of Capricorn.

So our eight year cycle is composed of *five successive inferior conjunctions* of Venus.

The sixth conjunction starts the new cycle.

It is the same as the situation with the musical octave. We hear "oct" and we think of eight notes. But an octave is really just seven notes, with the eighth note starting the next octave. Similarly, our Venus "octave" is composed of five notes, with the sixth one starting the cycle over again.

These five inferior conjunctions are evenly spaced in time, happening like clockwork every 584 days. They are also evenly *spaced*, more or less, *geometrically*. Each one happens approximately 215° ahead of the previous one.

Even more amazingly, if you plot all five of these inferior conjunctions on a zodiac ring, you will see that they make a slightly sloppy, but unmissable, five-pointed star: the famous – or infamous – *pentagram* of magical and occult practice.

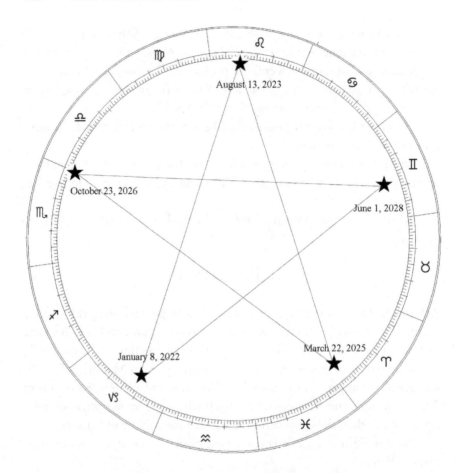

FIGURE ONE: THE VENUS PENTANGLE

Splitting hairs, as you can see in the listing of inferior conjunction dates above, that 215° is really just an average figure. Looking at the actual numbers, we see an advance of as little as 208° and as much as 222°.

Elliptical orbits – both our own and that of Venus – add these slight imperfections to the picture.

Our next step, while thinking of the number five, is to think of an astrological aspect which divides the zodiac into five equal pie-slices – the *quintile*, which is one-fifth of 360°, or 72°.

We looked at quintiles briefly in the two previous volumes of this series.

What does a quintile mean? In a nutshell, try dividing five into twelve in your head. You will notice that your head might blow up. Quintiles are like that – magical, mind-boggling, and miraculous.

In this eight-year Venusian cycle, we see the strong mark of the quintile aspect. Specifically, each successive inferior conjunction of the Sun and Venus occurs about one *tri-quintile* ahead of the previous one.

PENTANGLE – OR PENTAGRAM?

Enter "pentagram" in Wikipedia, and here are the first lines you will read:

> *Pentagrams were used symbolically in ancient Greece and Babylonia, and are used today as a symbol of faith by many Wiccans, akin to the use of the cross by Christians and the Star of David by the Jews. The pentagram has magical associations. Many people who practice Neopagan faiths wear jewelry incorporating the symbol. Christians once commonly used the pentagram to represent the five wounds of Jesus. The pentagram is also used as a symbol by other belief systems, and is associated with Freemasonry.*

Just mentioning that simple five-pointed star can drop us right into the eye of the culture-wars hurricane, in other words – witches versus born-again Christians, and so on.

As recently as the year 2000 in the state of Indiana, two practitioners of Wicca, Brandi Lehman and Shauntee Chaffin, were dismissed from a student-teacher program simply for displaying pentagram jewelry. They sued and they won. The headline of the Associated Press Wire Report dated Monday, May 1, 2000, reads, "Federal Judge Upholds Indiana Students' Right to Wear Wiccan Symbols.

Would they win the suit today? I don't know. That is not what this book is about, in any case. I just want to briefly point at a truly vast subject here, then quickly move on.

- Venus has traditionally been associated with the feminine, even though it is helpful to recall that men have Venus in their charts too. Let's not go too far with feminizing Venus, in other words.

- So-called "witchcraft" has often had a feminine association – although, once again, males have been involved too.
- Many people believe that "pagan" earth-and-sky religions survived despite persecution to the present day in the form of occultism, Wicca, and of course astrology. Women have played a disproportionate role in that survival, and have often paid a terrible price for it.

To me, it doesn't seem like much of a leap for us to connect the dots. The Venus pentangle in the sky is, I think, very likely the origin of the pentagram – and of many other things that still to this day frighten the pants off the patriarchy.

I also wonder why, despite the compelling beauty of this eight-year pentagonal Venus cycle, it is not more widely employed by astrologers.

Has this pan-cultural *Fear-of-Venus* affected even our own sacred craft?

SOLVING THE PRACTICAL PROBLEM WITH THE VENUS PENTANGLE

I find all of those historical ruminations plausible, but there may be a more down-to-earth explanation for why the Venus pentagram seems to be gathering dust among astrologers. As I mentioned a few lines ago, the problem is that this cycle simply cannot be made to work in the same ways that we are accustomed to seeing in conventional astrological practice. It doesn't form aspects in the usual ongoing way.

As we saw earlier, no one can say that "the Venus pentagram is making a trine to my Neptune in March." For everyone on the planet, we are looking at exactly the same dates and degrees. Furthermore, with five inferior conjunctions spread around the zodiac, while maybe one of them aligns with your Moon, at least two or three of the others are probably not making any important aspects to your natal chart.

The problem boils down to the fact that the Venus cycle doesn't seem to relate to your particular chart in a *personal* way. It just happens "up in the sky," more astronomical than astrological. Again, one of the five inferior conjunctions might happen to fall on a sensitive point for you. That is worth noting – but, really, it is just a fast-moving transiting conjunction of the Sun and Venus, hitting a natal planet, and quickly moving on.

There is no astrological reason to assume that the next conjunction nineteen months later, will also hit one of your buttons. And the odds are very long against all five of them falling on sensitive natal degrees.

So what is an astrologer to do?

In *The Book of Earth*, we delved into the Saturn cycle. Perhaps it provides an opening, or at least the beginning of one. We know that Saturn takes just under three decades to get around the Sun. So, for everyone universally, we have a Saturn Return as we approach the age of thirty and another one as we approach sixty. That is a powerful, impactful event. Critically, to know that it is happening, all we need to know is a person's age.

Could there be a similar eight-year rhythm hardwired into life and human consciousness?

Saturn is the Lord of Time, the planet of the Elder. It makes sense that Saturn returns mark turning points in the *maturational* process, specifically.

What kind of turning points would these every-eight-year "Venus returns" then mark? Presumably, they would bear strongly upon relationships and our capacity for intimacy. Ranging more widely, we know that Venus represents *taste* and *aesthetics, appearance, social skills, creativity, methods of re-establishing serenity* . . . might all of these areas of life hit evolutionary turning points on an eight-year rhythm?

We would be looking at reaching age eight, age sixteen, age twenty-four, and so on.

I want to be careful not to force the data here. Judge for yourself whether the simple *schema* which follows seems convincing and real. I am also aware as I write here that I am speaking in extremely broad generalizations. Please be aware of that too! With the Saturn cycle, we similarly generalized – helpfully, I believe – about the basic psychology of youth, mid-life, and the cycle of the elder. What follows here is painted in similarly broad terms too – and as with everything in astrology, there are ways to get these "Seasons of Venus" right and ways to get them wrong.

- Around age eight, we are generally expected to stop whining, learn to suck up our disappointments and frustrations, and to begin to exercise some sense of self-control and responsibility toward other people. Our social relationships – at school, for example – begin to

THE BOOK OF AIR

have "political" ramifications and complications, with much focus on hierarchy and status. We begin to compare ourselves to others outside the family.

- Around age sixteen, dating, courtship, and some degree of sexual expression are expected and generally culturally supported. All the mythology around turning "sweet sixteen" applies. Typically, around now we become obsessed with appearing to be *desirable* – and painfully afraid that we are not.

- Around age twenty-four, we have reached a plausible, socially-supported age for marriage and commitment, and perhaps for starting a family. We have now probably left home; our primary relationships have become voluntary rather than based on kinship ties. Life-long friendships are forming.

- Around age thirty-two, our sexual energies are probably peaking. Youthful liaisons end; dramatic sexual affairs are common. We retreat somewhat from "the crowd," and become more identified with our primary partnerships. The world begins truly to see us as adults, with all the attendant societal expectations. There is a good chance that we are parents.

- Around age forty, we are in the classic territory of the "mid-life crisis." We begin to realize the spiritual price we have paid for status – for getting other people to like us, to respect us, to fear us, whatever. Enormous psychic pressure arises either to surrender and accept our currently-established relationships, or to recoil in horror from them.

Up through this point (again, around age forty, which is the fifth return) I am feeling comfortable with everything that I have written. It all feels right to me; not forced, as if I were trying to twist reality into the shape of a theory.

As I began to think about turning forty-eight, fifty-six, and beyond, my words do begin to feel forced. I suspect the Venus cycle continues to have meaning, but individuation is so advanced by that point that it seems to eclipse the emergence, at least to my own mind, of any similarly simple statements.

Perhaps some of you readers can take it further. Perhaps many of you can add to the little bit that I have written here based on your own reflections about yourself and your friends.

I think that doing that would be good for astrology, and probably good for the world too.

Collectively, I think it is time that we got past our paranoia about pentagrams.

ANOTHER WAY OF LOOKING AT
THE VENUS PENTANGLE

Long ago in Egypt, a gentleman who went by the title of Thrice Majestic Hermes taught us the magical formula, "as above so below." In doing so, he laid the theoretical foundation for astrology. Sky and mind are like two mirrors facing each other.

That is why astrology works.

There is no reason that we cannot flip the equation, read it backwards, and have it be equally true. Why not say "as below, so above?" If two plus two equals four, then four must equal two plus two.

"Below" – meaning here in this world – everything gets confused and complicated. That is why we look to the simpler, more schematic structure of the heavens in order to try to figure out what is going on in our lives.

That's practical astrology.

But if we were having trouble understanding what is going on up in the sky, it makes sense that we might get some clues about it by considering what is happening right here at ground level. The way things are "here below" should logically cast some light on what is going on "above." Normally in astrological practice, the shoe is on the other foot, but here, with this cryptic Venusian cycle, might we learn something helpful by looking at the human world?

We just did that, in fact. As we try to crack the code of the Venus pentangle, we made some progress a few moments ago by setting birth as zero and then looking at ages eight, sixteen, and so forth.

But might this cycle operate in other ways as well? The question is a difficult one to ponder since we are not looking at the pentangle forming aspects or reaching turning points in any astrologically familiar way.

That does not mean that the Venus connection is not there; it only means that we cannot see it.

Let's try anyway.

Eight years is a simple number, easy to work with. My mind has often turned to a meditation upon the Venus cycle as I lie in my bed sleepless in the wee hours. I encourage you to try this little experiment too – if nothing else, it will help you sleep. And you might also make a helpful astrological discovery as well.

Here is how the experiment works.

Starting "below" – here on Earth – without any reference to astrology at all, I think of a specifically Venusian turning point in my own life: an actual event of an intimate nature. That could also be something artistic or something connected with returning to serenity, but the obvious choice would be a romantic milestone. Most of us have a few of those and they tend to loom large in our memories. We often remember dates too – our first meetings with significant people in our lives, marriages, divorces, and so on.

Such events are always heralded by more conventional astrological configurations, but I hypothesize that they might have some link to things I do not understand about the Venus pentangle – that *strings of such events might be linked in time* in a way that reflects the eight-year rhythm of the Venus cycle.

This is nothing but a plausible hypothesis – but like any honest hypothesis, there is a way to test it: just take a walk down Memory Lane. *I go back exactly eight years before one of those romantic events. I also go forward eight years into the future.* Then I ask the obvious question: *were those significant moments in my romantic life too?* Can I relate them to the Venus archetype as well?

Perhaps more importantly, *can I tie them all together in a developmental pattern, with significant, interconnected steps linked in meaning, but separated by multiples of eight years of time?*

If so, then I have found evidence for the eight-year rhythm of Venus having mysterious, thus far astrologically-inexplicable "zero points" – points of time that do not coincide with birth.

In other words, it is no longer about turning eight, sixteen, twenty-four, and so on. If this hypothesis works, it has become less generic, and a whole lot more personal.

More about that in a moment . . .

Looking at our own lives and comparing personal experience with our astrological charts is the eternal laboratory. There is nothing to be ashamed of in that; it is not egocentric; it is simply good astrological practice. We know ourselves; we can learn astrology from our own lives. There is no more honest mirror.

Also, because of the deeply personal nature of the planet Venus, much of people's actual experience in that category is not a matter of public record, making it more difficult to research these matters by using the life-stories of famous people. For one obvious example, the date of one's first experience of sexual intercourse could be a natural anchor-point in the Venus cycle, but Google as you will, you are still not likely to discover that information about anyone.

So that is why I am about to yack about myself again.

I can't think of anyone about whom I can yack as intimately – and given the nature of the subject matter, I would have no business talking about any of my clients either.

Before I launch into all of that, let me say a word or two about *orbs*. That is not exactly the correct word, but the question is, how "clockwork" do these events have to be? Perhaps we know the exact date on which we met someone who proved important to us. Astrologically, we know that exactly eight years later, minus a day or two, the hypothetical inner rhythm of the Venus cycle chimed again. *The odds are long against anything particularly significant happening on precisely that day.* But always in astrology, we allow orbs – tolerances – around those dates of exactitude. There is no reason to think that we would not do the same thing here.

With an eight year cycle, I find it plausible that we might allow an orb of a few months. That seems reasonable, and my experience suggests that it is also true.

THE OUIJA BOARD

In *The Book of Neptune,* I wrote a bit about my time working with the J.B. Rhine psychical research laboratories at Duke University. By day, these researchers were strictly scientists – but by night, things got a little weirder and a lot more open to possibilities.

One spring evening in 1968, when I was a college freshman, I was working a Ouija Board with a member of my cohort there at the Institute.

Walt and I had the experience of the planchette seemingly moving of its own accord, guided by some invisible entity. Being nineteen years old, I asked the spirit about my prospects for finding a girlfriend. The spirit, using the planchette, spelled out that I would meet her "very late in May."

At about 11:45 pm on Friday, May 31, 1968, I arrived home with a couple of pals. My sister Jan was down in the basement entertaining a few of her own friends. That's where I met Mary Jo – and I immediately fell in love – "very late in May."

At the time, I wasn't even thinking of the spirit's prophecy on the Ouija board. Those goosebumps only hit me much later.

Mary Jo and I were kids; our relationship did not last. But I still think of her fondly. We represented important developmental milestones for each other. I can honestly say that it was with her that I first felt anything like the deep *soul-seeing* kind of love that characterizes healthy adult intimacy.

We lost touch with each other long ago, but I think that she might say the same thing herself.

Now watch what happens:

I go back in time eight years from that date in "very late May" of 1968 I had just turned eleven years old – and the roaring 1960s had just begun. I have one of those "diamond" moments of lucid memory. I was at a New Years' Eve party with my church youth group. The Ball fell in Times Square – and I looked at my friend Janice. Our eyes met. I saw beyond myself into another soul, probably for the first time.

I remember that moment as if it were yesterday. The great goddess Venus awakened something in me.

I was only eleven. Janice and I never even kissed. But I think that, in that lucid Venusian moment, I began to learn *why* people kiss.

I would be the first to admit that all this is very subjective. I can only say that it is honest. Nothing about my saying any of this feels forced. Again, this New Years Eve memory of meeting Janice's eyes is one of those "diamond moments" in my memory of my own life. And it is utterly Venusian – and happened eight years, plus five months, before "very late May 1968."

A little earlier, I spoke of why using our own charts and lives as learning tools is not only legitimate, but also absolutely necessary. How could I possibly have access to "data" such as these two deeply personal stories by using the life of some movie star or political figure?

This kind of material is mostly too intimate ever to be part of anyone's public record.

Going eight years *forward* in time from that anchor-point with Mary Jo brings us to mid-1976. Shortly thereafter, my girlfriend, Michele, and I quit our jobs, bought a sailboat and went cruising down the east coast. Those months changed my life forever.

Before that sailing adventure, I "had jobs." Afterwards, I was a full-time astrological counsellor – and that is "Venus work" too.

And, Venus-fashion, Michele and I got married about five months after that peak. It didn't last long, but hey . . .we were young.

Eight more years forward, and it is 1984. In January of that year, I married Jodie Jensen, with whom I spent almost an entire Saturn cycle.

Eight more years brings us to 1992. The Uranus-Neptune conjunction landed smack on my natal Sun, so it was a colorful time for me in a lot of ways. Career-wise, it was a breakthrough period. The "performance" aspects of public speaking began to activate in me, and of course I was an astrologer – which is to say, a counsellor, and again that's Venus territory too.

My focus on the arts was another Venus-signature at that time. I wrote the first draft of my novel, *Stalking Anubis*. I composed my first rock opera, *The Rhymer and the Ravens*, based on Jodie's novel of the same name. My band Dragonship formed to perform it, along with a troop of dancers. We often had big audiences.

All of that bears the fingerprints of Venus; I was getting older, so my life was no longer quite so narrowly focussed on romantic intimacy, but rather on the arts and friendship.

Eight more years brings us to late May, 2000. In that year, astrologer Jeffrey Wolfe Green and I published the first of our two *Measuring The Night* volumes. The synergy between his audience and mine, along with his work and mine, triggered a critical-mass burst of interest in evolutionary astrology as a separate, new field within the larger framework of astrological practice. Back then, people often called me the "Pluto Brothers;" I am not sure it was always intended as flattery – but one can easily detect the unmistakable fingerprint of Venus: a significant partnership arose in my life.

At that time, I was also about one year away from seeing the Anza-Borrego desert for the first time, where I've lived for many years since. Jodie and I were feeling itchy in our North Carolina home, thinking of moving or buying a second home in the mountains – nothing much more to add to my narrative in that regard, except that . . .

Eight more years brings us to late May, 2008 – and just eight weeks later, we left North Carolina and moved into our new home here in Borrego Springs, where Jodie decided to leave our marriage. Venus has a fierce and painful face sometimes too.

And by the next return in 2016, I found myself in a new home and a new relationship.

All that I recount here "works for me" in convincing fashion, but I suppose it could all be dismissed as anecdotal and personal – and indeed, before anything deserves to be read into the record as an astrological gold standard, it must demonstrate that it is reliable and generalizable. I'm not making that big claim here.

"Works for me" is not enough to justify saying that it will work for everyone – but it is strong enough evidence that I am happy to put it out there and encourage you to see if it works for you too.

My guts tell me that this "floating" Venus pentangle – *anchored to turning-point biographical events rather than to technical aspects* – has a future in our craft.

Next time you have insomnia, give it a try. It's easy – all you have to do is to remember your own life, and be able to add and subtract the number eight.

FORTY YEARS IN THE WILDERNESS

Beyond the eight year Venus cycle we have been exploring, there is another, longer cycle – although to recognize it, we need to include Venus's downtown neighbor, Mercury. Again, as with the Venus pentagram, our journey starts out with dry numbers – then becomes eye-popping.

First, let me define the term *synodic*. As we have seen, Venus makes an inferior conjunction with the Sun, then 584 days later, it repeats that conjunction. That is Venus's *synodic period*.

- The average synodic period of Venus is 583.92 days
  ... times 25, that equals 14,598 days.
- The average synodic period of Mercury is 115.87754 days
  ... times 126, that equals 14,601 days.

Now, forgetting about synodic cycles, add the more familiar annual cycle we call the year. Commonly described as 365 days, it is actually 365.2423 days long.
  ... times 40, that equals 14,610 days.

Note that all of those final figures fall within less than two weeks of being the same length. So, to extremely close tolerances, forty years equals twenty-five Venus cycles and 126 Mercury cycles.

In practical terms, that means that, after forty years, all three will be back to their previous starting point.

This Sun-Venus-Mercury synchrony creates a repeating pattern in the sky. Here is how it works – and please bear with a little tedium.

There was, for example, an inferior conjunction of Venus and the Sun on September 8, 1935 at 14°46' of Virgo.

About ten days earlier, on August 28, 1935, Venus was conjunct Mercury at 20°39' of Virgo. On that day, the Sun was in about 4° of Virgo. Since the Sun was in an earlier degree, it went down first. As it set, Venus and Mercury were still low in the western sky.

Both were "evening stars," in other words

Almost exactly forty years later, on August 27, 1975, there was another inferior conjunction of Venus and the Sun, this time at 3°39' of Virgo.

Ten days earlier, on August 17, 1975, Venus was conjunct Mercury at 9°15' of Virgo. On that day, the Sun was in about 24° of Virgo – so once again the Venus-Mercury conjunction was an evening star in Virgo, visible in the west just after sunset.

Thus every forty years, nearly exactly, Venus, Mercury, and the Sun hit the reset button and start their endless cycle over again. This dance of Mercury, Venus, and the Sun is reliable and consistent.

- The Venus pentangle has five points. Repeat the pentangle another five times, and you get another cosmic "reset" in the sky.

There are forty *days*, more or less, of Venus retrograde – and forty *years* for this second, more subtle cycle.

Could this be why forty years and forty days comes up so often in Christian, Jewish, and Islamic spiritual literature? And, more pressingly, what could it mean for us personally? A forty-year cycle is a big chunk of life. Can I conjure up a connection between my meeting Mary Jo and moving to the desert almost exactly forty years later?

Actually, I can, in a way that is meaningful to me – but I am also wary of becoming too facile here. Astrology is powerful enough that we don't need to go scraping for subtle, shaky techniques.

Still, has anyone ever told you that "turning forty" passed right by them, unnoticed?

Or turning eighty?

VENUS HESPERUS, VENUS LUCIFER

Here's an observation to file under "duh"– *the first degree of Gemini rises before the last degree of Gemini.*

Any questions?

It follows that a *planet* in the first degree of Gemini rises earlier than a planet in the last degree of Gemini. And if the planet in the last degree of Gemini happens to be the Sun, then the planet at the beginning of Gemini *must rise just before dawn.*

- If your natal Venus is in an earlier zodiacal degree than your Sun, then at your birth, Venus rose before sunrise. It was "the morning star" – what the ancients called *Venus Lucifer* . . . not meaning Satan, but rather "Light-bringer."
- If your natal Venus is in a later zodiacal degree than your Sun, then at your birth, Venus was "the evening star" – what the ancients called *Venus Hesperus.*

The entire *Venus Lucifer cycle* lasts around nine and a half months – 292 days. That is the midpoint of the circuit. Around that time, Venus reaches *superior conjunction* – and it is again lost in the solar glare, but this time it is *behind the Sun*, on the other side of the solar system, as far from Earth as it can get.

When Venus emerges from the blinding sunlight, it is now the *evening star* – *Venus Hesperus*. About thirty-six days before the next inferior conjunction, it is at its brightest, casting shadows on the ground.

Three weeks or so before the end of the cycle, Venus stations and turns retrograde, and begins its descent into the Sun, only to start the whole dance over again.

It is the stuff of mythology. Ask a Babylonian, a Greek, or a Mayan.

But what does it mean in the context of modern astrological practice?

SHOULD YOU TRUST YOUR HEAD OR YOUR HEART?

In romantic affairs, that is an age-old question. People who answer it rigidly one way or the other tend to get into trouble. Some people say that we should trust neither one of them – those people stay safe, and lonely.

Smart people might say "trust both of them."

And the wisest ones probably say, "trust both – but make sure that neither one trusts the other."

A woman falls into passionate, romantic love – and gets her heart broken. She repents of passion, swearing that from now on she will only make logical choices in love. Perhaps she enlists a matchmaking service. "Bachelor #3" is a perfect match – logically.

But there is something about the twinkle in the eye of bachelor #4 . . .

Tempting – but no: she remembers what happened the last time she trusted her heart. This time she goes with her head, trusting logic and reason – bachelor #3 is her man. They vote the same, eat the same food, listen to the same music, love cats, hate dogs, want children someday. They even keep their homes at the same temperatures . . . perfect.

Three months later they break up – sadly but peacefully. They both agree that, as much as they *like* each other, there is just no magic, no chemistry. They could make good friends – or even siblings – but never partners.

The poor woman's heart is broken again. She feels defeated, tempted by bitterness. Her heart failed her. Her head failed her. Maybe she should trust neither of them ever again.

Or maybe, like our wisest ones, she should trust both of them – and make sure that each one keeps a suspicious eye on the other one.

As I suspect you have already figured out, in this little anecdote, Venus is the heart and the Sun is the head. When people stimulate our Venus, we feel instant fondness and affection toward them. We think they are "cute." Attraction often arises. If you are heterosexual, that ancient mammal in the base of your brain says, "let's make babies." And if you are gay, you don't have to worry about that – but you still have to worry about everything else.

When, on the other hand, our *Suns* are in harmony with other people, we tend to *get along well*. We share basic values. We respect each other. We can be friends. We simply like each other's company. We can talk. We can do projects together.

Venus and the Sun are not opposites, but they are birds of different feathers. Any long-term partnership that leaves you richer rather than poorer needs some of both of these energies.

We can achieve such balance, but it often requires some work – and maybe some heartbreak – to get us there. Many of us find ourselves, especially early in life, with a dangerous tendency to leap into love, blindly trusting the heart.

Others find themselves in the opposite dilemma: cautious, suspicious, and guarded to the point of starving the heart. Love is indeed risky. Ask your head about it, and it shows you a yellow caution light, if not a red stoplight.

Determining a person's tendencies in these intimate areas requires multi-dimensional astrological analysis. Issues around love, trust, and sexuality press all of our psychological, physical, and spiritual buttons. But Venus Hesperus and Venus Lucifer play a decisive role here – one that astrologers often underutilize.

At the Ascendant, we "dawn on life." It is a point of action, impulse, and automatic reflex. That simple point is the fulcrum of our thinking. In your chart, which planet rises first, Venus or the Sun? On the day you were born, which one hit the Ascendant first?

Do you lead with your head or your heart, in other words?

Remember: no matter where Venus falls in your chart, if it is in an earlier zodiacal degree than the Sun, it rises first. In that case, you have Venus Lucifer – *even if Venus was setting in the west at the moment of your birth.* Keep it simple: which planet was in an earlier degree, Venus or the Sun? Nothing else matters.

- Everything else in the chart being equal, a person born with Venus Hesperus tends toward caution and reason in matters of the heart – and must guard against living behind mental walls and only experiencing intimacy as an abstraction.

- Everything else in the chart being equal, a person born with Venus Lucifer tends toward impulsiveness, along with a reflex of quick trust in matters of the heart – and must guard against romantic folly, both in terms of personal heartbreak and in terms of breaking the hearts of others by committing prematurely to impossible, flawed, or tragic relationships.

CATS AND DOGS

Some years ago, I counseled a couple who were struggling with their relationship. A helpful metaphor arose in our dialogue – that, in matters of the heart, he was like a dog and she was more like a cat. Energetically, he would jump in her lap and lick her face – and if you have a cat, you know how cats react to that kind of sudden intrusion. She needed to be approached with more subtlety. Her affections needed to be won on a day-to-day basis. Unlike a dog, you "couldn't buy her affections with a steak."

Lest I sound overly partisan to cats, when he said "I love you," he meant it. He was not going to make her earn his love anew each day. Like the family dog, he was devoted, committed and enthusiastically unambivalent about loving her.

Their marriage didn't make it.

And you probably already know where this is going.

This couple taught me what I've written here about Venus as the morning star versus Venus as the evening star.

Mr. Dog had Venus Lucifer, while Madame Cat had Venus Hesperus.

22

CELESTIAL NAVIGATION III: URANUS TIMES, AQUARIUS TIMES

Planets enter Aquarius, and when they do, they take on the innovative, questioning, independent qualities of that sign. They are tired of Capricorn's rules and structures. Suddenly they are filled with a compulsion to enter public buildings through the exit doors and, out of sheer rebel pluck, to remove those "Do Not Remove" tags from their furniture.

They are, in other words, sick and tired of being told what to do. They light up with a desire to act purely for themselves for a change – and, meanwhile, your opinion of their behavior is none of their business.

Uranus, the modern ruler of Aquarius, steps into the spotlight by entering a new house of your chart or by forming an aspect to a natal planet. When that happens, a bit of standard astrological advice is that you should immediately begin to "expect the unexpected." And that is actually true – although if you stop and think about it for two seconds, the advice is quite impossible to follow. Often the best we can do with that line is to think – in retrospect – that I never would have expected *that*. I guess I should have expected it.

Still, it is true that strange and unpredictable events do tend to occur in Uranian times. Life's wild cards are turned over. For people who believe in randomness and chance, these are the times that fuel their beliefs – but, wait a minute, what if so-called "randomness" turns out to be predictable via Uranus transits . . .?

You begin to see where this goes.

Saturn, of course, co-rules Aquarius, and we take that connection seriously. We covered its transits and solar arcs in chapter twenty-two of *The Book of Earth,* along with the all-important cycle of Saturn Returns in chapter twenty-three of that same volume. Here, for the sake of completeness, we will only review some of the Saturn basics. For space reasons, we will not repeat that material in detail. It is important, though, and very much a part of our Aquarian picture. Please do review those chapters in *The Book of Earth* if you are fuzzy about Saturn.

TRANSITS AND SOLAR ARCS OF URANUS

Uranus is a slowboat, taking about eighty-four years to circle the Sun – 84.0205 years, if you want to split hairs. That works out to exactly 30,688.5 days – which explains why we need not concern ourselves with Uranian progressions. They unfold at the stately pace of about two and a half millennia per sign.

Another way to say all of this is that *for every full Uranian orbit around the Sun, it progresses only about one degree in your chart.* So we forget about it. Uranian progressions are something that only glaciers, tectonic plates, and God can understand.

No worry, that still leaves us with two powerhouses of astrological symbolism in the form of Uranian transits and solar arcs.

With an eighty-four year orbit, *Uranus takes about seven years to transit through a sign.* Its orbit is eccentric, so that figure varies, but only slightly. That pace works out to an advance of about *four degrees per year.* That figure is of course complicated by retrogradation. In practice, Uranus is direct for about seven months, then retrograde for about five.

At the end of a year, it is about four degrees further ahead in the zodiac.

As with all the planets, *watch out for those Uranian stations:* they are times of radically intensified impact – and great times to "expect the unexpected."

By *solar arc*, Uranus – in a way that is distinctly *uncharacteristic* of its rebellious nature – moves peacefully along with the herd at about one degree per year, never questioning the solar authorities.

Saturn is the next planet inward toward the Sun from Uranus. Its orbit takes just under thirty years to complete. Neptune is the next one out; it needs 165 years to make the circuit. As we have seen, Uranus falls right in the middle, requiring eighty-four years – a figure strikingly close to the average human lifespan.

That equivalency between a Uranian cycle and a human life-cycle is such a pivotal piece of our understanding of Uranian motion that it merits its own complete chapter, just a few pages ahead of where we are now.

I WOKE UP THIS MORNING AND . . .

. . . I realized that I couldn't stand being a dentist anymore.
. . . I realized that I didn't love my partner anymore.
. . . I realized that I just wasn't a Republican anymore.
. . . I realized that I couldn't live in the city anymore.

Every one of those statements is a vignette taken out of a true story about a client experiencing some kind of Uranian stimulation.

Here is a statement that is not:

. . . I woke up this morning and I decided to have scrambled eggs.

Eggs for breakfast is no shock. Eggs yesterday and more eggs tomorrow is a stable lifestyle choice. Depending on who you believe, maybe eggs will shorten your life by a year or lengthen it by a year, but figuring that out is your own business.

Try this one: I woke up this morning and realized that I would never eat another egg in my life – there's the Uranian signature again: *sudden, surprising change.*

Let's take one of these vignettes at random – "I realized that I couldn't stand being a dentist anymore" – and use it as a template for grasping the evolutionary impact of Uranian episodes on the human psyche.

So someone decides to become a dentist. Thank you, we need dentists in this world. She is in graduate school, studying dentistry. Her friends invite her to a wild, fun-filled beach weekend, redolent with prospects for college-style romance and debauchery . . . but no: our poor thing needs to stay home and read a book about molars.

But it's worth the sacrifice. She loves dentistry . . .

Down the road a few years, she is already in debt from dental school, and now she has to go even deeper in debt in order to afford all the equipment she needs for her new office.

Meanwhile, her friends think she is getting rich . . .

But it's worth the sacrifice and the projections and the misunderstandings. She loves dentistry . . .

Another patient with toxic bad breath . . .

But it's worth it. She loves dentistry . . .

Another person looks at her in terror and loathing, as if she were a torturer for the Spanish Inquisition.

Another spoiled child bites her finger.

Another patient comes back a year later, having spoiled her dental work by not brushing or flossing properly.

But it's worth the sacrifice. Our hero still loves dentistry . . .

Then, one rainy Thursday afternoon, one more patient arrives with bad breath, bad dental hygiene, and a bad attitude. At 6:30 on that following Friday morning, right after her alarm clock rings, she hears herself saying, *"I woke up this morning and I realized that I couldn't stand being a dentist anymore."*

She has reached a Uranian . . .

TIPPING POINT

Call me a Capricorn, but here in my opinion is the key to sanity, not to mention how to live a meaningful life: *make your stand in this world.* Commit to something or someone. At some point, hopefully fairly early in your life, you realize you have to stop trying to keep all your options open. You realize that life is short and finite, and that you are either going to "do it" or you are going to fail to do it. Otherwise you just drift. Otherwise you are like a flower that never opened.

As the song says, "freedom's just another word for nothing left to lose."

Making a stand anywhere – a spiritual path, a career, a relationship, a community, a moral crusade, an art form – requires a *decision*. And it also requires *ego-strength* in order to sustain the commitment. The human ego – which in this case is our spiritual friend, not our spiritual enemy – says, "this, but not that, that, or that." We make our choices and, hopefully, we stick to them and follow through on them.

Our aspiring dentist chose to read about molars instead of enjoying a weekend at the beach. That took focus and determination. That took *ego* – and here we are again using that slippery word honorably and precisely. Ego is actually what allows us to say "this, but not that." Ego is what *lets* us make a stand in this world. A healthy ego is what fights off other desires, fears, and impulses as they try to grab the steering wheel of our life.

Here is another way to express exactly the same idea: *ego suppresses the unconscious mind*, keeping it in its place.

The line between "the unconscious mind" and the soul is a fine one. Sometimes those rebel desires, fears, and impulses are truly the voice of the soul. *And sometimes they accumulate, rejected by the ego, in the unconscious dungeons of the psyche – until they reach a tipping point.*

Once again, on one rainy Thursday, one more patient has bad breath, bad dental hygiene, and a bad attitude. And the next morning, our dentist frightens herself by hearing herself say, "I woke up this morning and I realized that I couldn't stand being a dentist anymore."

None of this is just about dentistry, of course. That tale just provides us with a concrete illustration of a far bigger – and very Uranian – territory. Anyone, for example, who has stayed in a relationship for more than a year knows that sometimes remaining there is more about faith and commitment than it is about romantic feelings and sexual excitement.

To me, that sentence is almost the definition of the word "maturity."

Still, even in a relationship, here is a Uranian "earthquake" perspective: one more moment of emotional disconnection or misunderstanding, one more dismissive eye-rolling glance, one more broken promise . . . one more straw on the camel's back, one more drop of water behind the dam . . .

Tipping points abound in relationships, not to mention on camels' backs and in weakening infrastructures.

- During Uranian times, *the actual reality of the Self asserts itself,* breaking through the ego's prior commitments and previous self-image, creating the possibility of an existential tipping point.

I say "possibility" because frighteningly powerful forces are arrayed, psychologically, morally, socially and practically, against this breakthrough ever happening, even when it is absolutely necessary.

Think of our poor dentist again. Her situation is genuinely complicated. Maybe she is forty-five years old. Maybe she is two decades into her career. Maybe she has family and responsibilities.

"I know that I can't stand being a dentist anymore, *but . . .*

. . . if I am no longer a dentist, what will I do?

. . . if I am no longer a dentist, my debts do not automatically disappear.

. . . if I am no longer a dentist, how can I care for my children?

. . . if I am no longer a dentist, everyone will think I went crazy or that I failed.

. . . if I am no longer a dentist, what happens to my patients?

BREAKTHROUGH OR BREAKDOWN

When I was ten years old, if you had asked me what I wanted to be when I grew up, here is an answer I might actually have given you: *I want to go to South America and work for a big corporation.* OK, I am a Capricorn. But as you might imagine, there was an "influence" in operation. The handsome, commanding grown son of a sweet older woman who lived across the hall – a woman whom I called grandma – had done exactly that. He lived in Brazil and was a big success there. Everyone seemed quite impressed with him for it.

Since I was only ten years old, clueless about myself, and eager for other people to be impressed with me as well, I figured that I would simply play copycat. I would do what he had done.

There is no inherent moral culpability in working for a company with offices in a different country. Many good people find themselves in such a position. But if today I woke up in some nightmarish parallel universe in which that childhood dream of mine had come true, what would I feel like? In a word, *alienated.* I would feel as if I were living a life that had no roots in the actual nature of my soul.

That is the emotional condition that arises in the wake of a failed response to Uranian times: we become dissociated, detached from our own lives.

My childhood fantasy of working in South America ultimately proved groundless, but it is helpful to realize that it served a positive purpose for me at the tender, unformed age of ten. As *career* advice, it had no value whatsoever. But as *psychological* advice, it was sound: it provided me with a basis, at least in my fantasies, for the notion that I was perhaps capable of actually making a stand in this world. I might "be somebody" someday.

At age ten, that was helpful.

Subsequent Uranian passages helped me to let go of that childhood fantasy and come closer to understanding who I actually was meant to be. With transiting Uranus, for example, opposing my Moon from my tenth house, I changed my college major from Economics to Religion. For me, that was a major step on the road to becoming an astrologer – and of course, it also bore the classic Uranian signature of being an unexpected move.

Since I had no intention of becoming a minister, everyone – myself included – thought I was doing something very impractical. What could I possibly do with a degree in Religion except maybe wait on tables?

Now, in my seventies, I feel good about having devoted myself to astrological work. But I keep coming back to my nightmarish fantasy – what if I had woken up in a parallel universe and I was actually a corporate executive attempting to exploit a South American country? What would I do? *What would have happened to me, in other words, had I failed every Uranian passage of individuation in my life?*

Two possibilities enter my mind. The first is that I would blow my brains out, or at least some variation on that theme – drink myself to death, chase women who could be my daughters.

The second possibility is that I would simply turn off my own heart and go about living life as if I were as cold as a ghost.

In Uranian times, we all face that same choice: it boils down to *breakthrough* or *breakdown*.

There is no culpability in failing to be true to yourself *until you actually know yourself*. The arrival of that self-knowledge changes all of the moral and spiritual parameters. You then have "tasted of the fruit of the tree of the knowledge of good and evil." You cannot go back to the garden of innocence – or to thinking that you might be happy as an corporate executive in South America.

In Uranian times, you reach that tipping point: *the reality of who you are, what you feel, and what your path needs to be looms up out of your deep psyche.* You "realize that you can't stand being a dentist any longer." That pressing Uranian *pulse of individuation* erodes any defenses against the truth which your ego, however innocently, has erected.

Once you have tasted the fruit of the tree of the knowledge of who you truly are, you cannot un-taste it. From then on, you either follow the path that has been revealed to you – or something inside of you becomes resigned to the fact that for the rest of your days, your life will be a work of fiction, and rather pedestrian fiction at that.

EXPECT THE UNEXPECTED

Earlier we mentioned that one feature of Uranian times is that unusual or unpredictable events tend to occur. Telling a client to "expect the unexpected" is a catchy line – you can almost visualize it on a coffee mug or a bumper sticker. But of course it is impossible to expect something that we do not expect. The words ring the right emotional bells, but that is really the full extent of their value.

To understand this "wild card" dimension of the Uranian archetypal field, we need every piece of the deeper theoretical foundation we have been laying for the last few pages.

Here is the whole thing in a nutshell:

- If you are brave enough to be true to yourself during a Uranian time, the universe works at the outer edges of the laws of probability in order to open pathways forward for you – pathways that no reasonable person would ever predict.

"That will never happen – the odds against it are a million to one." Anyone who makes that statement needs a quick lesson in statistics and probability. Saying that the odds against something are a million to one actually means that it will *definitely* happen – just don't hold your breath waiting for it.

Weird things happen all the time. Plot twists that would have us rolling our eyes in a movie actually occur regularly in real life. An old college friend of mine, for example, at the tender age of twenty-two, applied for a prestigious editorial position. She quickly got one of those "thank you for your interest in publishing" letters, rejecting her. Three years later, that same publishing house called her in for an interview. An editor had abandoned ship in an angry huff in the middle of a big project with a looming deadline. They were desperate to hire someone. They looked at their stack of old applications, saw the one from my friend, realized that she was at least witty, and they decided to take a second look at her.

She and I lost touch long ago, but the last I heard she was still employed by that same publisher.

The point of this story is that it is "not realistic" to think that a young, inexperienced person without connections would ever be offered such a prestigious editorial position.

But it happened – at the same time that Uranus was transiting across her Ascendant.

In my early thirties, I briefly considered going to graduate school and getting my doctorate in psychology. Back then, I had begun bedeviling myself, worrying that I might become "really old, like forty, and still be the hippie astrologer in the town where I went to college."

I laugh now, but I was not laughing then.

Then my true self broke through the lather of my social conditioning. I realized that I actually loved being an astrologer. I decided that if astrology was my path in life, so be it.

Roll the dice, in other words.

That inner argument happened with Uranus transiting over my own Ascendant. A year or so later, the planet retrograded back and made a station just 3° beyond my Ascendant – well within the orbs of a conjunction. Again, always watch out for those stations! Two weeks earlier, my telephone rang. It was a literary agent in New York – one who had recently experienced enormous success representing Mario Puzo's blockbuster, *The Godfather*. She had heard about my work through a mutual client. She wondered if I might ever be interested in writing an astrology book that she would represent on spec. Six weeks later, I signed the contract for what would become *The Inner Sky*.

Whoever first said "you cannot make this stuff up" was surely in the midst of a Uranian transit.

MAGIC

The correct term, by the way, for the high Uranian processes we are talking about here is *magic*. What can that word mean except the idea that through inner work on consciousness, we might change the conditions we encounter in the world?

And that is exactly what we are talking about. Have faith, be true to your heart, and doors will open – at least in Uranian times.

Being true to oneself can be frightening. We need a little of that Uranian magic on our side. Remember the long list of fears and worries that our dentist had – all the reasons, practical and psychological, why she *had* to remain in that profession, even though it was leaching the life out of her soul.

In Uranian times, such is the face that reality presents to us. It is as if we are being asked how *badly* we want to be true to ourselves and what we are *willing to pay* for the privilege. If we make our stand, if we *commit to authenticity* no matter what price it might exact from us . . . well, then the universe sits back for a while, testing our resolve, making sure that we are sincere.

And if we pass the test, if we make our stand and *stick to it*, doorways open which no sane person would ever predict or expect.

Work on consciousness that alters the nature of reality: if that is not magic, I do not know the meaning of the word.

Uranus is the Magician.

Make an ally out of it, and you can be a magician too.

WHAT ABOUT SATURN?

Saturn rules Aquarius just as surely as does Uranus. Chapter twenty-two of *The Book of Earth* is a full exploration of its symbolism. Here, in these pages, I only want to reiterate the main points. Saturn's transits and solar arcs boil down to these seven areas of focus.

- *Maturation* – you are invited to move forward to the next developmental chapter in your life. This is another step in the endless process of growing up. Get it wrong, and you will soon be bored with yourself.

- *Great Works* – you have come to a point in your life where you need to commit to some massive effort that expresses the best in you. If you are unwilling to get exhausted, you will surely get depressed. The "great work" and the maturational process are inseparable – in accomplishing the great work, you transform your own nature. You grow up.
- *Solitude* – time spent alone is fertile ground now. Circumstances arise that thrust solitude upon you. Help may be available and necessary, but in the final analysis, successful navigation of this period is up to you alone.
- *Sacrifice* – you will be asked to make some sacrifice. You are likely to find yourself in a position in which you must request sacrifices from other people as well.
- *Duties and Responsibilities* – extra weight is on your shoulders now for the duration of this transit or solar arc. Make sure that you have actually *chosen freely* to take it on, as opposed to having internalized someone else's expectations of you.
- *Moral tests* – your integrity is likely to be tested. Be true to your own principles and values – but simultaneously be wary of other people attempting to define what is right and what is wrong for you.
- *Ageing* – the physical processes connected with ageing tend to be accelerated in Saturn times. Attend to your body. Stretch and try to maintain flexibility. Stay hydrated. Be mindful of the heightened possibility of muscular or skeletal damage. Caution helps.

ENTERING AQUARIUS

Sooner or later, all the planets pass through Aquarius, one way or another. As they do, they take on the values and psychological orientation of that sign. They become very different than they were while they were animated by Capricorn – or by Pisces, if they happen to have entered Aquarius via the back door.

Each sign is a reaction against the excesses of the previous one. Capricorn tends to follow the rules. Nothing pleases Aquarius more than the sound of rules breaking. Capricorn appreciates propriety and tradition. Aquarius is irreverent and inclined toward revolution. Capricorn works hard. It would not be fair to say Aquarius is inherently lazy – but if you tell it to go to school, you guarantee that it will play hooky. If you hand it a "honey-do" list, none of it will ever get done.

Laziness is not the issue; being "told what to do" is the issue.

Aquarius is, above all, the astrological correlate of the *process of individuation* – the process whereby we sort out our own natural path forward through life from all the background noise of unsolicited advice, guilt-trips, clueless parenting, conventionality, social judgement, and cultural training, as well as all of the lies-agreed-upon that constitute "common sense."

When a planet enters Aquarius, it feels a powerful impulse to *start thinking for itself.*

A child's Moon progresses into Aquarius. His *attitude* – that is always an evocative word for the Moon – becomes *rebellious.* Suddenly the boy's favorite word is *no.* Previously, with his Moon progressing through Capricorn, he had probably been better at maintaining his status as "a good boy." His attitude was more obedient then.

Understandably mom and dad are feeling some frustration.

Kids need discipline and there's no magic bullet here – but some clear understanding of what is going on developmentally for the child can be a big help. With that Aquarian progressed Moon, he is learning about independence and how to think for himself. *In reality, he is not very skillful at either of those things yet* – that's *why* he needs to learn them.

"No" is a valuable word in life and it is time for him to add it to his vocabulary.

From an evolutionary perspective, the scariest possibility here is that this child passes through this period *obediently.* That would suggest that he is learning nothing about Aquarius at all, except possibly its shadow-side: *dissociation.*

For obvious reasons, parents prefer obedience. What they might miss is the fact that in the "obedient" scenario their kid is on the road to becoming a sheep – a man who never found his own path in life, simply doing what others told him to do. Nascent individuality is a delicate, tentative thing, easily rebuffed. And as it begins to spread its wings inside the child, he is likely to overreach and behave clumsily out of sheer inexperience – and thus elicit a rebuff.

From the kid's point of view, an order might come from above, such as "clean your room." And he says No. Battle lines are drawn. The parents are holding most of the high cards. In the end, they probably win. Clean your room – or else: no TV, no dessert, no trip to Disneyland.

The room gets picked up. *But at what cost?*

It might be tempting to read what I have written so far as a suggestion that we should take a totally *laissez faire* attitude toward the child's misconduct. And it is true that a conscious parent faced with a kid's Aquarian passages benefits everyone by being mindful and not issuing too many arbitrary, unimportant, unnecessary rules and restrictions.

Still, children do need discipline and firm guidance. It is better that they learn discipline early from loving parents rather than having the world teach them these same lessons the hard way later on.

Here's the key: *the issue for that little boy is not really about whether he picks up the junk in his room. The issue is pure Aquarius: he is learning to defend his right to autonomy.*

And that is precious, and worth defending.

How can parents support their child spiritually and at the same time maintain a certain standard of hygiene and order in the home? Again, there is no magic bullet – but here is a little trick that just might work. *"Jason, you can clean up your room any time that's convenient for you – right now, tomorrow, even this weekend would be OK. It's up to you."*

Will that little manipulation actually get him to obey the house rules? Obviously, it would be disingenuous of me to guarantee anything, but there is a certain elegance in the gambit. We still want his room straightened up, but we have been wise enough to express it in a way that is not a direct abrogation of the child's right to make his own choices.

We have left some breathing room for his autonomy.

Implicit in these words is the critical insight that Jason is not really "defending his right to live in a pig-sty," even though that may be exactly what he appears to be doing. What feels threatened in him is not his right to live in squalor, but rather his right to Aquarian freedom – a drive that might be mollified by emphasizing that he can "clean up his room *whenever he wants.*"

Let's take young Jason's story a couple of steps further.

Let's say that his Saturn lies in Aquarius right on his astrological Descendant – smack on the cusp of his seventh house, in other words. With any planet in his seventh house, we know that Jason cannot do what he has come into this Earth to do without some very specific help. He is dependent upon the triggering effect of encountering – and recognizing – the right human partnerships.

With Aquarius in the picture, for him even to *recognize* such partners, he must first *individuate*. His natural soulmates, soul-friends, and partners in life tend to lie on the other side of various kinds of consensual-reality dividing lines. These people probably "look wrong for him" ethnically, economically, even perhaps in terms of their physical appearance. They just don't *appear* to be good fits.

- With enough Aquarian individuation, Jason will see through that socially-engendered delusion and actually recognize his true partners.

- Without the support of true Aquarian freedom, he is likely to fall into intimacy with people who cannot supply him with the proper evolutionary catalysts.

Of course, a conventional astrologer, seeing that "malefic" Saturn in the "house of marriage" would offer a fountain of discouraging predictions – predictions that would very probably come true, were Jason to fail the Aquarian test of true individuation.

That particular Aquarian Saturn can play out in a lot of different ways. Here is one of them: *Jason's natural partner is ten years older than he is. They meet when he is twenty-two.*

Immediately we see the fingerprints of Aquarius:

Everybody knows that she is "too old for him."

Everybody knows that she is "robbing the cradle" and that *he must have mother issues.*

Everybody knows that he will leave her as soon as he truly becomes a man.

Even more insidiously, Jason himself might have internalized all those toxic ideas. In that case, it is possible that when he met his soulmate, *he would not even recognize her.* To make that life-critical connection, Jason must first individuate.

Meanwhile, fifteen years earlier, his Moon progressed into Aquarius and there was a bit of a tussle with his parents over picking up his room . . .

You see where this goes.

It would be simplistic to imagine that if Jason's mom and dad "made him clean his room," that they also destroyed his prospects for a happy marriage later in life. The multidimensional complexity of our evolutionary journeys goes far beyond that kind of "single-issue" thinking. Hundreds of other transits, progressions, and solar arcs involving Aquarius or Uranus would be relevant, all of them potentially helping to lead Jason to the critical moment of that meeting.

Still, as the great psychic Edgar Cayce said repeatedly, "mind is the builder." We are nothing but the accumulation of our thoughts. As astrologers, we might translate that idea into the notion that we are nothing but the accumulation of our responses to all of our transits, progressions, and solar arcs. That is just another way of saying exactly the same thing.

It is true for Jason, and it is true for you and me.

Being a conscious parent often seems like an impossible task. Astrology can certainly help. But that could be another book.

THE ELEVENTH HOUSE

When a significant planet enters the eleventh house, we can expect two kinds of developments.

- First, that there will be some kind of underlying *reorientation of our relationship to the future.* In other words, plans and intentions are likely to change – although typically circumstances arise which restrain their immediate implementation.
- Second, that new alliances are likely to present themselves – alliances which can support the realization of those changed plans and intentions.

Our job, from an evolutionary perspective, is first simply to recognize all of that. A planet entering the eleventh house invites us to be mindful of our own changes. We are not who we once were; our needs and desires are becoming different.

Meanwhile, because of those personal changes, our "old crowd" might begin to feel stale and predictable.

All of this might suggest that we are ready to move onward into a new chapter of our lives. That, indeed, is often exactly how we feel. But, as we will soon see, the situation is usually more complicated than that. In reflecting on those complications, we come to the paradoxical heart of the eleventh house: *while it is about creating the future, it also often keeps us imprisoned in the past for a little while longer.* You might recognize Saturn's hand in that last piece of the puzzle – and another reminder that we should never ignore Saturn's natural rulership of this house, alongside the very evident hand of Uranus.

Deeper understanding begins with a very simple observation: since there are only twelve houses, *the eleventh house represents a very advanced stage of any cycle.* We can learn a lot about it by reflecting on the late stages of another cycle – the eleventh month of the year: November.

In the northern hemisphere, that month is a time marked by *harvest festivals.* Here in the United States, Thanksgiving is the obvious example, but there are many others.

During any harvest, we famously reap what we have sown. If you planted squash seeds, you are not going to be eating tomatoes.

In the eleventh house, the past is similarly catching up with us. Good news or bad news? Much depends on what seeds you planted.

The cycle of the houses naturally begins at the Ascendant. That is when we plant the seeds. A planet entering the eleventh house suggests that we are *harvesting the results of those precise previous actions.*

This phenomenon is often transparently obvious biographically with the transits of Jupiter or Saturn, or even sometimes with Uranus. It also leaps out with the progressed Moon.

The reason I put those four bodies in the spotlight is that the lengths of their cycles range from twelve years to nearly thirty years. The result is that, unless we are young, we can readily trace the previous alignment of these bodies with the Ascendant. That way, we can get some insight into the nature of the seeds we planted. That practical principle is a reliable workhorse in the counselling room with Jupiter, Saturn, and the progressed Moon. Uranus, however, with its eighty-four year cycle takes an average of seventy years to make it from the Ascendant to the eleventh house cusp. Most of us will not live long enough to experience that particular seed-to-fruit cycle.

What about, for example, the Sun progressing into the eleventh house? To know when it hit your Ascendant, we would have to go back into history – back to a time before you even *had* that Ascendant. In average terms, that progression would have happened approximately three centuries ago.

What seeds were planted then? How can we know? Well, if you find yourself harvesting yellow squash, you know that you didn't plant petunias. It just gets a lot more metaphysical with the slower planets.

I suspect that with slower bodies hitting that eleventh house cusp, we are looking at the ripening of karma. As usual, in matters of reincarnation, facts are slippery and hard to ascertain. There is one indirect piece of evidence, however, and it leads us to understand another dimension of the eleventh house: the "hand of fate" often makes itself felt when this house is stimulated.

"Fate" is not my favorite word, but I do use it here, with some caution. Nothing in astrology is rigid or totally predetermined. Still, actions always have consequences, even if those consequences are delayed in appearing. What seeds did you plant centuries ago in a prior lifetime? Whatever they were, it is now time for the harvest festival. Instances of *luck* – in both its attractive and unfortunate faces – can make themselves felt during times of eleventh house stimulus.

Much of our karma is interpersonal; that is why "fated" meetings are common during any of these eleventh house episodes.

Before we can move forward in fresh directions, we must *finish what we have started.* That insight – and inescapable limitation – is central to grasping the "delays and side tracks" that are often characteristic of eleventh house periods. Metaphysical perspectives – karma again – can help us understand what is happening. They help to explain parts of the eleventh house experience that otherwise might seem inexplicable and random.

There is much about the eleventh house and "finishing what we have started" that makes sense in a straightforward, practical way. We do not always need to be thinking in terms of unresolved karma to understand what is happening. Fresh plans do form, *but their implementation is often delayed by the need to resolve existing entanglements.*

That is why I opened this section by saying that when a significant planet enters the eleventh house, there is a reorientation of our relationship to the future, but I added that typically circumstances arise which restrain their implementation.

- You can retire – but not for three more years.
- You are going to move to Arizona, but only after Jane graduates from high school.
- You are going to plant some yellow squash, but not until May.
- You will marry – but only after a complex divorce is finalized.

GOING TO SEED

We might describe a person as having let herself "go to seed." It is not a flattering statement, but the metaphor does have a solid basis in botany. When a plant goes to seed, it doesn't look very good. Typically, leaves are lost. Usually the plant becomes leggy.

The reason is simply that all of its life force is being concentrated in those seeds. As they ripen, the seed pods burst. Seeds are scattered in the wind.

And the mother plant dies back.

At the risk of sounding breathless, in a sense, the plant has given its life in order to assure the future of its species.

Similarly, when your eleventh house is stimulated, life might request that you too "go to seed." This does not mean that you suddenly forget to change your underwear or to brush your teeth. *What it means is that you are invited to offer gifts of wisdom and experience to your tribe* – and that you might very well do that without realizing that is what you are doing. You might, for example, get into a conversation with a stranger on a train. You make some throwaway comment which, unbeknownst to you, changes that person's life. You might say, for example, that "life is short."

You are only talking about a pricey vacation you are going to take; it is really not a big deal. Your words, as you say them, do not exactly feel like the wisdom of the ages.

That night, the stranger asks for a divorce. Or quits his awful, dead-end government job. Or she decides to go ahead and move to New Mexico and just "see what happens there."

That all happens because he or she really, really needed someone *in that very moment* to say, "Life is short."

Your seed was carried away in the wind – and landed on very fertile ground. And of course, you have no idea of the importance of your words – no more than a dandelion knows where the wind will carry its seeds.

Lately, people talk about Chaos Theory. The standard metaphor is that a butterfly flaps its wings in South America and a hurricane forms three weeks later. Effects and consequences ramify in fractal ways, rendering prediction futile.

Chaos Theory and the eleventh house have a lot in common. When a planet is stimulating your eleventh house, *you are that butterfly*.

You may detect the fingerprints of the planet Uranus in that observation.

In an eleventh house time, it is both true and a considerable comfort, to accept the fact that *you are being used by a higher intelligence*. Your seeds are being scattered. Even though you cannot understand it, *surrendering to this higher intelligence is one of the ways in which you are finishing your business*. This is one of the ways that unresolved karma finds balance and resolution.

Meanwhile, you are feeling that tug toward a different kind of future. When the planet triggering your eleventh house finally reaches the Ascendant, you can fully implement those changes. With Jupiter or the progressed Moon, that might only be two or three years in the future. With any of the other progressions or solar arcs, those changes will not happen in this lifetime.

But, either way, long ago you made some promises that you are bound to keep. Those bills are due – and paying them actually feels like a liberation.

23

URANUS TIMES, AQUARIUS TIMES: THE BUILDING BLOCKS

In the course of its eighty-four year passage around the birthchart, transiting Uranus will make every aspect it can possible make and pass through every house – *once*. Obviously, not everyone lives to be eighty-four, so this is only an impressionistic statement. Still, it sets the right tone. *These Uranus transits are once-in-a-lifetime opportunities.* Even if we live to be a hundred years old, only a few of them will ever come around again.

- If you get these Uranian transits right, you win the grand prize: *your real self becomes the navigator of your life.*
- If you fail, it is as if you were born to get to Paris, but somehow you wound up in Philadelphia. You may have lived a fine life by all outward standards. Trouble is, it was not your life.

As we saw in the previous chapter, we ignore the *progressions* of Uranus because they are so slow. Meanwhile, we do pay close attention to its solar arcs. And of course its transits are very much at the heart of the matter. By transit, Uranus is slow enough to sink deeply into you, while being fast enough to be a very active player on the stage of your life.

In the pages that follow, we will look at Uranus as it forms aspects to each one of the other planets. We will also consider its entrance into each house and into each sign.

All of that material will reflect both transits and solar arcs. The two techniques are not exactly interchangeable, but in the "cookbook" material that follows, they are close enough in meaning to be bunched together. As we've seen before, stock paragraphs such as these are only starting points. To see the integrated nuances, you either need to add them yourself as you develop astrological experience – or find an astrologer who can sit with you in a personal way.

URANUS CONTACTING THE SUN

Where I am all wrong about myself: Some of the basic values by which I have been navigating my life have their origin in my family or in my subsequent social training rather than in my true essence as a human soul. It is time for me to weed out those distorting influences, and make a major correction in my existential course. In other words, it is about time that I did something truly for myself for a change.

The Cure: Paying discriminating, precise, honest attention to any feelings of emptiness or boredom that arise in me as I face my daily existence, and noting what *specific parts of my life* trigger those kinds of emotions. Then I boldly resolve to figure out a way to withdraw from those contracts. Learning to be at peace with the idea that as I claim the right to live my own life, inevitably there are people who will judge me – or worry about me. I will not be manipulated by their judgments or their concerns. This is, after all, my life, not theirs.

How the universe helps: Strange, unexpected events happen, opening doorways to freedom – doors that may never open again.

The active face of failure: I become contrary, arguing over things that do not really matter. I get into fruitless, pointless trouble with figures of authority.

The passive, dissociated face of failure: I unconsciously resolve to go through the motions of a life that no longer has meaning for me. I look through my eyes at a life with which I am no longer identified.

URANUS CONTACTING THE MOON

Where I am all wrong about myself: We all think of our feelings, our emotional needs, and our attitudes as very personal, but the reality is that much of what I *believe that I am feeling or needing* has in fact been scripted into me by external forces: family training, television, the mythology of the world. What they have taught me to anticipate will make me happy often fails to work. If I am wise and pay attention, this is a game-changer.

The Cure: Paying close attention to the gap between my expectations that happiness will arise from a given event versus the emptiness I actually feel when it happens. Resolving to feel what I actually feel, even if people then indicate that they think that "my feelings aren't working right – that *anyone* would be sad, satisfied, angry, jealous . . . whatever." My feelings are my own, and no one else has a right to script them for me.

How the universe helps: I get what I think I want and it fails to satisfy me, thus offering me the opportunity to re-think my desires. Disruptions and changes occur, especially in relation to home and family life – disruptions and changes which open doors to greater freedom for me.

The active face of failure: I allow unprocessed feelings of rebellious frustration to steer my life. I make dumb, emotionally-driven miscalculations. I throw the baby out with the bathwater.

The passive, dissociated face of failure: I become numb. A mood of simply not caring about anything takes hold of my heart. I find myself saying, "whatever . . ."

URANUS CONTACTING MERCURY

Where I am all wrong about myself: My thinking is skewed. Somewhere my sense of what is going on and the actual nature of events unfolding before my eyes have come adrift from each other. Where? The sign and house of my natal Mercury offer important clues. Even my words are affected: out of rote habit, I am making speeches in which I do not believe – and, half the time, I am not even aware that I am doing it.

The Cure: Listening critically to my own lectures. Scrutinizing every strong or adamant opinion I hold, realizing that this very quality of exaggeration is a clue about where my errors lie and what folly I am defending. I resolve to speak up and state my views, even if they are unpopular. In doing that, I promise myself never to lose sight of the possibility that I might be wrong.

How the universe helps: Shocking or surprising new information comes to light. All the messages I need to hear are right there before me in the form of overheard conversations, misdirected texts or emails, statements blurted out by other people. Omens and synchronicities abound.

The active face of failure: I defend myself against learning anything, perhaps simply by talking all the time or by interrupting others before they can tell me anything important. I become obsessed with trivial interests, which I soon forget.

The passive, dissociated face of failure: I surrender to the idea that since no one will ever understand me anyway, why should I bother trying to express myself? I allow opportunities to learn what I actually need to learn to slip through my fingers, fearing that if I pursue those interests, everyone would think I was crazy.

URANUS CONTACTING VENUS

Where I am all wrong about myself: Half of who I believe myself to be derives from other people's projections and their habitual expectations of me, which I have unwittingly internalized. This error operates in an unholy alliance with my own need for their approval or with the sense of safety which they – equally unwittingly – offer me in return for falsifying myself.

The Cure: Realizing that while partnerships are sacred contracts, they are up for renewal from time to time. Are my relationships still serving the purposes of my soul? I have come to a time when it is as harmonious and dharmic *as it can ever possibly be* to reconsider certain details in my agreements with other souls – or possibly to realize the contract has been fulfilled or expired.

How the universe helps: Elements of change – wild cards, chaos, the unexpected – disrupt the flow of "business as usual" in my intimate life and my partnerships. Mindfulness and surprising realizations arise as the context of these relationships shifts.

The active face of failure: I "act out," behaving foolishly, childishly, or selfishly with someone about whom I care. I confuse impulse with insight.

The passive, dissociated face of failure: Without realizing that I am doing it, I allow friendships or partnerships to die without them actually falling over. We become automatic and predictable in our interactions, having failed to update each other about who we have actually become.

URANUS CONTACTING MARS

Where I am all wrong about myself: Without my having noticed it, some of my old angers and resentments have simply run out of fuel. They are only operating on past momentum and mental habits. New enthusiasms are knocking on my door, while old entanglements which no longer fill me with any true passion are blocking me from allowing them to dawn in my consciousness and my life.

The Cure: Letting myself walk on the wild side for a little while. Trusting my impulses – and trusting my ability to improvise survival in the face of change. I resolve simply to roll the dice, to take a chance, and thereby to make a brave bid for greater freedom and authenticity in my life. I will not let my sexuality grab the steering wheel, but I resolve to listen to it and to be true to what it is telling me.

How the universe helps: Sudden crisis – or at least unexpected developments – arises, briefly opening avenues of escape from the tyranny of routine and predictability. Occasions of passions – anger, the call of adventure, sexuality – present themselves. Disruption breeds opportunity.

The active face of failure: I act out in angry, hurtful ways, "kicking the dog" or "slamming the door" instead of harnessing this fiery energy in service of liberating my own existence.

The passive, dissociated face of failure: An essential spark flickers out in me. I slip in the general direction of depression. I lock the jail and throw away the key – with me inside it.

URANUS CONTACTING JUPITER

Where I am all wrong about myself: Not only have I underestimated myself, but I have also pursued dreams and ambitions foisted upon me by external forces. My very definition of the word "success" is flawed. Achieving such vacuous success leaves me feeling empty and cheated – that is how I recognize its falseness. I gain the applause of people about whom I do not particularly care. Their values feel trivial to me, if only I stop and truly think about them.

The Cure: I resolve to redefine the meaning of the word success for myself: it is that which allows me to feel at liberty to be myself and to feel that I am truly living my best life in a spirit of radical authenticity. I live for freedom and truth, not for applause.

How the universe helps: If I am brave and humble enough to recognize the delusions within myself that have led me to put enormous energy into meaningless accomplishments, then the universe offers me strokes of luck. I "win contests" – that is to say, doors open; resources become available; allies appear.

The active face of failure: Against the odds, I "get what I want" – and it turns to cotton candy in my mouth.

The passive, dissociated face of failure: I sleep through opportunity's knock. Resignation and dissociation blind me to genuine possibility. In the end, when I look back on this missed chance, I believe that "nothing happened."

URANUS CONTACTING SATURN

Where I am all wrong about myself: I am a responsible person; the problem is that I have allowed other people to define my responsibilities. Part of what I interpret as "my duty to do," I do not actually *need* to do. If I let go of these erroneous definitions of my responsibilities, others will either learn to take care of themselves or other people will rise up to a level where they can take over for me. That would benefit them – and also liberate me to pursue my own true and natural path through life – to climb mountains worthy of what I have now become.

The Cure: Having faith that if I put my burdens down, the world does not end. I must learn to say "enough." I have fulfilled many of my contractual obligations at the spiritual level. I resolve to recognize that natural "expiration date," and to trust Providence to take care of whatever comes next.

How the universe helps: Sudden changes in circumstance have the effect of putting my existing duties in a different light. Responsibilities may simply come unexpectedly to endings and resolutions. These events may hit me like a lightning bolt. They help me to realize that I have graduated to a new level of maturation – one that entails the need for parallel maturation in the nature of my responsibilities themselves. Old ones must be let go in order to make way for new ones of which I am now worthy.

The active face of failure: As a result of delay in recognizing the need for these changes in how I define my duties, I reach a kind of breaking point. I am "being good," I am "being good," I am "being good" – until one day, I explode.

The passive, dissociated face of failure: I volunteer for slavery. I define myself as a public utility. I survive by disciplining myself to not feel what I am actually feeling.

URANUS CONTACTING URANUS

Note: the next chapter is a detailed analysis of the all-important relationship of Uranus to its natal position, focusing especially on the squares, oppositions, and Uranian return.

URANUS CONTACTING NEPTUNE

Where I am all wrong about myself: Religion – which is to say my beliefs about the nature and purpose of my life – has gotten in the way of true spiritual progress. I am too much of "the expert philosopher" in such matters. I need a miracle to blow up in my face – and blow up my vaunted "wisdom," allowing it to break through to a new level. Similarly, my imagination has become constrained by habitual patterns. My creativity is in danger of becoming rote and predictable.

The Cure: I need to shock my soul. I need to subject it to some radically different context of experience: a new place, new teachings – anything that forces me to reinvent myself in the fierce reality of the present moment and in the face of radical and fresh soul-stimulus.

How the universe helps: Miracles happen. Visitations of energy arise. Questions enter my mind that shatter my pre-existing assumptions. Experiences arise that I cannot explain. My mind stops in its tracks, struck silent by sheer awe.

The active face of failure: Resistance to change and growth takes the form of "fundamentalist" defense mechanisms related to old beliefs. Other people's questions bring angry responses from me rather than thought. Mental breakdowns can occur.

The passive, dissociated face of failure: "Agnosticism" can mean that a person is simply too lazy to be bothered to think about any matters deeper than navigating the trivial call-and-response of daily life. In that sense, I become "agnostic."

URANUS CONTACTING PLUTO

Where I am all wrong about myself: While it is fair enough to say that everyone, myself included, is at least a little bit crazy, I am wrong about the exact *definition* of my madness. That is because I have internalized other people's psychiatric accusations; I am not as far off the mark as they have tricked me into believing I am. Meanwhile, other unrecognized madnesses have been taking a bite out of my existence – while everyone praises the "wisdom" of my choices.

The Cure: I begin by realizing that it is insane to allow crazy people – not to mention, a world gone mad – to define the nature of my own sanity for me. I resolve to think fiercely courageous thoughts about how I will look back on the life-shaping decisions that I am making now from the perspective of my deathbed. That is precisely the quality of sanity that I now claim and on which I will base my decisions in life from this moment forward.

How the universe helps: Dramatic circumstances arise suddenly and unexpectedly, revealing insights – often painful or difficult ones – into the true nature of my own motivations, not to mention the motivations of others. It is all laid out before my eyes, if only I am willing to accept what I see. If I do accept it, I am liberated.

The active face of failure: Misdirected anger and resentment lead me to attack innocent or otherwise inappropriate targets. I behave in ways which later fill me with the emotion of shame.

The passive, dissociated face of failure: I recoil from the strong emotions which are arising in me, and instead of feeling them, I take refuge in numbness and dissociation. Free-floating anxiety, paranoia, and a vague, unspoken sense of impending tragedy quietly come to dominate my thoughts.

Uranus Through The Houses By Transit Or Solar Arc

URANUS PASSING THROUGH
THE FIRST HOUSE

The arena in which I am presently fighting for my freedom: I have a right to act unilaterally – even in ways which might be perceived by others as selfish – in order to remain true to my own authentic path. If anyone wants to judge me, criticize me, or try to bend my decisions to his or her own plans, that is their choice. It does not mean I need to pay them any attention.

My best ally: Independence and autonomy, salted with a sense of life's brevity. Being uppity.

Current synchronistic correlates: If I am true to my own heart, unpredictable opportunities arise. They seem to involve me painting myself into an existential corner, but if I have faith, doors open soon after.

The energy squandered or misdirected: My urge to live my own life in my own way must be founded upon a genuine process of independent self-inquiry. If I skip that psychological and spiritual work, then I inevitably fall into the contrarian trap of taking cues from everyone around me: specifically, if they suggested I turn left, I turn right – and I mistake mere contrariness for true freedom.

URANUS PASSING THROUGH
THE SECOND HOUSE

The arena in which I am presently fighting for my freedom: The basis of my own authentic dignity and self-respect is the real issue. What resources and accomplishments must I have in order to maintain those positive attitudes towards myself? Where "freedom" comes into the mix is the extent to which I have internalized other people's judgments – I must be free of those in order to truly think for myself about what actually supports my self-esteem. Attaining or maintaining financial freedom may be part of the question now. What does financial freedom actually mean? Here is a hint: rich people are just as likely to be enslaved to money issues as are poor ones. It's not about a maximum bank account; it is about balancing one's life and one's material needs.

My best ally: Self-confidence and self-respect. A recognition that spiritual success is not a popularity contest. The only office for which I am running is president of my own life.

Current synchronistic correlates: Fluctuations and unexpected developments in my practical or financial circumstances create openings for fresh goals and strategies in my life. New resources arise; the only question is, do I recognize them?

The energy squandered or misdirected: Lacking boldness and audacity – and perhaps worrying too much about other people's opinions of me – I fail to seize an opportunity to prove myself to myself in a more free-spirited, radical way – one that better suits what my soul is actually trying to become.

URANUS PASSING THROUGH
THE THIRD HOUSE

The arena in which I am presently fighting for my freedom: To say that "in my soul I am free" is a good start, provided that I really mean it – but the arena in which I am facing my real test is the question of whether I am actually speaking with my own true voice. Do I verbalize my thoughts and perceptions, even if they lead to other people disapproving of me? Do I say what I truly see?

My best ally: The realization that all geniuses are misunderstood, at least at first. I do not have to think of myself as a genius in order to believe the messages of my own eyes and ears.

Current synchronistic correlates: I am noticing clues that tell me that "what everybody knows" is not necessarily true. Cracks in the "collective lie" are appearing; the delusions-agreed-upon are wearing thin. Surprising information arrives from unexpected directions, changing everything.

The energy squandered or misdirected: I find myself saying things, not because I believe that they are true, but rather simply to shock people or in order to get their attention – although once I have their attention, I really have no idea what to do with it except perhaps to shock them further. Crackpot ideas and conspiracy theories attract me; something inside of me wants to believe them because they make me feel special, *so I do.*

URANUS PASSING THROUGH
THE FOURTH HOUSE

The arena in which I am presently fighting for my freedom: First and foremost, I am fighting for my freedom to feel what I actually feel, rather than what I am expected or required to *pretend that I feel*. It is dawning on me that my genuine emotions are actually substantially different from the ones that I have imagined that I had, and which other people – perhaps family members in particular – have expected me to have. Simultaneously, I am fighting for my freedom to live in my natural soul-home among those whom I recognize as my natural soul-family.

My best ally: Emotional honesty with myself. A physical home that supports me energetically – and home here might mean the roof over my head or, equally, the spirit of the land under my feet. "Home" also includes the idea of my *true family* – people who may or may not be related to me by conventional kinship standards.

Current synchronistic correlates: Some instability in my living circumstances is bubbling up. Is a change of address being pressed upon me by circumstances? Or is there some psychic need for a change in my physical home? In either case, my accepting these outward changes is linked synergistically to breakthroughs in my understanding of my own personal identity and purpose.

The energy squandered or misdirected: Thoughtless, impulsive changes in my domestic situation – that is to say, in my home or my family, or both. Half-baked, unconsidered emotions of rebellion lead me to make impulsive decisions which are difficult to reverse.

URANUS PASSING THROUGH
THE FIFTH HOUSE

The arena in which I am presently fighting for my freedom: My right to restore my spirit with activities which give me genuine joy. My creativity – a renaissance is trying its best to bloom in any arts I practice. My relationship with my own inner child. My right to choose partners and intimate friends by my own standards, rather than from the list of "appropriate choices" provided to me by those who have appointed themselves as guides, judges, and authorities in my life.

My best ally: A pagan attitude toward pleasures in general, whether they are of the mind or the flesh – there is no room for Puritanical judgments or repressions here.

Current synchronistic correlates: Pivotal meetings with "outlaws" and others who encourage me simply to be myself. Brief, transformative affairs are possible – and these relationships are not necessarily sexual, although they may be. Triggers and opportunities for my creativity appear.

The energy squandered or misdirected: Human societies always have many customs designed simply to regulate people's tendencies to get in trouble with their own appetites. While all such customs can be legitimately questioned now, it is important for me not to simply do the opposite, mistaking mere contrariness for freedom. People saying, "Do not drink alcohol before 5 o'clock in the afternoon" does not mean that anyone with true individuality starts drinking at 11 o'clock in the morning.

URANUS PASSING THROUGH
THE SIXTH HOUSE

The arena in which I am presently fighting for my freedom: I have a right to define the nature of the responsibilities which I accept as my own. At the same time, I have a right to refuse responsibilities which others attempt to thrust upon me. In the past, I have signed contracts which I should not have signed. As I withdraw from them, I am likely to incur judgments. I accept that reality; I apologize where appropriate – but I affirm my natural right to rewrite all such contracts based on who I now know I truly am. I also have a right to define my own health-related behaviors in my own way. I can question medical authorities. I can seek alternative treatments, if that is what I feel guided to do.

My best ally: An imperviousness to anyone trying to manipulate me with guilt or shame. I affirm that I have a right to change the rules about what I feel that I owe anyone, and that no one has a right to forbid me from doing so.

Current synchronistic correlates: Role models appear, showing me the steps on the more rebellious and questioning path that I need to follow now. My aim is not "to be just like them," but rather to see where their footsteps have led them and then to make my own decisions. Disruptions arise in my working environment or in the framework of my general responsibilities towards other people. These disruptions open doors.

The energy squandered or misdirected: I develop a bad attitude towards my duties, but I do not do anything about it. I grumble; I am derelict in minor ways – I am late, for example, or I am slightly "off" in my speech or my dress. All of the energy that should be going into real change instead is dissipated in inconsequential symbolic rebellions.

URANUS PASSING THROUGH THE SEVENTH HOUSE

The arena in which I am presently fighting for my freedom: Can I simultaneously be true to myself and still behave honorably in my existing relationships? If I am committed to another human being, I must now assert the reality of who I have actually become – that, or the relationship eventually simply runs out of fuel. The only future in my being dishonest right now is a dishonest relationship in the future; I reject that possibility. Changing partners? Or time for changes *within* a partnership? Or, if I am single, opening in a fresh way to the possibility of partnership?

My best ally: Self-knowledge expressed directly and honestly – and then tempered with patience. It took me a while to discover who I had become; I allow others a similar length of time to adjust to my changes. I am clear about them, but I am not impatient.

Current synchronistic correlates: Changes in the lives of friends and partners; changes in circumstance which de-stabilize relationships – and do that in potentially helpful, creative ways. There are people in my life who have been a true support to me, and *vice versa*, but with whom now there is a natural parting of the ways. Our directions in life have simply become different. Perhaps I am the first one to see that reality.

The energy squandered or misdirected: Relationship dramas that create more pain than insight or joy for all concerned. Blaming others for not understanding me when I have not truly made the effort even to understand myself.

URANUS PASSING THROUGH
THE EIGHTH HOUSE

The arena in which I am presently fighting for my freedom: I need a clear sense of my own woundedness, free from other people's versions of "my issues." I need to welcome my sexuality to speak to me with its true voice. I resolve to feel what I actually feel, no matter where those realizations lead me. If I am in partnership, I need more room to be myself within the context of that commitment.

My best ally: Nothing so adds urgency and honesty to the process of individuation as the realization that death is inevitable and always just around the corner.

Current synchronistic correlates: Changes in the lives of my deeper partners. Changes in the circumstances of my relationships. Intimate deaths, or the threat of their possibility. Near-miss accidents that serve as wake-up calls. Encounters with "mysterious energies." Occult experience.

The energy squandered or misdirected: Acts of rebellion against social norms of behavior, but acts which are driven by my own unresolved and unowned psychological projections rather than by genuine insight. Pointless risks.

URANUS PASSING THROUGH
THE NINTH HOUSE

The arena in which I am presently fighting for my freedom: Hindus grow up and think like Hindus; ditto for Christians and Muslims – not to mention Scientists. I resolve to transcend the belief-system into which I was initiated. I will think for myself. I will escape the bondage of my cultural training. My morals are my own business; I will define what is right and what is wrong for myself rather than aiming to win anyone else's "Good Boy" or "Good Girl" prize.

My best ally: A willingness to ask questions. An openness to doubt. An eagerness for adventure and for experiences outside my own familiar comfort zone. An interest in life's "big questions."

Current synchronistic correlates: Opportunities to travel outside my culture. Encounters with people who have a different understanding of life than my own. Education – especially in areas where the particular knowledge is taboo or discouraged. (Hey, look at you: at this very moment, you are reading an astrology book. It looks as if you're doing fine.)

The energy squandered or misdirected: Cranky beliefs espoused for their shock value. Defensiveness around pre-existing belief systems. Conspiracy theories. Journeys undertaken for the wrong reasons and which go badly awry.

URANUS PASSING THROUGH
THE TENTH HOUSE

The arena in which I am presently fighting for my freedom: I am ready to break out of the stultifying patterns of my existing public role in the world. My job might be suffocating me. My reputation and the community's expectations of me have taken on a life of their own – one that is increasingly remote from anything that is actually meaningful to me. I am ready to redefine myself.

My best ally: A willingness to lose status in the eyes of people whose values I do not actually share. An openness to being judged, laughed at, or even called crazy. I value my integrity and my authenticity above maintaining any public image. A refusal to "know my place."

Current synchronistic correlates: Unexpected changes in my professional, relational, or social status in the community. Doors open which offer me a chance to reboot my public identity, making it looser and freer. I remove a pair of tight shoes that I have been wearing – other people's expectations of my "appropriate" role. .

The energy squandered or misdirected: I hare off in every direction. Without a plan, any self-insight, or serious forethought, I impulsively rebel against all structure, routine, and authority in my life. Or worse, I do nothing – and thereby resolve to become a zombie going through the motions of a role in the community which long ago lost any connection to anything which truly feeds my soul.

URANUS PASSING THROUGH
THE ELEVENTH HOUSE

The arena in which I am presently fighting for my freedom: I am realizing that I have an unknown number of precious seconds left on this planet. I resolve to use them in my own way without wasting a single one of them.

My aspirations and intentions for my future are my own business – and my strategies for achieving them are not designed to please other people. I resolve to free myself from any "tribal tyranny" that might stand between me and my living the life I was born to live from now on.

My best ally: The realization that I have the power to create my own future. Immunity to collective delusions about "what will make me happy" – for example, money, security, and winning the respect of boring people. I need to form supportive alliances with tribes of fellow rebels and dissidents.

Current synchronistic correlates: Disruptions in my present social circumstances which offer me a chance to change my direction in life. Opportunities to connect with groups of like-minded people who are operating outside the mainstream of conventional society.

The energy squandered or misdirected: Crazy, utopian, or otherwise impossible "plans for the future" arise – plans which inevitably go nowhere and only serve to dissipate my energy. "Get rich quick" schemes. The company of ungrounded people; "bad influences."

URANUS PASSING THROUGH
THE TWELFTH HOUSE

The arena in which I am presently fighting for my freedom: I resolve not to let any preconceived ideas, including religious ones, stand between me and my experience of the Transcendent. In spiritual matters, I will trust my own mind and my own senses, no matter how far they drift from the lies-agreed-upon that pass for "God's Truth." I am fighting for my spiritual freedom, and I am ready for it.

My best ally: Radical independence of perception. A willingness to appear as if "I have gone off the deep end" in pursuit of spiritual insight. Faith that I will be guided and protected so long as I am true to myself. An independent attitude of "no guru, no method, no teacher."

Current synchronistic correlates: Sudden unexpected losses may arise which allow me the freedom to reinvent myself. Breakthroughs in consciousness. Weird psychic events. Existential or intellectual shock which triggers cascading insights.

The energy squandered or misdirected: Letting my attachment to odd beliefs stand between me and genuine evolution. Chasing rainbows; delusions defended as if I were thereby defending my link to the Divine. Mistaking the robes for the path.

ENTERING AQUARIUS

Most planets will enter Aquarius one way or another in the course of your lifetime. It may be via transit, or via progression or by solar arc. When they do, their underlying agenda shifts in the direction of more independence, along with increased suspicion regarding external authorities.

Do they then begin to truly think for themselves – or, like most people who mistake mere rebellion for thought, do they go down rabbit-holes that our great-great grandparents scoped out ages ago? Or invent brand new rabbit-holes?

As ever, there is higher ground and lower ground, and it is our own mindfulness that determines where we land.

In what follows, we offer some core insights into the meaning of each planet's passage through Aquarius. When we consider the Sun and the Moon, along with Mercury, Venus, and Mars, it is their progressions and solar arcs that carry the lion's share of the evolutionary significance. Their transits are meaningful, but they operate over shorter time-scales and do not have quite the same moxie.

Sometimes a planet will enter Aquarius via retrograde motion – that is to say, it enters Aquarius from Pisces. In much of what follows, the underlying assumption is that the planet is making its exit from Capricorn, leaving that more structured and focussed environment – and therefore feeling more like a kid on the brink of summer vacation.

THE SUN ENTERING AQUARIUS

What part of myself now needs a bracing dose of freedom? My entire self-image is constrained by expectations which others have projected onto me and which I have unwittingly allowed myself to internalize. My path through life is my own business – I need to have more faith in that free-spirited perspective.

What kinds of values best serve my soul at this time? I resolve to care less what other people think of me. My truth is my truth. I resolve to become more immune to the effects of criticism and manipulation. For the sake of my sanity, I am willing to "look crazy" in the minds of other people. Life is too short for any other attitude to make sense.

What happens to me now if I waste this energy? I become cranky and contrary in unimportant matters, defending trivial freedoms while sacrificing the important ones. I put a wall of ice between myself and others. I begin to live in my head.

THE MOON ENTERING AQUARIUS

What part of myself now needs a bracing dose of freedom? The question is, what actually makes me feel happy? Not "what have I been tricked into *thinking* will make me happy" – but rather what do I truly need if I want to feel genuinely happier? Clue: the answer is not likely to win me any popularity contests.

What kinds of values best serve my soul at this time? I realize that from an early age we are trained to feel jealous, afraid, happy, or sad based on social scripts and collective interpretations – for example we conventionally celebrate births and mourn deaths, while they say that "angels do the opposite." I recognize this training and the grip it has on me; I realize that it alienates me from the reality of my own heart; I resolve bravely to feel what I actually feel.

What happens to me now if I waste this energy? My heart withdraws from itself. A strange mood of unreality and disconnection arises in me. Life starts feeling like a pointless movie that I am watching and considering turning off.

MERCURY ENTERING AQUARIUS

What part of myself now needs a bracing dose of freedom? People always believe that they are thinking for themselves. That is how I once viewed myself – but I realise that such *independence of thought and perception* is only now bursting upon my consciousness. I am finally free to see – and to say – what is actually before my eyes.

What kinds of values best serve my soul at this time? I allow myself to think anything. No thought, however weird, unprecedented or heretical, is forbidden. Only within the limits imposed by kindness, I have a right to express myself in any way I please. In recognizing the truth, I do not require anyone else's agreement in order to believe it.

What happens to me now if I waste this energy? My mind becomes reflexively contrarian. I mistake simply "doubting everything" for intellectual or cognitive independence. The unreflective assumption that everything I hear is somehow wrong blinds me to truth as it is presented to me.

VENUS ENTERING AQUARIUS

What part of myself now needs a bracing dose of freedom? Love in all its forms is potentially the greatest treasure we have on earth, but like everything else, it has a shadow: predictability, habit and expectations blinding us to our own changes. In all of my relationships now, I need to express myself freshly, making sure that the ones I love are supported in updating their files about who I have actually become. It is my responsibility to give them that information.

What kinds of values best serve my soul at this time? Commitment, maturity, and fidelity need to be honored – but also balanced with the realization that every contract between souls comes up for renewal and reevaluation from time to time. That freshness is half of what keeps love alive.

What happens to me now if I waste this energy? I allow friendships and partnerships to slip into predictable ritual. History blinds me to the present, holding me – and us – back in a past we have actually both outgrown.

MARS ENTERING AQUARIUS

What part of myself now needs a bracing dose of freedom? My right to express anger, pique, frustration, and resentment. That sounds terrible, but here is a worse reality: holding those poisons inside of myself where they fester and gather interest, turning me petty and resentful. My sexual energy needs less constraint now too.

What kinds of values best serve my soul at this time? The understanding that interpersonal friction is an inevitable part of human existence. I accept it, recognizing that holding it inside of myself in the holy names of forgiveness or maturity only makes it more dangerous.

What happens to me now if I waste this energy? An edgy, potentially-destructive part of myself gets split off from my conscious self and begins to operate indirectly in my life in the form of little signs of aggression: teasing, eye-rolling, sarcasm. These forces erode both the quality of my human interactions, and my own mental health.

JUPITER ENTERING AQUARIUS

What part of myself now needs a bracing dose of freedom? I want a meaningful victory in my life now – but figuring out exactly what such a victory actually looks like requires me to think outside the box. Standard definitions of success are not working for me. To figure out what will truly enhance my level of enthusiasm for my own future, I must sort through what I have been *taught* will work: status, power, money, enhanced sexual desirability. Any one of them may be on the list – I just have to make sure that the list is my own rather than someone else's.

    What kinds of values best serve my soul at this time? Faith in myself and my ability to do something that impresses even me. That it might impress other people as well is part of the formula, but I need to be careful there – if I try to impress *everyone*, I will likely be pandering to the *status quo* – and that will lead me to fail in actually impressing myself.

    What happens to me now if I waste this energy? Others see me and imagine me to be proud and grateful for my life, while in reality I feel detached, deriving little real pleasure or satisfaction from much of what I have done or won.

SATURN ENTERING AQUARIUS

What part of myself now needs a bracing dose of freedom? My hunger to get my teeth into worthy projects requires a new, more independent direction at this point. I also need to re-consider any promises that I have made and any responsibilities that I have taken on – many of them no longer suit what I am becoming, and instead only serve to bind me to the past.

    What kinds of values best serve my soul at this time? In the end, my sense of my own dignity depends upon only two questions: that I *knew* my own values and standards, and that I *lived up* to them. The moral approval or disapproval which others might afford me is irrelevant. I also need to understand that expectations that I am carrying about other people's responsibilities toward me are only "premeditated resentments."

What happens to me now if I waste this energy? I slip into a time-serving attitude of resignation, as if I am destined by forces beyond my control to "pull the plow through the mud forever." I begin to feel very much alone in the world as the archetypes of the Exile and the Hermit come together in my heart.

URANUS ENTERING AQUARIUS

What part of myself now needs a bracing dose of freedom? Since Uranus rules Aquarius, the answer is "pretty much every part of myself." That does not mean that every aspect of my life must go topsy-turvy – only that every aspect of my life must be interrogated in terms of its honesty, authenticity, and continued relevance to what I am in the process of becoming. No area of my life is sacrosanct.

What kinds of values best serve my soul at this time? The three values that have animated geniuses and rebels since the beginning of time are my most helpful values now – a relentless fidelity to the truth, a suspicion of "what everybody knows," and a distaste for the word "impossible."

What happens to me now if I waste this energy? I lose track of the precious trail of breadcrumbs that I have been following into the deep dark forest of life. A critical step in the process of my individuation is missed. On my journey west, I turned north – and I did not realize my mistake.

NEPTUNE ENTERING AQUARIUS

What part of myself now needs a bracing dose of freedom? My spirituality would thrive on a more direct kind of mystical experience – and probably needs less intervening religion trying to explain it. My fantasy-life must become less constrained; if I let it go where it wants to go, I will learn a lot about myself from it. My imagination and my creativity are trying to take a turn in a more innovative direction.

What kinds of values best serve my soul at this time? The realization that, while moral and ethical principles have an important place in my decisions about what I actually do, that in my daydreams, nightdreams, and fantasies I can enjoy greater freedom and fewer rules. It is there that my soul experiments with new possibilities – and one fruit of that experimentation is the realization that certain experiences which I have been trained to condemn might actually turn out to be good for me.

What happens to me now if I waste this energy? Meditation becomes a scripted, predictable experience. My imagination ceases to function as the leading edge of my life. My inner soul-compass loses track of "magnetic north."

PLUTO ENTERING AQUARIUS

What part of myself now needs a bracing dose of freedom? My relationship with my own Shadow is being re-negotiated. Parts of myself which *others* have declared to be "bad" – *and I believed them* – are being rehabilitated now. Other behaviors which were collectively declared to be "fine and normal," I am now seeing as morally culpable, at least for myself. Essentially, I am switching over to *internal guidance* in all questions of right and wrong.

What kinds of values best serve my soul at this time? Moral independence. A willingness to look at my own dark side, but to do so from the context of my natural values rather than those arising from any other source. Here are two specific illustrations about this kind of moral re-orientation – although yours will be your own: first, certain religions have tried to make people feel guilty for having sexual feelings. I reject such poisonous stupidity. Second: our culture teaches us that it is fine and natural that animals are to be used and dominated. I reject that kind of poisonous stupidity too.

What happens to me now if I waste this energy? I punish myself for parts of my life where there is no actual reason for guilt, while blinding myself to places where life-force is draining from me, only because it is draining from everyone else in the same way and there is a collective agreement to pretend it is not happening.

24

THE URANIAN LIFE-CYCLE

U ranus takes eighty-four years, plus one week, to make a circuit of the Sun. And, if you take care of yourself, it would not be too surprising if it took you a similar length of time to make the circuit from infancy to the end of your life.

That simple symmetry between the Uranian orbital period and our own physical life-cycle leads us directly to one of the most useful tools in astrology. Less familiar than the cycle of Saturn Returns which we explored in *The Book of Earth*, the four-cornered Uranian cycle is really just as important – not to mention a lot more fun to talk about.

Obviously, when it comes to the length of your own life, the odds are against your dying exactly on schedule at age eighty-four. People with healthy lifestyles sometimes fall over dead in their fifties, while we always see articles about centenarians who attribute their longevity to vodka and cigars.

As I write in 2019, in the country of Monaco, the average lifespan is currently 89.32 years. They hold the record. Japanese people are famous for their long lives, but Japan is actually in second place, considerably behind Monaco, at 85.77 years – just slightly beyond the Uranian rhythm.

Meanwhile, the United States is way back in the pack, languishing in fifty-third place at 79.38 years. (Perhaps that is due in some left-handed way to the vast treasure that disappears into our for-profit healthcare system every year.) In Australia, the average length of life is 82.46 years. In the United Kingdom, it is a few days short of eight-one years. China is in 112th place at 75.87 years.

The poor Namibians are in last place, at 50.89 years.

You get the picture: even the average figures for the human lifespan are all over the map. There is no rigid way to link any planetary cycle to the length of a particular human life. But the cycle of Uranus comes closest, and there is no real competition, especially in the industrialized world. Saturn – the next slowest planet – takes only three decades to get around the Sun. Even those poor Namibians would feel bad for someone who didn't live to see his or her thirtieth birthday.

Neptune is the next planet out, and it needs 165 years to circle the Sun. If someone dies on his or her 165th birthday, I suspect all concerned, including the deceased, welcome the change of pace. There is such a thing as too long in this world.

So: let's set one Uranian orbital cycle *symbolically* equal to one human life-cycle. That is our premise in this chapter.

Watch where it carries us.

THE URANIAN CYCLE

Half of eight-four is forty-two. That means that when Uranus is halfway around its orbit – in opposition aspect to its own natal position, in other words – we are forty-two years old.

More or less.

The "more or less" part derives from the fact that the Uranian orbit is not a perfect circle. It is an *ellipse*, which means the planet goes a little faster when it is closer to the Sun, and a little more slowly when it is further away. The effect is not very dramatic, but our age at the *Uranian Opposition* varies a bit as a result. There is a *generational* oscillation that moves like a wave through the whole orbital cycle. One cohort of human beings might enter the Uranian Opposition as early as age thirty-eight, while another group, born forty-two years later, experiences it as late as age forty-four.

You really have to look it up, in other words – although if you look it up for even one of the people with whom you went to grammar school, his or her age at the Uranian Opposition will closely match your own and that of everyone else in your graduating class.

If you are not an astrologer, it of course wouldn't even cross your mind to look up the date of your Uranian Opposition – but don't worry, it will get your attention anyway. It is one of the more impactful elements in the entire arsenal of astrological symbolism. One folkloric name for the Uranian Opposition is the *mid-life crisis* – although I promise we will explore it more deeply and respectfully, with less reliance on pop-psychological clichés.

Still, the "cartoon" version of a mid-life crisis serves a helpful purpose for us – if you get the Uranian Opposition wrong, sure enough, you will have one of those embarrassing mid-life episodes like the ones that you see in television situation comedies.

But get it right, and ... well, read on.

Twenty-one is one quarter of eighty-four, so at approximately age twenty-one, Uranus *squares* its natal position for the first time. It squares it again when it is three-quarters of the way around the Sun, at around age sixty-three.

As you might imagine, those two squares are significantly different in nature, even though both of them could be described as "transiting Uranus square natal Uranus." We distinguish them from each other by naming the first one the *Waxing Uranian Square* and the second one the *Waning Uranian Square*.

As with the Uranian Opposition, they are both powerhouses of astrological meaning. They bowl you over, in other words. Again, because of the elliptical nature of the Uranian orbit, the age at which we experience these two transiting squares also varies, although not so dramatically as with the opposition. I've seen the waxing square happen as early as age eighteen or as late as age twenty-three. I've seen the waning square as early as age sixty-one or as late as sixty-four or sixty-five.

For all of us, pretty much like clockwork, a *Uranian Return* happens around our eighty-fourth birthdays, as Uranus comes home again. Some of us don't make it that far, but many of us do.

It is worth waiting for, as you will learn in a few more pages.

RETROGRADATION

As is typical with outer planet transits, Uranus advances for about seven months, then makes a station and turns retrograde for another five months or so. The effect is that generally each of these three pivotal Uranian cycle aspects happen, not once, but three times, all within a period of a year or so. There is a direct hit, followed by a retrograde hit, followed by a final direct one.

Occasionally we see only a single exact aspect form – but when that is the case, watch out for those nearby Uranian stations. They always happen very close to the position of the exact aspect, and as ever, a stationary planet is pumping out high amperage energy. Don't be fooled: even if the stationary near-square or near-opposition is not exact, it may well be even more powerful than the exact one.

In counselling room practice, I have found that each of these Uranian events is best understood as *operating developmentally over a period of three years or so.* Give them a year on either side of the period of exactitude, in other words. In the typical three-hit situation, generally there is a span of only about nine months between the first one and the final one, but if you limit your attention to that period, you will miss quite a lot of the action happening before and after the dates that your computer shows you.

THE HEART OF THE MATTER

With the planet Uranus, no matter what it is doing, the heart of the matter is always *individuation* – the endless process of sorting out who you really are from who you have been conditioned to think you are. Humans are social creatures, so for every one of us, there is always a gap between those two selves.

Here's the problem: asking you to sort them out is like asking the rat to guard the cheese. That is because the thing we call "you" *is* the problem and cannot be relied upon to solve it.

That might sound like a dead-end, but it turns out that there is a way around the problem.

Here is an illustration of why we can't trust the rat of the false self to guard the cheese of the real one. In this story, I play the role of the rat.

When transiting Uranus made a square to my Ascendant, my father died suddenly under bizarre circumstances. One image will convey the "expect the unexpected" part of his passing: *the last place I ever saw him alive was on the quay in George Town harbor on Grand Cayman in the Caribbean.* He was being evacuated from a cruise ship where we were celebrating my mother's eightieth birthday. We knew he was ill, but none of us had any idea how seriously.

My last words to my father there on the gurney in the harbor were, "See you soon." I still get goosebumps remembering that part.

At the time I said them, I thought I meant that I would see him in a few days.

Only later did "see you soon" take on metaphysical overtones.

My dad was a boatbuilder. He and I had always sailed together, and so seeing each other for the last time in that fabled pirate harbor was kind of fitting. I was lucky with him too. We loved each other in our Capricornian ways. Our relationship had always been easy, with lots of humor. He once told me that I had become his best friend. His death was clean and fairly quick, and there were no rusty psychological razor blades separating us.

Despite the shock, my father's death was as good as death gets, in other words.

Here is the point of this story: at his memorial service, *I did not cry* – and remember, the Ascendant is about *outward behavior*. To cry, or not to cry, that is the question. There were two voices in my head, one critical, and one supportive.

Voice number one: "Dammit, Steve: cry. This was your beloved father, you emotionally-constipated old Goat! By the way, even worse, you are acting like a *totally typical American male* – unable to express your emotions, even now. What are you afraid of? Probably you were shamed for crying when you were a little boy and you've been unable to express your feelings ever since. You are pitiful."

Voice number two: "Death is part of life. Your father was eighty-three years old and he died fairly easily, with love surrounding him. It doesn't get much better than that. On top of it, you, Steve, are a man of faith – the idea that consciousness continues after physical death is real for you. Death is an illusion, and you know it. Crying is just the expected social script here. Your *not* crying is actually more honest, and shows your wisdom and your understanding . . ."

The point is, there at my father's memorial service, I was having a classic Uranus-square-the-Ascendant experience: *who am I, really?* Was

I not crying because of social conditioning or because of true spirituality? What answer might I possibly give that would be honest and sure?

It was, as we saw back in the Libra Clan chapter, a real tail-twitcher.

See what I mean about the rat guarding the cheese? *How can I know which part of myself was in the captain's chair: the real self or the false, conditioned one?*

IT MAY BE IMPOSSIBLE ... BUT DON'T WORRY, HERE'S HOW IT WORKS

In any Uranian time – broadly, and not just in the Uranian cycle we are exploring in this chapter – here in just twelve words is how the psyche breaks through the cognitive logjam we just described.

Energy is transferred to the real self. Meanwhile, the false self is untouched.

- Everything real and true about yourself becomes *charged with excitement.*
- Everything false becomes *insufferably dull* by comparison.

If, instead of trying to sort it all out intellectually, you simply follow those slender threads of energy, you find the golden city of your true individuality at the end of the process. *Trust the excitement and engagement.* Follow the energy – and in those areas that have grown dull, *ask yourself why you are choosing to remain bound to them.*

The answer is that those dull areas were never truly yours in the first place; life just tricked you into believing that they were.

Again, all that I write here is about Uranian times *in general.* The Uranian Squares, Opposition, and Return reflect these same principles, but, as we will soon see, in very specific ways.

- All three are linked to specific ages, so they happen to everyone at the same stage of life, and thus they reflect turning points in the underlying, universal developmental logic of the entire maturational process.
- All three are purely Uranian, so they are 100% about the process of sorting out soul-signal from background cultural noise. Your true self is empowered and energized, while the socially-conditioned self simply flatlines.

- Being purely Uranian, in such times weird, unpredictable events are very likely to occur – events that are linked helpfully and synchronistically to your process of individuation. Doorways to liberation open up, in other words. You are free to pass through them – or not.
- If you get these Uranian passages right, some people will think you are crazy, wrong, or even dangerous to yourself. If you get them wrong, the irony is that you will be wined and dined, offered respect, money, widespread approval, sexual gratification, and improved status.
- These three turning points build on each other. If you get the waxing square right, you are far less likely to have a comedic "mid-life crisis" at the opposition, and so on through the Waning Square and the Return.

Let's unpack these biographical milestones, one at a time, starting with . . .

THE WAXING URANIAN SQUARE

"Turning twenty-one" – the phrase is loaded with meaning, both psychologically and, quite often legally as well. After that birthday, in many societies we are deemed fit to drink alcohol and to vote and to enter into binding contracts as adults in full.

Why "twenty-one" rather than the nice, round sound of "twenty?"

For at least one obvious reason, It would be far too glib to claim that the custom of marking twenty-one this way originated with the cycle of the planet Uranus: the planet was not even discovered until 1781.

Still, even long before Uranus was discovered, it was up there in the sky, hitting those same four corners for everyone. People could feel its effects, even without understanding their astrological origin.

Maybe that has something to do with the mythology around the twenty-first birthday.

Down in Australia, I have a beloved god-daughter named Claire. When she turned twenty, she didn't like it much. She began declaring to everyone that she was now "twenteen."

That worked for her with some degree of psychological authenticity – but only for another twelve months or so. At twenty-one, Claire knew that she was . . . not "over the hill" exactly, but certainly over a major waterfall.

There was no going back to being a teenager.

Turning twenty-one "changes everything." A lot of reflective people would agree with that statement – but remember, it is not the number itself that casts the magic spell: it is the effect of the waxing Uranian square.

That event, as we have seen, does not always happen exactly when a person hits "three times seven." It might occur a little earlier or a little later, depending on where you were born in the long orbital cycle of the planet.

I will refer to "twenty-one" a lot in what follows, but remember: you have to look it up to know exactly when it is happening for an individual. Twenty-one is only the average figure.

It is also helpful to recall that it is practical and effective to frame the Waxing Uranian Square as a *three-year period* that is centered on the nine months during which the aspect is exact. One's twenty-first birthday is always included somewhere in the process – and that fact is reinforced by all the social and legal mythology associated with that particular milestone.

Eternal questions about chickens and eggs have relevance here.

LEAVING HOME

There is something unspeakably tragic about a twelve year old street-kid without a family. There is also something tragic about a twenty-eight year old man or woman still living at home with the parents, depending on their support, unable to find his or her way in the world.

At some point in between those two ages, a child must do something very difficult, something he or she has no idea how to accomplish: that is, to *grow up*. That means leaving the nest. That means standing on his or her own two feet in the adult world.

Most of us succeed. But by the time that we are launched on the stormy seas of adult life, we have often forgotten how difficult the transition was. *We go from being protected to being unprotected, from being fed to needing to feed ourselves, from having "no need to worry about money" to being responsible for paying our own bills.*

Sometimes we go in the blink of an eye from *being* children to *having* children.

It is a frightening initiation and none of us are born knowing how to do it. The ego must "muscle up," Uranian-fashion, to pull off its Great Escape – and that is something that it is not even totally sure that it *wants* to do.

The process often sounds something like this:

At Twenty-One: "I love my mother and father, but I would *never* want to live the way they have chosen to live. I just *had to get away from them* before they drove me completely crazy.

At Twenty-Five: "My mom and dad have grown up *so much* in the past four or five years that I barely recognize them ...

The giggle is fairly obvious. Hidden within it is the heart of the Waxing Uranian Square. We are *individuating in relation to our family of origin*. It is not an easy task, and it often requires diverting a lot of energy to our egoic deflector shields.

If I had to make only one single point about it, I would say that the Waxing Uranian Square is about *leaving home*.

Often that particular piece of the puzzle works out quite literally – it is common during this three-year period that a young person first goes off to college or gets a job, which leads to renting his or her first apartment, having a roommate or two, and so on.

In the past, the Waxing Uranian Square often signaled marriage – leaving the family of origin and starting a family of one's own. The median age of marriage has of course been climbing in recent decades, and to a considerable extent, marriage has been replaced by less formalized coupling arrangements, especially among younger adults.

Still, certainly no one would be surprised at young people having their first "serious relationships" around the time of the Waxing Uranian Square – and, whatever the fate of such a relationship might turn out to be, the bond does signal a door closing on "life with mom and dad."

"Leaving home" is more than a literal biographical fact at this turning point in the Uranian cycle; it is also, even more fundamentally, a *psychological initiation*. Behind every concrete observation we have just made is a *symbolic turning point* in any young person's life. The phrase *you can't go home again* once more comes to mind. Young people, often far more than they realize, have the gestures, humor, quirks of speech, and values of their parents. That is natural and understandable – but at this evolutionary juncture, the core self is energized and becomes much more assertive in the character.

A developmental imperative arises that we separate our own identity from that of our parents.

Again, this classic piece of Uranian individuation is not easy. There is much to like about life in the familial nest – security, free room and board, and so on. The weight of social custom – plus an entire legal system – declares that it is the duty of your parents to meet your basic needs, free of charge, no matter how difficult you are.

It is a sweet deal while it lasts, and it is hard to let it go.

Still, those who cannot separate their own identities from the parental nest become pitiful, lost creatures, as if they need to be called "junior" for the rest of their lives.

Sometimes in order to make the break, the youthful ego needs a dangerous ally: *the energy of anger.* Doors are slammed. Hard words are spoken.

- "I can't stand another day of your damned tyranny, dad!" (*"Then move out and get a job, son."*)
- "Mom, you have no right to judge me!" (*"Under this roof, I do."*)

Sometimes bridges are dynamited in ways that can never be repaired. Even though that is one of the saddest realities in the world, maybe that definitive break is actually necessary – as I write these sentences, the word "imperative" keeps forming in my mind. The psyche simply *must* "leave home." Otherwise failure cascades into catastrophe. It is unacceptable. Any price is worth paying. And, during the Waxing Uranian Square, it *feels* that way too: imperative.

Needless to say, grace, patience, and psychological understanding on the part of parents is a precious support here.

Some of us get lucky that way; some of us don't.

As my own Waxing Uranian Square was starting, I had just arrived at Morrison Dorm as a freshman at the University of North Carolina in Chapel Hill. I immediately fell into a piteous state of despair. I loved my family. I missed my home and my mother and my father desperately; I longed pathetically for Thanksgiving vacation when I could at least briefly return to 15 Apple Orchard Lane, even if only for a week or so.

Just a few weeks later, after I had returned to school, Christmas vacation loomed – and Uranus had begun to work its magic. My emotions had turned around completely. I now *dreaded* going home and facing those expectations and strictures. I still loved my parents, but their lifestyle and their *rules* . . . I had grown to really appreciate sharing a tiny, bilious green cement-block dorm room with another male. That freedom was intoxicating – at least compared to the state of domestic servitude that I had previously known.

Ah, such freedom!

I laugh now, but those few months were the beginning of my own Uranian journey. I left home – and, like everyone else, once I did, there was no way to go home again.

THE URANIAN OPPOSITION

When I am doing readings for people during their Uranian Oppositions, I point out that if they were to suddenly pass away, during the eulogy someone might very well say that they died "in the middle of their lives."

Then I add that a truly clueless person might object, pointing out that, objectively speaking, they had actually died at the *very end* of their lives.

The "middle of life" is a psychological, not a mathematical, term, in other words. And when transiting Uranus opposes natal Uranus, regardless of the ultimate length of our lives, we have come to *midlife*.

In common speech, "midlife" can mean anything from age thirty-five to seventy, depending on who is talking. But astrologically, midlife is not a long, vaguely-defined period, but rather a discrete *developmental event* with very specific features. It unfolds over a period of about three years, as Uranus swings through an opposition aspect to the position it occupied when you were born.

Even though mid-life is about very different issues, it has many analogies with passing through *puberty*. Primary among them is that it *changes everything*.

Note that I am not saying "midlife *crisis*"– not yet, at least. There are many higher evolutionary possibilities here. But they all come down to the recognition that we have crossed a major developmental equator. We have left the hemisphere of our youth and entered the hemisphere of our mature years. Every cell in our bodies understands that fact. One way of saying it – and again, this is a psychological, not mathematical statement – is that *we are now closer to death than we are to birth*.

Putting it in those "closer to death" terms might seem dark or morbid, leading us to imagine that the Uranian Opposition is depressing. Actually, it is quite the opposite: usually, it is highly *stimulating*. It fills the psyche with *urgency*, not despair. Something deep inside us realizes that we have been wasting time, that an ancient clock is ticking, and that we had better *get on with it*.

But what exactly is "it?"

There is a phrase – literal words – that people often find themselves saying during their Uranian Oppositions: *it's about time I did something for myself for a change*.

You can hear the adamance in the phrase, as if these folks are challenging anyone to *dare* to contradict them. If they were Clint Eastwood, they'd be saying, "make my day."

Break down the word "myself" in the obvious way, and you are carried right in the heart of the matter:

It's about time I did something for my *Self* for a change.

MIRRORS

Each one of us was born for an evolutionary purpose – something our higher Self understands perfectly well. But we get distracted. Our souls may have a plan, but the trouble is that everybody else has a plan for us as well. They get us when we are very young and they begin training us. We are encouraged to be "normal" or to be "practical." And we are threatened that if we step too far outside the framework of social expectations, we will be punished.

Meanwhile we are rewarded with security, comfort, and pleasure if we conform.

All together, these societal pressures tend to pull us all away from our true evolutionary purpose, replacing it with "monkey business" – the predictable daily grind of feeding ourselves, doing what is required of us, and maybe stealing a few moments of release or escape.

To punch right through to the heart of the matter, there is another line I often use with clients. I ask them to make a guess about *how much time they have spent so far in this lifetime standing in front of mirrors, trying to be sexually attractive to people with whom they do not want to have sex*.

Everyone giggles, of course – and understands. Youth and its obsession with mirrors: there's a matched set. Whether we respond to what we see in the mirror with vanity or with shame, despair and self-criticism ultimately matters very little. Either way, it is all about hours logged in front of mirrors.

Our concern with how we look is miles beyond anything to do narrowly with our sexual needs. Sexual attractiveness is about *status* too – impressing the rest of the monkeys, in other words. Status opens many doors that would otherwise be closed, and status is hard to separate from appearance, especially when we are young.

Appearance is only part of it. There are also questions of how "cool" we appear to be, how rich we are, and so forth. Before we are forty, most of us have put a whole lot of time and energy into our campaign for the prestigious *monkey-of-the-year* prize. George Bernard Shaw once quipped, "Youth is wasted on the young." Not fair perhaps – but his comment is relevant to our understanding.

The point is that at the Uranian Opposition, something profound in us comes to understand that *we have somehow gotten off our correct evolutionary track*. We have been wasting the most precious treasure we have: *time itself*.

Compounding the problem is the fact that young people almost universally *over-estimate the length of life*. To them, "eighty years" seems like a metaphor for "forever."

Ask someone who just turned fifty.

Turn forty, and you can then *feel intuitively* what "forty more years" means. You may not die at exactly eighty, but you never know. In your bones, you begin to grasp a sense of life's brevity. Once again, at the Uranian Opposition, we realize that we are "closer to death than we are to birth" – and that we had better make up for lost time. Urgency and stimulation tend to arise rather than *angst*.

With that clock ticking, you don't even have time for angst.

Remember our mantra?

It is about time I did something for myself for a change.

MEANING – OR MEANINGLESSNESS

Always, underlying the Uranian Opposition, there is a *crisis in meaning* in our lives. In that sense, it is always a *spiritual crisis*. The issue is not whether we are Methodists, Muslims, or Hindus. Our spiritual crisis is not about religion. It is about the presence of – or the absence of – a *visceral sense of whether or not our lives are aligned with our souls*.

In the light of impending death, there is no room for anything now except the truth. We have, of course, always known that we would die someday; the difference now is that we can see it coming. If we live the years we have already lived, there we are, at death's door – and again, that is not a mathematical statement; it is a psychospiritual one.

THE MID-LIFE CRISIS

As is ever the case with Uranian times in general, energy is now pumped directly into the true core of our beings, while the false, socially-conditioned self finds that it has run very low on fuel. We have no enthusiasm left for waste and triviality. These principles are radically stark at the time of the Uranian Opposition. The "dentist" wakes up one morning and realizes that she "cannot stand being a dentist anymore."

But what must she become instead? What is the alternative to everything she has always known?

There are good answers to that question, and there are bad answers too. All of the bad ones reflect the dark side of the planet Uranus: *impulsive, unconsidered actions undertaken in a cold spirit of rebellion against the needs and views of everyone around us.* These bad answers constitute most of the "situation comedy" versions of the midlife crisis – although laughter only comes easily if we are watching the action from a safe distance.

- Our dentist slams the door on her office, deciding precipitously to "move to Los Angeles and become a rock star."
- Long marriages break up, often as a result of affairs.
- Impulsive "geographical cures" abound, solving nothing.

In many of these midlife crisis scenarios, there is a very specific psychological fingerprint: *the person is behaving in a way that would have made sense many years earlier.*

A married father experiences transiting Uranus opposite natal Uranus. He is forty-two years old, and he feels as if it is *about time he did something for himself for a change.* On schedule, he falls in love with a much younger woman – say, she is twenty-one. He abruptly leaves his wife of twenty years and abandons his children. He buys a sports car. He takes on the clothing styles and language of a much younger man. He is in the market for hair implants and botox treatments.

His friends are either all furious with him, worried about him – or they are simply laughing at him behind his back. He has become a ridiculous figure, but not an unfamiliar one. You have seen him on television many times, complete with a running laugh-track.

Note how so far, despite the tragic dimensions of the story, there is something undeniably cartoonish about it. Again, we have all seen this passion play before. *Our protagonist is closely following the standard script for a generic midlife crisis.* He believes that he is acting autonomously, finally "doing something for himself for a change."

But really, *as everyone except himself can plainly see,* he is completely and utterly in the grips of a dark archetype.

Part of the script requires that he be resentful because "no one understands him or supports him" – and yet, the irony is abundant: in fact, *everyone understands him perfectly well.*

They also know more or less how the story will inevitably play out. They have seen it all before.

It is easy for us to judge this man. If we are his wife or his children, it is understandable that we would be furious with him. As astrologers, however, we can fathom some deeper waters.

- At the Uranian Opposition, core insights typically follow when we ask one incisive question: *at what age would this man's behavior have made perfect sense?*

Please understand that what I am about to say is impressionistic, just a starting point for deeper thoughts. I will base a perspective on purely *average,* purely *conventional,* assumptions – in other words, assumptions that actually work pretty well most of the time, but which do not apply to everyone all of the time. They are not moral; they are merely statistical.

In the heterosexual population, how old might a man be for it to be completely appropriate and unworthy of notice that he is courting a twenty-one-year-old woman? At what age would no one raise an eyebrow?

Twenty-three, give or take?

Fair enough?

In the counseling room, if this man came to me with these "biographical symptoms" during his Uranian Opposition, I would begin by asking him *what he was doing when he was about twenty-three years old.*

My underlying assumption would be that somehow *at around that age, he got off track in life.* I would speculate that something inside of him, in falling in love with a younger woman, is trying to *go back to when he was twenty-three years old* in an attempt to make it right.

This is why so often during a Uranian midlife crisis, the person's behavior bears the fingerprints of *immaturity.* It seems that there arises then an unconscious drive to return to the *time in life* when we somehow made a wrong turn. Hints about exactly *when* that error occurred are often hidden in the evidence of the "immature" action.

To keep perspective on this hypothesis, all I would add is that, while it is not always relevant or productive, it is a sufficiently reliable pattern that it is always worth considering. Try it; it might work for you, in other words.

The moral of the tale is that if you come to a fork in the highway and you guess wrong about which way to go, after a few miles you realize your mistake, reverse course, go back, and take the right road.

That works great in an automobile – but life, alas, lacks a reverse gear.

One more point: even though such errors can occur at any point in the first half of life, in practical terms, it is worth spotlighting the particular dangers of the time around the Waxing Uranian Square, when we are "turning twenty-one." As we learned a few pages ago, this is a volatile period in everyone's life. We are beginning to breathe the heady air of adult freedom. You might say that the gun is now loaded. Precipitous marriages, ill-advised career choices, too-early parenthood – all are abundant errors around that age.

Sometimes it takes those missed turns two decades to fully catch up with us.

Still, remember what they say about babies and bathwater: even in the "mid-life crisis" scenario, something in the soul is at least *trying* to get back on track.

There is something beautiful, if tragic, in our desire to make it right.

So far, we have been reflecting on cautionary examples. Let's look at a happy one. Soul-recovery can happen at the Uranian Opposition too.

That, in fact, is its true purpose.

CLIMBING THE MATTERHORN

A woman is born with a soul-intention to climb the Matterhorn in Switzerland. She is a solar Aries with a strongly placed Mars, so she comes by such a bold dream naturally. Accordingly, at the evolutionary level, her underlying *spiritual aim* in getting to the top of that mountain is all about the *development of courage.*

Her fiery, passionate nature takes her down a different road, however. Instead of using that damn-the-torpedoes audacity to climb a tall mountain, she instead uses it to get herself unintentionally pregnant at the tender age of twenty-one.

It is not a tragedy. She marries; she and her husband love each other and their child. It is not a sad story in any simple sense. Warrior-like, she will not fail either one of them, her husband or her child. She has made her stand. Soon she is pregnant a second time.

The practical, domestic, and psychological realities of being a wife and mother mean many things to her, not all of them unhappy or unfulfilling. But among them is a goodbye to mountaineering. *She will not climb the Matterhorn in this lifetime.* She will probably not even allow herself to think about it. That milk is spilt.

Years later, at her Uranian Opposition, it happens that this woman and her family visit the Sierra Nevada mountains in California. While there, on impulse, she finds herself climbing hand-over-hand up a ten-foot rock face – it is not the Matterhorn exactly, but there is a symbolic connection.

Her husband turns around from the photograph he is taking, sees her, and is totally horrified, worried that she will fall.

When she climbs back down, she is beaming. She tells him that *she has not had so much fun since she was nineteen years old.* Remember our Uranian principle: follow the slender threads of your emerging enthusiasm.

Her *real self* – the self that was supposed to climb the Matterhorn – is now asserting itself. There's the signature of the planet Uranus in opposition to its own natal position, charging her *authentic, unlived self* with energy.

So far, so good.

How long does it take to ascend to the peak of the Matterhorn? I Googled the answer: "four or five hours" was the figure that came up. But here is a better answer: *many years.*

Climbing the mountain itself is one thing; *learning to be a mountain climber* is another.

Not to be rigid or dogmatic here, but for our woman in this story, it is now simply *too late for her to climb the Matterhorn.* She does not have the skills, nor is she likely to acquire them. After all, she is forty-two years old. She is not in appropriate physical shape. She has responsibilities in life on which she cannot turn her back, nor would she choose to. One of them is staying alive for her children and her husband.

In reality, getting to that lofty peak in Switzerland is simply not going to happen.

Here is what does happen instead.

That vacation in the Sierra Nevada at her Uranian Opposition sows a seed in our protagonist, one that resonates powerfully and magnetically in her psyche. In scampering up that ten-foot rock wall, *something awakened in her spirit.* She returns frequently to those stunning mountains. She takes up hiking, eventually graduating to backpacking.

One day, some years later, she makes it to the top of Mount Whitney, the highest peak in California. Climbing that mountain does not involve ropes, ice axes and crampons the way climbing the Matterhorn does, but it is still a significant accomplishment, especially for someone nearing fifty.

Remembering that astrology is fundamentally about the evolution of consciousness, here is the point of this story:

Scenario number one. (This is the one that did not happen.) She stands on top of the Matterhorn, spiritually exultant at the age of twenty-seven.

Scenario number two. (This is the one that did happen.) She stands on top of Mount Whitney, spiritually exultant at the age of fifty-two.

These are obviously different stories. But don your wizard's hat and compare them from the evolutionary viewpoint five hundred years into the future: *How much difference is there between these two soul-triumphs from the perspective of evolving consciousness?* Ultimately, they serve similar developmental purposes.

In the final analysis, it was the *integration of greater courage* in this lifetime that mattered to this woman, not which mountain peak she had to stand on in order to claim it.

The Uranian Opposition does not have to be a mid-life crisis. Instead, its true aim is to serve as a *mid-course correction* in the middle of our lives. To navigate it gracefully and consciously, we must:

- Pay attention to the unsettled feelings that arise in us, realizing that they are trying to convey a message to us from the core of the Self – a message regarding wrong turns that we have taken, usually in the name of pleasing other people or of fulfilling their expectations of us.
- Avoid *acting impulsively* based on those unsettled feelings. Reason and common sense must form an alliance with those emotions. Each side needs an equal vote. Neither one can succeed alone. Our impulses – and a realistic appraisal of where we are in life – must *pay attention* to each other.
- Take *bold action*, in a way that is appropriate given your age and your actual situation, to move in a new and more meaningful direction in your life.

You may not get to the top of the Matterhorn, but the top of Mount Whitney will be good enough. In the end, it is all about what you take out of this world with you, not what your body did while you were here.

THE WANING URANIAN SQUARE

In *The Book of Earth*, we explored the second Saturn Return, which represents the heart of our initiation into the Cycle of the Elder. The Waning Uranian Square, occurring shortly thereafter at around age sixty-three, is part of that same "eldering" process. As we will see, it sort of puts the frosting on the cake.

At the second Saturn Return, we learned that our "passion for madness" is markedly reduced, opening the way to a quieter kind of happiness than we have ever before known, along with a clearer, more stable form of wisdom.

It is a commonplace understanding that people sometimes become "addled" as they age. Fair enough. That does happen sometimes – but what is never said is something that true Elders see very clearly: that younger people also tend to be "addled" in their own way.

The poor things – the way their sexual hormones drive them to acts of folly, the way they seem compelled to chase after glitter in the wind, the way they imagine life to be so much longer than it actually is . . .

There is, in other words, much to celebrate and appreciate in our initiation into elderhood.

Still, there is no way around it: we are talking about "getting old." That is not an unambivalently merry topic for anyone. In many ways, as we will soon see, the Waning Uranian Square puts the finishing touches on our passage into the Cycle of the Elder, adding a corrective to Saturn's unremitting seriousness: a welcome and redeeming dollop of fun, mischief, and sparkle.

The best way I know to get to the essence of this critical Uranian passage around age sixty-three lies in my belaboring the obvious for a few moments. A familiar set of ideas will offer us a template for understanding some insights that are less familiar.

Everyone knows instinctively that if we have a baby, we need to hold the baby and we need to look deeply and lovingly into his or her eyes. Touch is critical too. It all boils down to "love" – but loving a baby *in principle* is never enough; we have to effectively *convey* that love to the child. We might make mistakes with nutrition or medicine; the child will survive all that. But a lack of love? We might survive that physically, but emotionally such scars run very deep.

This knowledge hardly needs to be stated; it is hardwired into the human psyche.

To ask ourselves *exactly why* it is so important to love a child is where I risk belaboring the obvious.

Let's do it anyway. It will soon help us to understand the Waning Uranian Square. Start by conjuring up an image of a "sane person" in midlife.

- Because he felt loved as a child, he has *learned to love himself.* His life reflects that happy fact. He has treated himself well. He is living a meaningful life.
- Because she was loved as a child, she learned how to *offer love.* Because she was touched, she is *not afraid of touching and being touched.* Her intimate life echoes the love she experienced as a baby.

The point is that we can make a very direct logical connection between being treated lovingly as an infant and becoming a sane person in midlife. No one needs logic to understand any of this – once again, this knowledge is simply built into the human psyche. It comes pre-installed. Unless we were damaged terribly in our own childhoods, we know it without anyone needing to explain it to us.

In this founding principle of child psychology, we have a *template* for understanding the Waning Uranian Square. It is like a formula in physics – $E=MC^2$ for example. You can plug any values you want into it, and the relationships still hold.

- In infancy, our aim is to support the child arriving at life's long middle as a sane adult.
- At the Waning Uranian Square, the aim is to lay the proper foundation for becoming . . .

A REALLY COOL OLD PERSON

We certainly know one when we see one. "Really cool" old people are fun to be around; they are magnetic; they radiate a kind of naughty wisdom completely devoid of pretense or the compulsion to offer anyone any unsolicited advice. They are delightful companions. They manage to teach us important things about living without ever appearing to be teaching.

Critical to our understanding here is that such appealing older people *utterly epitomize and embody the nature of the planet Uranus.* That is to say, *they are exactly what they are.* If you like them, they are delighted. And if you disapprove of them, while they probably find your prim attitudes amusing, they are still exactly who they are anyway.

You cannot change them – not to say that they do not change. They do, but only in response to the inner winds of their own evolutionary impulses, never simply to manipulate anyone else's opinion of them.

We naturally think well of that kind of older man or woman. Tellingly, he or she probably thinks that *you are fine just the way you are too.*

Getting many paragraphs ahead of myself here, the process of becoming such a *free-spirited elder* is the goal of the Uranian Return, which lies down the road at age eighty-four, and which we will explore in detail very soon.

Right now, suffice to say that the Waning Uranian Square lays the foundation for getting there.

It is the *infancy of your old age.* And that sixty-three year old "baby" needs care too – but of a rather different kind.

My term "a really cool old person" is obviously street language, not the language we encounter in anyone's psychology PhD program. I choose those informal words intentionally, with an aim toward keeping all academic pretence out of our astrological equations.

Still, even though referring to someone as "a really cool old person" sounds lightweight, the term invokes an *archetype* – a point which is easily proven with a little thought experiment.

Gather up a hundred people with brains in their heads. Feed them the words, "a really cool old person," then ask them quickly to jot down their impressions. Collect the papers, read through them – *and you will soon realize that those one hundred people are all in fairly detailed agreement about exactly what the phrase signifies.*

Five simple words – and a hundred people independently write "the same book" about such elders. And that is essentially what the word "archetype" actually means; *it is a complex psychic structure built into human consciousness pretty much universally in pretty much the same way in everyone.*

In a few pages, when we consider the Uranian Return, we will revisit the "really cool old person" in detail. There, we will see the full realization and integration of that archetype emerge as something very close to the purpose of human existence.

Right now, our "really cool old man or old woman" serves a simpler purpose. *It stands in relation to the Waning Uranian Square in exactly the same way that becoming "a sane person in mid-life" stands in relation to infancy.*

It is a north star that orients us in a moment of pivotal, creative uncertainty. One's early sixties are a magical, powerful time, as well as a pivotal turning point in the evolution of the soul.

THE GATEWAY TO WHAT LIES AHEAD

"The infancy of your old age" – that phrase is not just me being cute with words, as if I were saying something trite, like "today is the first day of the rest of your life." Instead, the phenomenon occurring now is quite objective, and it happens only once in life.

Just as with infancy, experiences that we encounter at the Waning Uranian Square have a profoundly shaping impact upon the rest of our days. As with infancy, it behooves us to get it right.

That child who was never touched can go on to live a loving and productive life – *after about fifteen years of psychotherapy, twice a week,* that is. Those words may not be literally true, but they do represent a serious and inescapable truth: that recovery from cold or incompetent parenting is a monumental undertaking. Anyone who heals from that kind of failure is a hero.

How much more efficient than fifteen years of psychotherapy would it have been for that poor child simply to have gotten a hug at the right time?

Here, at the Waning Uranian Square, our aim is no longer to become "a loving, self-actualized person in midlife." All that is behind us now, water under the bridge.

The aim at this juncture is to become "a really cool old person" – that is to say, a *wild man* or a *wild woman,* fully Uranian, *fully individuated,* with our souls and our outward biographies lined up so perfectly that you could shoot an arrow through them and not touch a thing.

- To get this process of radical, final individuation off on the right foot, it is critical that during the Waning Uranian Square we *break some rules.* We must, in other words, flex the muscles of our nascent freedom. We must begin to spread the wings of our wildness.

- Undoubtedly, here in our early sixties, we are beset with people who have expectations of us. *It is critical that we disappoint at least a few of them.* The aim is not to hurt or upset anyone; the aim is to claim our right to operate outside the bounds of social strictures *because now, if we have lived consciously, we are wise enough to do that without transgressing the immutable moral laws of nature and consciousness.*

Now that we have reached a certain age, certain proprieties are widely assumed to apply to us in terms of our dress, conduct, sexuality, and so forth. If we do not break some of those rules, we are truly doomed. Either that *sense of our right to be ourselves* will lock in now – or the door will close on its *ever* locking in. Failure here means that we will become one of those predictable old people straight out of Central Casting, talking about our bodily complaints and how much better everything was fifty years ago.

Here is one of my favorite words in describing a strong response to the Waning Uranian Square: *naughtiness.* At this time, it is imperative that we are "naughty" in at least a few gossip-worthy ways. *If we are not naughty now, it will be very difficult for us to ever again enjoy being naughty in this incarnation.* We will be just as stuck in the mud of other people's expectations of us as that poor infant who was not touched and is now trapped in loneliness.

"Naughty" is of course a kid's word, one which we would normally use in the context of criticizing a child's behavior. For children to "win the naughty prize," they must pass two tests. First they must *know* the rules, and second, they must *choose to ignore them* anyway.

Similarly, as we get older, we are besieged by another set of rules: pressures to behave "properly," in expected ways, and to fade quietly and passively into irrelevance.

Don't let it happen to you or to anyone you love!

A few paragraphs back, I promised that The Waning Uranian Square would add a welcome and necessary dollop of fun, mischief, and sparkle to the "Elder" mixture.

Are we having fun yet?

A SAMPLER OF WANING URANIAN SQUARE VICTORIES

- A prosperous single man with lazy, predatory children counting on their big inheritances decides to marry a woman he loves and who loves him – and to leave his entire estate to her.
- A chaplain in conservative Oklahoma who used to play in rock bands dusts off his old Les Paul guitar and starts a Sex Pistols tribute band.
- A woman puts her sickly but parasitic mother in a Senior Care facility so that she can go live in Ireland for a few months and work on completing her novel.
- Two people of the same gender decide to make a home together – and they get a big laugh out of everyone wondering whether they are gay or not.
- A popular senator chooses not to run for re-election, preferring to live in obscurity in some western wilderness.
- A stockbroker becomes a Buddhist monk.
- A single woman of sixty-three has an affair with a single man who is thirty-nine. Neither one anticipates marriage. They just *like* each other, and it's no one's business but their own.
- Someone stops going to church; another person *starts* going to church: either way, there are people standing in judgement of them. All such judgements are ignored.
- The Abstract Expressionist starts painting realistic still-lifes: bowls of fruit, vases of flowers. Her collectors are shocked. The gallery owner is appalled.
- The old hippie gets a haircut; the conservative banker grows a beard.

Each one of these sketches is "inspired by a true story" taken from my counseling practice. Each one of these people is well on their way to becoming a fully-realized "really cool old person."

Their success with "the infancy of their old age" has now launched them colorfully – and perhaps irreversibly – in the direction of a victorious Grand Finale in their response to . . .

THE URANIAN RETURN

The name Jenny Joseph may not ring a bell for you, but I can almost guarantee that you know some words that she wrote way back in 1961. She is the author of one of the more frequently quoted – and perhaps most beloved – poems of the twentieth century. It is called "Warning," but if I hadn't Googled it, I wouldn't have even known its title. I sure knew the poem though – and I bet you do too.

Here are some excerpts from the first verse. I quote them because they gloriously nail the feisty spirit of the Uranian Return:

> When I am an old woman I shall wear purple
> With a red hat which doesn't go, and doesn't suit me . . .
> I shall sit down on the pavement when I'm tired
> And gobble up samples in shops and press alarm bells
> And run my stick along the public railings
> And make up for the sobriety of my youth . . .
> And pick flowers in other people's gardens
> And learn to spit.

Jenny Joseph was British, living in Minchinhampton, Gloucestershire. Fittingly, she had Uranus conjunct both Mercury and Mars in edgy Aries – hence her delightfully acerbic humor. She passed away in January 2018 at the (*telling; synchronistic*) age of eighty-five.

I never had the great pleasure of meeting Ms. Joseph, but I would bet my life that she epitomized all of the wild piss-and-vinegar of a brilliant Uranian Return. I am sure that her dream of "learning to spit" was fully realized, at least metaphorically. (She was, after all, a British lady.)

Old age has been something of a taboo topic for a long time. It frightens people. In our collective tendency to avoid talking about it, ageing is perhaps second only to the obvious *alternative* to reaching old age.

No one wants to talk about death either.

With more people living to their Uranian Returns, and with the generally more open and psychological language that characterizes the modern world, there is simply a crying need for positive conversation around the final quarter of life.

Interestingly, Jenny Joseph's poem surfed that wave of welcome change in the collective consciousness. Even though it was written in 1961 and first saw print the next year, it did not become really well-known until the 1980s. By the time we reached 1996, in a poll by the BBC, it was voted the most popular post-war poem in Great Britain.

Progress!

Astrology can help us so much here as we attempt to build a more in-spiring map for the final decades of life – a map that might fill people with positive anticipation rather than dread and gloom around the mysterious and potentially liberating terrain that lies beyond age sixty.

Planetary cycles provide a perfect map for the developmental steps we all need to take if we want "getting old" to be a joy rather than a source of fear or embarrassment. The second Saturn Return, followed by the Wan-ing Uranian Square, are two-thirds of the map we need – and in *The Book of Water*, we will complete the picture by exploring the third leg of the tripod: the all-important Second Lunar Return. (That passage happens in our middle fifties, and it sets off this whole seven or eight year process of eldering.)

URANUS FINALLY COMES HOME

Around our eighty-fourth birthdays, Uranus pulls its final rabbit out of the hat: it conjuncts its own natal position. We may live on for many years after that moment – but from that moment forth, all the aspects which Uranus makes in our charts are aspects which it has already made once before, back in our childhoods.

As we reflect upon that simple fact, we can grasp something very close to the central purpose of human life. *Each time that Uranus forms an aspect, the planet it contacts experiences a pulse of individuation.*

By the time of the Uranian Return, you have had every opportunity to truly *become yourself.*

And that is what it is all about.

Earlier in this book, buried in one of the cookbook sections, I quoted a line from David Bowie. It is brilliant enough to bear repetition, so here it is again. *"I think ageing is an extraordinary process whereby you become the person you always should have been."*

Bowie only made it to age sixty-nine, but I feel that I can guarantee that he would have made a really cool old guy. His words prove that he understood the Uranian process very well.

Will every stage of this eighty-four year Uranian process be successful? That is, will we get every transit right? Probably for most of us the right answer is sometimes yes, sometimes no. To hold ourselves to the standard of perfection is the ultimate cruelty imaginable. We are, after all, souls in the process of *learning* these things – we cannot be expected to hit the target each and every time.

If that were true, there would obviously be no need for us to learn them at all.

Still, the passage of Uranus around your chart gradually *lifts the fingerprints of your soul into visibility.* Wise young people might be highly individuated – but they are very likely to be even more individuated decades down the road.

How could it be otherwise, unless death or addiction stops them in their tracks?

The Uranian goal of life – which can potentially be realized at age eighty-four – is to be flawlessly, unapologetically ourselves. The soul is then fully incarnate in the personality. We are not swayed by anyone's praise or anyone's blame. We do not need anyone's approval. We engage generously with the world, but we are liberated: *we feel no need to lie*, except perhaps in the name of kindness, ever again in our lives.

And isn't that synonymous with true liberty?

Stick around. It is worth waiting for.

25

AFTERWORD: THE BRIDGE OF LANGUAGE

My students often ask me if their chart supports the possibility of them becoming professional astrologers. As with most such questions, there are limits to how definitive an answer can be given in purely astrological terms. For one thing, astrology is a complex, intellectually-demanding system. I doubt that someone with below average intelligence could succeed at it. And intelligence is not something that can be determined reliably from any astrological configuration. But my students tend to be bright, as do most people drawn to learning the system.

Wisdom helps too – but once again, wisdom is not something that can be seen reliably in a chart.

Still, the question is a fair one. Astrology might not be able to provide an answer in any ultimate way, but it can cast helpful light on the terrain.

Blind reflexive supportiveness rarely does anyone much good in the long run. I would not want to don my wizard's cap and encourage anyone to pursue *any* career in which I suspected they would face failure or humiliation. Obviously, that would be the opposite of being helpful.

Beyond what I have just written, here is how I respond when people ask me if "they have what it takes" to be a successful astrologer. I tell them that before I would recommend that anyone pursue astrology as a profession, I want to see three personal qualities strongly supported by their natal charts.

- First, I look for the virtue of *caring*. This is not about abstract Neptunian compassion for the human condition. These are *Venusian* qualities of genuine interest and engagement with other people, along with *Lunar* qualities of nurturing and kindness. If we are not fundamentally loving people, the strain – and frankly the sheer repetitiveness – of human dramas and tragedies simply wears us down in a way that is not sustainable. That clients come to an astrologer for insight is a given; that they also come for the human touch of caring, support, and genuine concern is equally relevant. If we only care about people with whom we already have an intimate connection, we should look elsewhere for our mission in the world.

- Secondly, I look for *Saturnian* indications of independence and self-sufficiency, along with the *Uranian* ability to tolerate misunderstanding or even ridicule without unduly internalizing it. Those specifically Saturnian qualities are virtues I would actually like to see in the chart of anyone pursuing *any* form of self-employment. The Uranian qualities come into play because, with astrology, there is still some social prejudice against taking it seriously, along with no shortage of ignorant, negative projections. The situation has improved dramatically in my lifetime, but it still exists. Anyone who is not wired to live with some teasing or disrespect will have a hard time being identified publicly as an astrologer. Saturn returns to the picture when we realize that you've got to be able to get yourself out of bed in the morning under your own power and actually run a business.

- Thirdly, I look for *skill with language*, as indicated by prominent *Mercurial* energies. We must recall that this quality is as much about listening as it is about talking – and, even with a strong Mercury, the presence of the Venusian and Lunar energies we listed above helps to keep listening in balance with talking. The bottom line is that astrology, along with all other forms of counseling, is a *verbal art*. Not everyone is born equally skillful at translating the raw realities of the human heart into vocabulary, grammar, and syntax. Without an easy relationship with language, the budding astrologer would be like a very short person with ambitions as a professional basketball player. You cannot do the craft of astrology without linguistic fluency.

That third point – language skills – is very much in the domain of the Air element. Words – which are an outward manifestation of the Air processes happening inside us – are what I want to write about here. Words, ultimately, play a pivotal role in how we humans actually *pay attention* to each other.

In the three points I just made about the make-up of a good candidate for the profession of astrology, I mentioned five planets: Venus, the Moon, Saturn, Uranus, and Mercury.

All of them except the Moon have rulership over an Air sign.

(By the way, in keeping with the general themes of this series of books, when I speak of "Mercury," I am also thinking of Gemini and the third house – a person might not have Mercury in a very prominent position, but with two planets in Gemini and three more in the third house, he or she is still a "word person.")

The claim that astrology is an "Air sign discipline" is perhaps defensible, but I would not go quite that far – the other three elements have roles to play as well. *Still, Air is resonant with the concept-forming parts of human consciousness, and we humans form our concepts with words.* In that trait, we are unlike bulls and rams and scorpions. Remember: as we saw back in chapter one, Air signs are the only ones where *human beings* figure in the symbolism. All the rest of the signs are animals.

Animals do of course communicate, some of them in fairly elaborate terms. But there's never been, so far as we know, a Shakespeare among the ravens nor a Maya Angelou among the wolves.

HUSH

Sometimes in meditation, I encounter a space that is beyond language. Probably you do too. It feels like a very pure, exalted state in which I would love to live forever. But then, almost immediately, I get so excited that I start thinking, "Gee, this wordless place is pretty cool. Look at me, I'm practically in *satori* or cosmic consciousness or something . . . or, what's that other word? . . . oh yeah, I remember: *shunyata* . . . yeah, *shunyata*, that's me . . ."

I hope you get the joke. It's on me. Words can rescue us sometimes. But sometimes they do exactly the opposite.

Still, I can barely imagine my consciousness without words animating it. Maybe you cannot imagine yours in a state of endless silence either. It seems – *inhuman*. Stopping that internal dialog is a very advanced spiritual practice.

There is a Libran paradox here: I suspect that most successful astrologers have a highly-activated "inner talker." They are "word people." Words are how astrologers build those bridges to their clients. Words are how they pay attention. The paradox arises when we realize that almost all of our most profound insights come rising up out of the silent, mysterious depths of consciousness.

If we can't be quiet, we can't hear them.

We explored the "wise silence" of Taurus in *The Book of Earth* and we will explore many parallel psychic and intuitive mysteries in *The Book of Water*. Here, in *The Book of Air*, we have been contemplating the part of the human mind that creates the kinds of *verbal, conceptual understandings* which are so essential to astrological practice. That process unfolds in the tricky domain of language, where we can quickly tie ourselves up in knots of words – or release ourselves from prisons of error with a single, insightful phrase. Furthermore, if we "serve the Dark Lord," armed with seductive words, we can tie other people up in knots as well.

Another point lies a cognitive inch and a moral mile away: if we are aligned with the Higher Power, we can reach the highest goal of astrological practice – we can perhaps find the perfect phrases and ideas that help to liberate those who come to us for counsel from their own soul-cages.

In every case, it comes down to language. Words are the steel, stone, and mortar of the bridge that all counseling astrologers have been trying to build since the first one of us looked to the sky for understanding, then turned her or his face toward a person in need.

STORIES, IMAGES, AND METAPHORS

I would be a lot richer today if it weren't for my addiction to stories, images, and metaphors. I marvel when I hear of other astrologers who do half hour sessions with their clients. My sessions always require at least four times that long. I suspect that those quicker astrologers are often helpful and effective; I am not trying to make them wrong. I would also be the first to say that their "business model" compares favorably to my own.

But I could not do what I do without taking time to stretch out into a tale or two. That is why I need at least a couple of hours with anyone.

That approach is not for everyone. Some clients want a consultation that is like a five-minute newscast. There are astrologers for those people too.

I did a reading for a woman in North Carolina once. She apparently got something out of it because she asked me for a follow-up on her transits and progressions. But she wondered if I could do a briefer version, just presenting the high points of the material "in bullets."

I told her no, I can't do that – and referred her to a more telegraphic colleague.

Even though they take time, I use stories, images, and metaphors for a lot of reasons. The main one is simply that they *connect directly with the heart as well as with the intellect.* A more short-winded astrologer might, for example, press someone with lots of Libran planets in the seventh house simply to "be wary of codependent tendencies."

Fair enough; that is good advice.

Instead of spelling it out so literally, I might instead say, "I once knew a woman who could have been a great writer, but her husband had ambitions in that same direction. Even though he wasn't very talented, she didn't want to emasculate him by risking becoming more successful as a writer than he was. She died with her unpublished novel under a secret code name on her hard drive."

Notice how that story has a lot more punch than mere advice to "avoid codependency?" In story-form, the client's heart *feels it and integrates it.* That is because she *identifies with the character.* Simply saying "don't be codependent" is more likely to go in one ear and out the other – agreed, but undigested.

Stories create *identification.* That is why they work so well. Intellect *understands* – but to add a story is to add the heart. Identification triggers something more integrated and multi-dimensional than mere conceptual insight.

SPYCRAFT

I like stories, images, and metaphors for a second reason – they *sneak behind people's defenses*. Picture a devoted father who is a solar Capricorn with a Virgo Moon and natal Saturn on his Ascendant. Perhaps an astrologer exhorts him to be careful about coming across to his kids as "controlling, judgmental, or defensive."

The guy probably loves his children. He is probably sensitive about anyone questioning his relationships with them. It is easy to imagine that father feeling offended by the astrologer's "personal attack" on him – and maybe also trying to *control the truth of what that astrologer was saying by being voluminously defensive about it.*

A jury of this father's peers would get a laugh out of him, and never convict the astrologer. But that astrologer would have failed utterly as a counselor. *Skillful counselling is about doing your best to make sure that you are heard and that what you say is actually helpful.* It is never simply about "being right" – and Lord knows it is never about winning arguments with your clients.

So, faced with this father, I would choose a different strategy. I would think more like a spy than like a lawyer arguing a case. Perhaps I would not even *mention* that he might be controlling or defensive. Instead I would approach the territory indirectly, using a story *about someone else.* I would set up a "straw man," in other words – and rather than attacking the father, I attack the metaphor. Maybe I would say, "I once knew a good, hardworking guy who had built a lucrative business selling tires. He really wanted his son to take over the shop someday. He was proud to be able to give his kid such a good career opportunity. Trouble was, the boy loved horses and wanted to be a veterinarian – but whenever the son shared that dream with his dad, he only heard discouraging words.

The kid eventually became a veterinarian in Wyoming – *and the last time his father saw him was four years ago.*"

That last line is the zinger. But note that we didn't zing that father *directly.* We let his ego and his pride remain intact – like spies, we snuck behind his defenses and quietly planted the necessary insight.

Will this story help that father generate self-awareness and maybe get past his controlling side? Who knows? Maybe. Possibly. That's actually all we can ever hope for.

We can also console ourselves with one certainty: compared to the more confrontive approach, at least we did no harm.

These kinds of stories, images, and metaphors take longer to spell out than more direct, literal or didactic presentations. I think they are worth the extra time. I believe that they constitute "skillful means" in our craft. I believe they have a more integrated, multidimensional, long lasting, healing impact upon our clients.

And I believe that they are far less dangerous.

THE BOTTOMLESS WELL

Where do we find all this helpful imagery? You of course create some of it on your own. But you are not alone in this quest for metaphors. Our collective human appetite for it is so vast that it verges on insatiable. People have been creating such stories since the days when we were *all* Africans fifty thousand years ago. Once you realize how valuable and empowering such imagery is for us as astrologers, you become an avid collector. You really start paying attention when any metaphor catches your fancy. You remember it. You know that you will use it someday.

For pretty much every astrological configuration that could possibly exist, I have a tale or two – or maybe three or four. If I always use the same stories, I find I get bored with myself, and a bored storyteller is invariably a bad storyteller. Where do I get them – at least the ones I don't simply invent myself? For me personally, *reading novels* helps. I am constantly encountering grist for the mill that way.

Here's an example – and again, it is from a work of fiction written purely for entertainment. This one is from a murder mystery. Once, in one of Robert B. Parker's early novels, his private detective, Spenser, is unfaithful to his girlfriend. After the sexual encounter, he looks glum. His paramour, a Hollywood starlet, asks him why. He says, "Susan Silverman is going to hate this."

Starlet: "Why tell her?"

Spenser: "Because we have an honest relationship."

Starlet: "But you don't really *have* to tell her ..."
Spenser: *"But then we wouldn't have an honest relationship anymore."*

Wham! Isn't that last line absolutely great? *Spenser himself wanted to be in an honest relationship* – and he understood what it was going to cost him in order to maintain it. I have lost count of the number of times I have recounted that anecdote in the counseling room. I should give Parker's estate a royalty. *Sixty-eight words, and boom: a profound point is made about the nature of healthy Plutonian intimacy.*

I quoted that sequence from memory, and I probably have some of the words wrong. It doesn't matter. I always credit Parker – and in the bargain, my Plutonian clients get a very punchy sense of the kind of relationship that would work for them, not to mention the price they might have to pay in order to deserve one and preserve it.

Feel how much more deeply all this sinks in compared to just saying "you need to be in an honest relationship?" That is the power of a story. The client is likely to remember it for a long time.

In another murder mystery, this one by Jonathan Kellerman, I read a wonderfully compact line that I've probably quoted at least a hundred times in my private work: *"Religion makes good people better and bad people worse."*

I could make that same point myself, but it probably would take me five hundred words to say it. So, thank you, Jonathan Kellerman, both for the wise words and their elegant economy.

Detective novels are not everyone's cup of tea – but the point, once again, is that you can find these stories everywhere. The world has been full of wise, eloquent storytellers ever since we built the first campfire. Books of philosophy or psychology – or serious astrology – might strengthen our theoretical grasp, but it is often in works of fiction that we encounter the pithy phrases and rich human examples that can enliven our language. Pay attention to them – and you have found a powerful way to help your clients pay attention to you.

FOLKLORE

The spiritual literature of the world's various religious traditions can be hugely helpful in our quest for stories, images, and metaphors. Early in this book, I quoted one of my favorites. It is a proverb from India, and beautifully conveys something fundamental about Mercury, Gemini, and the third house: *"When the pickpocket meets the saint, he sees pockets."*

Everyone laughs when they hear that line – but they also experience a critical pulse of insight about how our interests and our biases impact everything we see.

The Muslim folk culture line, *"Trust Allah, but tie your camel"* comes to mind. Feel the way it quickly gets the Libran notion of paradox across?

Back to India: *"When the flower opens, nobody has to call the bees."* Ten words, and another fundamental insight is conveyed. I use that line all the time in talking about someone's tenth house mission, and how his or her job is *to become the person who is worthy of that mission*, then the universe does the rest. The "bees" find the open flower.

Building a huge arsenal of these phrases gives you fluency and effectiveness as an astrologer. To find them, all you really have to do is *pay attention*. Guaranteed, it would be a rare week in which you were not offered one or two such treasures.

Learning to collect them and to keep them ready to roll out at the right moment is purely Air work – conceptual and verbal – as we build the only bridge we really have to our clients: *the bridge of language.*

THE LITERATI

Oscar Wilde was a master of pithy metaphors. I've got dozens of his quips in my head, ready to be deployed at any moment.

The dark side of Jupiter? *I can resist anything except temptation.*

The bright side of Uranus? *Be yourself. Everyone else is taken.*

The evolutionary purpose of Gemini? *Consistency is the last refuge of the unimaginative.*

Mark Twain provides another treasure chest. Here's some Neptunian insight from him: *When I was young, I could remember anything, whether or not it had actually happened.*

Maybe a little perspective on the fifth house? *Go to heaven for the climate, hell for the company.*

Self-forgiveness and humility? *Giving up smoking is the easiest thing in the world. I know because I've done it thousands of times.*

THE BIBLE AND OTHER MYTHOLOGIES

I grew up in church, so I know a lot of Bible stories. For many years, I found them useful in the counseling room. In days gone by, everyone else knew those same stories too. They were part of our common heritage, back when America was a simpler place. Talking to a client who was facing a long slog through Saturn times, for example, I would often invoke "The Book of Job." The client would immediately understand the point: *there is an end to all of this difficulty. Keep the faith, and it will all be worth it once you get through it.*

That Biblical reference used to work well. People knew what I meant right away. That story was in their bones; all I had to do was to sound a note on the same frequency and something inside of them that went all the way back to their childhoods would resonate with it.

The usefulness of these Bible stories lasted maybe until I was in my forties. Fortunately I paid attention, Gemini-fashion, to the way the world was changing. When I mentioned tales from the Bible, I noticed more blank looks, especially on the faces of my younger clients – *many of whom had never had any church experience at all.* They were the first wave of the current "spiritual but not religious" generation.

"The Book of Job," said the baffled younger client. "Was that about that Apple computer guy?"

In our increasingly secular society, younger people are vastly less familiar with the Bible than in previous generations. That is a complex subject, but for practical purposes here, it just means I tend not to use Bible stories anymore.

Our aim as astrologers is effective communication, not social engineering.

For similar reasons, despite their astonishing power I rarely use Greek myths. In avoiding them, I am unlike many contemporary psychological astrologers. The trouble is, most people are not familiar with those myths anymore. *"Gee, you seem to be having a real Ariadne moment there. That's quite a Gordian knot you are facing. What you need is some Alexander to come along with his merry sword."*

How many people today are actually going to understand that line?

Again, our aim is *communication* – and it is a disaster to leave clients feeling dumb, or, even worse, insulted, as if you have put them down by lording your scholarship over them.

Myths, whether they're Greek or Hopi or Ashanti, never die. They are, after all, archetypes and thus fundamental to the fabric of the cosmos for all of time. They are always reborn and re-invented. To communicate effectively in the modern world, you just have to find their contemporary incarnations. That is why, today, if I invoke Darth Vader of *Star Wars* fame in order to conjure up the feeling of Pluto, almost everyone instantly resonates with my meaning. When I need to vividly convey the elder-wizard side of Saturn, all I have to do is to say "Dumbledore" or "Gandalf."

People's level of familiarity with those current mythic figures may change as the cultural wheels continue to turn, but for now they work very well – while poor Job and Ariadne seem to be mostly forgotten. Our central skill here lies in paying attention to *each generation's re-invention* of these ancient, fundamentally immutable, archetypes.

The word "immutable" is very close to accurate here, but not quite. We just have to remember that there is in fact one mutable element in the picture: the *name* we assign to the archetypal figure.

Here, for example, is a lineage, with each phase symmetrical, more or less, with the previous one:

Dedi, back in the days of Pharaoh Khufu . . .

begat *Medea* . . .

begat *Seimei* . . .

begat *Merlin* . . .

begat *Gandalf* . . .

begat *Dumbledore* . . .

Look them up, if you want. But you don't really need to. If you know one of them, at the most fundamental level, you already know the rest. More importantly, you can ring the *Dedi* bell in your client today by saying *Dumb-ledore*, knowing that it is far more likely to convey the intended understanding. *A skillful astrologer learns whatever mythic names are current, and uses them.* Paying attention that way is how we maintain the bridge of words. Yesterday's bridge might not work anymore – and the comforting irony is that today's bridge is essentially the same as yesterday's bridge anyway.

In all of this, it is only intellectual pride and academic attachment that tricks astrologers into blundering with their clients, leaving them confused, and robbing them of what might have been a life-changing inspiration or understanding.

I've never seen or read *Game of Thrones*, but I gather that the books and the television series have had enormous impact on a lot of people. Doubtless, characters in that story correspond with planets and signs – literally any successful story conforms with that prediction. For that reason alone, I am confident that *Game of Thrones* can provide astrologers with a gold mine of useful, evocative metaphors – but a skillful astrologer counseling *me* would hopefully detect the blank look on my face when he or she invoked "Brienne of Tarth" or "Rhaegar Targaryen."

My blank look should trigger an immediate retreat to other kinds of imagery.

It is the Air element that we are talking about, and Air is always about *paying attention.* That includes paying attention to glazed-over eyes and other signs of befuddlement in our clients if our choice of words is simply not working.

YOUR OWN STORY

There is one story you know inside-out, and that one is your own. Can you use it to help build the word-bridge to your clients? Yes indeed, and you probably should – but with one major *caveat.* No client wants to hear you saying,"and another thing about me, and another thing about me, and another thing ..."

A little self-revelation goes a long way, in other words. Still, used judiciously and sparingly, your own story can be helpful. Here's why. A skillful astrological reading can feel like an X-ray of a person's soul. It *should* feel that way, in fact. Being seen so clearly, with many of one's flaws and vulnerabilities revealed, can be an emotionally threatening experience. Standing naked before a stranger who was dressed in evening clothes would feel weird and uncomfortable for almost anyone.

Maybe it would help a bit if the stranger were naked too.

That is one place where a little self-revelation on the part of the astrologer can be helpful. Immediately we can see the particular utility of using a few *embarrassing* personal stories. They may not be your favorites, but they do humanize you in the client's eyes. There is much that is instructive in the mistakes that you have made *and from which you actually learned something.* Sharing some of those *when the client is facing parallel issues* can serve two useful purposes:

- First, you serve splendidly as an illustration of the cost of a weak response to an astrological challenge.
- Secondly, such revelations *warm and humanize the room.*

When I was about twelve, I had a little card taped up over my bed. It had come packaged with some bubble gum I'd bought. The card depicted a dejected man in a striped prison uniform, complete with a ball and chain. The caption read, *"Cheer up! You can always serve as a bad example."*

You can too.

Most of the books I have written have some personal, autobiographical material in them. Anyone who has been reading my work over the past thirty-five years or so has learned a lot about me. In my early books, there were just a few anecdotes – the powerful impact of my visit to the Van Gogh museum in Amsterdam played a part in *The Changing Sky*, for one example. For another, some reflections on the experience of night-sailing my old wooden trimaran *Nimble Hope* on the Neuse River estuary in North Carolina opened *The Night Speaks*.

There was nothing particularly revealing personally in those stories; certainly nothing that was embarrassing to me. They were simply colorful metaphors that worked well with the flow of those books.

By the time I got to writing *Yesterday's Sky*, I was older and bolder. In those pages, I told a revealing past life story that definitely passes the "embarrassment test."

Here it is again:

When I was a young man, I went backpacking in Europe for a few months with my partner. In the deserted ruins of Pompeii on a gray November day, we encountered a guard. With his eye on my pretty blonde girlfriend, he told me with a wink that I, as a man, should not miss the fine murals in the ruins of the old brothel. Lamentably, said he, women were not allowed in there due to the stimulating nature of the art – but that I should not worry a moment because he would protect my girlfriend for me while I was gone.

Even at that tender age I saw through his deception – but the weird thing was that as soon as he launched into giving me directions to the brothel, I finished his sentence for him.

I knew where the brothel was in ancient Pompeii!

There is obviously some naughty, if somewhat metaphysical, fun in that tale. The clear evidence that I had probably been a regular customer in a whorehouse a couple of millennia ago perhaps does not put me in the brightest light from a spiritual perspective.

It was long ago enough that I no longer take the revelation very hard. Whatever karma I created for myself back then as a result of those actions has dissipated – I've never paid anyone for sex in this lifetime, and the whole notion today strikes me as weird, impossibly awkward, and alienating.

But that personal past-life story serves a very real purpose, far beyond its entertainment value. That is why I felt it deserved some ink in *Yesterday's Sky*, and maybe bears repetition here in these pages. Behind the embarrassing fun of my Pompeiian interlude is a serious point about soul-growth over time. The purpose of life – and therefore of reincarnation – boils down to the evolution of consciousness. One corollary of that point is that in each lifetime, *we evolve and we learn*. We may learn and evolve very slowly, or perhaps very rapidly, but every experience is grist for the mill. There is a second corollary: it follows that, in previous lifetimes, you were *less evolved* than you are presently. The way I like to express it with my clients is, *"You were even dumber in your past lives than you are today."*

That last line never fails to get a laugh, but it also underscores three serious points:

- That you are more conscious now than you have ever been in the history of the universe.
- That you have learned at least as much from your mistakes as you have learned from the things you have gotten right.
- That wisdom and self-forgiveness are inseparable.

With a client or with my students, I could simply spell out those three points didactically the way I just did. Likely, they would be accepted with a nod – and just as quickly forgotten. But *Steven Forrest used to frequent a whorehouse in Italy* – that is a mental image that the client or the student is less likely to forget.

Each one of those three points is built into my past-life story.

And the story is what is going to make them stick.

ANOTHER REASON OCCASIONALLY TO USE PERSONAL ILLUSTRATIONS

With his progressed Sun just half a degree away from a perfect sextile to his natal Midheaven, Barack Obama was inaugurated as President of the United States. That is a fine example of practical astrology at work. We have the single most powerful factor in developmental astrology – the progressed Sun – making a supportive aspect to the Midheaven – which is universally understood to be related to one's career or position in society.

Quod erat demonstrandum: astrology works.

In astrological teaching, it is common practice to use the charts of famous public figures, such as Barack Obama, as illustrations. Because they are famous, most of us know their stories, or at least the outlines of them. In comparing astrological symbols to biographical reality, we can begin to learn how the symbolism works. Our skills improve. And a side benefit sneaks into the mix as well: our faith in astrology deepens. Every time we see it working, we become more convinced of its efficacy.

And it always works.

Whether we are teaching astrology or simply doing a private consultation with a client, there is nothing wrong with the approach of using public figures as astrological illustrations. I often do it myself. *Together, those famous people constitute a big part of our current collective mythic vocabulary.* They are part of how we know ourselves as a society. These public figures serve the same purpose that was once served by Zeus – or our old friend, Ariadne – on Mount Olympus.

Still, even though the practice of illustrating astrological configuration this way is nearly universal and often effective, there is an insidious danger in relying on famous people as examples. Only by being mindful of it can we avoid succumbing to it. Let me take us straight to the heart of that danger with some not-so-simple questions, starting with, *what did it feel like to be Barack Obama on January 20, 2009?* What was his *internal experience?* What did becoming the President of the United States mean for him in *spiritual* or *evolutionary* terms? How would we have *counselled* him on that fateful day?

Looks really good for your career lately, Barack! Is that what we would say to him? Let us all pray that astrology – and astrologers – can go more deeply than that. With more profound astrological analysis, we can certainly get closer to addressing these more serious kinds of questions. But the bottom line is that only Barack Obama himself could ever really answer them definitively and authoritatively. When it comes to the journey of his soul, he has the best seat in the house.

And when it comes to the journey of your own soul, you have the best seats in the house too.

It is that last point that gives us another, perhaps even better, reason to use ourselves as examples from time to time. *Unlike with famous people, you have access to the interior experience of an astrological configuration, not just to the events and behaviors.*

The insidious danger in *only* using the charts of famous people is that it forces a kind of superficiality on us. We inevitably wind up focusing on outward facts alone – "the blows of destiny," as Carl Jung once put it. We often find ourselves using such charts to "prove astrology," even though that proof may no longer be necessary for the majority of us.

"See? Look – the progressed Sun sextiles Obama's Midheaven and he becomes the President!"

Yes – but we already knew that.

Outward biographical facts are not off-limits. They are not a taboo subject. We just have to be careful not to let them seduce us away from capitalizing on astrology's greatest strength, which is its ability to hold a mirror before the evolution of consciousness.

The mere *facts* of life are secondary. They are only the vehicle your soul is riding.

This might be the single most compelling reason to use your own story occasionally in your work with clients: *you know its inner meaning.*

That is true of your victories – and your self-administered catastrophes as well. What you have learned, how you learned it – *and what it felt like to learn it* – may very well be generalizable to another person who is faced with *a parallel set of issues,* either existentially or astrologically.

Of course, all of this can only be true if you yourself are living an examined life – and even then, only if you are using astrology as the lens through which you are examining it. You can only go as deeply into a client's soul as you are willing and able to delve into your own.

Used in this way, astrology emerges as a true spiritual practice. And unless you are traveling down that road yourself in the humble privacy of your own psyche, you have no business being an evolutionary astrologer.

And if you are using astrology personally that way, welcome to our ancient guild, and thank you for helping us to keep its sacred flame burning.

– Steven Forrest
Borrego Springs, California

LEARN ASTROLOGY WITH STEVEN FORREST

Interested in learning more about Steven's unique approach to astrology? For a listing of lectures and workshops that are available in a variety of audio and video formats online for instant viewing and download, visit https://www.forrestastrology.com/store.

Better yet, join the many successful students who have completed Steven's Astrological Apprenticeship Program, where he teaches both the specific techniques of interpretation and the style of presentation that have made him one of the most successful and influential astrologers in the world.

Steven takes great joy in passing on the teachings and strategies that have worked for him over the years through his Apprenticeship Program, and in 2018 was honored with the prestigious Regulus Award for his years of dedication in the field.

The Apprenticeship Program presents students with a rare opportunity to learn astrology in a supportive environment of like-minded individuals, who together create a feeling of community and connection, leading to bonds that last throughout life. Some come to the program to train professionally, while others come for personal or spiritual enrichment.

Learn more at www.forrestastrology.com.